Contemporary Social Work F

Series Editor
Christina E. Newhill

For further volumes:
http://www.springer.com/series/8853

Michael G. Vaughn · Brian E. Perron

Editors

Social Work Practice
in the Addictions

 Springer

Editors
Michael G. Vaughn
Saint Louis University
St. Louis, MO, USA

Brian E. Perron
University of Michigan
Ann Arbor, MI, USA

ISBN 978-1-4614-5356-7 (hardcover)   ISBN 978-1-4614-5357-4 (eBook)
ISBN 978-1-4614-9385-3 (softcover)
DOI 10.1007/978-1-4614-5357-4
Springer New York Heidelberg Dordrecht London

Library of Congress Control Number: 2012950336

Printed on acid-free paper   *

Springer is part of Springer Science+Business Media (www.springer.com)

Preface

Several important developments motivated us to pull together a volume on social work practice in the addictions. First, social workers represent the largest body of addiction and mental health service providers in the USA and many other countries. Consequently, a growing interest in issues of addiction in schools of social work throughout the USA and abroad is being observed. This is exemplified by an increased number of addiction-related courses, certificate programs, field placements, research projects, and peer-reviewed articles. Despite these developments and the impact that addictive behaviors have on client populations, the field of social work lacks authoritative resources to help ensure social workers receive training based on the best available knowledge and interventions in addictions. Quite simply, social workers are not being exposed to the most current developments in the field of addiction research. Existing texts are not sufficiently comprehensive and not based on the cutting-edge information. As such, the flowering of evidence-based science in this domain is inhibited.

The absence of an authoritative book on addictions specifically written for social workers is critically needed. Thus, this volume fills the gap by providing a comprehensive evidence-based guidebook that can serve as the cornerstone for courses in the addictions at schools of social work. Cutting-edge yet user-friendly, this book can be used by not only graduate and undergraduate students in social work but also researchers and practicing social workers who seek to update their knowledge. This volume is designed to provide state-of-the-art information that can be used as a reference guide that will facilitate the advancement of knowledge in social work and beyond.

Several issues bear mention that pertain to terminology and the future of diagnostic systems. We use the term addictions as an umbrella term in this volume to include substance use, abuse, and substance-related problem behaviors and not solely dependence. The reason for this is substance dependence is intimately connected to these other categories either by prior progression and relapses or by the myriad behavioral consequences of dependence. Thus, several chapters discuss and present information pertaining to the use and abuse of intoxicants and related behaviors. Although we realize that many behaviors such as compulsive video game playing and exercise dependence can be considered under the general rubric of addictions, our focus is on alcohol and other drugs. However, much of what is covered in this volume is applicable to these emerging areas of addiction. At the time this volume was completed DSM-V has not been implemented. As is the case with the classification of mental health disorders we realize that the revisions to substance use disorders are projected to be significant. In order to maintain relevance especially to information consistent with DSM-V we will add updated supplemental materials to the web site for this book. This will be especially useful for instructors who adopt the volume for their courses and wish to remain current.

Contributing authors represent many of the leading social work addiction researchers. Additionally, we include researchers from other allied fields, including psychiatry, psychology, and epidemiology, to ensure a strong interdisciplinary focus. In short, this is an impressive lineup of distinguished scholars and rising stars. Unlike other texts on addiction outside of the field of social work, this book is infused with content relating to social justice and practice with diverse communities to represent the knowledge base of social work. Further, we add chapters on the etiology and epidemiology of addiction and alcohol and drug policy, elements typically not included in social work books on addictions. We include these elements because in our view social workers benefit from an understanding of the causes of addiction, their prevalence, and patterns, and the policy context in which alcohol and illicit drug use, abuse, and dependence occurs. Thus, this volume is comprehensive, social work friendly, and interdisciplinary.

The structure of the volume is divided into four major parts. Part I covers foundational material related to the various perspectives on addiction, epidemiology, and explanatory theories. In Chap. 1, "Historical and Contemporary Perspectives," Howard, Garland, and Whitt document the rise of perspectives on addictions including important developments that formed addictions as a professional and academic field. They also describe the various models of addiction and substance abuse such as the moral, educational, spiritual, psychological, sociocultural, biological, public health, and neurocognitive. The distribution of addiction and its mental health comorbidities particularly with respect to services for afflicted persons is taken up by Michael Fendrich in Chap. 2, "Epidemiology." In Chap. 3, "Etiology," Michael Vaughn uses a cell-to-society framework to provide an explanation of the genetic and environmental causes of substance abuse and addiction.

Part II brings together the major components of assessment, diagnosis, and treatment. In Chap. 4, "Assessment Strategies for Substance Use Disorders," Michael Mancini elucidates the assessment process as acquiring and synthesizing information but most importantly establishing a productive therapeutic alliance in order to engage them in treatment and to develop an understanding of the role substances play in a person's life across multiple psychosocial domains. In Chap. 5, "The Language of Diagnosis," Ahmedani and Perron focus on using the Diagnostic and Statistical Manual (DSM) as a basis for diagnosis in social work practice. They provide an overview of the DSM, including basic information on the multiaxial assessment and diagnostic coding including making distinction between substance use disorders (i.e., abuse and dependence) and substance-induced disorders (i.e., intoxication, withdrawal, and substance-induced mental disorders). Recent years have witnessed the rise of briefer motivation-based interventions in the addictions' field. In Chap. 6, "Brief Motivational Interventions to Change Problematic Substance Use," Ilgen and Glass examine the empirical evidence supporting brief motivational interventions and explain the essence of motivational interviewing. They argue that social workers employed in a variety of practice settings (e.g., substance abuse treatment, mental health or medical settings) are well positioned to identify individuals who could be appropriate for brief motivational interventions. In Chap. 7, "Cognitive Behavioral Therapy with Substance Use Disorders: Theory, Evidence, and Practice," Granillo, Perron, Jarman, and Gutowski tackle the cognitive behavioral therapy (CBT) paradigm as applied to substance use disorders. CBT represents a broad class of interventions that take into account how learning processes are involved in developing and maintaining maladaptive thought patterns, emotional reactions, and behavioral responses. The final chapter in Part II examines the recovery process. In Chap. 8, "Philosophy and Practice of AA and Related Twelve-Step Programs," Pickard, Laudet, and Grahovac discuss the often misunderstood 12-step programs that are voluntary, nonprofessional, self-directed groups that use peer support to promote recovery from an addiction. As these authors astutely point out social workers possess minimal training in the philosophy and practice of 12-step programs, preventing them from maximizing the benefits of this important resource.

Part III is unique in providing cutting-edge information on specific populations. In Chap. 9, "A Framework for Integrating Culture, Diversity, and Social Justice in Addictions," Castro and Gildar recognize the important role that culture and diversity plays in addiction. They outline a multidimensional framework for integrating culture into addiction. Next, in Chap. 10, "Empirical Status of Culturally Competent Practices," Marsiglia and Booth examine effective prevention and treatment programs that are rooted in each individual client, their families, and their larger social and cultural networks. This chapter considers the role of culture of origin in relation to resiliency and protection from substance abuse and addiction processes. Substance use and abuse during adolescence is the focus on Chap. 11, "Adolescents," by Bender, Tripodi, and Rock. These researchers survey the empirical literature and highlight numerous concerns during this developmental period vis-à-vis substance abuse. These concerns include psychosocial problems, cognitive deficits, and reduced motivation to succeed academically. In Chap. 12, "Women and Families," Bonnie Carlson draws comparisons between males and females with respect to alcohol and drug use problems with particular attention to treatment admissions, stressful life events, childhood and/or adult interpersonal victimization, pregnancy issues, and impaired parenting. Carlson outlines and discusses available best practice guidelines for providing services for women who abuse or are dependent on substances. Finally, in Chap. 13, "Older Adults," Sacco and Kuerbis point out that greater numbers of older adults will need treatment for substance-related conditions. To prepare practitioners for these trends, this chapter specifies the unique challenges and age-specific risks regarding assessment and treatment of unhealthy substance use, including prescription drug use, among older adults.

Social work practice in the addictions occurs within a definite policy context. Thus, Part IV focuses on key developments in alcohol and drug policy. Building a bridge between policy and practice is the overall goal of this section. In Chap. 14, "Alcohol Policy," Jennifer Price-Wolf and Lorraine Midanik provide a critical appraisal of policies surrounding the use, abuse, and dependence of alcohol including biomedicalization, prevention, and harm reduction. Importantly, these authors demonstrate the links between these larger social issues and how they impact social work practices such as assessment. In Chap. 15, "Drug Control Policies: Problems and Prospects," Maayan Schori and Eli Lawental confront issues of drug policy. More specifically, Schori and Lawental place special emphasis on historical, economic, legal developments as well as treatment and rehabilitation policies. These authors conclude, among other things, that real change in drug policy is difficult without a major shift in public perceptions about drug use.

In sum, this volume is designed to provide and enhance the knowledge and skill set of social workers about the addictions' arena. Given the enormous number of persons affected by substance use disorders and substance-related problem behaviors it is our hope that this volume contributes to increased effectiveness by social workers in this often neglected domain of practice.

St. Louis, MO, USA   Michael G. Vaughn
Ann Arbor, MI, USA   Brian E. Perron

Contents

Contributors

Brian K. Ahmedani Henry Ford Health System, Detroit, MI, USA

Kimberly Bender University of Denver, Denver, CO, USA

Jaime Booth Arizona State University, Tempe, AZ, USA

Bonnie Carlson Arizona State University, Tempe, AZ, USA

Felipe González Castro Department of Psychology, University of Texas-El Paso, TX, USA

Michael Fendrich Center for Applied Behavioral Health Research, Helen Bader School of Social Welfare, University of Wisconsin-Milwaukee, Milwaukee, USA

Eric L. Garland Trinite Institute on the Addictions, College of Social Work, Florida State University, Tallahassee, FL, USA

Natalie J. Gildar Arizona State University, Tempe, AZ, USA

Joseph E. Glass School of Social Work, University of Wisconsin-Madison, Madison , WI, USA

M. Teresa Granillo The University of Texas at Austin, Austin, TX, USA

Ivana D. Grahovac The University of Texas at Austin, Austin, TX, USA

Sarah M. Gutowski University of Michigan, Ann Arbor, MI, USA

Matthew O. Howard University of North Carolina at Chapel Hill, Chapel Hill, NC, USA

Mark A. Ilgen Department of Veterans Affairs Healthcare System, VA Serious Mental Illness Treatment Research and Evaluation Center, Ann Arbor, MI, USA

Christopher Jarman Michigan State University, Lansing, MI, USA

Alexis Kuerbis Research Foundation for Mental Hygiene, Inc, New York, NY, USA

Department of Psychiatry, Columbia University College of Physicians & Surgeons, New York, NY, USA

Alexandre Laudet National Development and Research Institutes, Inc., New York, NY, USA

Eli Lawental Tel Hai College, Haifa, Israel

Michael Mancini Saint Louis University, St. Louis, MO, USA

Flavio F. Marsiglia Arizona State University, Tempe, AZ, USA

Lorraine T. Midanik University of California at Berkeley, Berkeley, CA, USA

Brian E. Perron University of Michigan, Ann Arbor, MI, USA

Joseph G. Pickard University of Missouri at St. Louis, St. Louis, MO, USA

Jennifer Price Wolf University of California at Berkeley, Berkeley, CA, USA

Jacoba Rock University of Denver, Denver, CO, USA

Paul Sacco School of Social Work, University of Maryland-Baltimore, Baltimore, MD, USA

Maayan Lawental Schori University of Pennsylvania, Philadelphia, PA, USA

Stephen Tripodi Florida State University, Tallahassee, FL, USA

Michael G. Vaughn Saint Louis University, St. Louis, MO, USA

Ahmed Whitt University of North Carolina, Chapel Hill, NC, USA

Part I
Overview and Foundations

Understanding the major perspectives, distribution in the population and causes of addiction provides a powerful context and foundation for social work practice. Part I begins with coverage of the historical and contemporary perspectives on addictions beginning in the eighteenth century and moving through contemporary times and includes moral, biological, psychiatric, sociological, social work, and public health perspectives. The emphasis is on how persons with addictive behaviors were viewed and treated over time. Next, we attend to epidemiology. Specifically, the patterns of addictive behaviors in the population focusing mainly on alcohol, tobacco, and illicit drug use (including cannabis, inhalants, cocaine, and prescription medications) patterns. Finally, the causal processes of addiction are examined. In our view, knowledge of the etiologic factors that contribute to the development and expression of addictive behaviors is foundational for social workers. Taking a cell to society perspective, the interplay between genes, neuroscience, personality, and social factors and their effects on the pathways toward addiction are discussed.

Chapter 1
Historical and Contemporary Perspectives

Matthew O. Howard, Eric L. Garland, and Ahmed Whitt

> Cassio: *"O thou invisible spirit of wine, if thou hast no name to be known by, let us call thee devil."*
> Iago: *"Come, come. Good wine is a good familiar creature, if it be well used."*
>
> (Shakespeare, Othello, Act 2, Scene 3).

Intoxicant use and related social and health pathologies are among the defining features of human civilization. It is virtually impossible to find an historical epoch, geographical area, or sociodemographic subgroup that has escaped the ravages of substance abuse. Archeological discoveries indicate that the Sumerians were cultivating poppies, which they termed the "joy plant," as early as 3000 BC (Crocq, 2007); the identification of Stone Age beer jugs suggests that the use of fermented alcoholic beverages dates to the Neolithic period (ca. 10000 BC) (Arnold, 2005).

Reasons for substance use have varied widely within and across cultures and over time. The Navajo and pre-Columbian indigenous populations used peyote (*Lophophora williamsi*) for purposes of spiritual reflection, whereas the Ebers papryas, among the oldest (ca. 1500 BC) medical documents in existence, recommends opium juice for the treatment of refractory crying in infants (Crocq, 2007; Westermeyer, 1988). Despite the widespread use of intoxicants' for religious and medical purposes, psychoactive substance use for social and recreational reasons has been associated with significant problems in contemporary and historical cultures.

M.O. Howard (✉) • A. Whitt
University of North Carolina at Chapel Hill, Chapel Hill, NC, USA
e-mail: mohoward@email.unc.edu; ahmedw@email.unc.edu

E.L. Garland
Trinite Institute on the Addictions, College of Social Work,
Florida State University, Tallahassee, FL, USA
e-mail: egarland@fsu.edu

M.G. Vaughn and B.E. Perron (eds.), *Social Work Practice in the Addictions*,
Contemporary Social Work Practice, DOI 10.1007/978-1-4614-5357-4_1,
© Springer Science+Business Media New York 2013

Among the developments that have dramatically increased the severity of substance use problems over the past 150 years are the ever-increasing potency of psychoactive agents and more efficient (faster and more dangerous) routes of drug administration. Advances in modern analytical and synthetic chemistry allowed for the extraction of morphine from crude opium and subsequent synthesis of heroin from morphine (Page, 2009). Likewise, "crack" and powder cocaine are significantly more potent than the coca leaves and coca paste from which they are derived (Page, 2009). Distillation of wine and other fermented liquids increased the percentage of alcohol in beverage alcohol from a high of approximately 14% to more than 90% in some cases (Hanson, 2009). Such distilled beverages led to the London Gin Epidemic in the first half of the eighteenth century and to the first reports of fetal alcohol syndrome in neonates of women who drank heavily while pregnant (Warner, 2002).

Depending on the drug taken and historical setting, routes of administration have included chewing, sniffing/snorting, smoking, enemas, suppositories, and ingestion. Among the most important of the historical developments encouraging illicit drug use was the introduction of the hypodermic needle in 1858 by Dr. Fordyce Baker (although intravenous injection using a bladder and quill was reported as early as 1656). Intravenous drug use, needle sharing, and associated blood-borne infections (especially malaria) became endemic in North America in the early twentieth century (Zule, Vogtsberger, & Desmond, 1997).

Detailed histories are available describing pre-historic, pre- and post-Columbian, and post-industrial and modern substance use patterns and associated problems (Jay, 2010). These reviews examine anthropological, economic, and geopolitical factors related to the spread of substance use including the effects of sea travel, the agricultural revolution, and rural to urban migration (Westermeyer, 1988). The focus of this chapter, however, is on contemporary developments related to substance abuse research and practice occurring since the explosion of drug use that marked the decades of the 1960s, 1970s, and 1980s. Courtwright (2010) noted that "what was alarming [about this epidemic] was the scale of the problem; the spread of illicit drug use to groups such as middle-class students or American military personnel, which had not been heavily involved before; and the fast growth of the drug-related crime" (p. 116).

Institutional, regulatory, organizational, research, social, and treatment-related developments since the 1960s have profoundly shaped contemporary social work practice in the addictions. This chapter examines key developments in these areas over the past half-century and their implications for social workers who work with psychoactive substance users. Contemporary and historical conceptualizations of the substance abuser are also reviewed, with particular emphasis on the continuing influence of these perspectives on public and professional responses to persons with problems related to drug and alcohol abuse and dependence.

Institutional Developments

The National Institute of Alcohol Abuse and Alcoholism and National Institute on Drug Abuse

The National Institute of Alcohol Abuse and Alcoholism (NIAAA) was created in 1970 with the enactment of the Comprehensive Alcohol Abuse and Alcoholism Prevention, Treatment, and Rehabilitation Act (P.L. 91-616). This act placed NIAAA under the aegis of the National Institute of Mental Health within the Health Services and Mental Health Administration (Hewitt, 1995). P.L. 91-616 mandated that NIAAA "develop and conduct comprehensive health, education, research, and planning programs for the prevention and treatment of alcohol abuse and alcoholism and for rehabilitation of alcohol abuse and alcoholics" (p. 1). P.L. 91-616 included key provisions to prevent employment-related discrimination against "recovering" alcoholics, assist the states in providing more effective prevention and treatment programming, provide for the treatment of federal civilian employees with alcohol problems, and require that all public and private hospitals receiving federal funds provide alcohol dependence treatment to persons needing it.

NIAAA was recognized as an independent institute within the newly created Alcohol, Drug Abuse, and Mental Health Administration when P. L. 93-282 was passed in 1974. In 1974, the annual appropriation to NIAAA was $84.6 million. The 2011 appropriation to NIAAA is approximately $460 million, a 544% increase over the 1974 funding level, which includes monies for more than 700 research project grants along with significant funding for alcohol research centers, career training, and intramural research.

P.L. 93-282 also established National Institute on Drug Abuse (NIDA) as an independent institute in 1974. NIDA appropriations were $65.2 million in 1974, approximately one-third of which funded research grants. NIDA appropriations for 2011 were $1.1 billion (a nearly 17-fold increase over the 1974 funding level), which includes funding for more than 1,300 research projects.

Dramatic increases in federal funding for prevention and treatment research over the past 35 years have reflected the growing national recognition of the importance of substance abuse as a social problem. With more than 2,000 research projects currently funded annually by NIAAA and NIDA, practice-relevant scientific knowledge has accumulated rapidly in the substance abuse area. This accumulation of knowledge has provided fertile ground for the identification and dissemination of "evidence-based practices" in diverse areas of addiction practice (Miller, Sorenson, Selzer, & Brigham, 2006). Currently, serious consideration is being given, for cost savings and scientific reasons, to unifying NIAAA and NIDA under one umbrella organization referred to by some observers as the National Institute on Substance Use Disorders (Grabowski, 2010).

Substance Use Surveillance Surveys

The 1970s also ushered in several ongoing national surveys of substance use designed to estimate the prevalence of drug use and allow for the early detection of emerging drug problems. The Drug Abuse Warning Network (DAWN) and National Household Survey on Drug Abuse [currently the National Survey on Drug Use and Health (NSDUH)] surveys were initiated under the Special Action Office for Drug Abuse Prevention in 1972. DAWN includes two national survey efforts. The first is a surveillance system to monitor drug-related visits to a nationally representative sample of hospital emergency rooms. A related DAWN survey examines national trends in drug-related deaths investigated by medical examiners and coroners. The NSDUH is a nationally representative annual household survey of approximately 67,500 U.S. residents aged 12 and older and assesses the prevalence of substance use and related attitudes and behavior (e.g., perceived risk and availability of select substances and age at initiation of use of specific drugs).

In 1975, the Monitoring the Future Survey (MTF) (also known as the High School Senior Survey) was initiated to provide an annual indication of the prevalence of substance use among 12th graders nationally and trends in such use over time. At present, the MTF also includes 8th and 10th graders, such that a total of 46,500 youth participated in the 2010 MTF survey selected from more than 400 secondary schools nationally. DAWN, NSDUH, and MTF remain key sentinel surveys for the detection of emerging drug problems in the USA (albeit with important methodological modifications since their inception) and have provided data for thousands of scientific and media reports about substance abuse. Findings of these surveys have also underscored how prevalent and costly substance abuse is to the U.S. polity and have provided policy makers with critically important information for legislative and policy decision-making.

Organizational Developments

Research Society on Alcoholism and College on Problems of Drug Dependence

Shortly following the creation of NIAAA and NIDA, two of the leading organizations of substance abuse scientists were founded. Research Society on Alcoholism (RSA) was established in 1976, comprised of former members of the National Council on Alcoholism and American Medical Society on Alcoholism (Israel & Lieber, 2002). The initial membership directory included 197 researchers; current RSA membership exceeds 1,600 (cf., www.rsoa.org).

The creation and growth of RSA and College on Problems of Drug Dependence (CPDD) served many purposes, including supporting young substance abuse researchers and their work, recognizing outstanding substance abuse research and researchers, and legitimizing the efforts of researchers who chose to focus their careers on substance use disorders. RSA established the influential journal *Alcoholism: Clinical and Experimental Research*, whereas CPDD's official organ is the journal *Drug and Alcohol Dependence*. RSA and CPDD, the journals they publish and annual conferences they convene, remain among the signal developments in the history of addiction science and practice. Prior to the creation of NIAAA and NIDA and founding of RSA and CPDD, research on substance abuse problems was not highly regarded, nor was scientific work actively pursued in this domain of inquiry. These organizations stimulated dramatic increases in the amount and quality of practice-relevant research in the addictions, which now provides the basis for the evidence-based practice movement in this clinical area.

Recent years have also witnessed the emergence of professional specialty groups such as the American Society of Addiction Medicine (www.asam.org), American Academy of Addiction Psychiatry (www3.aaap.org), International Nurses Society on Addictions (www.intnsa.org/home/index.asp), and state and national bodies that certify chemical dependency counselors and practitioners active in areas such as pathological gambling (i.e., the Council on Problem Gambling, www.ncpgambling. org) and sexual addiction (i.e., International Institute for Trauma and Addictions Professionals, www.iitap.com).

Legislative and Regulatory Developments

Critical developments in the "war on drugs" between 1960 and the present have been detailed elsewhere (Campbell, 2009). Notable for the purposes of the present chapter were President Johnson's consolidation of several agencies into the Bureau of Narcotics and Dangerous Drugs in 1968, President Nixon's establishment of the Office of Drug Abuse Law Enforcement in 1972 and Drug Enforcement Administration in 1973, and President Herbert Walker Bush's appointment of William Bennett to head the new Office of National Drug Control Policy in 1989. These agencies were primarily enacted with law enforcement aims in mind and to consolidate antidrug efforts operating previously across various levels of government (Campbell, 2009).

Since the 1980s, European governments have largely adopted "harm reduction" initiatives to minimize adverse consequences of drug abuse including HIV transmission, drug overdoses, and widespread incarceration of drug-using offenders (Courtwright, 2010). The USA has generally failed to enact legislation reducing legal penalties for drug possession or to provide for readily accessible needle exchange programs or safe injection areas whereby disease transmission and overdose might be prevented. Courtwright (2010, p. 117) asks, "Why did U.S. [addictions] science develop in one direction, U.S. policy in another? Why deepening medical insight and intensifying punishment?" The answer to this question, from Courtwright's (2010) perspective, is that Republican politicians adopted a policy of selective reaction to the developments of the 1960s that included the promotion of severe penalties for criminal offenses, the related war on drugs, and welfare reform.

Legislative developments of this era were consistent with Courtwright's perspective. P. L. 104-121 denied Supplemental Security Income and Social Security Disability Insurance payments to persons who applied because of their substance use disorder (Sowers, 1998). P.L. 104-121 was passed due to concerns that public monies were being used to purchase drugs, but had the effect of denying housing, health-care services, and treatment to persons attempting to recover from substance use disorders. P.L. 104-193 (Section 115) had the further effect of excluding persons convicted of drug-related felonies from receipt of food stamps or general welfare and assistance (Sowers, 1998). For various reasons, these laws reduced the availability of treatment and other rehabilitative services for substance users, and had inadvertent adverse consequences on the health and well-being of substance users and their families. A recent positive development on the legislative front is the adoption of the Paul Wellstone and Pete Domenici Mental Health Parity and Addictions Equity Act (MHPAE) of 2008, which aimed to require "parity" for mental health and addictions treatment benefits vis-à-vis medical and surgical benefits in private health insurance plans (Barry, Huskemp, & Goldman, 2010). Although MHPAE is a notable exception, a fair conclusion is that substance abuse-related legislative and policy developments of the past 50 years have not been especially enlightened and have often had the effect of punishing, stigmatizing, and further marginalizing substance abusers.

Research Developments

Growth of Substance Abuse Research

By virtually any metric, substance abuse research has grown dramatically in scope and sophistication over the past half-century. Identified 56 English-language addiction journals and 27 addiction journals published in languages other than English. In 1965, there were only 10 English-language/non-English-language substance abuse specialty journals worldwide; by 2008, this figure had increased to 88. Approximately half of all the substance abuse research articles are published in addiction specialty journals.

Although no specific data are available to our knowledge, we believe the number of substance abuse articles published in professional and disciplinary journals has also increased dramatically. A review of reports indexed in the *PubMed* and *PsychInfo computerized bibliographic* databases between 1960 and 2010 reveals substantial growth in the substance abuse literature. For example, in 1960, 235 reports were indexed in *PubMed* addressing alcohol abuse and 674 addressing drug abuse. Comparable figures for 2010 were 3,042 and 14,455. Thus, a total of 909 substance abuse reports were indexed in *PubMed* in 1960, compared to 17,497 in 2010—an increase of more than 19-fold. *PubMed* and *PsychoInfo* are among the leading biomedical and psychological bibliographic databases in the world. Findings from these databases document exponential growth in the substance abuse literature, such that more than 20,000 new substance abuse research-related reports enter the scientific literature each year.

Social Developments

Mass Incarceration, Epidemic HIV-AIDS, and Ever-Emerging Drugs of Abuse

The law enforcement- and punishment-oriented approach of the Regan–Bush era contributed to a notable increase in the number of prison inmates nationally. Whereas the daily census of prison inmates had been relatively stable at 1/1,000 adults between 1925 and 1975, the comparable census figures between 1975 and 2000 showed an increase of 500% (Courtwright, 2010). By 2002, two million U.S. citizens were incarcerated. Courtwright (2010) observed that "nothing like it had occurred in the history of the country or of any other advanced democracy" (p. 116). The personal, social, and economic costs of incarceration on this level cried out for effective policy, prevention, and treatment practices in relation to youth and adults at risk for substance-related offending.

The roughly coincident development of tests for HIV in 1985 and hepatitis C (HCV) in 1989 increased awareness of these emerging epidemics and greatly spurred interest in intravenous drug use as a vector for blood-borne disease transmission. Intravenous drug use was thought to contribute directly to risk for HIV via needle sharing and indirectly via disinhibition of high-risk sexual behavior. More recently, identification of sexually transmitted human papilloma virus (HPV) infection causing cervical, anal, and throat cancers in men and women and the possible transmission of HPV by sharing of marijuana "joints" and other substance use behaviors (Zwenger, 2009) have further underscored the dangerousness of unbridled sexual activity fueled by substance-related behavioral disinhibition.

Mini-epidemics, oscillations in the nature and frequency of drug use, and the continual emergence of new psychoactive agents complicate efforts to address drug abuse on individual and societal levels. For instance, in just the past few years, "spice," an extremely potent and synthetic form of marijuana, has come on the market (Savage, 2010), "bath salts" containing the stimulant mephadrone have been widely abused and associated with a number of deaths (Ross, Watson, & Goldberger, 2011), and highly concentrated extracts of the plant *salvia divinorum* became a legally available hallucinogen (*Salvia divinorum* Research and Information Center, 2011). The Internet has enhanced ready access to these and other psychoactive drugs and to the plethora of online pharmacies selling prescription drugs of abuse (Janofsky, 2004).

Clinical Developments

Evidence-Based Treatment and Prevention Practices

The exponential growth of practice-relevant substance abuse research has also led to the identification and dissemination of a number of "evidence-based treatments" for addictive disorders (Miller et al., 2006). Similarly, the growth of "prevention science" and founding of a journal and organization specifically devoted to study of prevention interventions has the potential to significantly improve the efficacy of prevention efforts in the USA and elsewhere (cf., Society for Prevention Research, www.preventionscience.org). It is not only simply that treatment and prevention studies have grown far more numerous, but also that the methodological rigor of these investigations has increased significantly in recent years.

Nosological Advances

Standardized criteria for the diagnosis of substance use disorders and related conditions (such as intoxication and withdrawal syndromes) have also been extensively studied, such that a wealth of knowledge has accrued in this area since the publication of the *Diagnostic and Statistical Manual of Mental Disorders-Third Edition* in 1980. In addition, more than 500 rating scales, interviews, questionnaires, and other screening and assessment instruments are currently available to assess virtually every conceivable facet of substance abuse, behavioral addictions, comorbid family, social, and psychiatric disorders, and substance-related problems. Many of these instruments are cost free, well studied, and can be accessed at the web site of the University of Washington's Alcohol and Drug Abuse Institute (see www.adai.washington.edu/instruments/).

Conceptualizations of Substance Abuse and Substance Abusers

Moral Model

The notion that substance use is a volitional act undertaken by an agent who knows, or should know, that dependence and other adverse consequences may follow, was prevalent in antiquity and remains so today. Modern adherents of this perspective support criminal justice, law enforcement, and moral persuasion responses to substance abusers, although, as the following Biblical verses make clear, historical treatment of substance abusers was occasionally even more Draconian:

If a man have a stubborn and rebellious son, which will not obey the voice of his father, or the voice of his mother, and that, when they have chastened him, will not hearken unto them: then shall his father and his mother lay hold on him, and bring him out unto the elders of his city, and unto the gate of his place;

And they shall say unto the elders of his city, This our son is stubborn and rebellious, he will not obey our voice; he is a glutton and a drunkard.

And the men of his city shall stone him with stones, that he die: so shalt thou put evil away from you; and all Israel shall hear and fear (Deuteronomy, 21: 18–21).

Many practitioners regard the moral model as anachronistic, stigmatizing, and simplistic, ignoring the multifactorial nature of addiction, wherein biopsychosocial factors contribute to the etiology of substance abuse and attendant problems. However, surveys reveal that many members of the general public and professional groups continue to regard substance abusers as "weak willed," characterologically defective, and as fully deserving of the criminal penalties that accompany acts such as driving while intoxicated (Howard & Chung, 2000). Complexities of the moral model have been examined and this perspective continues to exert powerful influence over criminal justice treatment of the substance user even to this day (Fingarette, 1988; Morse, 2004; Peele, 1989; Satel, 2001).

Temperance Model

In the early decades of the twentieth century, alcohol was regarded by many U.S. citizens as a potent and pernicious substance, capable of producing severe dependence and related diseases. Some activists in the Temperance movement promoted moderate use of alcohol, whereas others advocated for a total ban on alcohol. In 1919, the Volstead Act was passed as the 18th amendment to the U.S. Constitution, which prohibited the sale and transportation of alcoholic beverages. This act, though successful in reducing health and social consequences of alcohol abuse, was repealed in 1933 by the 21st amendment to the Constitution. These contradictory amendments, enacted over a relatively brief span of 15 years, reflected the ambivalence of the U.S. populace toward alcohol use—an ambivalence that is apparent even today.

Educational Model

Educational models view substance abuse as arising from a deficit of knowledge about addiction and its deleterious consequences. Prevention and treatment programs for persons arrested for driving under the influence, for example, often include a prominent educational component. Although purely educational interventions have rarely shown strong evidence of effectiveness, widespread promulgation of the harmful effects of cigarette smoking may have played a key role in the dramatic reductions in cigarette use in the USA in recent decades. Most treatment and prevention interventions continue to include educational components, consistent with the tenets of educational deficit models.

Spiritual Model

The spiritual deficit model of addiction, perhaps best exemplified by Alcoholics Anonymous, but characteristic of a number of the world's religious and spiritual orientations, emphasizes the role that spiritual deficits can play in the individual's attraction to and powerlessness over substance abuse. Advocates of the spiritual model believe it is unlikely that substance abuse can be successfully overcome without the assistance of a "higher power"; however, one may conceive it.

Psychological Models

Psychological models span a broad expanse of perspectives including personality, self-medication, conditioning, social learning, and cognitive theories. Each of these perspectives is briefly addressed below.

Perhaps the best known of the personality models are psychoanalytic perspectives that regard substance abuse as a symptomatic expression of underlying character and psychosexual-developmental problems. In some psychoanalytic theories, latent homosexuality, fixation at the "oral" stage of development, or a thirst for omnipotence and control are viewed as the underlying causes of substance abuse. Other theorists emphasize the pervasive and predisposing influences of low self-esteem and the overreliance on primitive defense mechanisms commonly employed by substance abusers, such as denial and rationalization. In more modern and empirically based formulations, traits such as impulsivity, novelty or sensation seeking, and fearlessness have also been described as characteristic features of substance abusers (e.g., Howard, Kivlahan, & Walker, 1997). The key commonality of all these approaches is that they emphasize the etiological role of personality and temperament in substance abuse. Typically, psychotherapy (including its more confrontational variants) and promotion of parenting, relational, and family management practices that may enhance psychological health are perceived as key approaches to the prevention and treatment of substance use disorders.

Substance abusers are commonly afflicted with co-occurring psychiatric disorders that complicate their treatment. Mood, anxiety, psychotic, and other psychiatric disorders may be linked with a range of different patterns and types of substance abuse through a complex network of associations. Substance abuse and dependence can precede, follow, or occur contemporaneously with co-occurring psychiatric disorders. In some cases, it may be apparent that substance abuse was the cause or consequence of a co-occurring psychiatric disorder like depression; in other cases, a "third factor" (such as traumatic childhood experiences) may appear to give rise to each of the co-occurring disorders. Proponents of the self-medication model regard substance abuse, at least in some persons, as a conscious or unconscious effort on the part of the afflicted individual to amerliorate noxious symptoms of anxiety, depression, psychosis, or other psychiatric conditions that disproportionately afflict the substance abuser. Adequate treatment of the dually diagnosed client calls for targeted interventions directed at comorbid psychiatric disorders. From this perspective, if co-occurring disorders are effectively treated, then it is probable that substance abuse will diminish significantly in frequency and intensity or abate altogether.

Skinner popularized the "experimental analysis of behavior" and the notion that behaviors were more likely to be repeated in the future if they had been positively reinforced in the past. That is, Skinner (1969) held that prior contingencies of reinforcement shaped future behaviors, such that positive reinforcement following substance use could lead to positive expectancies about the outcomes of future substance use. Potential reinforcing outcomes of substance use could be increased relaxation due to the anxiolytic effects of some depressants, increased focus, attention, and productivity along with euphoric mood in stimulant abusers, and increased conviviality with friends and family due to the disinhibiting and euphorigenic effects of alcohol abuse. As an outgrowth of this learning theory perspective on substance abuse, operant conditioning-based interventions have been applied to the treatment of substance abuse, including chemical and faradic (i.e., shock) aversion, although these treatments have also been conceptualized in terms of classical or Pavlovian conditioning and taste aversion learning paradigms (the latter in the case of chemical aversion therapy).

Classical conditioning models emphasize the pairing of an unconditioned stimulus (e.g., a drug) with a neutral conditioned stimulus in the environment. Through repeated pairings, the neutral stimulus acquires the capacity to elicit an unconditioned response formerly elicited only by the unconditioned stimulus. Thereby, formerly neutral cues within the environment, and even interoceptive (i.e., pertaining to the sense of the physiological condition of the body) cues within an organism, can acquire the capacity to evoke craving responses that lead to continued substance abuse. For many substance abusers, a host of cues acquire the capacity to increase the likelihood of substance abuse. Cue exposure treatments based on Pavolian conditioning models present substance abusers with substance-related cues to elicit a craving response, and then subsequently prevent the treated client from engaging in actual substance use (Drummond & Glautier, 1994). These interventions are thought to "extinguish" stimulus–response associations and have proven useful in the treatment of some substance users.

Social learning theory has been conceptualized as a model that synthesizes principles of cognitive and learning theory (Maisto, Carey, & Bradizza, 1999). Key constructs of the theory are vicarious learning, also referred to as "modeling," differential reinforcement [i.e., the notion that the nature and intensity of the reinforcement one receives following a behavior is contingent on the stimulus condition (i.e., socio-environmental setting in which the behavior is carried out)], cognitive processes (conceptualized as mediating setting and behavior relationships), and reciprocal determinism (i.e., the notion that behavior can control and be controlled by environmental conditions). With regard to substance abuse, social learning theory (Bandura, 1999) emphasizes the effects of peer modeling of substance use, the teaching of new coping or adaptive skills, and altering those conditions of an individual's environment that promote substance use. Similarly, sociocognitive models have received significant research attention in recent years, particularly models that explore the effects of positive substance-related outcome expectancies on substance use or that examine the role of abstinence violation expectancies on relapse to substance use (Marlatt & Donovan 2005). Cognitive interventions such as mindfulness training (e.g., Garland, in press; Garland, Gaylord, Boettiger, & Howard, 2010) and cognitive-behavioral therapy are increasingly used to address dysfunctional cognitions and to equip substance abusers to better cope with urges to use substances.

Sociocultural and Family Systems Models

Sociocultural and family systems models view individual behavior, including that related to substance abuse, as embedded in a larger complex of micro, mezzo, and macro-level influences. Systems at each of these levels seek to maintain homeostasis and resist change through negative feedback processes (Bateson, 1972). Macro-level social influences include laws, regulations, norms and mores that influence availability, consumption, and consequences of substance use. For example, the geographical location of a nation, its socioeconomic standing and political stability, as well as its religious traditions may greatly influence the likelihood of substance abuse and related problems. Families are embedded in social systems and may, themselves, promote or discourage substance abuse among their members. Family systems or family interactional models highlight factors that perpetuate substance abuse among family members over time and even intergenerationally. Family systems models are also frequently invoked to explain the diverse roles that children and adult children of substance abusers assume in families affected by substance abuse. Family therapy treatments are considered the preferred intervention from the family systems perspective because any change in the substance user's use of substances is likely to reverberate through the family resulting in disruption and distress (e.g., Szapocznik & Williams, 2000). Proponents of family systems models regard substance abuse as a "family disorder" and believe the entire family should be involved in treatment.

Biological Models

A host of biological models have emerged historically and in contemporary theorizing in the substance abuse area. Biological models include those that emphasize genetic, metabolic, and neuropsychopharmacological factors that may render some persons vulnerable to substance dependence or that may greatly increase the dependence liability of some psychoactive substances. Novel evolutionary, behavior genetic, and neurobiological models have emerged in recent decades.

Over the past decade developments in neuroscience, evolutionary biology, and the social sciences have allowed scientists to begin asking why and how biopsychological features of humans evolved in such a way as to make them vulnerable to substance abuse and dependence (Hill & Newlin, 2002). Evolutionary theories have sought to explain fundamental drives to use psychoactive substances and to engage in high-risk behaviors including pathological gambling and binge eating. Evolutionary psychobiology (i.e., functional analyses of psychobiological processes examining the evolution of biological mechanisms that mediate behavior) emerged in the late 1970s with the work of Chagnon and Irons (1979) and Daly and Wilson (1978). In the 1990s, Nesse and Nesse (1994) and Nesse and Berridge (1997) argued that contemporary problems with substance misuse have stemmed largely from the availability of potent psychoactive agents capable of greatly enhancing dopaminergic neurotransmission in mesolimbic brain structures designed to reinforce adaptive behavior related to eating, drinking, and sex.

Public Heath Model

The public health model conceptualizes substance abuse and related problems as outcomes of host, agent, and environmental interactions. Host vulnerabilities might include a genetic predisposition to alcohol dependence or other addictive disorders. Different substances of abuse (i.e., agents) also carry different risks for substance dependence, referred to as their abuse liability, and different risks for various other adverse biopsychosocial outcomes. Finally, environments differ considerably in the extent to which they promote risks for substance abuse and related problems.

For example, practitioners operating from a public health perspective interested in reducing HIV transmission among intravenous opioid users might target highly impulsive and/or risk-taking persons (i.e., host factors), encourage such users to take an oral, long-acting opioid-agonist substitution therapy (i.e., agent factors), and encourage public support and funding for needle exchange and needle sterilization programs (i.e., environmental factors).

The Disease Model

The disease model, also referred to as the "two populations" model, incorporates the view that alcohol or drug-dependent persons are qualitatively different from their nondependent counterparts (Fingarette, 1988). Like pregnancy, proponents of this approach believe one either does or does not have the "disease of addiction." Prominent signs and symptoms of this disease are held to be loss of control over substance use and habitual use of denial as a defense mechanism. Further, although one may "recover" from the disease of addiction via absolute abstinence from psychoactive substance use, the condition is incurable.

Widespread adoption of the disease concept of alcohol and drug dependence following the Repeal of Prohibition served the purpose of medicalizing substance abuse behaviors, while allowing undiagnosed persons free license to use the psychoactive substances they desired. This alibing of alcohol consumption on the part of "non-alcoholics" also served the interests of alcohol beverage manufacturers. Prevention efforts based on disease model conceptualizations focus on early identification of persons at risk for the disease of alcoholism and abstinence-based treatment, often delivered by other persons in recovery from alcoholism. The disease concept has grown enormously more influential over the past 75 years and has been extended to drug dependence and behavioral addictions. A number of theorists have referred to these developments as the "diseasing of America" (Peele, 1989).

Neurocognitive Models

For the past two decades, findings from cognitive neuroscience have informed our understanding of addiction. The view emerging from a number of lines of research is one in which addiction is considered the result of interacting neurocognitive processes. Individuals differ substantially with regard to their vulnerability to the acquisition, maintenance, and reinstatement of addictive behaviors; these individual differences have been linked to variation in neurocognitive functions that have been modeled in recent multisystems conceptualizations (Garland, Boettiger, & Howard, 2011; George & Koob, 2010). Candidate neurocognitive processes include attention, automaticity, reward processing, emotion regulation, and inhibitory control, among others. These processes, which appear to be central in regulating the cognitive, affective, and autonomic mechanisms underpinning addiction, are subserved by a widely distributed network of cortical and subcortical brain regions with distinct anatomical and functional linkages.

Recurrent substance use is thought to impart incentive salience to cues associated with substance use through a learned motivational response subserved by sensitization of mesocorticolimbic brain regions (Robinson & Berridge, 2008). Because substance use results in pleasure and an experience of reward mediated by dopaminergic activations in basal ganglia structures (Feltenstein & See, 2008), these substance-related cues come to elicit a powerful, conditioned motivational response coupled with a "wanting/craving" for substances (O'Brien, Childress, Ehrman, & Robbins, 1998; Robinson & Berridge, 2001). By virtue of classical conditioning principles as outlined earlier in this chapter, cues associated with substance use can come elicit a constellation of physiological reactions. These conditioned responses, known as cue-reactivity, likely impart compulsivity to substance-seeking behaviors, motivating the individual to consume drugs and alcohol even after long periods of abstinence and despite countervailing motivations to remain abstinent, particularly under conditions of stress and negative affect (Garland, Boettiger, et al., 2011).

The appetitive cognitive and behavioral response to substance-related cues is thought to be coordinated by drug-use action schemas (i.e., memory systems that compel consumption of drugs through automatized sequences of stimulus-bound, context-dependent behavior) (Tiffany, 1990; Tiffany & Conklin, 2000). Such schemas develop from repeated substance use in much the same way that other over-learned behavioral sequences become automatized through repetition (e.g., riding a bike) (Shiffrin & Schneier, 1977). After hundreds of repetitions of consistent responses to a given stimulus, attending and responding to that stimulus become automatic, leading to rapid processing in neural circuits involved in executing the behavioral response (Schneider & Chein, 2003). During formation of automatic habits, a neurobiological shift occurs in which behaviors that were originally guided by associative prefrontal cortical networks which compute predicted behavioral outcomes become controlled by sensorimotor cortico-basal ganglia networks (Yin & Knowlton, 2006). Once substance-related cues have acquired incentive salience through conditioning, substance-use action schemas deploy attention to search for and focus on such cues as a means of satisfying the goal of drug use.

When drug-related cues become the focus of attention, motivation for drug use increases which, in turn, amplifies the salience of such cues (Franken, 2003). Thus, there is a mutual excitatory relationship between addiction attentional bias and craving (Field, Munafo, & Franken, 2009), which may compel drug use even in the absence of the desire or intent to use drugs. Hence, the addict may find him or herself consuming drugs without consciousness of the motive or intent to use, in much the same way that other complex thought-action repertoires such as goal-pursuit can be engaged without conscious volition by conditioned contextual cues (Bargh & Chartrand, 1999). This notion corresponds with anecdotal reports of addictive binges in which alcoholics describe having the intent to take a single drink and "the next thing I knew, the bottle was empty," previously abstinent "crack" addicts describe being "lost" for days in a crack house after relapsing by taking a single hit, or the common occurrence of sitting in front of the television with a bag of potato chips only to discover 30 min later that the whole bag has been eaten.

Moreover, the addict may experience difficulty inhibiting the compulsive, automatic addictive response, particularly under conditions of stress and negative affect. Indeed, persons with substance use disorders and behavioral addictions have been shown to exhibit impaired response inhibition, that is, the ability to withhold an automatized response under conditions which typically elicit that response (Goldstein & Volkow, 2011). Thus, as the ability to inhibit drug-related appetitive and consummatory responses becomes impaired due to the neurocognitive changes that occur with escalating addiction, the individual struggling with addiction progressively loses more and more control over the addictive habit.

In an attempt to regulate mounting addictive urges, such individuals may employ "willpower" to suppress urges to engage in the addictive behavior. Suppression of substance-related thoughts and urges evokes "rebound effects," resulting in attentional fixation on drug cues and increased intrusiveness of substance-related mental contents (Klein, 2007; Palfai, Monti, Colby, & Rohsenow, 1997). In turn, suppression of thoughts of substance use and eating leads to greater enactment of such behaviors (Erskine & Georgiou, 2010; Erskine, Georgiou, & Kvavilashvili, 2011). Chronic suppression of addictive urges appears to deplete the neurocognitive resources for self-regulation, resulting in an inability to inhibit substance-related cognitions and an attentional bias towards substance-related cues (Garland, Carter, Ropes, & Howard, 2011). Ultimately, exhaustion of regulatory resources that occurs during sustained suppression of urges may result in relapse.

In sum, from the neurocognitive perspective, a person becomes addicted through basic human learning processes gone awry. In the case of an addiction to a psychoactive substance, learning processes become hijacked due to the neuropharmacologically rewarding properties of the drug itself (Hyman, 2007). The once-intentional behavior to seek and consume drugs becomes rapidly engrained as an automatic, compulsive habit, one that becomes increasingly more difficult to inhibit. As the individual addict struggles to regain control over his or her behavior, he or she becomes hypervigilant for cues such as the sight of a bar, an old hang-out spot, or a familiar "drinking buddy," which can reflexively trigger uncomfortable physical sensations and a strong desire to consume substances, even after extended periods of abstinence. When such cue-reactivity is amplified by life stress, the urge to use may become overwhelming, and misguided attempts to suppress such urges only make them worse. Eventually, the addict relapses, which strengthens the addictive habit through processes of conditioning.

Hence, treatment approaches offering effective alternatives to the maladaptive strategy of suppressing the urge to use substances in the face of relapse triggers may free neurocognitive resources for effective regulation of emotional distress and concomitant urges. Behavioral interventions that can target the neurocognitive processes outlined in the previous section may be effective treatments for addiction. Treatments involving mindfulness training such as *Mindfulness-Based Relapse Prevention* (Bowen et al., 2009; Bowen, Chawla, & Marlatt, 2010) or *Mindfulness-Oriented Recovery Enhancement* (Garland, in press; Garland et al., 2010) are especially promising. These interventions provide instruction in coping with addictive impulses through cultivating metacognitive awareness and acceptance rather than suppression.

Conclusions

Intoxicant use is an age-old human problem of profound complexity and perniciousness. Recent years have witnessed the establishment of federal institutions and professional societies devoted to substance abuse research and a dramatic accumulation of research on all facets of addictive disorders. Research-related developments related to assessment, treatment, and prevention of substance use disorders have greatly improved the standard of care for persons with substance use disorders. A notable diversity of conceptualizations has emerged over the past two thousand years in relation to the substance abuser. Moral condemnation and simplistic unidimensional theories are gradually giving way to more complex models incorporating recent biopsychosocial research findings

Social work practitioners in the addictions, by virtue of the aforementioned developments, are well placed to provide key evidence-based assessment, prevention, and treatment services to persons with substance use disorders. Given the vulnerable and disadvantaged populations they work with, social workers commonly encounter substance abuse in their day-to-day professional interactions. Thus, it is important for social workers to examine their own attitudes toward substance abuse and substance abusers, and to prevent such perceptions from impeding their work with stigmatized client groups.

References

Arnold, J. P. (2005). *Origin and history of beer and brewing: From prehistoric times to the beginning of brewing science and technology.* Cleveland: Beer Books. ISBN 978-9662084-1-2.

Bandura, A. (1999). A sociocognitive analysis of substance abuse: An agentic perspective. *Psychological Science, 10,* 214–217.

Bargh, J. A., & Chartrand, T. L. (1999). The unbearable automaticity of being. *American Psychologist, 54,* 462–479.

Barry, C. L., Huskamp, H. A., & Goldman, H. H. (2010). A political history of federal mental health and addiction insurance. *Milbank Quarterly, 88,* 404–433.

Bateson, G. (1972). *Steps to an ecology of mind.* New York: Ballantine.

Bowen, S., Chawla, N., Collins, S. E., Witkiewitz, K., Hsu, S., Grow, J., et al. (2009). Mindfulness-based relapse prevention for substance use disorders: A pilot efficacy trial. *Substance Abuse, 30,* 295–305.

Bowen, S., Chawla, N., & Marlatt, G. A. (2010). *Mindfulness-based relapse prevention for addictive behaviors.* New York: Guilford Press.

Campbell, H. (2009). *Drug war zone: Frontline dispatches from the streets of El Paso and Juarez.* Austin, TX: University of Texas Press.

Chagnon, N. I., & Irons, W. (Eds.). (1979). *Evolutionary biology and human social behavior: An anthropological perspective.* North Scituate: Duxbury.

Courtwright, D. T. (2010). NIDA, this is your life. *Drug and Alcohol Dependence, 107,* 116–118.

Crocq, M. (2007). Historical and cultural aspects of man's relationship with addictive drugs. *Dialogues in Clinical Neuroscience, 9,* 355–361.

Daly, M., & Wilson, M. (1978). *Sex, evolution, and behavior: Adaptations for reproduction.* North Scituate: Duxbury.

Drummond, D. C., & Glautier, S. (1994). A controlled trial of cue exposure treatment in alcohol dependence. *Journal of Consulting and Clinical Psychology, 62,* 809–817.

Erskine, J. A., & Georgiou, G. J. (2010). Effects of thought suppression on eating behaviour in restrained and non-restrained eaters. *Appetite, 54,* 499–503.

Erskine, J. A., Georgiou, G. J., & Kvavilashvili, L. (2011). I suppress, therefore I smoke: Effects of thought suppression on smoking behavior. *Psychological Science, 21,* 1225–1230.

Feltenstein, M., & See, R. (2008). The neurocircuitry of addiction: An overview. *British Journal of Pharmacology, 154,* 261–274.

Field, M., Munafo, M. R., & Franken, I. H. (2009). A meta-analytic investigation of the relationship between attentional bias and subjective craving in substance abuse. *Psychological Bulletin, 135,* 589–607.

Fingarette, H. (1988). *Heavy drinking: The myth of alcoholism as a disease.* Berkeley: University of California Press.

Franken, I. H. (2003). Drug craving and addiction: Integrating psychological and neuropsychopharmacological approaches. *Progress in Neuropsychopharmacology and Biological Psychiatry, 27,* 563–579.

Garland, E. L. (in press). *Mindfulness-oriented recovery enhancement: Reclaiming a meaningful life from addiction and stress.* Washington, DC: NASW Press.

Garland, E. L., Carter, K., Ropes, K., & Howard, M. O. (2011). Thought suppression, impaired regulation of urges, and Addiction-Stroop predict affect-modulated cue-reactivity among alcohol dependent adults. *Biological Psychology.* doi:10.1016/j.biopsycho.2011.09.010.

Garland, E. L., Gaylord, S. A., Boettiger, C. A., & Howard, M. O. (2010). Mindfulness training modifies cognitive, affective, and physiological mechanisms implicated in alcohol dependence: Results from a randomized controlled pilot trial. *Journal of Psychoactive Drugs, 42,* 177–192.

George, O., & Koob, G. F. (2010). Individual differences in prefrontal cortex function and the transition from drug use to drug dependence. *Neuroscience and Biobehavioral Reviews, 35,* 232–247.

Goldstein, R. Z., & Volkow, N. D. (2011). Dysfunction of the prefrontal cortex in addiction: Neuroimaging findings and clinical implications. *Nature Reviews Neuroscience, 12*(11), 652–669.

Grabowski, J. (2010). Sun-downing and integration for the advancement of science and therapeutics: The National Institute on Substance Use Disorders (NISUD). *Addiction, 105,* 2044–2049.

Hanson, D. J. (2009). Historical overview of alcohol use. In R. T. Ammerman, P.J. Ott, & R. E. Tarter (Eds.), *Prevention and societal impact of drug and alcohol abuse* (pp. 31–45). Psychology Press/Taylor & Francis, London.

Hewitt, B. G. (1995). The creation of the National Institute on Alcohol Abuse and Alcoholism: Responding to America's alcohol problem. *Alcohol Health & Research World, 19,* 1–6.

Hill, E. M., & Newlin, D. B. (2002). Evolutionary approaches to addiction: Introduction. *Addiction, 97,* 375–379.

Howard, M. O., & Chung, S. S. (2000). Nurses' attitudes toward substance users. I. Surveys. *Substance Use & Misuse, 35,* 347–365.

Howard, M. O., Kivlahan, D., & Walker, R. D. (1997). Cloninger's tridimensional theory of personality and psychopathology: Applications to substance use disorders. *Journal of Studies on Alcohol, 58,* 48–66.

Hyman, S. E. (2007). The neurobiology of addiction: Implications for voluntary control of behavior. *American Journal of Bioethics, 7,* 8–11.

Israel, Y., & Lieber, C. S. (2002). The Research Society on Alcoholism. *Addiction, 97,* 483–486.

Janofsky, M. (2004, March 18). Drug fighters turn to rising tide of prescription drug abuse. *New York Times.*

Jay, M. (2010). *High society: The central role of mind-altering drugs in history, science, and culture.* New York: Park Street Press.

Klein, A. A. (2007). Suppression-induced hyperaccessibility of thoughts in abstinent alcoholics: A preliminary investigation. *Behaviour Research and Therapy, 45,* 169–177.

Maisto, S. A., Carey, K. B., & Bradizza, C. M. (1999). Social learning theory. In K. E. Leonaard & H. T. Blane (Eds.), *Psychological theories of drinking and alcoholism* (2nd ed., pp. 106–163). New York: Guilford Press.

Marlatt, G. A., & Donovan, D. M. (2005). *Relapse prevention, 2nd ed. Maintenance strategies in the treatment of addictive behaviors.*: New York: Guilford Press.

Miller, W. R., Sorensen, J. L., Selzer, J. A., & Brigham, G. S. (2006). Disseminating evidence-based practices in substance abuse treatment: A review with suggestions. *Journal of Substance Abuse Treatment, 31,* 25–39.

Morse, S. J. (2004). Medicine and morals, craving and compulsion. *Substance Use & Misuse, 39,* 437–460.

Nesse, R. M. (1994). An evolutionary perspective on substance abuse. *Ethology and Sociobiology, 15,* 339–348.

Nesse, R. M., & Berridge, K. C. (1997). Psychoactive drug use in evolutionary perspective. *Science, 278,* 63–66.

O'Brien, C. P., Childress, A. R., Ehrman, R., & Robbins, S. J. (1998). Conditioning factors in drug abuse: Can they explain compulsion? *Journal of Psychopharmacology, 12*(1), 15.

Page, J. B. (2009). Historical overview of other abusable drugs. In R. T. Ammerman, P. J. Ott, & R. E. Tarter (Eds.), *Prevention and societal impact of drug and alcohol abuse* (pp. 47–63). Psychology Press/Taylor & Francis, Pittsburg, PA.

Palfai, T. P., Monti, P. M., Colby, S. M., & Rohsenow, D. J. (1997). Effects of suppressing the urge to drink on the accessibility of alcohol outcome expectancies. *Behaviour Research and Therapy, 35*, 59–65.

Peele, S. (1989). *The diseasing of America*. Boston: Houghton-Mifflin.

Robinson, T. E., & Berridge, K. C. (2001). Incentive-sensitization and addiction. *Addiction, 96*, 103–114.

Robinson, T. E., & Berridge, K. C. (2008). The incentive sensitization theory: Some current issues. *Philosophical Transactions of the Royal Society of London, 363*, 3137–3146.

Ross, E. A., Watson, M., & Goldberger, B. (2011). "Bath salts" intoxication. *New England Journal of Medicine, 365*, 967–968.

Salvia divinorum Research and Information Center. www.sagewisdom.org. Accessed 23 November 2011.

Satel, S. L. (2001). Is drug addiction a brain disease? In P. B. Heyman & W. N. Brownsberger (Eds.), *Drug addiction and drug policy: The struggle to control dependence* (pp. 118–143). Cambridge: Harvard University Press.

Savage, M. W. (2010, July 10). The growing buzz on "spice"—The marijuana alternative. washingtonpost.com/wp-dyn/content/article/2010/.../AR2010070903554.html. Accessed 23 November 2011.

Schneider, W., & Chein, J. M. (2003). Controlled and automatic processing: Behavior theory, and biological mechanisms. *Cognitive Science, 27*, 525–559.

Shiffrin, R. M., & Schneier, W. (1977). Controlled and automatic human information processing. II. Perceptual learning, automatic attending, and a general theory. *Psychological Review, 84*, 127–190.

Skinner, B. F. (1969). *Contingencies of reinforcement: A theoretical analysis*. New York: Appelton-Century-Crofts.

Sowers, W. E. (1998). Parallel processes: Moral failure, addiction, and society. *Community Mental Health Journal, 34*, 331–336.

Szapocznik, J., & Williams, R. A. (2000). Brief strategic family therapy: Twenty-five years of interplay among theory, research, and practice in adolescent behavior problems and drug abuse. *Clinical Child and Family Psychology Review, 3*(2), 117–134.

Tiffany, S. T. (1990). A cognitive model of drug urges and drug-use behavior: Role of automatic and nonautomatic processes. *Psychological Review, 97*, 147–168.

Tiffany, S. T., & Conklin, C. A. (2000). A cognitive processing model of alcohol craving and compulsive alcohol use. *Addiction, 95*(Suppl. 2), S145–S153.

Warner, J. (2002). *Craze: Gin and debauchery in the age of reason*. London: Random House.

Westermeyer, J. (1988). The pursuit of intoxication: Our 100 century-old romance with psychoactive substances. *American Journal on Drug and Alcohol Abuse, 14*, 175–187.

Yin, H. H., & Knowlton, B. J. (2006). The role of the basal ganglia in habit formation. *Nature Reviews Neuroscience, 7*, 464–476.

Zule, W. A., Vogtsberger, K. N., & Desmond, D. P. (1997). The intravenous injection of illicit drugs and needle sharing: An historical perspective. *Journal of Psychoactive Drugs, 29*, 199–204.

Zwenger, S. R. (2009). Bogarting that joint might decrease oral HPV among cannabis users. *Current Oncology, 16*, 5–7.

Chapter 2
Epidemiology

Michael Fendrich

Introduction

This chapter is a brief introductory perspective on epidemiology—in particular psychiatric epidemiology—a field which encompasses the study of both addiction and mental illness. This perspective is in contrast to the typical clinical perspectives held by many social workers whose primary interest is in directly treating or addressing problems at the individual or family level. Clinicians are critically important—but epidemiologists count—literally. This chapter presents some recent data on trends in rates of disorder and unmet treatment need. It concludes by highlighting the critical importance of epidemiology as a perspective focused not just on describing rates but on searching for causes. In particular, epidemiology's role in articulating the importance of "place" and how multilevel research models—models accounting for both individual and community level risk factors—can facilitate more effective prevention strategies.

Background

Psychiatric epidemiology is the study of the distribution, burden, and causes of mental illness and psychological distress in the community. The key word here is "distribution"; epidemiologists identify and sort cases by time and place in order to ultimately make inferences about causality. From its early days, psychiatric

An earlier version of this chapter was presented as part of the Helen Carey Memorial lecture in September, 2009 at the Milwaukee County Division of Behavioral Health.

M. Fendrich (✉)
Center for Applied Behavioral Health Research, Helen Bader School of Social Welfare,
University of Wisconsin-Milwaukee, Milwaukee, USA
e-mail: fendrich@uwm.edu

M.G. Vaughn and B.E. Perron (eds.), *Social Work Practice in the Addictions*,
Contemporary Social Work Practice, DOI 10.1007/978-1-4614-5357-4_2,
© Springer Science+Business Media New York 2013

epidemiology was focused on the impact of location—the physical and social environment—on the development of psychiatric disorders and symptoms.

According to Susser et al.'s recent comprehensive review (Susser, Schwartz, Morabia, & Bromet, 2006), the Durkheim cross-national European investigation first published in the late nineteenth century of suicide may be considered early example of psychiatric epidemiology. Using official records of recorded suicides, Durkheim found elevated rates in so-called Protestant countries compared with Catholic countries (Durkheim, 1987). Durkheim surmised that behavior was affected by the contrasting patterns of interpersonal connections and social support—the varying social structures—characterizing and countries with different religious orientations (Susser et al., 2006).

In the early part of the twentieth century, the Chicago School of Social Ecology led by Faris and Dunham conducted a series of studies focused on exploring the geographic distribution of mental illness in Chicago neighborhoods. Their research showed that patterns for the distribution of schizophrenia contrasted with patterns for the distribution of manic depression. The highest rates of schizophrenia were in inner city neighborhoods characterized by high levels of residential instability and social isolation and lowest rates in more affluent suburban areas. In contrast, manic depression was highest in the suburban areas and lowest in the inner city neighborhoods (Faris & Dunham, 1939). Thus, as illustrated by the early work of Durkheim and Faris and Dunham, the field of psychiatric epidemiology has its roots in an ecological approach—one that emphasizes community characteristics as opposed to individual level risk factors in the etiology of psychiatric disorders (including both mental illness and substance abuse).

Methodology

Over the course of subsequent decades and continuing to the present, psychiatric epidemiologists have mainly focused on the use of large-scale social surveys to measure rates of distress and psychiatric disorder (Susser et al., 2006). Through responses to these surveys, they have identified individual-level risk factors for these outcomes, such as socioeconomic disadvantage, exposure to stress, impairments in social relationships, or adverse family history and experiences. A number of studies involve surveying randomly selected residents of urban households about drug use, high-risk sexual behavior, and psychiatric symptoms.

Surveys, especially those that involve the collection of data on sensitive topics from randomly selected individuals in a targeted geographic areas, are typically very expensive—costing hundreds of thousands of dollars to execute in a scientifically valid manner. Social surveys are usually long and detailed measures that ask people questions that may seem sensitive and make respondents uncomfortable. For example, respondents often do not provide valid responses to when questioned about issues such as drug abuse history (Fendrich, Johnson, Sudman, Wislar, & Spiehler, 1999). Furthermore, survey researchers are challenged by declining response rates (Groves et al., 2006). It is often hard to get people in the community to answer the door or telephone or respond to inquiries on the Internet. And once contacted by survey researchers, many people do not want to be burdened with a lengthy set of intrusive questions.

Given these challenges, many clinicians may wonder why epidemiologists do not rely on the collection of treatment information obtained from social service systems. Why don't researchers just approach social service agencies and treatment centers to gain access to clinic records patients for interviews to find out about prevalence, risk factors, and disease course?

Even if HIPAA regulations were not a barrier, the need to base conclusions about prevalence, etiology and course on nonclinically derived samples is perhaps best supported by the concept of the clinician's illusion (Cohen & Cohen, 1984). This is the notion—well established in other areas of epidemiology and sometimes called "Berkson's Bias"—that those with a specific type of disorder or illness that actually seek clinical treatment tend to be quite different, especially while they are in the midst of receiving treatment, than others who have the disorder. Compared with other cases, patients in a treatment-based sample tend to be more impaired, to have higher rates of comorbidity, a longer disease course, and, overall, to have a much worse prognosis. Cohen and Cohen (1984) cite as examples the disputed, overly pessimistic prognoses that clinicians typically ascribe to alcoholism, schizophrenia, and heroin addiction. Dire prognoses derived from cross-sectional research employing clinical samples have been consistently contradicted by longitudinal research with nonclinical samples. The most famous example of such a contradiction derives from Lee Robins' study of Vietnam Veterans.

> Perhaps even more striking is the view of clinicians, widely shared by the public, of opiate addiction as an incurable state for most if not all users. This view was forcefully contradicted by Robins and associates, who found that of a sample of Vietnam veterans who were addicted to heroin when interviewed after their return to the USA, 71% were drug free 21/2 years later, often without great effort. Of all those who became addicted in Vietnam, even a larger proportion, 88% avoided relapse over the three years following their return (Cohen & Cohen, 1984: p. 1179).

As empirically supported and concisely summarized by Cohen and Cohen (1984), the clinician's illusion is the "attribution of the characteristics and course of those patients who are currently ill to the entire population contracting the illness… it is the consequence of using a prevalence sample as a substitute for an incidence sample" (p. 1180). While it might be far more convenient for me to study a clinic or residential treatment-based population of those treated for opiate addiction, cases in the clinic are not like those in the community. We cannot get a true sense of a disorder's onset, course, long-term prognosis, correlates, or etiology without doing community-based health surveys.

Epidemiological Survey Results

The survey work that epidemiologists do today builds on a tradition started in the middle of the twentieth century, beginning with a number of survey-based community studies—including Srole's "Midtown Manhattan" study and the Leightons' study of Nova Scotia residents (Leighton, Harding, Macklin, MacMillan, & Leighton, 1963; Srole et al., 1962). Early on in psychiatric epidemiology, researchers did not have the tools to derive precise diagnoses and instead focused on nonspecific indicators of psychological impairment or distress. These studies found that symptoms of psychological distress were quite common, with over 80% of the population reporting them (Susser et al., 2006). About 20% of the population had symptoms that were judged by psychiatrists reviewing the data as indicative of *severe* impairment. Risk factors for impairment included being female, having lower socioeconomic status, and experiencing greater socioeconomic adversity (Susser et al., 2006). These rates seem unreasonably high at first blush, and, accordingly, were met by both researchers and the public with considerable skepticism (Susser et al., 2006).

In the mid-1980s, the technology of survey research developed to the point where diagnostic specific survey tools were available and validated for use by lay interviewers in large-scale community surveys. In the early 1980s, employing one such tool, the Diagnostic Interview Schedule (DIS), the National Institute of Mental Health-supported Epidemiologic Catchment Area study determined the diagnostic status of some 20,000 adults sampled from selected neighborhoods of five U.S. communities. This was followed with two rounds of the Kessler's National Comorbidity Survey (one in 1991–1992; and one in 2001–2002) which employed the Composite International Diagnostic Interview (CIDI) in a national probability sample.

These two sets of studies, when taken together, suggest that somewhere between 15% and 25% of adults ages 18–64 years currently suffer from one or more mental disorders (Susser et al., 2006). The data suggest that disorders are highly comorbid with one another and that many of these disorders typically have symptoms that began in childhood or adolescence. Also note that these diagnostic-focused national studies provided further support for the high prevalence of psychiatric impairment (previously met with public skepticism) and provided additional evidence that gender, social class, family dysfunction, and environmental adversity are key correlates of psychiatric disorder onset.

Increasingly, epidemiologists are concerned with and have documented the prominent role that psychiatric disorders have in the total pattern of morbidity and mortality nationally and worldwide as part of the World Health Organization's (WHO's) Global Burden of Disease initiative. Beginning in late 1990s, a revised version of the CIDI was administered in 30 countries worldwide. Based on these data, the specific burden of mental disorders on the USA was most recently summarized by Buka (2008: p. 977):

> …according to the World Health Organization's estimates for 2002 (which have been sustained in more recent updates), mental health disorders are the leading cause of disability in the USA and Canada, accounting for 25% of all years of life lost to disability and premature mortality. Worldwide, it is estimated that mental disorders account for 12% of disability-adjusted life years. In terms of mortality, suicide alone is the 11th leading cause of death in the USA, with approximately 30,000 deaths per year.

Figure 2.1 reflects recent work by Eaton et al. (2008) that summarizes the global burden of psychiatric disorder by first indicating the worldwide 1 year prevalence of

Mental disorder	Median 1-year prevalence	Interquartile range	No. of studies found	No. of studies included
Panic disorder	0.9	0.6-1.9	486	33
Social phobia	2.8	1.1-5.8	296	30
Simple phobia	4.8	3.5-7.3	296	25
Major depressive disorder	5.3	3.6-6.5	3,935	42
Obsessive-compulsive disorder	1.0	0.6-2.0	293	19
Drug abuse/dependence	1.8	1.1-2.7	1,417	11
Alcohol abuse/dependence	5.9	5.2-8.1	1,646	14
Personality disorders	9.1	9.0-14.4	620	5
Schizophrenia	0.5	0.3-0.6	2,637	23
Bipolar disorder	0.6	0.3-1.1	865	16
Dementia (age >65 years)	5.4	3.2-7.1	2,979	25

Eaton et al. *Epidemiol Rev 2008;30:1-14*. Reprinted with permission from Oxford University Press.

Fig. 2.1 Prevalence of mental disorders* in adults in the 12 months prior to interview

major psychiatric disorders by diagnosis; these estimates are based on an extensive review of multiple US and international prevalence studies. Highlighting the most prevalent major psychiatric disorders, the estimates suggest that about 6% of the adult population suffered from alcohol abuse or dependence during the past year, over 5% of the adult population suffered from depression; and among the adult population over 65, more than 5% suffered from dementia.

Eaton et al. (2008) estimated the global burden of disease (GBD) for each of the diagnostic categories listed in Fig. 2.2. This includes an estimate of the GBD disability weight for certain disorders (based on expert rankings of symptom vignettes), as well as an indicator of the percentage of those with each disorder who have marked impairment on the Sheehan Disability Scale (which was administered as part of the WHO collaborative surveys). More importantly, they provide an estimate of the cost per year in the USA for each of the disorders.

Thus, for example, the score of 83 for bipolar disorder indicates that among those who suffer from this disorder, 83% report a severe disability in one or more of the four areas on the Sheehan Disability Scale. With respect to the Global Burden of Disease weight (GBD), for comparison sake, we know that multiple sclerosis has a GBD weight of 0.41, deafness 0.33, and blindness 0.62. The schizophrenia GBD weight of 0.50, the bipolar GBD weight of 0.40, and the major depressive disorder GBD weight of 0.35 underscores the severity of these relatively prevalent psychiatric disorders. The last column of the table highlights the US costs associated with each of these disorders. The costs are staggering. The costs associated with both alcohol abuse/dependence and drug abuse/dependence in the USA exceeds $200 billion. The costs for major depression approach $100 billion. By conceptualizing the burden of psychiatric disorders in terms of the years of disability that they cause, the WHO projected that depression will be the second leading cause of disability in the world by the year 2020, right behind cardiovascular disease (Susser et al., 2006; Üstün et al. 2004).

Mental disorder	GBD disability weight*	CPES % severe SDS disabiltiy†	Cost per annum in US dollars (billions)
Panic disorder	0.17	47	30.4
Social phobia	NA§	36	15.7
Simple phobia	NA	19	11.0
Major depressive disorder	0.35¶	58	97.3
Obsessive-compulsive disorder	0.13	47	10.6
Drug abuse/dependence	0.25	39#	201.6
Alcohol abuse/dependence	0.16¶	14#	226.0
Personality disorders	NA	NA	NA
Schizophrenia	0.53¶	NA	70.0
Bipolar disorder	0.40¶	83	78.6
Dementia (age >65 years)	NA	NA	76.0

*Global Burden of Disease (GBD) disability weights from Murray and Lopez, annex table 3, untreated form, age group 15-44 years.

† Percentage with marked or extremely severe impairment according to the Sheehan Disability Scale (SDS), as used in the Collaborative Psychiatric Epidemiologic Surveys (CPES). The SDS estimate for bipolar disorder was based on the most severe of the SDS rating for depression and mania. Bipolar disorder and its SDS estimate were present in the National Comorbidity Survey Replication (NCS-R) and National Survey of American Life (NSAL) components of the CPES. Obsessive-compulsive disorder and simple phobia and their SDS estimates were present in only the NCS-R component of the CPES.

§ NA, not applicable.

¶ Disability weights from Mathers et al. (2006); depression level is "moderate."

Dependence only.

Eaton et al. *Epidemiol Rev 2008;30:1-14.* Reprinted with permission from Oxford University Press.

Fig. 2.2 Disability and cost associated with mental disorders

The WHO report also underscores the extent to which treatment need is not met. Strikingly, the report points out that in developed countries, between 36% and 50% of those who were identified as having serious mental illness on the CIDI survey were untreated in the year before their interview; the gap is even greater in developing countries where over three quarters of serious cases received no treatment (The WHO World Mental Health Survey Consortium, 2004).

The cross-national variation is informative for another reason: it reminds us that when we aggregate across countries we may lose sight of critical differences that may relate to specific countries and specific diagnoses (recalling Durkheim), so it might be best to refocus with some U.S. specific data, and if possible, on specific disorders.

For example, the review by Mojtabai et al. (2009) suggests that with respect to those meeting the criteria for a diagnosis of schizophrenia in the USA 40% report not having received mental health treatment in the previous 6–12 months. Among those who report getting treatment, these authors indicate that their treatment falls short of the benchmarks set by evidence-based practice guidelines and that a lack of meaningful psychosocial treatments (as opposed to medication treatment) and a lack of continuity of care are particularly striking.

Epidemiologists have produced specific estimates related to prevalence of serious mental illness and unmet treatment need in the US general population in the

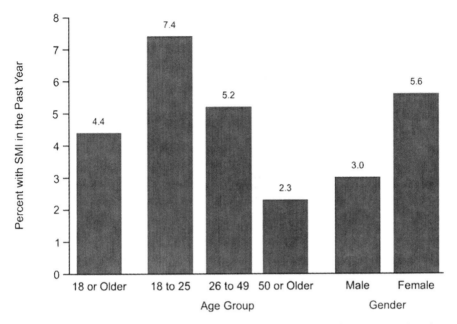

Fig. 2.3 Serious mental illness in the past year among adults aged 18 or older, by age and gender: 2008. http://www.oas.samhsa.gov/nsduh/2k8nsduh/2k8Results.cfm#8.1.1

annual National Survey on Drug Use and Health (NSDUH). In the last decade, the NSDUH survey has added questions about depression and serious psychological distress (via the K6 Scale) to its extensive and comprehensive national assessment of substance use problems in children and adults. In 2008, further modifications and enhancements were made to the survey (including additional questions about disability and follow-up clinical interviews with a sample subset) that facilitated estimates of what the US Office of Applied Studies terms "serious mental illness." The NSDUH surveyed over 67,500 people ages 12 and older in randomly selected households in the USA using audio computer-assisted self-interviews (Substance Abuse and Mental Health Services Administration, 2009). In 2008, NSDUH estimated that about 4.4% of the adult population ages 18 years and older experienced serious mental illness (having a mental disorder plus "impairment" in functioning) during the past year (based on model estimates; see Fig. 2.3). That represents about 9.8 million adults. The figure shows that among the subgroups in the population, the 18–25 years old group experienced the highest rates and that women experienced higher rates than men. Also, not shown, the rates of SMI were higher among adults who were unemployed (8%). Respondents meeting the criteria for serious mental illness (SMI) reported significantly higher rates of substance dependence or abuse. Among adults with SMI in 2008, 25.2% were dependent on or abused illicit drugs or alcohol—this compares with 8.3% for non-SMI adults.

Overall, the NSDUH survey indicates that 2.5 million adults were estimated as having had both SMI PLUS substance abuse and dependence during the past year

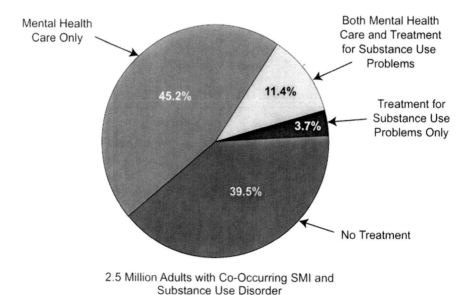

2.5 Million Adults with Co-Occurring SMI and
Substance Use Disorder

Fig. 2.4 Past year mental health care and treatment for substance use problems among adults aged 18 or older with both serious mental illness and a substance use disorder: 2008. http://www.oas. samhsa.gov/nsduh/2k8nsduh/2k8Results.cfm#8.1.1

in 2008. The pie chart in Fig. 2.4 underscores the limited nature of treatment being provided to those most in need of it. Nearly 60% reported receiving some type of treatment during the past year—most of the treatment was restricted to mental health services (i.e., their substance abuse was not directly addressed). Most strikingly, nearly 40% of this group with dual diagnosis issues received no treatment at all during the past year. While the rates of serious mental illness in this study are somewhat lower than we have seen in CIDI-based studies, these findings regarding unmet treatment need are consistent with the WHO data presented earlier.

Figure 2.5 is based on follow-up questions regarding reasons for not seeking treatment among those who self-identified as having an unmet need for treatment or counseling who also reported not receiving mental health services during the past year. Among the 5.1 million adults who reported an unmet need for mental health care and who *did not* receive mental health services in the past year (see Fig. 2.5), the primary barrier to care—affecting nearly 43% of these respondents—was affordability. Interestingly, nearly one in five within this group cited not knowing where to go for care as a reason for not receiving needed services.

Clearly, there may be important differences in location that may influence the nature of psychiatric disorders; it may not be completely valid to aggregate data across the 50 states. NSDUH provides statewide estimates of elevated rates of serious psychological distress (based on the average of multiple survey years) and of major depression alone (based on K6 algorithms; Hughes, Sathe, & Spagnola, 2009).

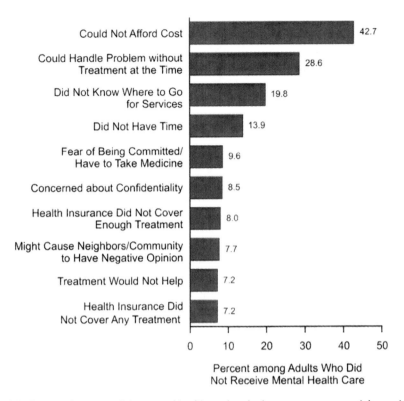

Fig. 2.5 Reasons for not receiving mental health services in the past year among adults aged 18 or older with an unmet need for mental health care who did not receive mental health services: 2008. http://www.oas.samhsa.gov/nsduh/2k8nsduh/2k8Results.cfm#8.1.1

The declining budgets in State Mental Health and Substance Abuse Systems treatment services locally and nationally have also been well documented. The National Association of State Mental Health Program Directors (NASMHPD), based on a survey of 42 states, determined that state mental health budget cuts of at least nearly 5% are evident in 32 states for FY 2009 and over 8% for FY 2010. We are also seeing increasing reports in the media that the criminal justice system is bearing a great deal of the burden for mental health care. A recent report in the New York Times documented the fact that juvenile justice systems around the country are being flooded with youths with severe mental illness—youths who previously may have been treated through their states' mental health systems (Moore, 2009).

The Search for Cause: The Importance of Place

A core focus of epidemiology—part of the definition provided earlier—is the search for causes. We use that search to guide prevention strategies so that ultimately we can have an impact in reducing rates and preventing serious mental disorder from occurring or persisting. Importantly, there has been renewed attention to the importance of this search. As part of this search, there has been renewed concern about the importance of "place" in the variability and distribution of disorder. This is reflected in three recent comprehensive summaries of the psychiatric literature appearing in the 2008 volume of Epidemiological Reviews. One paper focuses on the role of "place" in psychosis (March et al., 2008). Another focuses on neighborhood and depression (Kim, 2008). A third shows variability in rates of schizophrenia by region (McGrath, Saha, Chant, & Welham, 2008). These papers return the discipline of psychiatric epidemiology to its Durkheimian roots.

In his review of neighborhood and depression, Kim notes, "Across studies, the evidence generally supports harmful effects of social disorder and, to a lesser extent, suggests protective effects for neighborhood socioeconomic status" (Kim, 2008: p. 101).

An extensive and growing body of social science research underscores the conclusion that the qualities and characteristics of our neighborhoods can powerfully influence our life course. Recent research suggests that neighborhoods not only can affect the onset and course of severe mental illness, but they can also affect long-term academic achievement, sexual risk behavior and the prevalence of sexually transmitted diseases, the use of illicit drugs such as marijuana and cocaine and even high-risk drinking behavior among college students.

This focus on place—and other macro-level variables is coming at a time of great methodological and statistical advancement that has been facilitated by a set of methods called "multilevel modeling." Previously, the approach to modeling risk factors for psychiatric outcomes had been primarily targeted toward individual level risk factors—variables that were measured at the person level—or characteristics of individual persons for whom behavioral outcomes were being studied (e.g., socioeconomic status, relationships with family members, personality characteristics and sociodemographic variables such as age, gender, and race/ethnicity).

Techniques for modeling causation at the individual level, however, have now advanced to the point where researchers can explore both individual and macro-level neighborhood influences simultaneously. For example, in recent work on high-risk college drinking outcomes in college students, researchers have used multilevel models to explore the influence of exposure to prevention programs, student achievement, and the availability of alcohol outlets and venues in the areas around campus (so-called alcohol outlet density; e.g. Scribner et al., 2008). Epidemiological researchers are advancing the field to search for causes through more complex models that systematically and centrally incorporate "place."

Thus, the data and methodology are beginning to point to the notion that improving "place" or changing neighborhoods may be critical to transforming lives. This may be easier said than done. Neighborhood boundaries are subjective, complex, and unstable. In this era of twitter, texting, cell phones, blogging, and the Internet, the notion of what constitutes "place" is even more confusing and challenging. These new cyber communities may actually create new barriers, challenges, and risk for those with serious mental illness and those with limited access to technology. And these cyber places are distinct from the "real" places which desperately need our attention.

We can move forward in reducing the ever growing and seemingly insatiable demand for psychiatric services in the long run by understanding the mechanisms of neighborhood impact and the processes that lead to neighborhood improvement. This is not completely reduced to a monetary resource issue. Policy makers, researchers, and service providers are increasingly discussing strategies for improving local levels of "social capital"—community characteristics that promote participation in groups, activities and social networks for mutual benefit (see Putnam, 2002). Neighborhoods high in social capital are those where residents have high levels of trust in one another and where there are an abundance of activities characterized by voluntary efforts and reciprocal exchanges. Epidemiologist need to continue to develop, and refine this concept, systematically track social capital's level and variation across neighborhoods and thoroughly investigate—through multilevel modeling procedures—its association with health and behavioral outcomes.

The idea of connecting those with serious mental illness in treatment or those who are reentering from treatment facilities (and prisons) to supportive networks and meaningful voluntary activities in the community—an idea that is clearly consistent with social capital theories—is probably as old as the discipline of social work itself. Many social workers are probably well aware of pockets of strength, where supportive community networks thrive despite dismal socioeconomic conditions.

Conclusions

Treatment providers' insights regarding social capital are valuable to epidemiologists as we focus our work on describing neighborhood level risk and protective factors and statistically assessing their impact on mental health and other behavioral outcomes. As researchers we need to continue to clearly communicate our findings to you—to describe how variation across places and individuals affect the onset and course of psychiatric disorder. We also need to communicate our findings to the communities where we do the research and directly engage communities as much as possible in our research. The joint and collaborative efforts of epidemiologists, clinicians and social work practitioners, and community members, supported by enhanced federal funding for epidemiological and intervention research, may provide sufficient conditions for genuine improvements in the quality of place, ultimately *reducing* the burden of mental illness in our community.

References

Buka, S. L. (2008). Psychiatric epidemiology: Reducing the global burden of mental illness. *American Journal of Epidemiology, 168*, 977–979.

Cohen, P., & Cohen, J. (1984). The clinician's illusion. *Archives of General Psychiatry, 41*, 1178–1182.

Durkheim, E. (1987/1897). *Le Suicide*. New York: Free Press.

Eaton, W. W., Martins, S. S., Nestdat, G., Bienvenu, O. J., Clarke, D., & Alexandre, P. (2008). The burden of mental disorders. *Epidemiologic Reviews, 30*, 1–14.

Faris, R., & Dunham, H. (1939). *Mental disorders in urban areas: An ecological study of schizophrenia and other psychoses*. New York: Hafner Publishing.

Fendrich, M., Johnson, T. P., Sudman, S., Wislar, J. S., & Spiehler, V. (1999). Validity of drug use reporting in a high risk community sample: A comparison of cocaine and heroin survey reports with hair tests. *American Journal of Epidemiology, 149*, 955–962.

Groves, R. M., Couper, M. P., Presser, S., Singer, E., Tourangeau, R., Acosta, G. P., et al. (2006). Experiments in producing nonresponse bias. *Public Opinion Quarterly, 70*, 720–736.

Hughes, A., Sathe, N., & Spagnola, K. (2009). *State estimates of substance use from the 2006–2007 National Surveys on Drug Use and Health*. Office of Applied Studies, Substance Abuse and Mental Health Services Administration, NSDUH Series H-35, HHS Publication No. SMA 09-4362, Rockville, MD.

Kim, D. (2008). Blues from the neighborhood? Neighborhood characteristics and depression. *Epidemiologic Reviews, 30*, 101–117.

Leighton, D. C., Harding, J. S., Macklin, D. B., MacMillan, A. M., & Leighton, A. H. (1963). The character of danger: Psychiatric symptoms in selected communities. In *The Stirling County study of psychiatric disorder and sociocultural environment* (Vol. III). New York: Basic Books.

March, D., Hatch, S. L., Morgan, C., Kirkbride, J. B., Bresnahan, M., Fearon, P., et al. (2008). Psychosis and place. *Epidemiologic Reviews, 30*, 84–100.

Mathers, C. D., Lopez, A. D., & Murray, C. J. (2006). The burden of disease and mortality by condition: data, methods, and results for 2001. In: Lopez, A.D., Mathers, C.D., Ezzati, M. et al., (eds). *Global burden of disease and risk factors*. Washington, DC: The World Bank, 145–240.

McGrath, J., Saha, S., Chant, D., & Welham, J. (2008). Schizophrenia: A concise overview of incidence, prevalence and mortality. *Epidemiologic Reviews, 30*, 67–76.

Mojtabai, R., Fochtmann, L., Chang, S. W., Kotov, R., Craig, T. J., & Bromet, E. (2009). Unmet need for mental health care in schizophrenia: An overview of literature and new data from a first-admission study. *Schizophrenia Bulletin, 35*, 679–695.

Moore, S. (2009). Mentally ill offenders strain juvenile justice system. *New York Times*. Retrieved August 10th, 2009 form http://www.nytimes.com/2009/08/10/us/10juvenile.html?pagewanted=all.

Murray, C.J.L., & Lopez, A.D. (1996). *The global burden of disease: a comprehensive assessment of mortality and disability from diseases, injuries, and risk factors in 1990 and projected to 2020*. Boston MA: Harvard University Press.

National Association of State Mental Health Program Directors Research Institute. (2008). *SMHA budget shortfalls FY 2009, 2010, & 2011. Results based on 42 states responding*.

Putnam, R. D. (2002). *Democracies in flux: The evolution of social capital in contemporary society*. New York: Oxford University Press.

Scribner, R., Mason, K., Theall, K., Simonsen, N., Schneider, S. K., Goberg Towvim, L., et al. (2008). The contextual role of alcohol outlet density in college drinking. *Journal of Studies of Alcohol and Other Drugs, 69*, 112–120.

Srole, L., Langer, T. S., Michael, S. T., Kirkpatrick, P., Opler, M., & Rennie, T. A. (1962). *Mental health in the metropolis*. New York: Harper & Row.

Substance Abuse and Mental Health Services Administration. (2009). *Results from the 2008 National Survey on Drug Use and Health: National Findings*. Office of Applied Studies, NSDUH Series H-36, HHS Publication No. SMA 09-4434, Rockville, MD.

Susser, E., Schwartz, S., Morabia, A., & Bromet, E. J. (2006). *Psychiatric epidemiology: Searching for the causes of mental disorders*. New York: Oxford University Press.

The WHO World Mental Health Survey Consortium. (2004). Prevalence, severity, and unmet need for treatment in the World Health Organization World Mental Health Surveys. *Journal of the American Medical Association, 291*, 2581–2590.

Üstün, T. B., Ayuso-Mateos, J. L., Chatterji, S., Mathers, C., & Murray, C. J. (2004). Global burden of depressive disorders in the year 2000. *British Journal of Psychiatry, 184*, 386–392.

Chapter 3
Etiology

Michael G. Vaughn

While previous chapters on historical and contemporary perspectives and epidemiology introduced the study of causes this chapter's sole focus is on knowledge of the causal factors that contribute to the development and expression of addictive behaviors and dependence syndromes. Although most social workers are involved in treatment and services components in the addictions arena, knowledge about causes provides a rich understanding about many of the factors that undergird problems with addictive substances. Taking a cell to society perspective the emphasis in this chapter will be on the interplay between genes, neuroscience, social cognition, and proximal and distal environments and their effects on the pathways toward addiction.

Understanding etiology is important for several reasons. Arguably, the most important reason is that knowing the causes for something allows us to target those causes for amelioration both in a policy and practice sense. Social work practitioners benefit from knowledge of causation of addiction by treating their clients in a more scientifically informed and humane way. Some of the negative biases that practitioners and policy-makers have with regard to those dependent on various substances are attenuated by a robust understanding of etiology. In other words, the values that helping professions have are made more sturdy by a scientific rendering of the causes of addiction.

Theories as to the causes of addiction vary. Older perspectives often emphasized addiction as a character flaw in need of correction before alcohol or drug use would terminate. Modern theoretical formulations tend to fall somewhere along the biosocial continuum meaning that a greater emphasis is placed on biological or sociological factors. However, most of these theories recognize that addiction is a multifactor phenomenon. Before moving into a fuller discussion of the etiology of addiction some basic definitional issues need to be examined.

M.G. Vaughn (✉)
Saint Louis University, St. Louis, MO, USA
e-mail: mvaughn9@slu.edu

M.G. Vaughn and B.E. Perron (eds.), *Social Work Practice in the Addictions,*
Contemporary Social Work Practice, DOI 10.1007/978-1-4614-5357-4_3,
© Springer Science+Business Media New York 2013

Definitional Issues

Although numerous definitions of addiction have been put forth, one contemporary definition that succinctly captures the essence of addiction has been articulated by Koob and LeMoal (2006, p. 25) who defined addiction as follows: "Drug addiction, also known as substance dependence, is a chronically relapsing disorder characterized by (1) a compulsion to seek and take the drug, (2) loss of control in limiting intake, and (3) emergence of a negative emotional state (e.g., dysphoria, anxiety, irritability) when access to the drug is prevented (defined here as dependence)." So Koob's definition points out three key features of definition that impact understanding causes (not to mention prevention and treatment): compulsive drug-seeking behavior, lowered self-control, and negative emotions. One additional factor that amplifies these three factors is that substance-dependent individuals often reach a level of tolerance in their substance intake. Tolerance is a physiological condition where the body requires an increase amount of a given substance in order to achieve desired effects. Given individual differences in executive governance and self-regulation and emotion coupled with environmental and situational variation, it is easy to see that addiction is a multiple factor process influenced by biological, psychological, and social variables.

Susceptibility Genes

Although incorrect, explanations of addiction in popular culture tend to suggest that the causal relationship between a gene (genotype) and some behavioral outcome (phenotype) is straightforward and direct. However, addictive disorders and behaviors are not inherited in a direct Mendelian way. In general, complex behaviorally oriented phenotypes such as binge drinking or drug dependence are indirectly predicted and less likely to involve a "gene for" explanation (Chakravarti & Little, 2003; Meyer-Lindenberg & Weinberger, 2006; Plomin & Rutter, 1998; Rutter, Moffitt, & Caspi, 2006). However, a number of genes have been found to play an important role in the causal nexus of addiction. Recent work, for example, from the Collaborative Study on the Genetics of Alcoholism has found that GABRA2 (expressed more strongly in men) is associated with dependence on alcohol (Edenberg et al., 2004). Importantly, several studies have since replicated this finding (Agrawal et al., 2006; Covault, Gelernter, Hesselbrock, Nellissery, & Kranzler, 2004; Fehr et al., 2006; Soyka et al., 2008; Xu et al., 2004). Dick et al. (2009) have hypothesized that GABRA2 may underlie susceptibility to not only alcohol and drug dependence but general externalizing behaviors as well. This notion was tested from childhood to adulthood using trajectory analysis from an original sample that consisted of 585 children. Results indicated that GABRA2 was indeed associated with elevated externalizing, however, parental supervision moderated the effect.

A gene, OPRM1, found in the endogenous opioid system (a system that produces molecules in the body similar to morphine and related opiates) is associated with increased sensitivity to the effects of alcohol (Ray & Hutchison, 2004). Findings relating OPRM1 to drug dependence have been less successful (see Dick & Agrawal, 2008). Other genes in the endogenous opioid system such as OPRK1 and OPRD1 have also been investigated with modest results (Dick & Agrawal, 2008). A gene in another system has also come under intense investigation. CHRM2, produced in the cholinergic system (a system that produces the excitatory neurotransmitter acetylcholine) has been associated with alcohol and drug dependence and has been replicated in multiple samples (Dick & Agrawal, 2008).

Another gene, the low-activity alleles of the monoamine oxidase A (MAOA) has been found to confer an increased risk to developing a range of antisocial behaviors including alcoholism (Guo, Wilhelmsen, & Hamilton, 2007). Samochowiec et al. (1999) tested whether length variation of the 30-bp repeat of the MAOA polymorphism was associated with variation in antisocial behavior and alcohol dependence using a clinical sample of 488 German males including 59 alcoholics with antisocial personality disorder. Findings showed that the frequency of the low-activity 3-repeat allele was significantly higher among the 59 antisocial alcoholics compared with 185 controls (51% vs. 35%, $p < .05$). The mechanism by which the low activity MAOA exerts its effects may be due to its weak regulatory function of the prefrontal cortex demonstrated by brain imaging analyses in male study participants.

Neurotransmitters: Dopamine and Serotonin

Neurotransmitters are chemicals that transmit a signal and facilitate communication between neurons in the brain. They are often classified as peptides, monoamines, and amino acids and are often functionally excitatory (e.g., go) and inhibitory (e.g., stop) in nature. Because of their basic importance to behavior and life itself, neurotransmitters are an important area of study with respect to addiction etiology. The biochemical mechanism by which substances increase addiction probability is partly due to the effects of increased dopamine levels in the brain. Dopamine is a type of neurotransmitter associated with reinforcement of natural rewards necessary for survival. Dopamine facilitates increases in communication between receptors in the brain associated with heightened states of joy and arousal. The close relationship between the reward pathway (more on this a little later) and dopamine activity has led many to refer to this circuit as the dopaminergic system. Numerous substances including cocaine and amphetamines, opiates, nicotine, alcohol, and cannabis involve the release of dopamine and implicate an important area of the brain in addiction known as the nucleus accumbens. The nucleus accumbens is a site in the reward pathway where major substances of abuse exert their reinforcing effects. Based on brain-imaging investigations low numbers of type 2 dopamine receptors (i.e., DRD2) have been found to be associated with heightened risk for addiction (Noble, 2000). Individuals with this risk allele have lower levels of dopamine in their brains. Because dopamine helps the brain experience feelings of pleasure—things associated with reward taking drugs of abuse increases dopamine in the brain. Conversely, it has been hypothesized that higher levels may be a protective factor or type of shield from addiction (Childress, 2006). Another dopamine gene, DRD4, has been explored due to its linkage with novelty seeking. Novelty seeking refers to a temperament trait in Cloninger's (1987) model, which is a dopaminergically modulated tendency toward exploratory behavior and excitement in response to new or novel things in the environment. Research by Vaughn and colleagues (Vaughn, Beaver, DeLisi, Howard, & Perron, 2009) has found a relatively robust association between DRD4 and binge drinking.

With respect to the neurotransmitter serotonin, alcohol use and aggressive behavior have been associated with decreases in serotonin activity. The reason for this is that serotonin is a key regulator of mood and aggression (Nelson & Chiavegatto, 2001). In particular, studies have implicated the low activity short allele polymorphism (5-HTT). These results have been found in western and non-western societies. However, not all studies have found this link. For example, Brown et al. (2007) performed PET scans among patients being treated for alcohol dependence and found no significant variations between patients classified as aggressive or nonaggressive in the densities of the serotonin transporter gene (5-HTT).

What Do Brain Scans Tell Us About the Causes of Addiction?

Much of the recent understanding and conceptualization of addiction as a disease of the brain (more to follow on this) has been facilitated by the rise of neuroimaging techniques. There are five major neuroimaging techniques that have been employed in varying degrees to unravel the mechanisms of addiction: structural magnetic resonance imaging, functional magnetic resonance imaging, magnetic resonance spectroscopy, positron emission tomography, and single photon emission computed tomography (see Fowler, Volkow, Kassed, & Chang, 2007). Each of these techniques possesses different advantages in gathering information on the effects of substance use and understanding the substance-dependent brain. The major advantage of these techniques is that they permit direct comparisons to be made between persons who are at varying levels of substance use and addiction with individuals who are not using. Other factors such as age, race, gender, socioeconomic status can be matched with these comparisons to further isolate the differences. Taken together, findings from brain scan studies indicate clear involvement of biochemical, structural, functional, and metabolic processes in the brain that have an influence on decision-making, planning, and craving. Brain imaging studies, although valuable, are cumbersome, expensive, and difficult to use on large samples and as such this impedes their impact on understanding the causes of addiction.

The Causal Role of the Brain's Reward Pathway

In a seminal essay appearing in the prestigious journal, *Science* in 1997 Alan Leshner, former director of the National Institute on Drug Abuse, declared that "Addiction is a Brain Disease, and it Matters." Leshner summarized 20 years of scientific research on addiction and revealed that most of the neural circuits affected by drugs of abuse and resulting receptor behavior are fairly well established. Much of the best research has found that there are major differences in the brains of addicted persons and nonaddicted persons. These differences are pronounced. Importantly, Leshner also recognized that the social environment that addicted persons find themselves in (i.e., brain is nested in a context of social relations) possess an important role in the development and course of addiction.

The main neural circuit that Leshner and many others have discussed is commonly termed the reward pathway. The reward pathway or specifically the mesolimbic reward system is of critical importance due to its role in survival. The reward pathway is the area of the brain that provides the positive reinforcement for eating, drinking, sex, and other functions basic to survival. Thus, the reward pathway is rooted in our evolutionary history. With respect to the ingestion of drugs of abuse, the reward pathway is flooded with dopamine to such a magnitude (e.g., above and beyond that of aforementioned food and sex) that the neural circuit becomes "hijacked" and compulsive drug seeking and craving follows due to the powerful pleasure and reinforcement effects. Craving is common in addiction and can be defined as the memory of the pleasurable and reinforcing aspects of drug ingestion and occurs during a negative emotional state (Koob & LeMoal, 2008; Markou, Kosten, & Koob, 1998). So why doesn't everyone who uses a psychoactive intoxicant become addicted given that the effects on the reward pathway are so great? One major answer has to do with the ability to exercise self-control, which serves as a counterbalance to our drive for pleasure. However, there is individual variation in the ability to exercise inhibitory control and some drugs of abuse such as cocaine and heroin powerfully overwhelm executive governance and the ability to plan and exercise judgment over one's actions. This is particularly the case among persons who may possess structural or functional deficits in this area of the brain.

Following an extensive examination of brain imaging, neuropsychological, and clinical outcome studies Lubman, Yucel, and Pantelis (2004, p. 1491) further specify these relations stating "The current literature suggests that in addition to the brain's reward system, two frontal cortical regions (anterior cingulated and orbitofrontal cortices), critical in inhibitory control over reward-related behavior are dysfunctional in addicted individuals. These same regions have been implicated in other compulsive conditions characterized by deficits in inhibitory control over maladaptive behaviors, such as obsessive–compulsive disorder."

One useful analogy used to understand the compulsion inherent is addiction is the "stop" and "go" conceptualization. Childress (2006) suggests that this analogy aids in gaining insight into the heterogeneity that exists in the etiology of addiction. The ancient reward pathway is the "go" system because of its involvement and sensitivity towards motivation related to natural rewards. The "stop" system is responsible for inhibiting behavior when the reward is dangerous or detrimental to survival. Extending this analogy further we can think of the reward pathway as the gas pedal of automobile and executive functions — components of the mammalian brain that in humans includes planning, decision-making, and impulse control, as the brakes. The variation in how this analogy expresses itself n different individuals is largely determined by inputs form genes and the social environment. Heterogeneity in the stop and go systems due to polygenic (i.e., multiple genes), neural deficits, and environmental input such as early trauma influence the response to addictive substances and resulting consequences for behavior. Not only is their individual-level variation but also developmental variation in these systems over the life-course.

One of these important developmental periods for addiction is adolescence, where drug experimentation and antisocial behavior is normative (Moffitt, 1993). During adolescence executive functions responsible for inhibitory control are not yet fully developed or mature, thereby creating a situation of a strong reward response coupled with a weak stop system (Childress, 2006). This situation is thought to account for why the period of adolescence is such a risky developmental period (Steinberg, 2007). Compounding existing addiction vulnerability substance use and abuse is also associated or comorbid with attention-deficit hyperactivity disorder and conduct problems. Although the causal status between conduct problems and addiction is unresolved, it is clear that each contributes to the other in myriad ways.

In sum, genetic and neuroscience reward pathway research points to disrupted control and compulsive substance seeking. The expression of neurobehavioral disinhibition even without the use of substances is often present in childhood and is related to aggression, inattention, exploratory sensation seeking and has been found to be powerfully associated with addiction risk as an adult (Tarter, 2002; Tarter, Kirisci, Habeych, Reynolds, & Vanyukov, 2003). As such, neurodisinhibition as a trait is causally related to addiction. Further impairment due to substance use amplifies this risk presumably due to "hijacking" of the reward pathway.

Social-Cognition

Social and cognitive aspects of addiction which involve thinking and behaving in interaction with others are a crucial point of contact between the biology and environment. Social cognitive perspectives build nicely upon the genetic and neurosciences of addiction etiology. One of the reasons for this has been articulated by Volkow (2003, p. 3): "We are beginning to understand that drugs exert persistent neurobiological effects that extend beyond the midbrain centers of pleasure and reward to disrupt the brain's frontal cortex – the thinking region of the brain, where risks and benefits are weighed and decisions made." Cognitive processes stand between our biology, on the one hand, and environmental input on the other. Within the social cognitive field two viewpoints have been dominant according to McCusker (2001), social learning theory and cognitive neuropsychology. Social learning theories of addiction are derived from the work of Bandura (1977, 1986, 1997) and essentially assert that cognitive biases aid in maintaining addiction and some form of cognitive structuring is needed to disengage the repeated and habituated thoughts and behaviors associated with an addictive lifestyle. Motivating the restructuring of belief systems related to addictive behaviors is considered a key component of change and the assessment of change is usually accomplished by employing some sort of self-report measure. In contrast, the cognitive neuropsychological approach uses performance-based measures such as the Stroop test. This test assesses frontal region and attention based on a participant saying the color of the word and not what the word says. So, if blue is written in green you would say green instead of blue. Despite some of the measurement shortcomings involving the overreliance on self-report measures, social learning theories have much to offer. Constructs derived from this theory such as cognitive mediation and self-efficacy help to explain many behaviors that are central to addiction. For example, if one's level of self-efficacy is high then their ability to govern themselves (refusal of drugs or stopping at one alcoholic beverage) in social situations where binge drinking or drug use is common is more likely. This is why some individuals persevere in the face of an external stressor. Although this may seem to be related to character flaw reasoning, the self-efficacy construct is intended as a neutral scientific concept and is not intended to cast judgments on any individual's character. Bandura thought of self-efficacy as personal agency and thus departed substantially from early deterministic behaviorist accounts where environment simply elicited responses from people (Scheier, 2010).

Proximal Environmental Factors

Proximal environmental factors represent variables such as peers, family, and neighborhoods that individuals have direct contact with and have a role in the development, maintenance, and desistance from addiction. Although it is common to invoke risk and protective factor schemes when speaking of proximal environmental effects (e.g., deviant peers are a risk factor for drug use). While this is true it is not an etiological theory. Over reliance on risk and protective factor parlance is not a substitute for an overall causal theory of addiction. Risk factors are not in and of themselves causes but are instead correlates unless tested and stated as such (i.e., causal risk factors). However, risk factors can be integrated into a theory of addiction. As Glantz (2010, p. 63) has stated "identifying risk factors is not the equivalent of a comprehensive characterization of vulnerability or etiology.......vulnerability is not just the degree of accumulation of risk factors." Research has identified peer effects in being associated with substance misuse (Gunning, Sussman, Rohrbach, Kniazev, & Masagutov, 2009; Nash, McQueen, & Bray, 2005; Poelen, Scholte, Willemsen, Boomsma, & Engels, 2007; Scholte, Poelen, Willemsen, Boomsmsa, & Engels, 2007) but how youth begin to have contact with deviant peers and how this leads to addiction are central questions that have etiological import. Some experimental use and minor delinquency acts over the life course can be viewed as normative but drug abuse and frequent delinquency is not (Moffitt, 1993, 2003). Proximal environmental factors such as peer effects can be thought of as a contagion whereby vulnerable youth may become initiated into an addiction lifestyle. Although some youth are pushed toward deviant peers, youth high on sensation seeking may look for them.

While environments act on individuals it is also likely that individuals seek out environments that enable them to satisfy their tendencies. For example, if a person has the capacity to sing, they may seek to join church choirs or bands in school. Peers are nested within families. There are several major pathways from which families exert causal effects vis-à-vis addiction. The first is via genetics, which we have already discussed. The second is social learning and modeling (e.g., family drinking and early initiation). Another factor is what parents do to their children. This includes aversive conditioning—too much or too little, lack of supervision and monitoring, and physical abuse (Castro, Brook, Brook, & Rubenstone, 2006; Tobler, Komro, & Maldonado-Molina, 2009). Are some of these parental variables tied to another layer of context? Theoretically, at least, the answer is yes. Families are certainly nested within neighborhoods and neighborhoods within socially disorganized areas that are experiencing weak bonds and concentrated disadvantage are related to a range of unhealthy outcomes including drug abuse (Lambert, Brown, Phillips, & Ialongo, 2004). Interestingly, the macro analog to self-efficacy, collective efficacy, has been found to be protective at least with respect to crime (Sampson, Raudenbush, & Earls, 1997). Overall, however, the causal effects of neighborhoods on addiction are unclear and likely indirect. Very little empirical research has demonstrated the association between neighborhoods, social processes, and addiction, particularly while controlling for the effect of biological vulnerability. One could theorize that a chain of causal effects whereby persons in distressed neighborhoods are also distressed themselves and become dependent on substance through self-medication. Despite the relatively common sense appeal of this idea, research has failed to convincingly show that this is the case.

Distal Environmental Factors

Proximal factors are nested in a larger context of distal environmental variables. Examples of distal factors germane to the etiologic study of addiction include climate, physical environment, transportation routes, soils and vegetation, political economy, and ideology. The supply of drugs such as heroin and cocaine are definitely tied to all of these variables. With respect to addiction, it is important to understand that psychoactive substances are processed, manufactured, and distributed and are facilitated by marketing factors such as formal and informal advertisements (television and billboards), availability of markets, and the political economy surrounding alcohol and drug production. Put in simple terms, an individual cannot become substance dependent if the drug either does not exist or is unavailable. For example, if an individual were alone on an uncharted island there would be no possibility to become addicted to alcohol or drugs. Another important cell to society fact is that certain illicit drugs such as heroin are derived from opium poppies which thrive in particular habitats around the globe. This is also true of another major drug of abuse, cocaine. The infrastructures of the countries and their political stability in which these plants are grown are often such that technological lag and related poverty

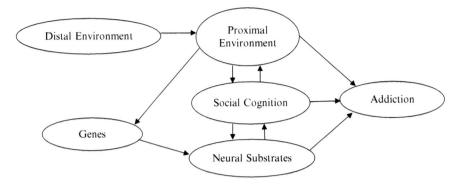

Fig. 3.1 Etiologic model of addiction

decrease participation in global economic exchange. Under these conditions it is fairly easy to understand how a bio-geographic plant resource such as opium poppies or coca can be elevated to a large monetary and strategic force in the underground economies of these countries. There exists relatively little research, however, into the distal influences that set many of the conditions for the individual susceptibility to addiction to be expressed. Future etiologic research should attempt to study these connections in empirically rigorous ways such as through the use of longitudinal and experimental designs. Putting it all together, Fig. 3.1 displays the relationships between these previously described factors in a full etiologic model of addiction.

From Bench to Trench: Incorporating Etiology into Prevention and Treatment

While the purpose of conducting prevention and treatment interventions is typically aimed at changing the antecedents (e.g., motivations, cognitive schemas) of substance use and thereby ameliorate abuse and dependence these types of designs are also useful for unraveling etiologica l processes. The reason for this is the effect of a causal marker such as a genetic polymorphism can be incorporated into the intervention design thereby enhancing its potential to isolate a treatment effect. Prevention trials can target these etiologic processes as they target risk factors that influence addiction outcomes. In addition, social work practitioners in the addictions area that employ cognitive-behavioral or brief interventions (e.g., Miller & Rollnick, 2002) can better understand the linkages that etiologic factors have in relation to components of change and use them for greater impact. In short, knowledge of etiologic processes of addiction enriches the applications (trench) and can in turn potential inform basic (bench) approaches that search for the causes of substance use, abuse, and dependence.

Summary and Conclusions

This chapter described the many causal factors for addiction along a "cell to society" continuum. Much more is known about the genetics and neuroscientific casual factors for addiction than the effects of neighborhood or larger macro units. However, because addiction crosses many disciplinary fields a transdisciplinary synthesis is critically needed in order to provide a fuller appraisal of the web of causation. This is also the case for other problem behaviors (e.g., Vaughn, 2007; Vaughn, Beaver, & DeLisi, 2009). Consequences of not utilizing such a framework includes a lack biological–environment integration leading to isolated studies not linking together, myopic states of explaining addiction strictly in terms of a singular disciplinary focus. Further, there can be associated reductions in new research methodologies and dissemination of important findings arising from knowledge fields not communicating with one another. Social workers benefit from an understanding of the genetic, neuroscientific, social cognitive, proximal and distal environmental factors that explain addiction.

References

Agrawal, A., Edenberg, H. J., Foroud, T., Bierut, L. J., Dunne, G., Hinrichs, et al. (2006). Association of *GABRA2* with drug dependence in the Collaborative Study of the Genetics of Alcoholism sample. *Behavioral Genetics, 36*(5), 640–650.

Bandura, A. (1977). *Social learning theory.* Englewood Cliffs: Prentice Hall.

Bandura, A. (1986). *Social foundations of thought and action: A social cognitive theory.* Englewood Cliffs: Prentice Hall.

Bandura, A. (1997). *Self-efficacy: The exercise of control.* New York: W.H. Freeman.

Brown, A. K., George, D. T., Masahiro, F., Jeih-San, L., Masanori, I., Hibbeln, J., et al. (2007). PET [11C] DASB imaging of serotonin transporters in patients with alcoholism. *Alcoholism: Clinical and Experimental Research, 31*(1), 28–32.

Castro, F. G., Brook, J. S., Brook, D. W., & Rubenstone, E. (2006). Paternal, perceived maternal, and youth risk factors as predictors of youth stage of substance use: A longitudinal study. *Journal of Addictive Diseases, 25,* 65–75.

Chakravarti, A., & Little, P. (2003). Nature, nurture and human disease. *Nature, 421,* 412–414.

Childress, A. R. (2006). What can human brain imaging tell us about vulnerability to addiction and to relapse? In W. R. Miller & K. M. Carroll (Eds.), *Rethinking substance abuse what the science shows, and what we should do about it* (pp. 46–60). New York: Guilford Press.

Cloninger, C. R. (1987). Neurogenetic adaptive mechanisms in alcoholism. *Science, 236,* 410–416.

Covault, J., Gelernter, J., Hesselbrock, V., Nellissery, M., & Kranzler, H. R. (2004). Allelic and haplotypic association of GABRA2 with alcohol dependence. *American Journal of Medical Genetics Part B: Neuropsychiatric Genetics, 129B*(1), 104–109.

Dick, D. M., & Agrawal, A. (2008). Genetics of alcohol and other drug dependence. *Alcohol Research and Health, 31,* 111–118.

Dick, D. M., Latendresse, S. J., Lansford, J. E., Budde, J. P., Goate, A., Dodge, K. A., et al. (2009). Role of GABRA2 in trajectories of externalizing behavior across development and evidence of moderation by parental monitoring. *Archives of General Psychiatry, 66,* 649–657.

Edenberg, H. J., Dick, D. M., Xuei, X., Tian, H., Almasy, L., Bauer, L. O., et al. (2004). Variations in GABRA2, encoding the alpha 2 subunit of the GABA(A) receptor, are associated with alcohol dependence and with brain oscillations. *American Journal of Human Genetics, 74,* 705–714.

Fehr, C., Sander, T., Tadic, A., Lenzen, K. P., Anghelescu, I., Klawe, C., et al. (2006). Confirmation of association of the *GABRA2* gene with alcohol dependence by subtype-specific analysis. *Psychiatric Genetics, 16*(1), 9–17.

Fowler, J. S., Volkow, N. D., Kassed, C. A., & Chang, L. (2007). Imaging the addicted human brain. *NIDA Science and Practice Perspectives, 3*(2), 4–16.

Glantz, M. D. (2010). Theories of substance dependence etiology. In L. M. Scheier (Ed.), *Handbook of drug use etiology: Theory, methods, and empirical findings*. Washington, D.C.: American Psychological Association Press.

Gunning, M., Sussman, S., Rohrbach, L. A., Kniazev, V., & Masagutov, R. (2009). Concurrent predictors of cigarette and alcohol use among U.S. and Russian adolescents. *Journal of Drug Education, 39*, 385–400.

Guo, G., Wilhelmsen, K., & Hamilton, N. (2007). Gene-lifecourse interaction for alcohol consumption in adolescence and young adulthood: Five monoamine genes. *American Journal of Medical Genetics Part B (Neuropsychiatric Genetics), 144B*, 417–423.

Koob, G., & LeMoal, M. (2006). *Neurobiology of addiction*. London: Elsevier Academic.

Koob, G., & LeMoal, M. (2008). Addiction and the brain antireward system. *Annual Review of Psychology, 59*, 29–53.

Lambert, S. F., Brown, T. L., Phillips, C. M., & Ialongo, N. S. (2004). The relationship between perceptions of neighborhood characteristics and substance use among urban African American adolescents. *American Journal of Community Psychology, 34*, 205–218.

Leshner, A. I. (1997). Addiction is a brain disease, and it matters. *Science, 278*, 45–47.

Lubman, D. I., Yucel, M., & Pantelis, C. (2004). Addiction, a condition of compulsive behaviour? Neuroimaging and neuropsychological evidence of inhibitory dysregulation. *Addiction, 99*, 1491–1502.

Markou, A., Kosten, T. R., & Koob, G. F. (1998). Neurobiological similarities in depression and drug dependence: a self-medication hypothesis. *Neuropsychopharmacology, 18*, 135–174.

McCusker, C. G. (2001). Cognitive biases and addiction: an evolution in theory and method. *Addiction, 96*, 47–56.

Meyer-Lindenberg, A., & Weinberger, D. R. (2006). Intermediate phenotypes and genetic mechanisms of psychiatric disorders. *Nature Reviews Neuroscience, 7*, 818–827.

Miller, W. R., & Rollnick, S. (2002). *Motivational interviewing: Preparing people for change* (2nd ed.). New York: Guilford Press.

Moffitt, T. E. (1993). 'Life-course persistent' and 'adolescence-limited' antisocial behavior: A developmental taxonomy. *Psychological Review, 100*, 674–701.

Moffitt, T. E. (2003). Life-course-persistent and adolescence-limited antisocial behavior: A 10-year research review and a research agenda. In B. B. Lahey, T. E. Moffitt, & A. Caspi (Eds.), *Causes of conduct disorder and juvenile delinquency* (pp. 49–75). New York: The Guilford Press.

Nash, S. G., McQueen, A., & Bray, J. H. (2005). Pathways to adolescent alcohol use: An examination of mediating and moderating effects. *Journal of Child and Family Studies, 9*, 509–528.

Nelson, R. J., & Chiavegatto, S. (2001). Molecular basis of aggression. *Trends in Neuroscience, 24*, 713–719.

Noble, E. P. (2000). Addiction and its reward process through polymorphisms of the D2 dopamine receptor gene: A review. *European Psychiatry, 15*, 7–89.

Plomin, R., & Rutter, M. (1998). Child development, molecular genetics, and what to do with genes once they are found. *Child Development, 69*, 1223–1242.

Poelen, E. A., Scholte, R. H., Willemsen, G., Boomsma, D. I., & Engels, C. M. (2007). Drinking by parents, siblings, and friends as predictors of regular alcohol use in adolescents and young adults: A longitudinal twin-family study. *Alcohol & Alcoholism, 42*, 362–369.

Ray, L. A., & Hutchison, K. E. (2004). A polymorphism of the μ-opioid receptor gene (*oprm1*) and sensitivity to the effects of alcohol in humans. *Alcohol: Clinical and Experimental Research, 28*(12), 1789–1795.

Rutter, M., Moffitt, T. E., & Caspi, A. (2006). Gene-environment interplay and psychopathology: Multiple varieties but real effects. *Journal of Child Psychology and Psychiatry, 47*, 226–261.

Samochowiec, J., Lesch, K. P., Rottman, M., Smolka, M., Syagailo, Y. V., Okladnova, O., et al. (1999). Association of a regulatory polymorphism in the promoter region of the MAOA gene with antisocial alcoholism. *Psychiatric Research, 86*, 67–72.

Sampson, R., Raudenbush, S. W., & Earls, F. (1997). Neighborhoods and violent crime: A multilevel study of collective efficacy. *Science, 277*, 918–924.

Scheier, L. M. (2010). Social-cognitive models of drug use etiology. In L. M. Scheier (Ed.), *Handbook of drug use etiology: Theory, methods, and empirical findings*. Washington, D.C.: American Psychological Association Press.

Scholte, R. H., Poelen, E. A., Willemsen, G., Boomsmsa, D. I., & Engels, R. C. (2007). Relative risks of adolescent and young adult alcohol use: The role of drinking fathers, mothers, siblings, and friends. *Addictive Behaviors, 33*, 1–14.

Soyka, M., Preuss, U. W., Hesselbrock, V., Zill, P., Koller, G., & Bondy, B. (2008). GABA-A2 receptor subunit gene (*GABRA2*) polymorphisms and risk for alcohol dependence. *Journal of Psychiatric Research, 42*, 184–191.

Steinberg, L. (2007). Risk-taking in adolescence: New perspectives from brain and behavioral science. *Current Directions in Psychological Science, 16*, 55–59.

Tarter, R. E. (2002). Etiology of adolescent substance abuse: A developmental perspective. *American Journal of Addiction, 11*, 171–191.

Tarter, R. E., Kirisci, L., Habeych, M., Reynolds, M., & Vanyukov, M. (2003). Neurobehavior disinhibition in childhood predisposes boys to substance use disorder by young adulthood: direct and mediated etiologic pathways. *American Journal of Psychiatry, 160*, 1078–1085.

Tobler, A. L., Komro, K. A., & Maldonado-Molina, M. M. (2009). Relationship between neighborhood context, family management practices and alcohol use among urban, multi-ethnic, young adolescents. *Prevention Science, 10*, 313–324.

Vaughn, M. G. (2007). Biosocial dynamics: A transdisciplinary approach to violence. In M. DeLisi & P. J. Conis (Eds.), *Violent offenders: theory, research, public policy, & practice* (pp. 63–77). Sudbury, MA: Jones & Bartlett.

Vaughn, M. G., Beaver, K. M., & DeLisi, M. (2009a). A general biosocial paradigm of antisocial behavior: A preliminary test in a sample of adolescents. *Youth Violence and Juvenile Justice, 7*, 279–298.

Vaughn, M. G., Beaver, K. M., DeLisi, M., Howard, M. O., & Perron, B. E. (2009b). Dopamine D4 receptor gene exon III polymorphism associated with binge drinking attitudinal phenotype. *Alcohol, 43*, 179–184.

Volkow, N. D. (2003). The addicted brain: Why such poor decisions? *NIDA Notes, 18*, 1–15.

Xu, K., Westly, E., Taubman, J., Astor, W., Lipsky, R. H., & Goldman, D. (2004). Linkage disequilibrium relationships among *GABRA* cluster genes located on chromosome 4 with alcohol dependence in two populations. *Alcoholism: Clinical and Experimental Research, 28*, 48.

Part II
Assessment, Diagnosis, and Treatment

Assessment, diagnosis, and treatment are the heart of effective practice in the addictions. This section covers the major topics germane to this area. The first chapter focuses on efficient and effective assessment as it is the foundation of selecting treatment strategies that can maximize client outcomes. The next chapter examines the information necessary for social workers to understand with respect to the diagnostic structure of substance use disorders. Next, the major evidence-based brief interventions and motivational strategies are presented, which are among the most important skills for social workers addressing addictive behaviors, not only for moving them through the change process but also for effectively engaging clients in the early stage of treatment. We then move to recovery and examine mutual aid groups (e.g., AA/NA) and long-term support services available to persons recovering from an addiction. Specifically, this chapter moves beyond simply describing these programs and provides practical strategies on how social workers can interface with these groups to improve referrals and client engagement. Finally, cognitive behavioral therapy is covered. This chapter covers the theory behind cognitive behavioral therapy, followed by instruction on practical skills and micro-interventions for addressing addictive behaviors within this framework.

Chapter 4
Assessment Strategies for Substance Use Disorders

Michael Mancini

The assessment of substance use disorders is a process of acquiring and synthesizing information on the impact of psychoactive substance use, which includes alcohol, illicit and prescription drugs, on the lives of consumers of human services.[1] The first goal of assessment is to begin the process of developing a productive therapeutic alliance with consumers in order to engage them in treatment. The second goal is to develop an understanding of the role substances play in a person's life across multiple psychosocial domains. The third goal is to explore how consumers understand their substance use and their readiness to change substance use behaviors. The final goal of assessment is to synthesize the above information into a collaborative plan of action designed to meet the short- and long-term goals as identified by the consumer.[2] This chapter includes the following topics: (1) an overview of how co-occurring substance use disorders and serious mental illness impact the assessment process; (2) discussion of five common components of a substance use assessment organized across three phases that include: screening, diagnosis, psychosocial assessment, functional analysis, and assessing readiness for change; and (3) the development of stage appropriate treatment plans based on assessment information using an illustrative case study.

---

[1] In this chapter, the term "substance" is used to refer to alcohol as well as illicit drugs such as marijuana, cocaine, heroin, and amphetamines and prescription drugs that are commonly abused such as benzodiazepines, pain killers, and barbiturates among others.

[2] The term "clinician" is used to refer to any human service practitioner including social worker, counselor, psychologist, case manager, nurse or psychiatrist in a health, mental health or substance abuse treatment setting. The term "consumer" is used to refer to any person receiving health, mental health, substance abuse, or other human services.

M. Mancini (✉)
Saint Louis University, School of Social Work, St. Louis, MO, USA
e-mail: mancinim@slu.edu

M.G. Vaughn and B.E. Perron (eds.), *Social Work Practice in the Addictions*,
Contemporary Social Work Practice, DOI 10.1007/978-1-4614-5357-4_4,
© Springer Science+Business Media New York 2013

Co-occurring Substance Use and Serious Mental Illness

Substance use is common in the general population. The 2008 National Survey on Drug Use and Health (NSDUH) estimates that approximately 50 % of all Americans report consuming at least one alcoholic drink within the last 30 days (SAMHSA, 2008). Several large-scale longitudinal studies have demonstrated that substance use disorders and serious mental illnesses such as major depression, bipolar disorder, schizophrenia, and PTSD among others commonly co-occur (Conway, Compton, Stinson, & Grant, 2006; Grant et al., 2004; Kessler et al., 1995, 1996, 1997; Regier et al. 1990; Swendsen et al., 2010). The presence of co-occurring disorders also complicates treatment for both sets of disorders due to lack of coordinated systems of care leading to the conclusion that systems of care for mental illness and substance use need to be integrated, stage-wise, coordinated and continuous (Drake, Mueser, Brunette, & McHugo, 2004; Minkoff, 2000; Mueser, Noordsy, Drake, & Fox, 2003). This requires clinicians to integrate screening, assessment, and treatment planning procedures in order to: (1) identify the presence of a severe mental illness and/or substance use disorder and understand the severity of the symptoms; (2) assess the relationship between substance use and mental illness and how each impact functioning in a variety of life domains; (3) understand the level of readiness of the consumer to engage in treatment; and (4) work with the consumer to develop, execute, and evaluate a plan of action that involves stage-based interventions that are tailored to meet the multidimensional needs of the consumer (CSAT, 2006; Mueser et al., 2003).

Serious and mental illnesses (SMI) are defined as a history of severe acute symptomatic episodes of one or more diagnosable psychiatric disorders as outlined in the Diagnostic and Statistical Manual of Mental Disorders (DSM) that result in long-term functional impairment that interferes with various activities of living and requires a high level of medical and psychosocial services (Mechanic, 2008; SAMHSA, 1993). A person who is classified as experiencing SMI exhibits symptoms from several Axis I disorders. Disorders that are routinely classified as fitting the criteria of SMI are the psychotic disorders schizophrenia and schizoaffective disorder, the major mood disorders of major depressive disorder and bipolar disorder, and the anxiety disorders obsessive compulsive disorder and post-traumatic stress disorder (APA, 2000). Symptom overlap between serious mental illnesses and substance use disorders can make differential diagnosis a challenge (see Tables 4.1 and 4.2 for a diagnostic overview of several serious mental illnesses and substance use disorders).

The common co-occurrence of substance use and these mood, anxiety and psychotic disorders is further complicated by the diagnostic categories of substance-induced disorders. A mood, anxiety, or psychotic disorder can be classified as substance induced if the etiology of the specific psychiatric symptoms can be traced back to the effects of a substance, or if the symptoms occurred due to the effects of intoxication and/or withdrawal of a substance (APA, 2000). It is important that a careful history of psychiatric symptoms and substance use be taken, particularly during times of abstinence. However, many times, differentiating between these two

Table 4.1 Summary of diagnostic indicators for serious mental illnesses that commonly co-occur with substance use disorders adapted from the DSM-IV-TR (APA, 2000)

Axis I	Diagnostic indicators
Major depressive disorder	A mood disorder characterized by a marked disturbance in mood characterized by at least 2 weeks of marked sadness, loss of interest or pleasure in activities (anhedonia), disturbances in concentration, sleep, and appetite, chronic fatigue, guilt, excessive feelings of worthlessness and/or guilt, and recurrent thoughts of death and dying. Can include psychotic features
Bipolar disorder	A mood disorder characterized by severe fluctuation in mood that is characterized by the presence of mania. A manic episode is a distinct period of at least 1 week of elevated, expansive, or irritable mood marked by grandiosity, euphoria, racing thoughts, pressured speech, decreased need for sleep, erratic or impulsive behavior and poor judgment. Can include psychotic features
Schizophrenia	A psychotic disorder characterized by significant disturbance in cognition, emotion, and social functioning. Persons with schizophrenia must have a history of symptoms of at least 6 months that include positive symptoms of hallucinations such as hearing voices or seeing things that are not seen or heard by others, delusions such as beliefs of paranoia, persecution or having special powers or a relationships, disorganized speech and behavior as well as negative symptoms including apathy, affectual blunting, and social isolation
Schizoaffective disorder	A psychotic disorder in which a person experiences the symptoms of schizophrenia concurrently with the symptoms of either major depressive disorder and/or mania. A person must experience psychotic symptoms in the absence of significant mood symptoms for a period lasting at least 2 weeks
Post-traumatic stress disorder	An anxiety disorder that results from the experience of a traumatic event. Traumatic events are unexpected, intense, and overwhelming events that cause a sense of intense fear or terror and are perceived as life threatening. Post-traumatic stress disorder involves a combination of persistent and intrusive thoughts about the traumatic event and re-experiencing the event through flashbacks and intense nightmares, increased arousal such as sleep difficulty, irritability and hyper-vigilance and persistent efforts to avoid activities, conversations, thoughts, feelings and places that remind the person of the event and/or the experience of detachment or emotional numbing
Substance induced mood disorder	The essential feature of substance-induced mood disorder is a prominent and persistent disturbance in mood such as depressed mood or markedly diminished interest or pleasure or elevated, expansive, or irritable mood. That is judged to be due to the direct physiological effects of a substance (i.e., a drug of abuse, a medication, other somatic treatment for depression, or toxin exposure)

(continued)

Table 4.1 (continued)

Axis I	Diagnostic indicators
Substance induced psychotic disorder	The essential features of substance-induced psychotic disorder are prominent hallucinations or delusions that are judged to be due to the direct physiological effects of a substance (i.e., a drug of abuse, a medication, or toxin exposure)
Substance induced anxiety disorder	The essential features of substance-induced anxiety disorder are prominent anxiety symptoms such as prominent anxiety, panic attacks, phobias, or obsessions or compulsions. (Criterion A) that are judged to be due to the direct physiological effects of a substance (i.e., a drug of abuse, a medication, or toxin exposure)

sets of disorders can be impossible. Nonetheless, when mental illness and substance use disorders co-occur both conditions should be considered primary and treatment for each disorder should be integrated (Minkoff, 2000; Mueser et al., 2003).

The American Psychiatric Disorder Diagnostic and Statistical Manual of Mental Disorders (DSM-IV-TR) lists 11 substances that could be linked to an Axis I substance use disorder. These substances include: Alcohol, amphetamines, caffeine (intoxication only), nicotine (dependence and withdrawal only), cannabis, cocaine, hallucinogens, inhalants, opioids, phencyclidine (PCP), sedatives/anxiolytics, and polysubstance dependence (not abuse) for multiple substances (APA, 2000). In the DSM-IV-TR, the four categories of substance use disorders are substance abuse, substance dependence, substance intoxication, and substance withdrawal. Substance abuse is characterized by a maladaptive pattern of alcohol or substance use that significantly interferes with at least one area of functioning (APA, 2000). Substance dependence is characterized as a physical and/or psychological loss of control over substance using behavior. Table 4.2 provides a diagnostic overview of major substance use disorder categories.

Strategies and Tools for Substance Use Assessment

The high comorbidity rate of mental illness and substance use disorders in clinical populations and the negative consequences that result require practitioners in clinical settings to routinely assess for both disorders. Assessment is an ongoing and multidimensional *process* consisting of an interrelated array of phases, skills and strategies with multiple purposes. This section will provide an overview of the assessment process broken down into three overlapping phases. The *early phase* of assessment involves engaging consumers and screening for substance use and mental illness. The *middle phase* of assessment involves accurately diagnosing any existing substance use and/or serious mental illnesses and developing a current and historical understanding of how substances have impacted a person's life across

Table 4.2 Summary of diagnostic indicators for substance use disorders adapted from the DSM- IV-TR (APA, 2000)

Substance abuse	A maladaptive substance use that causes clinically important distress or impairment, shown in a single 12-month period by one or more of the following: (1) failure to carry out major obligations at work, home or school because of repeated substance use; (2) repeated use of substances even when physically dangerous to do so; (3) repeated experience of legal problems; (4) continued substance use despite knowing that it has caused or worsened social or interpersonal problems
Substance dependence	Maladaptive substance use causes clinically important distress or impairment, shown in a single 12-month period by three or more of the following: (1) tolerance or withdrawal; (2) amount/duration of use greater than intended; (3) unsuccessful efforts to control or reduce use; (4) spending much time using a substance, recovering from its effects, or trying to obtain it; (5) reducing or abandoning important work, social or leisure activities because of substance use; (6) continued substance use despite knowing that it has probably caused ongoing physical or psychological problems
Substance intoxication	The development of a reversible substance-specific syndrome due to the recent ingestion of (or exposure to) a substance (Criterion A). The clinically significant maladaptive behavioral or psychological changes associated with intoxication (e.g., disturbances of perception, wakefulness, attention, thinking, judgment, psychomotor behavior, and interpersonal behavior)
Substance withdrawal	The development of a substance-specific maladaptive behavioral change, with physiological and cognitive concomitants, that is due to the cessation of, or reduction in, heavy and prolonged substance use (Criterion A). The substance-specific syndrome causes clinically significant distress or impairment in social, occupational, or other important areas of functioning

multiple psychosocial domains. The *late phase* of assessment involves understanding the antecedents, consequences, advantages, and disadvantages of substance use from the consumer's perspective and how motivated a person is to change substance using behaviors. Figure 4.1 outlines the phases and tasks of substance use assessment. These phases are meant to provide a general rubric of organizing general assessment tasks. The next sections will outline the tasks within each phase of the assessment process in more detail.

The Early Phase of Assessment: Engagement and Identification

In the early phase of assessment the consumer and clinician begin to forge their relationship. During this phase, it is important for clinicians to set a tone of collaboration and trust (Rapp & Goscha, 2006). It is also during this time that clinicians begin the assessment process by first screening for the presence of a substance use

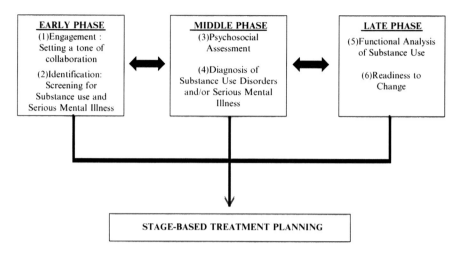

Fig. 4.1 Phases and the six tasks of substance use assessment

disorders and serious mental illnesses. The dual goals of engagement and screening occur simultaneously and require that clinicians skillfully obtain information in a way that communicates respect, honesty, trust, and unconditional positive regard (Rapp & Goscha, 2006). The following section will outline strategies and tools that can be used during this initial phase of assessment.

Engagement: Setting a Tone of Collaboration

While it has been historically difficult to engage and retain people with co-occurring disorders into services (Brunette, Mueser, & Drake, 2004), the length and intensity of engagement in services is an important predictor in treatment outcome (Fiorentine, Nakashima, & Anglin, 1999). A key component of engagement is the therapeutic alliance between clinician and consumer. Therapeutic alliance is broadly defined as the strength of a relationship between clinician and consumer that is based in collaboration, respect, and unconditional positive regard. This strength of this alliance has been found to have a moderate effect in treatment success (Martin, Garske, & Davis, 2000). Rapp and Goscha emphasize the importance of building a "trusting and reciprocal relationship" (p. 73) with consumers that is purposeful, reciprocal, friendly, trusting, and empowering (2006). Assessments that are conducted in an warm, genuine, nonjudgmental manner that focus on consumer strengths, acknowledge consumers struggles, seek out and support consumers' short- and long-term goals and provide a sense of hope will be more likely to lead to stronger therapeutic relationships and better consumer engagement in treatment. On the other hand, assessments that are overly problem-oriented, cold, one-sided interrogations will often lead to treatment relationships that are shallow, unproductive, and brief.

There are several strategies and approaches that can be effective in enhancing engagement during the assessment process. The first strategy is assessing for immediate needs of the consumer and providing practical support to address those needs (Mueser et al., 2003). A second strategy useful for enhancing engagement is assessing for client's short- and long-term goals for both treatment and for life. A third strategy is the use of basic motivational interviewing skills in the assessment process such as the use of open-ended questions, reflective listening and affirming consumers feelings and perspectives (Miller & Rollnick, 2002). Clinicians should also withhold advice giving and avoid confrontation, instead focusing on understanding how the consumer perceives the problem, what strategies the consumer has employed in the past to resolve the problem and what they are willing to do going forward. This gentle style of interaction can be effective in gathering quality information, while at the same time setting a collaborative tone, building self-efficacy, and establishing hope (Miller & Rollnick, 2002).

Identification: Screening for Mental Illness and Substance Use

The purpose of screening and detection is to identify signs of substance use problems and mental health issues that require further assessment. Screening and detection should occur at the earliest contact with consumers and should involve a broad range of substance use and mental health conditions. Screening and detection of co-occurring disorders should be a routine part of most clinical and nonclinical settings.

Screening for Mental Illness

When screening for mental illness, clinicians should ask consumers if they have ever had a history of mental health treatment including whether they have ever been prescribed psychiatric medications. Second, clinicians should ask if there is a family history of mental illness or suicide. A genogram may be a good tool to identify the presence of mental illness in the family. Third, clinicians should assess for the presence of symptoms that might indicate the presence of a mood, anxiety, or psychotic disorder and if the person has ever experienced trauma. The use of brief, yet comprehensive screening instruments should be used to assess for these disorders. Several tools exist that are easy to administer and score.

Three well-established scales that have good reliability and validity are the Brief Symptom Inventory (BSI) (Derogatis, 1993), the Symptom Checklist-90-R (SCL-90-R) (Derogatis, 1994) and the Modified Colorado Symptom Index (MCSI) (Conrad et al., 2001). Each scale measures a wide range of mental health issues including psychoticism, anxiety, and depression. The BSI is a 53-item scale that is relatively easy to administer and has shown good reliability and validity and correlates highly (>0.90) with its parent version, the Symptom Checklist-90-R (SCL-90-R) (Derogatis, 1994). This scale also comes in a modified 18-item short form (Derogatis, 2001). The SCL-90 is a 90-item scale that can be completed in less than 15 min in various settings and with clinical and nonclinical populations. This scale measures a broad array of symptoms across nine categories including depression, anxiety, psychoticism, paranoid ideation, and hostility. A Global Severity Index (GSI) score can be calculated that indicates overall psychological functioning and health (Derogatis, 1994). The MCSI is a brief 14-item scale that measures a broad array of mental health symptomology. In a study of 1,381 homeless persons, the scale was found to have good internal consistency and test retest reliability as well as high face, construct and criterion validity (Conrad et al., 2001).

A fourth instrument that is simpler and in the public domain is the Modified M.I.N.I. Screen (MMS) (Alexander, Haugland, Lin, Bertollo, & McCorry, 2008). The MMS measures mood, anxiety, and psychotic spectrum disorders as well as suicidality. While it lacks the sensitivity of the above tools, it does have good face validity and is generally reliable in a variety of settings (2008).

Screening for the Use of Substances

Given the high prevalence of comorbid substance use in clinical populations, it is advised that all clinicians routinely screen consumers for substance use. Clinicians must keep in mind the sensitivity and shame that accompanies problematic substance use and should ask questions about substance use in an open and nonjudgmental manner. Clinicians should not react with surprise or disappointment when consumers reveal substance use information, but should only encourage consumers to discuss their perspectives of use through the open-ended questioning and reflective listening techniques identified above. Clinicians should also refrain from any advice-giving at this stage until the assessment is complete.

When initiating the screening process, clinicians should begin by asking permission to discuss alcohol and substance use and assure consumers that screening for substance use is a routine part of the assessment process. Next, clinicians should identify the substances the consumer has used in the past month followed by the amount, duration and frequency of use for each substance. A tool called the follow-back calendar can be used to help consumers provide accurate descriptions of their substance use (Fals-Stewart, O'Farrell, Freitas, McFarlin, & Rutigliano, 2000). This tool asks the consumer to identify the type and amount of substances they use each day beginning with the most recent day and then "following back" on a calendar the previous 30 days. This can provide excellent data not only for the clinicians but also for the consumer (Mueser et al., 2003). Finally, clinicians should ask consumers to discuss their personal and family history of any problematic substance use and treatment.

Several effective screening tools for substance use are available. One of the most commonly used instruments is the C.A.G.E. (Ewing, 1984; Mayfield, McLeod, & Hall, 1974). The CAGE was originally developed to detect problematic drinking patterns, but has since been "adapted to include drugs" and is now referred to as the CAGE-AID to reflect this adaptation (Brown & Rounds, 1991). The CAGE-AID is a simple, yet effective screening tool that can be used to assess whether further assessment for alcohol or substance use disorders is warranted. The CAGE is an acronym for: (C) Have you ever tried to *cut down* on your drinking or drug use? (A) Have you ever been a*nnoyed* by anyone about your drinking or drug use? (G)Have you ever felt *guilty* or ashamed about your drinking or drug use? and (E) Have you ever had an "*eye-opener*" or used alcohol or drugs in the morning? Answering "yes" to any of these questions indicates an alcohol or drug use problem. This screen is primarily designed to assess alcohol or drug dependence and will miss up to 50 % of cases, but when combined with questions about frequency, duration and amount of consumption, it can be an effective screen for substance abuse.

Another screening tool for alcohol use disorders that has been shown to be effective, especially in medical settings, is the Alcohol Use Disorders Identification Test (AUDIT) (Babor, De La Fuente, & Saunders, 1989). The AUDIT is a 10-item scale that measures alcohol abuse, alcohol dependence, and hazardous alcohol use. Two other common screening instruments are the Michigan Alcohol Screening Test (MAST) (Selzer, 1971) and the Drug Abuse Screening Test (DAST) (Skinner, 1982). The MAST is a 22-item scale that measures problem drinking. The DAST is a 28-item screen that is similarly worded as the MAST to assess problematic use of drugs. It does not specify problems with particular drugs, but only indicates if further assessment is warranted. It can identify if substance abuse or dependence is likely depending on the score. The CAGE-AID, AUDIT, DAST, and MAST can all be found in the public domain.

Another screening instrument, the Dartmouth Assessment of Lifestyle Instrument (DALI) is a brief 18-item scale that measures risky behavior as well as recent substance use disorders related to alcohol, cocaine, and cannabis (Mueser et al., 2003; Rosenberg et al., 1998). It was specifically developed for co-occurring populations and has high reliability and specificity with this population. It is easy to administer, although scoring is more complicated than the previously mentioned screening instruments.

A final screening tool that has broad application and has been shown to have good reliability and validity is the Simple Screening Instrument for Alcohol and Other Drugs (SSI-AOD) (CSAT, 1994). This instrument was developed as part of the Substance Abuse and Mental Health Administration Treatment Improvement Protocol 11 (TIP-11). Since it is a government sponsored tool it is within the public domain. It has 16 items with scores ranging from 0 to 14. Answering "yes" to four or more questions indicates the possible presence of a substance use disorder. The SSI-AOD measures several domains of substance use including consumption, adverse consequences from substance use, preoccupation and loss of control, problem recognition and withdrawal and tolerance.

The Middle Phase of Assessment: Psychosocial Assessment and Diagnosis

If initial screenings indicate evidence for problematic substance use, then further assessment is warranted. The clinical goals in the middle phase of assessment are to understand how substance use impacts consumer functioning across several life domains through a comprehensive psychosocial assessment and to use this information to determine the presence of a substance use disorder diagnosis.

Domains of a Psychosocial Assessment of Substance Use

It is important at this stage for clinicians to continue to develop a collaborative and nonjudgmental tone relying on open-ended questions and reflective listening skills. The goals of assessment are not only to gather information, but also to continue to establish a working alliance with the consumer. Following a positive screen for substance use, clinicians should explore with the consumer the impact of substance use across several domains of psychosocial functioning. These domains are discussed briefly below.

Substance Use History

The first domain of functioning is understanding consumers' substance use history. Clinicians should get a full description of current use including frequency, amount and duration of use over the last 6 months. Questions within this domain include when consumers first began substance use and how this use has developed over time, any past treatment experiences, and a description of any periods when consumers did not use substances. This is particularly important in order to understand the successful and unsuccessful strategies that consumers have used in the past to achieve abstinence and how consumer functioning is different during times of reduced use or abstinence.

Medical and Psychiatric Treatment History

Clinicians should obtain a detailed history of any medical or psychiatric symptoms experienced by the consumer including past or current diagnoses, treatment history, and medication usage. A detailed account of current psychiatric symptoms and their severity is important in order to determine if a current Axis I disorder exists (APA, 2000). Equally important is for the clinician to ascertain how the consumer understands his or her psychiatric symptoms and their treatment. Several diagnostic tools exist for this purpose. One such tool is the Structured Clinical Interview for Axis I DSM-IV Disorders (SCID-I) (First, Spitzer, Gibbon, & Williams, 1997). This tool is a structured clinical interview form for making diagnoses for major Axis I disorders. This is a diagnostic tool with a high degree of sensitivity, reliability, and validity. It is a tool that can only be administered in 45–90 min by highly trained professionals only.

Identifying the presence of any medical conditions or chronic diseases (particularly those that are related to, or impacted by, substance use) is also important in order to develop treatment plans that accommodate multiple needs. The presence of a debilitating or life-threatening medical condition can also be a motivating factor for persons with substance use disorders and can be useful in treatment planning efforts. Continued substance use despite knowing that this use can worsen medical problems is also a sign of substance dependence.

Personal Relationships

Since it is common for persons with substance use issues to experience problems in various personal relationships with family, significant others, friends, and co-workers it is important to assess past and current status of interpersonal relationships for consumers with substance use issues. High levels of family or interpersonal conflict or increasing isolation are often signs of a substance use disorder. Improving interpersonal relationships is also a common motivating factor for persons seeking substance use disorder treatment. Clinicians should pay particular attention to patterns of conflict that surround fluctuations in use as well as any loss of relationships due to substance use as increased isolation can be a sign of substance dependence and can create or exacerbate psychiatric problems.

Legal and Financial

An assessment of past and current legal difficulties, especially those directly related to substance use (e.g., DUIs, fights, disorderly conduct, stealing, domestic violence), is also important in order to understand the extent of maladaptive substance use behaviors. The experience of legal difficulties directly or indirectly related to substance use can be a sign of substance abuse or dependence. Clinicians should also assess for the presence of financial problems that are either the result of substance use (e.g., spending all of one's money on drugs), or that provide stress in a person's life that can lead to increase substance use as a coping strategy.

Physical Health and Safety

When a substance use disorder is suspected, it is important to assess for threats to personal health and safety. Threats to personal health and safety include: (1) hazardous substance use such as using high amounts, use while driving or operating machinery, or sharing needles; and (2) risky behaviors associated with use such as unprotected sex, exchanging sex for drugs, using in dangerous situations, owing drug dealers, and being in abusive relationships. These threats to safety should be assessed and services designed to reduce these risks should be implemented immediately such as providing low threshold access to safe housing, medical care, condoms, clean needles, methadone, and basic needs such as food and clothing.

Recreational Activities and Spirituality

One of the most important areas of assessment involves understanding what gives people meaning and purpose in their lives. Many times, persons with substance use disorders and psychiatric conditions have forgotten or abandoned activities that they once found meaningful. It is important to understand what gives people meaning because it is this understanding that will drive the treatment planning process. Helping people work toward (re)engaging in meaningful activities will also be important in assisting them in achieving and maintaining treatment goals.

Diagnosis of Substance Use Disorders

Diagnosis of substance use disorders involves determining if a person meets criteria for substance use without impairment, substance abuse, or substance dependence. This is an important distinction that has implications for client education, treatment planning, and intervention. Table 4.2 outlines the specific diagnostic criteria for substance use disorders. It is important to note that a person may meet criteria for dependence for one substance, while meeting criteria for abuse or use without impairment for other substances. A person may also be dependent on more than one substance which is classified as polysubstance dependence in the DSM-IV-TR (APA, 2000). Therefore, diagnosis should occur separately for each substance of choice.

Two scales that can be useful in differentiating if a person exhibits alcohol or substance use or dependence are the Alcohol Use Scale Revised (AUS-R) and the Drug Use Scale-Revised (DUS-R) (Mueser et al., 2003). Both scales are based on the DSM-IV-TR diagnostic criteria for substance used disorders and focus on alcohol and/or drug use that has occurred over the past 6 months. Each tool provides a 5-point scale that ranges from: (1) abstinence; (2) use without impairment; (3) alcohol or substance abuse; (4) alcohol or substance dependence; and (5) dependence with institutionalization. Clinicians should rely on a variety of information sources to complete each scale including consumer self-report, lab results, historical records, and a range of collateral contacts. The areas measuring abuse include many areas of social and occupational role functioning, physical and psychiatric status, and use in dangerous situations. The scale also measures criteria for dependence such as using greater amounts of substances than intended, withdrawal effects, activities given up for use, tolerance, and continued use despite knowing it has caused significant problems.

Another popular and effective diagnostic tool that is useful is the Addiction Severity Index (ASI) (McLellan, Luborsky, Woody, & O'Brien, 1980). The ASI is a semi-structured interview that examines several areas in persons with suspected substance abuse or dependence issues. These areas include: medical status, employment and support, drug use, alcohol use, legal status, family/social status, and psychiatric status. The interview lasts up to 1 h and examines alcohol and substance use over the last 30 days and prevalence of lifetime problems in all areas. This tool has high test–retest reliability and sensitivity (Leonhard, Mulvey, Gastfriend, & Shwartz, 2000). The main drawback is that it can be a highly complex and overly technical tool that requires a fair level of clinical sophistication and patience on the part of the consumer.

The Late Phase of Assessment: Functional Analysis and Readiness to Change

The final phase of assessment has direct implications for treatment planning and intervention. In this phase, the clinician, in collaboration with the consumer explores the advantages and disadvantages of substance use in the consumer's life and the consumer's readiness to change substance use behaviors.

Functional Analysis

A functional analysis or payoff matrix of substance use is designed to help the person accurately and objectively assess the role substances play in their lives and the advantages and disadvantages of using and not using substances (Meyers & Miller, 2001; Miller & Rollnick, 2002; Mueser et al., 2003). The goal of the functional analysis is to understand the factors that maintain substance using behavior. This analysis will then be used to design a plan for intervention. Mueser et al. (2003) identify several characteristics to an effective functional analysis. These characteristics include: (1) focusing on behaviors rather than personality characteristics or flaws; (2) focusing on skill development to achieve goals rather than solely on substance use elimination; and (3) assuming that substances using behavior is due to controllable contextual factors (2003).

A functional analysis has four components. The first component is collaboratively exploring the *advantages of using substances*. Common responses may include that substances help a person feel high or euphoric. The second area for exploration is the *advantages of* not *using substances*. Common responses include healthier relationships, less legal, financial, health and relationship troubles. A third area for analysis is the *disadvantages of using substances*. Common response may be increased conflict with family and more financial legal or health problems. The last domain is the *disadvantages of* not *using substances*. Important information regarding the motivations for use and the beliefs that interfere with changing use patters can emerge in this domain. Common responses include lack of feeling high, loneliness, anxiety, the return of depressive or anxious symptoms, fear of losing friends, cravings, feelings of failure, poor concentration, and boredom.

Assessing Motivation to Change

The transtheoretical model of change is an integrative framework that views any kind of behavior change as a bidirectional, but ultimately a progressive, series of small steps (Prochaska, DiClemente, & Norcross, 1992). Behavior change can include the initiation, modification, and cessation of any behavior. In this model, behavior change progresses from an initial *precontemplation stage* where a person is not engaged in thoughts about changing a behavior to a *contemplation stage* where a person is seriously considering changing a behavior, but has not taken any steps to do so. From contemplation, a person move to the *preparation stage* where they have begun to solidify their commitment to change and have begun to plan to take action and may have begun to take small steps toward changing a behavior. The *action stage* is where a person has made a specific and sustained change in behavior. The *maintenance stage* is where a person has solidified gains and works to maintain and sustain gains through relapse prevention and other efforts (1992).

There are various ways to assess stage of change or readiness to change. One method is the use of The Stages of Change Readiness and Treatment Eagerness Scale (SOCRATES) (Miller & Tonigan, 1996). SOCRATES is a 32-item scale that measure alcohol and drug abuse. A shorter 19-item version has been developed (version 8D). The instrument yields three scores: Recognition (Re), Ambivalence (Am), and Taking Steps (Ts). It is a public domain instrument and may be used without special permission.

Another scale is the University of Rhode Island Change Assessment Scale (URICA) (DiClemente & Hughes, 1990). This is a 32-item scale that measures four areas including precontemplation, contemplation, action and maintenance using a 5-point Likert scale. It has good internal consistency and criterion, construct and content validity (Willoughby & Edens, 1996). The SOCRATES differs from the URICA in that SOCRATES poses questions specifically about alcohol or other drug use, whereas URICA focuses more on changing behaviors or problems more generally.

Putting It All Together: Guiding Principles of Treatment Planning

Treatment planning is a key activity linked to other activities along the continuum of community mental health practices (Adams & Grieder, 2005). It is derived from the process of psychosocial assessment and is both a product (i.e., a plan of action to achieve agreed upon goals and objectives) as well as a process consisting of ongoing interactions in which clinician and consumer partner to work toward a set of shared objectives and goals (Mueser et al., 2003; Rapp & Goscha, 2006). Treatment plans should be living documents that act as road map toward recovery for both substance use and mental illness.

Guideline # 1: Respect Consumer Choices and Needs

Treatment plans are most useful when they are structured around the aspirations and long-term goals of consumers and also meet their immediate needs (Rapp & Goscha, 2006). It is too often the case that treatment plans reflect preferred goals of the clinician, program, or system rather than consumers and that consumers with substance use issues are forced to wait or "jump through hoops" to get what they really want. These hoops can include treatment adherence, admitting a problem with substance use, abstinence, and compliance with program rules or medication. When this happens consumers become disengaged, resentful, and hopeless. What's worse, when these feelings lead to apathy, dependency, withdrawal or anger consumers are considered "resistant" or "noncompliant." Research indicates that when consumer preferences are respected and immediate needs are met through low-threshold access to practical help engagement increases (Mueser et al., 2003; Padgett, Henwood, Abrams, & Davis, 2008; Tsemberis, Gulcur, & Nakae, 2004).

Immediate needs that consumers with mental illness and substance use issues have can include personal safety, housing, employment, medications/healthcare, benefits, vouchers for transportation and food, clean injecting equipment (for injecting drug users), condoms, and day care among others.

Guideline # 2: Use the Functional Analysis to Determine an Appropriate Array of Interventions

The information gathered from a functional analysis should lead to treatment interventions that cut across four broad areas of intervention. The first area is reducing the positive effects of substances. This can include the use of medications such as naltrexone and methadone that reduce the body's ability to feel the euphoria of getting high.

The second area of intervention is increasing the negative effects of using substances. This approach usually relies on instituting negative consequences that are coercive or unpleasant. Intervention in this area usually involve movement to a restrictive settings, taking control of money through payeeships, the use of shame or guilt, or the use of medication such as Disulfiram (Antabuse), which make a person physically ill if they take a drink of alcohol.

Strategies for increasing the advantages of not using substances include using contingent reinforcement approaches such as the Community Reinforcement

Approach (CRA) (Hunt & Azrin, 1973). CRA is a behaviorally focused approach to alcohol and drug treatment that utilizes social, recreational, familial, and vocational reinforcers to assist consumers in creating rewarding sober lifestyles (Meyers & Miller, 2001). The majority of CRA work focuses on the amelioration of skill deficits though skills training in the areas of communication, problem solving and substance refusal, relationship counseling, job skills, recreational and social counseling, and relapse prevention.

Another strategy is the use of motivational interviewing strategies designed to help motivate the client toward behavioral change by helping them recognize how substances interfere with the achievement of their overarching goals (Miller & Rollnick, 2002).

Lastly, education about the effects of substances and mental illness are also good strategies to help people understand how substance use and mental illness interact (Mueser et al., 2003).

The last area of intervention is helping consumers decrease the disadvantages of not using substances. Interventions in this area can involve the use of individual or group-based cognitive behavioral therapy designed to help people cope with depressive or anxious symptoms. Cognitive behavioral approaches can also assist in developing treatment plans designed to reduce cravings and identify and cope with triggers that lead to relapse (Kadden et al., 1995; Monti, Kadden, Rohsenow, Cooney, & Abrams, 2002). In addition, 12-step programs and other self-help interventions can also be used in conjunction with these approaches. Medications such as selective serotonin reuptake inhibitors, mood stabilizers, and antipsychotics can be used to assist people in reducing psychiatric symptoms. Social skills training to help people deal with social anxiety and the fear they will be lonely or bored once they give up substance is another strategy (Mueser et al., 2003).

Guideline # 3: Choose Interventions That Are Stage Appropriate

A final consideration in treatment planning is choosing interventions that are appropriate for a consumer's stage of change for a particular substance. Interventions are most effective when they match a client's motivational intensity for change (Drake et al., 2004). Persons in earlier stages of change do not respond to forceful intervention efforts, confrontation or education/advice giving because they are not ready to make commitments or to take action on their behavior. A mistake of many substance abuse counselors is prescribing interventions that require a high level of planning and commitment and are thus more suitable for persons in preparation or action stages (e.g., going to AA, residential treatment, quitting use ...). The result is treatment drop-out and lack of engagement. It is important for clinicians to accurately assess a person's stage of change for each substance as readiness to change can be different for each substance used.

Interventions for persons in precontemplation include simply discussing substance use behaviors, providing practical assistance, outreach, and harm reduction approaches (Marlatt, 1996; Mueser et al., 2003). For persons in contemplation and preparation stages of change, motivational interviewing strategies designed to increase ambivalence about substance use and increase motivation to change behaviors are effective (Miller & Rollnick, 2002). For persons in action and maintenance stages of change, the use of CRA, CBT, family support, self-help, relapse prevention and medication-assisted treatment approaches are most appropriate.

Conclusion

Assessment for substance use disorders is a dynamic and multidimensional process. Given the high concordance rates of mental illness and substance use, clinicians should routinely screen and assess for both disorders. It is important for clinicians to gather information in a way that respects consumer choice and sets a collaborative tone for the therapeutic relationship. Assessment procedures that include screening, diagnosis, psychosocial assessment, functional analysis, and assessing readiness for change should inform the treatment planning process. Treatment plans should be developed collaboratively and interventions selected should assist consumers in achieving their long-term goals and meeting their immediate needs, while respecting their readiness to make changes in their lifestyles regarding substance use.

Appendix I Case Study: Jessica

Jessica, a 30-year-old Caucasian woman has been referred to your team for treatment by local law enforcement for assessment and treatment for mental illness and substance abuse.

Jessica is a bright, engaging, and humorous individual. Jessica likes to be in nature. She has enjoyed cycling and meditation in the past. She also enjoys reading and writing poetry. In college she was a business major until she dropped out in her junior year. She refers to this as, "my biggest mistake." She has dreamed of finishing her degree and going into marketing someday, as she states, "when I'm not such a nutcase." At this point she says, "I just want to get my life somewhat stable so I can work a little and keep an apartment and not kill myself or anyone else."

Jessica has been diagnosed with major depressive disorder. When she is depressed she often sleeps all day, refuses to see anyone, does not eat and becomes suicidal. Jessica has attempted suicide several times in the past Jessica states, "When I go through one of those periods my life is blown to pieces. The darkness comes and I go under. It's like I'm trying to keep my head above water in the darkest, scariest place on earth and there is no one there to save you. It swallows you up."

Jessica states that she began using cocaine when she was 20. By the time she was 24 she was using it every day and needing more and more of it to get high. She states that she has been in rehab for cocaine at least four times. She states that she often stops using for a while, but then starts back up. Once she starts using it is hard for her to stop. She states, "it (cocaine) takes over my life. I can't think about anything else but getting high." In the past year, she has lost 2 entry level jobs and has been forced to move twice due to her aggressive behavior and substance use. She states, "when I binge I don't show up to work, there's a lot of traffic in and out of my house and I tend to get a bit wild. That's when I lose my job or get thrown out of apartments." Currently, she has a studio apartment. She is not employed at the moment and is living off of some savings, support from parents and her small unemployment check from her last job which will run out in 1 month. Jessica's short-term goals are that she wants to find a job in order to pay her rent. Jessica had not used cocaine for the past 2 months. She has also reduced her alcohol intake, drinking only one or two drinks every other week during this time. During this time she has been steadily looking for work and has not had any problems with her landlord or the legal system. However, last 2 weeks Jessica has missed her appointments with you and did not call to cancel or reschedule. Today, Jessica shows up at your office without an appointment asking if she can see you for a session. She looks very tired and unkempt which is also unlike Jessica. Having a gap in your schedule you accommodate her request. The following is a description of the clinical interaction.

Clinician	Jessica, I'm glad to see you. I hadn't seen you in a while and was getting concerned. How have things been going lately?
Jessica	I used cocaine a bunch of times last week.
Clinician	You used cocaine last week?
Jessica	Yeah. I was out with friends at a bar. After the bar closed we went over to someone's house and out came the cocaine. I turned them down at first, but everyone was having such a good time and they kept asking me if I wanted any and what was wrong with me, and c'mon party with us and blah, blah, blah and after a while I just said the hell with it and before I knew it I was using.
Clinician	So you refused their offers at first, but they were persistent and you ended up using. What did you say to them when you refused?
Jessica	I just said something like, "Oh, I'm not really feeling like it right now." Which was a total lie. I wanted to get high—real bad. Everyone was just having a good time and I was feeling so lousy for so long that I just wanted to feel good for once. I thought I would be fine at first. I knew there was going to be coke where I was going, but I was feeling so good just to be out of the house and hanging out with people that I didn't want the night to end. I didn't want to go back to that apartment so I thought, "Well, I got two months clean—that should be enough to get me through this. I'll just say 'no' and that's it." Well, that didn't work so good.
Clinician	So on the one hand you didn't want to use at first and you thought that if it was there you could handle it. You just wanted to hang out with your friends. But on the other hand, when the coke came out you had a craving to use that was pretty strong and you ended up wanting it and using it. Is that right?
Jessica	Yeah, that's about right. Once the stuff came out, everyone was just using and after awhile I just wanted to join in and be a part of it and feel good. I didn't go there to use. I went there to hang out. I just got swept up. I should've known better—me being a screw-up, junkie and all.

(continued)

Clinician	So, tell me what happened next?
Jessica	Once the coke was gone I went home. Crashed the whole next day and felt worse than I had before I went out. Right back in the hole. And now I just blew two months of sobriety so I was feeling like, "Fuck it-why bother, you know?" "It's always going to be this way." I called my friend up and we scored some cocaine and some weed and went back to my apartment and got high again. The next day, crashed again. Then I really started to want to get high. I knew I was headed down that bad road again. So I said, I gotta get some help and I went to a couple of (NA) meetings. That was two days ago and now here I am. I haven't used since then. I really don't know what I want at this point. I just know I don't want to fall all the way back this time.
Clinician	Jessica, it takes lot of strength to recognize the situation you were in and take action. I don't think you're giving yourself enough credit for that and I want to make sure you know that I'm proud of you for recognizing the situation for what it was and seeking out help. And I'm glad you're here and that you're OK. You wouldn't have been able to do this a year ago. You mentioned a couple of times that you felt pretty lousy for a while before you used cocaine and that you didn't want to leave the party and go back to your apartment. Could you tell me about what was going on before the first time you used cocaine? Before you went to the bar—what was going on in your life?
Jessica	At first I was just really, really sad, you know? Sleeping all day. No showering. "Who cares?," you know. I can't find a job. I'm alone. It started with feeling sad and then I just shut myself off from the world and when I'm alone with myself for a long time. It gets pretty ugly.
Clinician	So things weren't going well for you and you got really depressed and you didn't know how to get out of it. What were you thinking?
Jessica	Well, after a while the voices started yapping. You know, from my past. "You're a piece of shit." And "You're ugly." "You're a whore." "No one loves you." "You should just die; You're never going to be anything." Oh, what else? "You're a loser." "You're a junkie." "Die. Die. Die." It wasn't the worse I've been. But it was pretty bad. Couldn't sleep at night. Slept all day. Stopped eating after awhile. And then—Chain smoking. Cable TV. Soda. Sleep. Repeat. And then after a while I just didn't really feel anything. Just zombied out.
Therapist	So it sounds like you started thinking a lot of really negative thoughts about yourself and this led to having trouble sleeping and just having a real hard time all around. It must have been awful. So, what did you do?
Jessica	I had a couple of drinks.
Therapist	You started drinking. And what happened?
Jessica	I started to feel better. I slept a bit. I felt less sad. I know what you're thinking, but, booze isn't my problem. I'm not a drunk like my father. I'm a junkie. Cocaine is my problem. Drinking and weed? I can take them or leave them. And sometimes they help me feel better. So after I drank a few beers I actually felt kind a good for the first time in over a week. I didn't want to kill myself. I felt like I wanted to see people and have a good time and so I called my friends, maybe the wrong ones, and asked them to go out. We went out and I felt alive for awhile and you know the rest. Say what you want—but if it wasn't for the cocaine—I could have been alright.

Appendix II Case Study Analysis: Jessica

The case of Jessica demonstrates a person with a number of strengths and who has survived a great deal and who has clear and important dreams. It is also clear that Jessica struggles with major depressive disorder and addiction. Jessica's cocaine addiction meets the criteria for Cocaine Dependence. She exhibits an extreme loss of psychological control that is the hallmark of this disorder. Jessica experiences physical and psychological cravings, spends a lot of time and money using substances, has unsuccessfully tried to cut down on her use, and engages in risky and unhealthy behaviors when using. It is unclear if Jessica experiences the physical characteristics of tolerance or withdrawal.

Jessica's alcohol use is also a concern due to her major depressive disorder. Alcohol, a depressant, can exacerbate depressive symptoms. Given the severity of her depressive symptoms and cocaine addiction, even moderate alcohol use can lead to significant consequences. As can be seen in the vignette, but may not be clear to Jessica at this point, is her attempts to cope with her depressive symptoms by using alcohol actually places her at risk of cocaine use relapse and probably increases her depressive symptoms over the long run despite giving her relief in the short term. Jessica's statements indicate that she is most likely in precontemplation regarding her alcohol use. In regard to Jessica's cocaine use, she is most likely in preparation or (early) action stage. She is motivated to stop use and has made attempts to do so. The fact that she came to the clinician's office despite feeling ashamed indicates a strong therapeutic bond and engagement.

Jessica's long-term dream is to return to school, finish her degree, and work in marketing. That is where treatment planning starts. The clinical goal will be to build a ladder to that dream through the achievement of short-term goals. The fuel to this process will be repeated affirmation, support, and celebration of successes. It is clear in Jessica's speech that she lacks hope and self-efficacy. One of the clinician's tasks is to build up Jessica's hope and self-efficacy through practical and emotional support. However, Jessica's immediate needs are to find employment, meet the requirements of her probation, and to regain her footing in her battle with cocaine addiction. Achieving both the short- and long-term goals must involve a conversation about Jessica's cocaine and alcohol use.

The threat of negative legal consequences is relevant since she is on probation. However, as can be seen, Jessica's addiction is powerful enough to override her fear of legal repercussion from her probation officer if she were to fail a drug test. One negative consequence that Jessica discussed is her sense of shame and despair over losing control over her use. This may be an area to tap into through open and honest discussion and may be a motivating factor in helping Jessica prevent future relapses. It is clear the Jessica could benefit greatly from the development of skills such as substance refusal skills, identifying triggers for relapse and craving management as well as ways to prevent relapse such as developing healthier recreational activities. Jessica could also benefit greatly from psychoeducation that would help her understand how her substance use and mental illness interact. The use of medication-assisted treatments to reduce her cravings may also be effective and relevant here. Equally important would be cognitive behavioral approaches designed to help her manage negative thoughts about herself and to cope with fears of loneliness that often accompanies sobriety by helping her develop sober supports either through self-help and/or reengaging in pleasurable activities.

Since Jessica is in precontemplation regarding her alcohol use, a treatment planning goal in this area may be simply to discuss her alcohol use for a few minutes each session and monitor her use. Psychoeducation may also be an option given her psychiatric symptoms (Mueser et al., 2003). An analysis of her recent relapse through motivational interviewing techniques may help to increase Jessica's ambivalence about her alcohol use. However, providing ways to relieve her depressive symptoms either through medication and/or other wellness activities are needed to replace the use of alcohol as a coping response.

References

Adams, N., & Grieder, D. M. (2005). *Treatment planning for person-centered care.* Boston: Elsevier Academic.

Alexander, M. J., Haugland, G., Lin, S. P., Bertollo, D. N., & McCorry, F. A. (2008). Mental health screening in addiction, corrections and social service settings: Validating the MMS. *International Journal on the Addictions, 6,* 105–119.

American Psychiatric Association. (2000). *The Diagnostic and Statistical Manual of Mental Disorders Text Revised* (4th ed.) (DSM-IV-TR). Washington, DC: American Psychiatric Association.

Babor, T. F., De La Fuente, J. R., & Saunders, J. (1989). *AUDIT: Alcohol use disorders identification test: guidelines for use in primary health care.* Geneva: World Health Organization.

Brown, R., & Rounds, L. (1991). *Conjoint screening questionnaires for alcohol and drug abuse: Two pilot studies.* Unpublished study.

Brunette, M. F., Mueser, K., & Drake, R. E. (2004). A review of the research on residential programs for people with severe mental illness and co-occurring substance use disorders. *Drug and Alcohol Review, 23,* 471–481.

Center for Substance Abuse Treatment. (1994). *Simple screening instruments for outreach for alcohol and other drug abuse and infectious diseases.* Treatment Improvement Protocol (TIP) Series 11. DHHS Publication No. (SMA) 94-2094. Rockville, MD: Substance Abuse and Mental Health Services Administration.

Center for Substance Abuse Treatment. (2006). *Screening, assessment and treatment planning for persons with co-occurring disorders.* COCE Overview Paper 2. DHHS Publication No. (SMA) 06-4164. Rockville, MD: Substance Abuse and Mental Health Services Administration, and Center for Mental Health Services.

Conrad, K. J., Yagelka, J. R., Matters, M. D., Rich, A. R., Williams, V., & Buchanan, M. (2001). Reliability and validity of a modified Colorado symptom index in a national homeless sample. *Mental Health Services Research, 3,* 141–153.

Conway, K. P., Compton, W., Stinson, F. S., & Grant, B. F. (2006). Lifetime comorbidity of DSM-IV mood and anxiety disorders and specific drug use disorders: results from the National Epidemiologic Survey on Alcohol and Related Conditions. *Journal of Clinical Psychiatry, 67,* 247–257.

Derogatis, L. R. (1993). *Brief Symptoms Inventory (BSI): Administration, scoring and procedures manual* (3rd ed.). Minneapolis: NCS Pearson, Inc.

Derogatis, L. R. (1994). *Symptom Checklist-90-R (SCL-90-R): Administration, scoring and procedures manual* (3rd ed.). Minneapolis: NCS Pearsons, Inc.

Derogatis, L. R. (2001). *Brief Symptom Inventory (BSI)-18. Administration scoring and procedures manual*. Minneapolis: NCS Pearson, Inc.

DiClemente, C. C., & Hughes, S. O. (1990). Stages of change profiles in alcoholism treatment. *Journal of Substance Abuse, 2*, 217–235.

Drake, R. E., Mueser, K. T., Brunette, M. F., & McHugo, G. J. (2004). A review of treatments for people with severe mental illnesses and co-occurring substance use disorders. *Psychiatric Rehabilitation Journal, 27*, 360–374.

Ewing, J. A. (1984). Detecting alcoholism: The CAGE questionnaire. *Journal of the American Medical Association, 252*, 1905–1907.

Fals-Stewart, W., O'Farrell, T. J., Freitas, T. T., McFarlin, S. K., & Rutigliano, P. (2000). The Timeline Followback reports of psychoactive substance use by drug-abusing patients: Psychometric properties. *Journal of Counseling and Clinical Psychology, 68*, 134–144.

Fiorentine, R., Nakashima, & Anglin, M. D. (1999). Client engagement in drug treatment. *Journal of Substance Abuse Treatment, 17*, 199–206.

First, M. B., Spitzer, R. L., Gibbon, M., & Williams, J. B. W. (1997). *Structured Clinical Interview for DSM-IV Axis I Disorders-Clinicians Version (SCID-CV)*. Washington, DC: American Psychiatric Press.

Grant, B. F., Stinson, F. S., Dawson, D. A., Chou, S. P., Dufour, M. C., Compton, W., et al. (2004). Prevalence and co-occurrence of substance use disorders and independent mood and anxiety disorders: Results from the National Epidemiologic Survey on Alcohol and Related Conditions. *Archives of General Psychiatry, 61*(8), 807–816.

Hunt, G. M., & Azrin, N. H. (1973). A community-reinforcement approach to alcoholism. *Behavior Research and Therapy, 11*, 91–104.

Kadden R., Carroll, K., Donovan, D., Cooney, N., Monti, P., Abrams, D. Litt, M., Hester, R., (Eds.). (1995). *Cognitive behavioral coping skills therapy manual: A clinical research guide for therapists treating individuals with alcohol abuse and dependence. National Institute of Alcohol Abuse and Addictions. Project MATCH Monograph Series* (Vol. 3). NIH Pub. No. 94-3724. National Institute of Health. Available at: http://pubs.niaaa.nih.gov/publications/MATCHSeries3/Project%20MATCH%20Vol_3.pdf.

Kessler, R. C., Crum, R. M., Warner, L. A., Nelson, C. B., Schulenberg, J., Anthony, J. C. (1997). Lifetime co-occurrence of DSM-III-R alcohol abuse and dependence with other psychiatric disorders in the National Comorbidity Survey. *Archives of General Psychiatry, 54*, 313–321.

Kessler, R.C, Nelson, C.B., McGonagle, K.A., Edlund, M.J., Frank, R.G., Leaf, P.J. (1996). The epidemiology of co-occurring addictive and mental disorders: Implications for prevention and service utilization. *American Journal of Orthopsychiatry, 66*, 17–31.

Kessler, R. C., Sonnega A., Bromet E., Hughes, M., Nelson, C. B. (1995). Posttraumatic stress disorder in the national comorbidity survey. *Archives of General Psychiatry, 52*, 1048–1060.

Leonhard, C., Mulvey, K., Gastfriend, D. R., & Shwartz, M. (2000). Addiction Severity Index: A field study of internal consistency and validity. *Journal of Substance Abuse Treatment, 18*, 129–135.

Marlatt, A. G. (1996). Harm reduction: Come as you are. *Addictive Behaviors, 21*, 779–788.

Martin, D. J., Garske, J. P., & Davis, M. K. (2000). Relation of the therapeutic alliance with outcome and other variables: A meta-analytic review. *Journal of Consulting and Clinical Psychology, 68*, 438–450.

Mayfield, D., McLeod, G., & Hall, P. (1974). The CAGE questionnaire: Validation of a new alcoholism screening instrument. *American Journal of Psychiatry, 131*, 1121–1123.

McLellan, A. T., Luborsky, L., Woody, G. E., & O'Brien, C. P. (1980). An improved diagnostic evaluation instrument for substance abuse patients: The Addiction Severity Index. *Journal of Nervous and Mental Disease, 186*, 26–33.

Mechanic, D. (2008). *Mental health and social policy: Beyond managed care* (5th ed.). Boston: Allyn & Bacon.

Meyers, R. J., & Miller, W. R. (2001). *A Community Reinforcement Approach to addiction treatment*. Cambridge: Cambridge University Press.

Miller, W., & Rollnick, S. (2002). *Motivational interviewing: Preparing people for change.* New York: Guilford Press.

Miller, W. R., & Tonigan, J. S. (1996). Assessing drinkers' motivation for change: The Stages of Change Readiness and Treatment Eagerness Scale (SOCRATES). *Psychology of Addictive Behaviors, 10,* 81–89.

Minkoff, K. (2000). An integrated model for the management of co-occurring psychiatric and substance disorders in managed care systems. *Disease Management & Health Outcomes, 8,* 250–257.

Monti, P., Kadden, R., Rohsenow, D., Cooney, N., & Abrams, D. (2002). *Treating alcohol dependence: A coping skills training guide* (2nd ed.). New York: Guildford Press.

Mueser, K. T., Noordsy, D. L., Drake, R. E., & Fox, L. (2003). *Integrated treatment for dual disorders: A guide to effective practice.* New York: Guilford Press.

Padgett, D. K., Henwood, B., Abrams, C., & Davis, A. (2008). Engagement and retention in services among formerly homeless adults with co-occurring mental illness and substance abuse: Voices from the margins. *Psychiatric Rehabilitation Journal, 31,* 226–233.

Prochaska, J. O., DiClemente, C. C., & Norcross, J. C. (1992). In search of how people change: Applications to addictive behaviors. *American Psychologist, 47,* 1102–1114.

Rapp, C., & Goscha, R. (2006). *The strengths model: Case management with people with psychiatric disabilities.* New York: Oxford University Press.

Regier, D. A., Farmer, M. E., Rae, D. S., Locke, B. Z., Keith, S. J., Judd, L. L., et al. (1990). Comorbidity of mental disorders with alcohol and other drug abuse: Results from the Epidemiologic Catchment Area (ECA) study. *Journal of the American Medical Association, 264,* 2511–2518.

Rosenberg, S. D., Drake, R. E., Wolford, G. L., Mueser, K. T., Oxman, T. E., Vidaver, R. M., et al. (1998). Dartmouth Assessment of Lifestyle Instrument (DALI): A substance use disorder screen for people with severe mental illness. *American Journal of Psychiatry, 155,* 232–238.

Selzer, M. L. (1971). The Michigan Alcohol Screening Test: The quest for a new diagnostic instrument. *American Journal of Psychiatry, 127,* 1653–1658.

Skinner, H. A. (1982). Drug Abuse Screening Test. *Addictive Behavior, 7,* 363–371.

Substance Abuse and Mental Health Services Administration. (1993, May 20). Definition of adults with SMI and children with SED. *Federal Register, 58*(96), 29422–29425.

Substance Abuse and Mental Health Services Administration. (2008). *Results from the 2007 National Survey on Drug Use and Health: National Findings.* Office of Applied Studies, NSDUH Series H-34, DHHS Publication No. SMA 08-4343. Rockville, MD: Substance Abuse and Mental Health Services Administration.

Swendsen, J., Conway, K. P., Degenhardt, L., Glantz, M., Jin, R., et al. (2010). Mental disorders as risk factors for substance use, abuse and dependence: Results from the 10 year follow-up of the National Comorbidity Survey. *Addiction, 105,* 1117–1128.

Tsemberis, S., Gulcur, L., & Nakae, M. (2004). Housing first, consumer choice, and harm reduction for homeless individuals with a dual diagnosis. *American Journal of Public Health, 94,* 651–656.

Willoughby, F. W., & Edens, J. F. (1996). Construct validity and predictive utility of the Stages of Change Scale for alcoholics. *Journal of Substance Abuse, 8,* 275–291.

Chapter 5
Language of Diagnosis

Brian K. Ahmedani and Brian E. Perron

The Diagnostic and Statistical Manual of Mental Disorders, 4th edition, Text Revision (DSM-IV-TR) [American Psychiatric Association (APA), 2000] is the current gold standard for mental health and substance use diagnosis.[1] Social workers in clinical settings need to be aware of the language of diagnosis, particularly as it relates to the major diagnostic system. This is necessary in order to ensure consistent application of diagnostic practices with our clients, communicate with service providers of other disciplines (e.g., psychiatry, psychology, and nursing), and facilitate reimbursement services from insurance providers. Although there is an abundance of criticisms and critiques of the DSM (e.g., Kirk & Kutchins, 1992; Kutchins & Kirk, 1988), it remains an essential tool for social workers at all system levels (Frazer, Westhuis, Daley, & Phillips, 2009; Martin, Chung, & Langenbucher, 2008; Ponniah et al., 2011).

The purpose of this chapter is to provide an overview of the DSM, and its basic information, in order to understand the classification of substance-related disorders. The reader is encouraged to pay careful attention to the different nuances of language and definitions in order to fully appreciate the complexities and importance of this diagnostic system. Given the breadth of this topic area, it is important to acknowledge that some important information has been excluded. However, the reader is

---

[1] A revision of this edition of the DSM was taking place at the same time this chapter was written. Although significant changes with respect to the diagnosis of substance use disorders are expected in the revision, these anticipated changes were not integrated into this chapter. However, an online supplement to this chapter will be available to highlight the changes.

B.K. Ahmedani (✉)
Henry Ford Health System, Detroit, MI, USA
e-mail: bahmeda1@hfhs.org

B.E. Perron
University of Michigan, Ann Arbor, MI, USA
e-mail: beperron@umich.edu

M.G. Vaughn and B.E. Perron (eds.), *Social Work Practice in the Addictions*,
Contemporary Social Work Practice, DOI 10.1007/978-1-4614-5357-4_5,
© Springer Science+Business Media New York 2013

encouraged to supplement his/her learning with the carefully selected references that are found throughout the chapter. Finally, it should be noted that the use of the abbreviation *DSM* in this chapter refers broadly to this particular diagnostic and classification system. Unless otherwise specified, this usage refers to the most recent version.

Overview of the DSM

The first version of the DSM was published in 1952 and was based largely on psychoanalytical theory (APA, 1952; Hyman, 2007). The next edition, DSM-II, also relied on the same theoretical framework (APA, 1968). But in 1980, DSM-III was released, which focused more on research and field testing of diagnostic criteria than psychoanalytic theory (APA, 1980, 1987). This approach also guided subsequent revisions, including the DSM-IV (APA, 1994) and DSM-IV-TR (APA, 2000). The "TR" represents "text revision," but this edition does not contain any conceptual differences from the DSM-IV. Rather, the major differences involve the text descriptions between the diagnostic criteria for the different disorders. While DSM-V is proposed to be released in 2013 (APA, 2010; O'Brien, 2011; Regier, Narrow, Kuhl, & Kupfer, 2009), the DSM-IV-TR, based on a medical diagnostic model (Fink & Taylor, 2008), is arguably the gold standard for diagnosis of mental health and substance use disorders in the USA at this point. Nonetheless, it is recommended that every social worker, particularly those in mental health and addiction treatment settings, carries and refers to the current DSM, since it is virtually impossible to memorize all the various disorders and respective diagnostic criteria.

Multiaxial Assessment

One of the core features of diagnosis using the DSM is the multiaxial assessment system (see Table 5.1). The system is comprised of five axes (I–V) that are used to establish a complete DSM diagnosis (APA, 2000; Zalaquett, Fuerth, Stein, Ivey, & Ivey, 2008). Axis I includes all major clinical disorders and other disorders that are the focus of clinical attention. This axis is where all substance-related disorders are listed, as well as other major mental health disorders such as mood, anxiety, and schizophrenia and psychotic disorders. Axis II refers specifically to personality disorders and mental retardation. Axis III is used for all general medical conditions. All medical conditions referenced here should correspond to the International Classification of Diseases (World Health Organization, 2007, 2011).

While the first three axes focus on diagnosable conditions, the last two axes are used for summarizing information on other related or contributing problems and overall functioning. Specifically, Axis IV is for listing information on psychosocial and environmental problems including (but not limited to) (1) occupation, (2) hous ing, (3) finances, (4) access to health care, (5) criminal involvement, (6) a limited primary

Table 5.1 Multiaxial Assessment in DSM-IV-TR (APA, 2000)

Axis I	Substance-related disorders
	Major clinical disorders
	Other conditions deserving major clinical attention
Axis II	Personality disorders
	Mental retardation
Axis III	General medical conditions (ICD-9-CM or ICD-10 Criteria)
Axis IV	Psychosocial and environmental problems
Axis V	Global assessment of functioning: score (0–100)

support group, and (7) social environment. Lopez et al. (2006) recommend that when determining which psychosocial/environmental issues to indicate on Axis IV, the clinician should also assess which psychosocial or environmental resources may help improve an individual's condition. In essence, determining a set of resources associated with each problem will allow the social worker to work with the client to create a treatment plan.

The final axis (Axis V) includes the Global Assessment of Functioning (GAF), which is commonly referred to as a *GAF score* in routine practice. The GAF score ranges from 1 (extreme danger of hurting self or others) to 100 (superior functioning). A score of 0 indicates that there is inadequate information to assess overall functioning. The GAF score varies based on the factors listed on the first four axes, but is primarily determined by a number of elements including whether or not the individual has suicidal or homicidal ideation or plans as well as attempts of either act. In addition, a social worker needs to assess factors related to affect, judgment, thinking patterns, mood, hygiene, and ability to communicate in order to determine a GAF score.

While GAF scores have shown some reliability in first time assessment, they must be used with caution to determine change over time (Söderberg et al., 2005). More specifically, it is important that GAF scores should reflect functioning rather than symptoms. This is particularly important when assessing individuals with disorders that exhibit significant variations over time (e.g., substance use disorders, schizophrenia-spectrum disorders; see Smith et al., 2011). Social workers, and other clinical staff, should receive in-depth training and supervision in order to use the GAF measure, as scores can often be wildly inconsistent if used without such experience (Vatnaland, Vatnaland, Friis, & Opjordsmoen, 2007).

Diagnostic Coding

The coding scheme used to indicate diagnoses in DSM-IV-TR correspond to those used in the International Classification of Diseases (ICD). Currently, the ICD is in its 10th revision, and plans for the 11th revision are under way with a final version due by 2015 (WHO, 2007, 2011). Nonetheless, some of the health-care arena in the USA still relies upon the ICD-9-CM. Several differences between the ICD-10 and

ICD-9-CM are noteworthy. For example, ICD-10 includes two additional categories having codes that start with letters instead of three digit numbers (Quan et al., 2008). Thus, it is important to recognize which version of the ICD is in use in each practice setting, so that clinical criteria can correspond accordingly. If the practice setting uses the ICD-10 classification, then social workers should reference the back of DSM-IV-TR (pp. 883–896) to find the equivalent code.

When making a diagnosis using DSM-IV-TR, several considerations are necessary. When a client arrives for a visit, either in the inpatient, emergency, or outpatient setting, the social worker should attribute a diagnosis that is associated with that particular visit. This diagnostic code is called the *principal diagnosis* and reason for the visit. When multiple diagnoses are present, which is common among persons with substance-related disorders, the conditions should be listed in order of treatment focus on their corresponding axes. The most prominent condition may also include the phrase "Principal Diagnosis" (inpatient) or "Reason for Visit" (outpatient). Similarly, if a social worker believes that a client may meet criteria for a disorder but still lacks some information, then a diagnosis may be listed along with the phrase "Provisional." As is often the case, clients may meet several, but not full, criteria for a disorder.

Sometimes a person may not exhibit full criteria for a given disorder, even though the criteria that are met are associated with clinically significant impairments or functioning. In this situation, a social worker may choose to give a "Not Otherwise Specified" (NOS) diagnosis that corresponds to the condition of concern. For example, a client who used cannabis and met some criteria, but not full criteria for a specific disorder may be given the following diagnosis: 292.9 cannabis-related disorder NOS. Specific codes used to reference NOS are available for each relevant diagnostic category (e.g., 291.9 alcohol related disorder NOS, etc.; APA, 2000).

Overview of Substance-Related Disorders

Substance-related disorders are separated into two specific categories in DSM-IV-TR: (1) substance use disorders (i.e., abuse and dependence), and (2) substance-induced disorders (i.e., intoxication, withdrawal, and other-induced conditions). These disorders, along with their corresponding diagnostic codes, are summarized in Tables 5.2 and 5.3, respectively. These disorders differentially apply to 11 different classes of substances: alcohol, amphetamines, caffeine, cannabis, cocaine, hallucinogens, inhalants, nicotine, opioids, phencyclidine, and sedatives/hypnotics/anxiolytics.

Two important clarifications need to be made. First, a general diagnosis of a "substance use disorder" is not permissible, unless the actual substance cannot be determined.[2] Instead, each diagnosis needs to correspond to the actual substance that the person is using. Some classes of substances have diagnostic codes specifically for different types of substances, which should be used if the exact substance can be reliably determined. For example, methamphetamines are contained within the amphetamine class. Thus, if a client meets diagnostic criteria for abuse of

---

[2] In this case, the diagnosis would be specified as an unknown "substance-related disorder."

Table 5.2 Diagnostic codes for substance use disorders by substance class (APA, 2000)

Substance	Abuse	Dependence
Alcohol	305.00	303.90
Amphetamines	305.70	304.40
Caffeine	N/A	N/A
Cannabis	305.20	304.30
Cocaine	305.60	304.20
Hallucinogens	305.30	304.50
Inhalants	305.90	304.60
Nicotine	N/A	305.10
Opioids	305.50	304.00
Phencyclidines	305.90	304.60
Sedatives/hypnotics/anxiolytics	305.40	304.10

methamphetamine, then methamphetamine should be identified along with the code corresponding to the general amphetamine class (i.e., 305.70; APA, 2000).

The second clarification refers to the differential application of disorders to substances. More specifically, not every substance has an associated abuse or dependence diagnosis, or a substance-induced disorder. For example, all the disorders can be applied to alcohol, but only a subset of disorders apply to caffeine—that is, an individual cannot be diagnosed with caffeine abuse or dependence, but can be diagnosed with caffeine intoxication. These nuances further underscore the need to refer regularly to the actual DSM when assigning a given diagnosis. Provided below is a more detailed description of the different disorders.

Substance Use Disorders

As indicated, the two major substance use disorders are abuse and dependence, and an actual diagnosis requires a specific class or type of substance. Another important consideration with respect to abuse and dependence is their *hierarchical relationship*. That is, substance abuse is considered to be the less severe of the two disorders for a given class of substances (e.g., alcohol abuse vs. alcohol dependence). Additionally, an individual cannot simultaneously hold both disorders for a given class of substances (e.g., alcohol abuse *and* alcohol dependence). If the individual meets criteria for both disorders, the more severe disorder (i.e., dependence) would be assigned. Finally, if an individual ever met criteria for dependence for any given class of substances, that individual cannot subsequently receive an abuse diagnosis for that class.

Substance Abuse

Substance abuse includes repeated or persistent problems related to substance use. While substance abuse can be associated with significant problems in a person's life, it is not characterized by withdrawal symptoms or compulsive use. To meet criteria for a substance abuse diagnosis, a client's substance use must result in one

Table 5.3 Diagnostic codes for substance-induced mental disorders by substance Class (APA. 2000)

Substance	Dementia	Amnestic disorder	Psychotic disorder with Del./Hal.	Mood disorder	Anxiety disorder	Sexual dysfunction	Sleep disorder
Alcohol	291.20	291.10	291.5/291.3	291.89	291.89	291.89	291.89
Amphetamines	N/A	N/A	292.11/292.12	292.84	292.89	292.89	292.89
Caffeine	N/A	N/A	N/A	N/A	292.89	N/A	292.89
Cannabis	N/A	N/A	292.11/292.12	N/A	292.89	N/A	N/A
Cocaine	N/A	N/A	292.11/292.12	292.84	292.89	292.89	292.89
Hallucinogens	N/A	N/A	292.11/292.12	292.84	292.89	N/A	N/A
Inhalants	292.82	N/A	292.11/292.12	292.84	292.89	N/A	N/A
Nicotine	N/A	N/A	N/A	N/A	N/A	N/A	N/A
Opioids	N/A	N/A	292.11/292.12	292.84	N/A	292.89	292.89
Phencyclidines	N/A	N/A	292.11/292.12	292.84	292.89	N/A	N/A
Sed./Hypn./Anxiol.	292.82	292.83	292.11/292.12	292.84	292.89	292.89	292.89

Sed. sedatives. *Hypn.* hypnotics. *Anxiol.* anxiolytics. *Del.* delusions. *Hal.* hallucinations

of the following four criteria being met within a 12-month period: (1) failure to fulfill major role obligations as a result of use, (2) use in situations that are physically hazardous, (3) repeated legal problems related to use, and (4) social or legal problems resulting from repeated use (APA, 2000). Social workers should note that there is not an existing code or condition related to abuse of nicotine or caffeine.

Substance Dependence

Substance dependence is considered more severe than substance abuse, as it is characterized by significant impairment or distress related to physiological, cognitive, and behavioral symptoms. In order to make a substance dependence diagnosis, a client must meet any three or more of the following seven criteria in any 12-month period: (1) tolerance (a need for more amounts to achieve the same effect and diminished effect after continued use), (2) withdrawal (physiological or cognitive syndromes related to substance use that may lead to social, occupational, or other impairment), (3) substance is used for longer periods or in larger amounts than intended, (4) unsuccessful attempts to stop or reduce use, (5) a significant amount of time is spent to obtain or recover from the substance, (6) reduced participation in normal social, occupational, or recreational activities due to use, and (7) use continues despite continuous problems related to the substance (APA, 2000). Although the DSM-IV-TR criteria for dependence do not include cravings for the substance, this should also be assessed.

When making a dependence diagnosis, the social worker must consider many other components. First, the diagnosis should be attached to the specific drug of abuse. Second, following the main dependence diagnosis, the social worker should always specify whether the condition is "with physiological dependence" or "without -physiological dependence." Physiological dependence means that the client is experiencing either tolerance or withdrawal (the first two criteria). Also, social workers should note that there is not an existing code or condition related to substance dependence regarding caffeine use.

Course Specifiers

A set of course specifiers are used for substance dependence. While course specifiers are available for other mental health disorders, the course specifiers for substance use disorders are unique. The first four specifiers relate to remission. "Early remission" should be used if a client with a specific dependence diagnosis met criteria for abuse or dependence within the past 1–12 months, but currently either does not meet any criteria (early full remission) or meets fewer criteria than what is necessary for an abuse or dependence diagnosis (early partial remission). In these cases, the individual maintains the dependence diagnosis with the appropriate specifier, even though the individual may have met criteria for substance abuse. If these same specifications are met for longer than 1 year, then a course specifier of either "sustained full remission" (no criteria are met) or "sustained partial remission" (fewer criteria met than needed for an active diagnosis) can be attached to a diagnosis (e.g., 304.20 cocaine dependence, sustained partial remission).

Two additional course specifiers can be attached to a substance dependence diagnosis are "on agonist therapy" and "in a controlled environment." "On agonist therapy" is used when a client is being treated with an agonist, such as methadone, and he/she has not met criteria (except withdrawal or tolerance to the agonist) for an active diagnosis for at least a month. Furthermore, "in a controlled environment" indicates that for at least a month the client is in a setting or environment without access to the drug of abuse, such as a locked and substance-free prison or hospital unit, and no longer meets criteria for an active diagnosis (APA, 2000).

Substance-Induced Disorders

The large category of substance-induced disorders is comprised of three main subtypes: substance intoxication, substance withdrawal, and substance-induced mental disorders. The clinical diagnostic codes from DSM-IV-TR for substance intoxication and withdrawal, by substance class, are summarized in Table 5.4. Also, it is important to recognize that there are several different forms of substance-induced mental disorders. These unique conditions are discussed in detail in DSM-IV-TR within the sections that correspond to the specific non-substance-related mental disorder (e.g., mood disorders; APA, 2000). Diagnostic codes for these conditions are shown in Table 5.4. Substance-induced disorders are discussed in more detail below.

Substance Intoxication

Substance intoxication generally occurs up to 1 day after a course of heavy use of a substance and does not require sustained use over a period of time. Three specific criteria are necessary for making a diagnosis of substance intoxication: (1) use or exposure to a substance resulting in a substance-specific syndrome, (2) maladaptive or psychological changes occurring as a result of the effect of the substance on the central nervous system, and (3) the corresponding symptoms cannot be due to a general medical or other mental health condition. A diagnosis of substance intoxication can be made for any of the substance classes except nicotine (APA, 2000).

Substance Withdrawal

The criteria for substance withdrawal are similar to the withdrawal criterion used in a substance dependence diagnosis. Therefore, it is important for social workers to recognize whether their clients' withdrawal symptoms are due specifically to substance withdrawal or whether they are part of a more severe substance dependence diagnosis. Three specific criteria are necessary for a substance withdrawal diagnosis:

Table 5.4 Diagnostic codes for substance intoxication and withdrawal by substance class (APA, 2000)

Substance	Intoxication	Withdrawal	Intoxication delirium	Withdrawal delirium
Alcohol	303.00	291.81	291.00	291.00
Amphetamines	292.89	292.00	292.81	N/A
Caffeine	305.90	N/A	N/A	N/A
Cannabis	292.89	N/A	292.81	N/A
Cocaine	292.89	292.00	292.81	N/A
Hallucinogens	292.89	N/A	292.81	N/A
Inhalants	292.89	N/A	292.81	N/A
Nicotine	N/A	292.00	292.81	N/A
Opioids	292.89	292.00	292.81	N/A
Phencyclidines	292.89	N/A	292.81	N/A
Sedatives/ hypnotics/ anxiolytics	292.89	292.00	292.81	292.81

(1) heavy or prolonged substance use leading to a substance-specific syndrome, (2) significant distress or impairment in social, occupational, or other areas of functioning related to the syndrome, and (3) the corresponding symptoms are not due to a general medical or other mental health condition (APA, 2000). In situations where a client meets criteria for substance withdrawal and substance dependence, a social worker should give the diagnosis of substance dependence. Different from substance intoxication, a diagnosis of substance withdrawal can only be made for the following classes of substances: alcohol, amphetamines, cocaine, nicotine, opioids, and sedatives/hypnotics/anxiolytics (APA, 2000).

Substance Intoxication Vs. Withdrawal Delirium

Beyond a standard diagnosis of either substance intoxication or withdrawal, delirium can also be the result of either condition and should be noted as such in a proper diagnosis. In circumstances when a client presents to a visit with symptoms consistent with either intoxication or withdrawal, then a social worker should assess for criteria consistent with delirium. A diagnosis of either substance intoxication delirium or substance withdrawal delirium should be made when the standard symptoms are present for each non-delirium condition with the addition of the following criteria related to delirium: (1) there is a significant disturbance of consciousness, (2) a corresponding change or perpetual disturbance in cognition, (3) the delirium symptoms occurred during or shortly after either substance intoxication or withdrawal. For a diagnosis of substance intoxication delirium, any of the substance classes can be noted except caffeine. A diagnosis of substance withdrawal delirium, however, can only be present for the substance classes of alcohol and sedatives/hypnotics/anxiolytics (APA, 2000).

Substance-Induced Mental Disorders

Substance use can result in a number of symptoms that are consistent with other mental disorders discussed in detail throughout DSM-IV-TR. In addition to delirium, there are seven different categories of mental disorders that can be substance induced. These categories include: (1) dementia, (2) amnestic disorder, (3) psychotic disorders, (4) mood disorders, (5) anxiety disorders, (6) sexual dysfunctions, and (7) sleep disorders. To make a diagnosis of a substance-induced mental disorder in one of these categories, the mental disorder symptoms must be the result of substance use. This is an important distinction that is often difficult to determine, since mental health symptoms can either come before or after substance use. More specifically, individuals with mental health conditions may use substances to ease the burden of their symptoms or mental health conditions may be the direct result of using substances. A careful social work assessment is necessary to determine whether the substance use preceded the mental health symptoms, in which case a substance-induced diagnosis can be made. For each diagnosis, the social worker should record the specific substance that induced the mental disorder along with any appropriate specifiers and subtypes (e.g., 291.89 alcohol-induced mood disorder, with depressive features, with onset during intoxication; APA, 2000). Table 5.3 provides a more detailed list of the diagnostic codes that are associated with each substance-induced mental disorder by substance class.

Substance-induced mental disorders can either be "persisting," "with onset during intoxication," or "with onset during withdrawal." Substance-induced dementia and amnestic disorder are always diagnosed as "persisting" only. This means that symptoms consistent with amnestic disorder or dementia must persist beyond the typical scope of substance intoxication or withdrawal and must not occur specifically during delirium. Substance-induced dementia and amnestic disorder can occur from using either alcohol or sedatives/hypnotics/anxiolytics. In addition, substance-induced dementia can result from inhalant use (APA, 2000).

The remaining substance-induced mental disorders can only occur with onset either during intoxication or withdrawal. In these circumstances, the criteria for substance intoxication or substance withdrawal must be met along with the corresponding symptoms for one of the five remaining mental disorder categories. First, substance-induced psychotic disorders can occur either with onset during intoxication (all substance classes besides nicotine and caffeine) or withdrawal (only for classes alcohol and sedatives/hypnotics/anxiolytics). In addition, if the psychotic disorder is associated with hallucinations or delusions, the predominant symptoms should be included as a course specifier (e.g., with hallucinations). Similarly, a diagnosis of substance-induced mood disorder should include the course specifier "with onset during intoxication (all substance classes besides nicotine, cannabis, and caffeine) or "with onset during withdrawal" (only for classes alcohol, amphetamines, cocaine, or sedatives/hypnotics/anxiolytics). In addition, one of the following subtypes may also be used under this category to indicate symptoms that correspond to depression, mania, or both: (1) with depressive features, (2) with manic features, or (3) with mixed features (APA, 2000).

Similar to substance-induced psychotic and mood disorders, substance-induced anxiety disorders can occur either "with onset during intoxication" (all substance classes besides nicotine, opioids, or sedatives/hypnotics/anxiolytics) or withdrawal (only for classes alcohol, cocaine, or sedatives/hypnotics/anxiolytics). In addition, in the case that substance-induced anxiety disorders are present with a specific set of symptoms consistent with the major anxiety disorders, then one of the following course specifiers can be used: (1) with generalized anxiety, (2) with panic attacks, (3) with obsessive-compulsive symptoms, or (4) with phobic symptoms. Substance-induced sleep disorders also occur either "with onset during intoxication" or withdrawal and have several subtype options. The following substance classes can cause onset during intoxication or withdrawal: alcohol, amphetamines, cocaine, opioids, and sedatives/hypnotics/anxiolytics. It is important to note that caffeine can result in a diagnosis of substance-induced sleep disorder with onset during intoxication, but not with onset during withdrawal. The following sleep disorder subtypes can be indicated as course specifiers along with the diagnosis: (1) insomnia type, (2) hypersomnia type, (3) parasomnia type, or (4) mixed type. Finally, substance-induced sexual dysfunctions can only occur with onset during intoxication and with the following substance classes: alcohol, amphetamines, cocaine, opioids, or sedatives/hypnotics/anxiolytics. Possible specifiers for this diagnosis correspond to the predominant type of sexual dysfunction occurring for the client. These specifiers include: (1) with impaired desire, (2) with impaired arousal, (3) with impaired orgasm, or (4) with sexual pain (APA, 2000).

Hallucinogen Persisting Perception Disorder

Hallucinogen persisting perception disorder is comprised of flashbacks related to the use of hallucinogens. This diagnosis is specifically unique to hallucinogen use only, and cannot be made for the use of other substances. There are three main criteria in a DSM-IV-TR diagnosis of hallucinogen persisting perception disorder: (1) re-experiencing perceptual symptoms, such as colors, flashes of light, hallucinations, and others, following the cessation of hallucinogen use, (2) significant impairment or distress associated with the symptoms, and (3) the symptoms cannot be the result of a general medical or other mental health condition.

Polysubstance Use and Other Substance Related Disorders

Beyond the specific diagnostic codes and criteria for substance use and substance-induced disorders, there are other conditions in DSM-IV-TR that are used for individuals who use more than one substance at a time or for individuals who use drugs of abuse that do not fit within the specified 11 classes of substances. First, in the circumstance that a client is using more than one substance, all substance disorders should be listed on Axis I (e.g., 304.0 heroin dependence; 305.90 amyl nitrate abuse). Nonetheless, if a client meets criteria for substance dependence and three or more different substances were used in which none were predominant, then the social worker should give the diagnosis—304.80 polysubstance dependence. To make this diagnosis, a social worker must ensure that criteria for dependence were met for all of the substances used. A diagnosis regarding polysubstance use can only be made for dependence, and therefore, cannot be made for another of the other substance-related disorders categories (e.g., abuse and intoxication; APA, 2000).

DSM-IV-TR also allows for situations in which a person uses substances that do not correspond to any of the main 11 classes of substances. Among these substances are anabolic steroids, nitrite inhalants, nitrous oxide, catnip, kava, betel nut, and other over-the-counter or prescription medications, among others. When a client presents in a clinical setting after using one or more of these substances, then a social worker should consider whether he/she meets criteria for a substance-related disorder. In addition, a client may meet criteria for a substance-related disorder, but it cannot be determined to which substance. In this case, the disorder is unknown. A diagnosis of other (or unknown) substance-related disorder can be made in any substance-related disorder category discussed earlier including dependence (304.90), abuse (305.90), intoxication (292.89), withdrawal (292.0), or any of the substance-induced mental disorders. If diagnosing a substance-induced mental disorder, then the social worker should determine whether it occurred with onset during intoxication or withdrawal. The specific substance being used should be listed if it is known; otherwise the social worker should indicate that the diagnosis is unknown.

Conclusions and Future Directions

This chapter highlights the complexities and nuances involved in the reliable and valid diagnosis of substance-related disorders from the perspective of the DSM. It is critical that social workers are fully informed of the system and understand its clinical utility in the context of known limitations. The DSM continues to evolve guided by science and statistical models, and the proposed changes to the current version of the DSM will likely improve its clinical utility. Social workers are encouraged to remain current with the scientific literature on proposed changes in order to effectively and efficiently respond to actual changes in the system. While in-depth study of diagnosis is essential, social workers can enhance their understanding of diagnosis with supplementary studies on assessment techniques, epidemiology, and theory. These supplementary areas can help further refine our understanding of the strengths and limitations of this diagnostic and classification system, which can ultimately lead to better services for clients being served.

References

American Psychiatric Association. (1952). *Diagnostic and Statistical Manual of Mental Disorders.* Washington, DC: American Psychiatric Association Mental Health Service.

American Psychiatric Association. (1968). *Diagnostic and Statistical Manual of Mental Disorders* (2nd ed.). Washington, DC: American Psychiatric Association.

American Psychiatric Association. (1980). *Diagnostic and Statistical Manual of Mental Disorders* (3rd ed.). Washington, DC: American Psychiatric Association.

American Psychiatric Association. (1987). *Diagnostic and Statistical Manual of Mental Disorders* (3rd ed., revision). Washington, DC: American Psychiatric Association.

American Psychiatric Association. (1994). *Diagnostic and Statistical Manual of Mental Disorders* (4th ed.). Washington, DC: American Psychiatric Association.

American Psychiatric Association. (2000). *Diagnostic and Statistical Manual of Mental Disorders* (4th ed., text revision). Washington, DC: American Psychiatric Association.

American Psychiatric Association. (2010). *DSM-5: The future of psychiatric diagnosis.* Retrieved from http://www.dsm5.org/Pages/Default.aspx. Accessed on June 1, 2011.

Fink, M., & Taylor, M. A. (2008). The medical evidence-based model for psychiatric syndromes: Return to a classical paradigm. *Acta Psychiatrica Scandinavica, 117,* 81–84.

Frazer, P., Westhuis, D., Daley, J. G., & Phillips, I. (2009). How clinical social workers are using the DSM-IV: A national study. *Social Work in Mental Health, 7*(4), 325–339.

Hyman, S. E. (2007). Can neuroscience be integrated into the DSM-V? *Nature Reviews Neuroscience, 8,* 725–732.

Kirk, S. A., & Kutchins, H. (1992). *The selling of DSM: The rhetoric of science in psychiatry.* Hawthorne, NY: Aldine de Gruyter.

Kutchins, H., & Kirk, S. A. (1988). The business of diagnosis: DSM-III and clinical social work. *Social Work, 33,* 215–220.

Lopez, S. J., Edwards, L. M., Pedrotti, J. T., Prosser, E. C., LaRue, S., Spalitto, S. V., et al. (2006). Beyond the DSM-IV: Assumptions, alternatives, and alterations. *Journal of Counseling & Development, 84,* 259–267.

Martin, C. S., Chung, T., & Langenbucher, J. W. (2008). How should we revise diagnostic criteria for substance use disorders in DSM-V? *Journal of Abnormal Psychology, 117*(3), 561–575.

O'Brien, C. (2011). Addiction and dependence in DSM-V. *Addiction, 106*(5), 866–867.

Ponniah, K., Weissman, M. M., Bledsoe, S. E., Verdeli, H., Gameroff, M. J., Mufson, L., et al. (2011). Training in structured diagnostic assessment using DSM-IV criteria. *Research on Social Work Practice, 21*(4), 452–457.

Quan, H., Lee, B., Saunders, L. D., Parsons, G. A., Nilsson, C. I., Alibhai, A., et al. (2008). Assessing validity of ICD-9-CM and ICD-10 administrative data in recording clinical conditions in a unique dually coded database. *Health Services Research, 43*(4), 1424–1441.

Regier, D. A., Narrow, W. E., Kuhl, E. A., & Kupfer, D. J. (2009). The conceptual development of DSM-V. *American Journal of Psychiatry, 166,* 645–650.

Smith, G. N., Ehmann, T. S., Flynn, S. W., MacEwan, G. W., Tee, K., Kopala, L. C., et al. (2011). *Psychiatric Services, 62,* 411–417.

Söderberg, P., Tungström, S., & Armelius, A. (2005). Special section on the GAF: Reliability of global assessment of functioning ratings made by clinical psychiatric staff. *Psychiatric Services, 56,* 434–438.

Vatnaland, T., Vatnaland, J., Friis, S., & Opjordsmoen, S. (2007). Are GAF scores reliable in routine clinical use? *Acta Psychiatrica Scandinavica, 115,* 326–330.

World Health Organization. (2007). *International Statistical Classification of Diseases and Related Health Problems, 10th revision (ICD-10).* Retrieved from http://apps.who.int/classifications/apps/icd/icd10online/. Accessed on Jan 24, 2012.

World Health Organization. (2011). *International Classification of Diseases, 11th revision is due by 2015*. Retrieved from http://www.who.int/classifications/icd/revision/en/index.html. Accessed on Jan 24, 2012.

Zalaquett, C. P., Fuerth, K. M., Stein, C., Ivey, A. E., & Ivey, M. B. (2008). Reframing the DSM-IV-TR from a multicultural/social justice perspective. *Journal of Counseling & Development, 86*(3), 364–371.

Chapter 6
Brief Motivational Interventions to Change Problematic Substance Use

Mark A. Ilgen and Joseph E. Glass

The misuse of alcohol and drugs represents a common and costly problem within the USA and around the world (SAMHSA, 2010; World Health Organization, 2010). Given the substantial prevalence of substance use disorders, social workers are likely to encounter a large number of patients with substance-related problems regardless of the setting in which they work. Clearly, social workers working within addictions treatment programs will see large numbers of patients with substance-related problems. However, even outside of specialty substance use disorder treatment settings, social workers frequently encounter clients who are struggling with problems related to the use of alcohol or drugs. Social workers employed in general mental health settings report that approximately one fifth of clients in their caseloads carry a DSM-IV diagnosis of a substance use disorder (Smith, Whitaker, & Weismiller, 2006). Brief motivational interventions provide a framework for treatment providers to intervene to reduce substance misuse. Below, we briefly review the data on the prevalence of substance use/misuse, describe the role of motivation in shaping behavior, and describe the existing evidence supporting the efficacy of brief motivational interventions. Given emerging evidence that brief motivational interventions can be effective even when delivered in non-specialty settings, such as primary care, social workers in all treatment settings have the opportunity to assess for and address problematic substance use in their patients.

M.A. Ilgen (✉)
Department of Veterans Affairs Healthcare System,
VA Serious Mental Illness Treatment Research and Evaluation Center,
Ann Arbor, MI, USA

Department of Psychiatry, University of Michigan, Ann Arbor, MI, USA
e-mail: marki@med.umich.edu

J.E. Glass
School of Social Work, University of Wisconsin-Madison,
1350 University Ave., Madison, WI 53706, USA
e-mail: jeglass@wustl.edu

M.G. Vaughn and B.E. Perron (eds.), *Social Work Practice in the Addictions*,
Contemporary Social Work Practice, DOI 10.1007/978-1-4614-5357-4_6,
© Springer Science+Business Media New York 2013

Prevalence

The use of alcohol and drug use is very common in the USA and around the world (SAMHSA, 2010; World Health Organization, 2010). Based on the data from the 2006 National Survey on Drug Use and Health, 23% of U.S. residents engaged in at-risk drinking in the last year, with an estimated 7.6% of the population of the USA meeting criteria for a diagnosable alcohol use disorder (AUD) (SAMHSA, 2007). It was also estimated that 20.2 million individuals over the age of 12 had used an illicit drug in the past month, which amounts to approximately 8.2% of the U.S. population. About half of those who used illicit drugs used cannabis. Further, 35.2 million individuals over the age of 12 had used cocaine in their lifetime (8.6 million using crack cocaine) and just over 6 million used cocaine in the past year (SAMHSA, 2007). The rates of substance use disorders are higher in certain clinical settings such as locations that provide emergency treatment to traditionally underserved or impoverished patients (Booth et al., 2011). Given the high prevalence of alcohol and drug use, it is not surprising that social work practitioners frequently encounter clients with active substance use disorders in their clinical practice (Smith et al., 2006).

Consequences

The problems related to the use of alcohol and illicit substances are highly relevant to the diverse populations that social workers serve. Consuming alcohol above recommended limits is associated with an increased risk of acute injury, psychosocial problems, chronic and acute medical problems, and terminal illness (Center for Disease Control and Prevention, 2009; National Institute on Alcohol Abuse and Alcoholism, 2005). Persons with substance use disorders report strained social relationships and negative perceptions from others in their social network (Midanik & Greenfield, 2000). Many families are familiar with the devastating effects of alcohol; one-quarter of all children under 18 years of age live in a household with someone who is alcohol dependent (Grant, 2000), and over one half of all adults have a family member who has had problems with alcohol (Dawson & Grant, 1998). Additionally, substance use disorders appear to have more deleterious effects for racial/ethnic minorities and women. The social consequences of alcohol are worse for African American and Hispanics as compared to whites, which may be attributed to harsher experiences of alcohol-related stigma among some racial and ethnic minorities (Mulia, Ye, Greenfield, & Zemore, 2009; Smith, Dawson, Goldstein, & Grant, 2010). Women who consume alcohol at unhealthy levels experience more psychosocial and medical problems as compared to men (Bradley et al., 2001). Those who are dependent on alcohol or drugs are subject to being devalued by their peers and experience discrimination. The public stigma towards those with alcohol and drug used disorders is even worse than the stigma towards those with schizophrenia or depression partially because those with substance use disorders are perceived as more violent and more at fault for their illness (Schomerus et al., 2011). Given the profession's spotlight on social justice, social workers are in a unique position to offer help to those who experience alcohol and drug problems.

Few of Those with Substance Use Disorders Receive Treatment

Despite the substantial prevalence of substance use disorders within the USA and consistent findings highlighting the beneficial effects of treatment, few of those with substance use disorders seek any formal or informal treatment services (Cohen, Feinn, Arias, & Kranzler, 2007; Glass et al., 2010; Ilgen et al., 2011). When asked why they have not received services, untreated individuals cite a number of reasons including: lack of social support or health insurance, negative stigma, low confidence in the efficacy of available AUD treatments, and the belief that a person should be strong enough to handle an AUD on his/her own (Cohen et al., 2007; Edlund, Booth, & Feldman, 2009; Grant, Hasin, & Dawson, 1996; Schober & Annis, 1996) These concerns are likely made worse by the fact that many addictions treatment programs have structural problems (cumbersome intake processes, high staff turnover) that make treatment-seeking less appealing to those with substance use disorders (Dunn, Deroo, & Rivara, 2001; McLellan, Carise, & Kleber, 2003; McLellan & Meyers, 2004).

The Role of Motivation in Behavior Change

Given the substantial gap between the potential need for addictions treatment and the rate of utilization of these services, strategies are needed to reach a larger number of individuals with problematic substance use and either help them to change their substance use or, in those with more severe substance-related problems, encourage them to utilize treatments provided by substance abuse specialists. Below, we provide a brief overview of a theory of how motivation influences behavior change and how motivational interventions increase the likelihood of behavior change. Additionally, we note how interventions that target motivation could harness the existing process of behavior change to increase the likelihood that an individual will reduce his or her substance misuse.

Conceptual Model of Behavior Change by Individuals with Problematic Alcohol or Drug Use

Changing entrenched problematic behaviors, such as frequent drug use, often seems daunting to both the patient and the treatment provider. Yet the process of behavior change for problematic substance use shares many common characteristics with other problem health behaviors (changing diet, exercise, medication adherence, problematic alcohol use, etc.) that have been the targets of successful public health interventions for years (Miller, 1998). Rogers' Protection Motivation Theory (PMT) of threat appraisals and attitude change describes a model for understanding the processes related to changing substance use and other health-related behaviors (Rogers, 1975; Rogers & Prentice-Dunn, 1997). In other words, the theory attempts to explain the factors which cause one to be *motivated* to *protect* him/herself from deleterious outcomes that are associated with risky behaviors. An integration of theory and findings from the brief intervention and motivational interviewing (MI) literature is necessary to explicate how screening and brief intervention strategies can facilitate change (Amrhein, Miller, Yahne, Palmer, & Fulcher, 2003; Dunn et al., 2001; Hettema, Steele, & Miller, 2005).

PMT is one of the most widely studied models of health behavior change (Floyd, Prentice-Dunn, & Rogers, 2000) and has been the basis of research on strategies to: reduce HIV risk behaviors (Fang, Stanton, Li, Feigelman, & Baldwin, 1998; Houlding & Davidson, 2003); increase adherence to cancer risk reduction protocols (McClendon & Prentice-Dunn, 2001; Wood, 2008); and increase exercise in those at elevated risk for cardiac disease (Reid et al., 2007). Additionally, it has been applied to the study of addictive behaviors in interventions designed to reduce the rates of driving while intoxicated (Ben-Ahron, White, & Phillips, 1995), alcohol use in older adults (Runge, Prentice-Dunn, & Scogin, 1993), and drug trafficking in inner-city African American youth (Wu, Stanton, Li, Galbraith, & Cole, 2005). A meta-analysis of 65 studies examined the impact of each of the primary components of PMT (perceived rewards, threat severity, vulnerability, etc.) and subsequent motivation to change problematic behaviors (Floyd et al., 2000). The effect of each of the components of PMT was moderate (Cohen's *d* of 0.5), despite the high degree of variability in sample composition, problems examined, and methods of measurement.

Figure 6.1 presents the core components of the PMT model, along with a representation of how brief motivational interventions are designed to directly address each of these components (e.g., self-efficacy, "response efficacy"). The figure also illustrates the role of motivationally based interventions on later factors related to behavioral change (e.g., intentions/commitment to change, development of a specific change plan). According to the PMT model, motivation to change risky behaviors (referred to as *Protection Motivation*) is a function of weighing the value of maintaining a maladaptive response versus implementing an adaptive response, and is predicted by *threat appraisal* and *coping appraisal*. *Threat appraisal* is hypothesized to reflect (A) the perception of the *rewards* of continued engagement in the problematic behavior, and (B) the perceived *severity* of problems if the behavior remains unchanged, and the perceived *vulnerability* to these problems. *Coping appraisals* reflect (C) the individual's perception of the overall *efficacy* of the strategy to reduce risk ("response efficacy") and the individual's *self-efficacy* to adhere to the change approach, and (D) the response cost, or perception of the unpleasant consequences of adopting the behavior change. Changing motivation is a matter of addressing both *threat appraisals* and *coping appraisals*. Individuals may be particularly amenable to changing their perception of their *threat and coping appraisals* during times of acute stress (considered to be a "teachable moment").

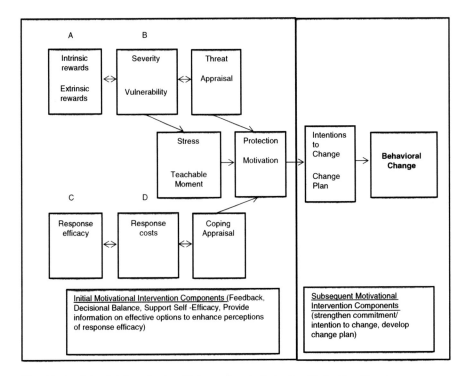

Fig. 6.1 Applying brief motivational interventions to Protection Motivation Theory

As depicted in Fig. 6.1, effective brief motivation-based intervention strategies address the components of the PMT model by: (a) incorporating "feedback" regarding potential consequences of problematic behaviors; (b) exploring the pros and cons of making changes versus the pros and cons of maintaining the status quo through the use of brief "decisional balance" exercises; (c) discussing an individualized menu of options that have been shown to be effective for making changes; and (d) supporting or bolstering participants' personal self-efficacy. Further, research and theories on mechanisms for behavior change illustrate that the likelihood of change can be enhanced by increased motivation coupled with elicitation of verbal or written commitment/intent to change and a specific behavioral change plan (Amrhein et al., 2003; Gollwitzer, 1999; Hettema et al., 2005)

Brief Motivational Interventions to Change Patterns of Substance Misuse

Thus, as described above, motivation to change is theorized to play an important role in influencing the process of behavior change. Understandably, interventions have been developed to target motivation to change. Most of these have grown out of the initial work on MI. Below, we review the history of MI as well as the evidence supporting the efficacy of this approach. Additionally, we describe two related interventions that have grown out of the substantial research on MI: Motivational Enhancement Therapy (MET) and Screening, Brief Interventions, and Referral to Treatment (SBIRT) approaches.

Motivational Interviewing

MI was developed by William Miller as a client-centered, directive method for enhancing intrinsic motivation to change by exploring and resolving ambivalence (Apodaca & Longabaugh, 2009; Miller & Rollnick, 1991). The general approach for MI encouraged the therapist to closely attend to the client's speech with an emphasis on evoking and strengthening the client's motivation for change. The therapist was encouraged to respond empathically to client's ambivalence to encourage the client, instead of the therapist, to articulate the reasons for making a change (Miller & Rose, 2009)

The four core principles of MI include: expressing empathy, supporting self-efficacy, rolling with resistance, and developing discrepancy (Smedslund et al., 2011). Expressing empathy involves seeing the world through the client's eyes and ensuring that the client feels understood and not judged for their behavior. Supporting self-efficacy reflects attempts by the therapist to increase the client's confidence that they are capable of making a change. The term "rolling with resistance" describes the therapists attempt to avoid direct confrontation and deflect any assertions from the patient that change is not possible and/or desirable. Finally, the emphasis on developing a discrepancy involves helping clients attend to the lack of congruence between their current behaviors and future goals.

Over the past three decades MI and related approaches have been well studied. Several recent empirical reviews and meta-analyses summarize the sizable body of literature supporting the efficacy of MI (Burke, Arkowitz, & Menchola, 2003; Lundahl & Burke, 2009; Lundahl, Kunz, Brownell, Tollefson, & Burke, 2010; Vasilaki, Hosier, & Cox, 2006), MI has been examined for treatment of problematic alcohol use and drug disorders; however, the largest body of evidence is for reducing problem alcohol use. Specifically, MI has been shown to be at least as effective as other treatments for problem drinking and significantly better than no treatment or waitlist controls. In their review, Lundahl and Burke (2009) estimate the difference in success rates for reducing problematic alcohol use in clients who received MI compared with untreated samples to be between 10% and 20% greater. When MI for alcohol misuse is compared to other active alcohol treatments, the difference in success rates was estimated to range from 0% to 20% in favor of MI. In the treatment of Marijuana Dependence, MI has been shown to be at least as effective as other treatments and significantly better than no intervention for individuals with marijuana dependence. Similarly, evidence suggests that MI is significantly more effective than no treatment for cocaine or heroin use (Lundahl & Burke, 2009).

Meta-analyses highlight that, although the between groups effect size was statistically different from zero and indicated superior outcomes for MI, relative to no-treatment controls, effect sizes were largest at first follow-up, suggesting MI's effects fade across time (Vasilaki et al., 2006) Additionally, MI was found to be more efficacious with treatment seeking samples although significant effects of lower magnitude were observed in non-treatment-seeking samples as well. These findings indicate that MI might be more effective in individuals who demonstrate at least some basic level of desire to change their substance use.

Motivational Enhancement Therapy

MET was developed by Miller and colleagues as a manualized, 4-session intervention for individuals with alcohol dependence (Miller, Zweben, DiClemente, & Rychtarik, 1992). This intervention included a greater emphasis on assessment and personalized feedback than standard MI. MET is likely best known for its role as one of the three interventions study in the early 1990s as part of Project MATCH (1993). Project MATCH was a large randomized controlled trial designed to study whether patient characteristics significantly influenced the efficacy of three intervention conditions: 4 sessions of MET, 12 sessions of Cognitive Behavioral Therapy (CBT), and 12 sessions of 12-Step Facilitation (TSF).

In the manualized version of MET from Project MATCH, the first session provided clients with feedback from the initial assessment on drinking level and alcohol-related symptoms. The goals of the first session were to help motivate the client to initiate or maintain positive reductions in their alcohol use. The second session was designed to help clients consolidate commitment to change. The third and fourth sessions of MET, delivered several weeks after the initial two sessions, were designed to monitor progress during this time period and further encourage positive behavior change (Project MATCH, 1993).

Project MATCH was not designed as a comparison between the three therapy sessions. The goal of Project MATCH was to determine whether various subgroups of alcohol-dependent clients would respond differently to three manual-guided, individual treatments. Participants in all treatment groups showed significant improvements on all drinking measures, with no consistent differences between treatment groups. In examining client x intervention interactions (to identify client characteristics that might make certain treatments particularly suitable for certain individuals), Project MATCH found that, for client's high on anger, MET outperformed the other treatments on both primary drinking outcome measures (percentage of days abstinent and average number of drinks per drinking day) at 1- and 3-year follow-ups (Project MATCH Research Group, 1997, 1998). Results from Project MATCH show that outpatient clients low in motivation ultimately reported greater benefit from MET than from the other two interventions. For clients less motivated to change, at the beginning of the post-treatment period, CBT appeared to be superior to MET. However, over the course of the follow up the outcomes for the two treatments reversed, with those who received MET reporting less alcohol use than those who received CBT; these results are consistent with a possible delayed effect for MET in those with low initial motivation to change (Project MATCH Research Group, 1997, 1998). Also, the performance of MET relative to CBT and TSF suggests that this 4-session, interventional has comparable outcomes to the other two 12-session interventions; thus, MET may be a more cost-effective treatment than either CBT or TSF (Project MATCH Research Group, 1997)

Screening, Brief Intervention, Referral to Treatment

Based partially on the success of the trials of brief motivational interventions described above, attempts have been made to deliver brief interventions within standard medical settings. These approaches are different from standard MIs in that they are typically delivered by nonmental health providers in settings where addictions-related services have not typically been available. These brief interventions are typically referred to as SBIRT interventions and are designed to address a range of alcohol use patterns and related consequences ranging from occasional risky substance use to substance dependence (Babor et al., 2007).

Previous research has shown that brief interventions for at-risk or hazardous drinking are effective in reducing drinking levels across a variety of health-care settings (Babor & Grant, 1992; Chick, Lloyd, & Crombie, 1985; Fleming, Barry, Manwell, Johnson, & London, 1997; Harris & Miller, 1990; Wallace, Cutler, & Haines, 1988). Meta-analyses of randomized controlled studies have found that these techniques generally reduce drinking compared to control conditions (Dunn et al., 2001). Brief intervention approaches have been also used among emergency department (ED) patients admitted to hospitals (Dyehouse & Sommers, 1995; Welte, Perry, Longabaugh, & Clifford, 1998) and with injured patients in the ED (Bazargan-Hejazi et al., 2005; Blow et al., 2006; Gentilello et al., 1999; Harvard, Hill, & Buxton, 2008; Longabaugh et al., 2001; Mello et al., 2005). A recent meta-analysis of ED studies concluded that ED-based interventions significantly reduce alcohol-related injury but do not necessarily decrease alcohol consumption (Harvard et al., 2008). Although a number of studies address the need for and use of brief interventions for drug use (Baker, Kochan, Dixon, Heather, & Wodak, 1994; Compton, Monahan, & Simmons-Cody, 1999; Dunn & Ries, 1997; Greber, Allen, Soeken, & Solounias, 1997; Lang, Engelander, & Tracey Brooke, 2000; Weaver, Jarvis, & Schnoll, 1999), there are few published randomized controlled trials with drug users. Despite some differences in existing studies, such as duration of the interventions, promising treatment results have been shown in studies investigating the effectiveness of brief interventions among cocaine, heroin, and amphetamine users recruited from a variety of non-ED based settings (Baker et al., 2004; Bernstein et al., 2007; Bernstein, Bernstein, & Levenson, 1997; Stotts, Schmitz, Rhoades, & Grabowski, 2001). For example, Bernstein et al. (2005) reported that a brief intervention for heroin and/or cocaine users recruited from several walk-in non-emergent clinics (urgent care, women's clinic, and a homeless clinic) that included a motivational intervention session delivered by trained peer educators and a subsequent booster call 10 days later, led to a reduction in heroin and cocaine use, and an increased likelihood of abstinence from these drugs at 6-month follow-up visit. Taken together, the literature generally supports SBIRTs as potentially effective interventions to reduce substance use following a medical visit.

Conclusions

Overall, large numbers of adults within the USA report some form of recent problematic alcohol use and/or drug use. However, many of these individuals never utilize formal additions treatment services. Current theories of behavior change highlight the potential importance of motivation as an important determinant of the decision to decrease or cease substance misuse. In order to better harness an individual's intrinsic motivation, several strategies have been developed to increase motivation in a non-confrontational manner. Over the past three decades of study, research has generally supported the efficacy of these brief motivational interventions in their ability to help individuals reduce their substance use. Additionally, a growing body of research supports the utilization of these brief interventions outside standard addictions treatment settings. Broadening the settings in which these services are delivered as well as delivering interventions that are shorter and potentially more appealing than more-traditional addictions treatment services increases the likelihood that individuals with substance-related problems will receive the assistance that they need to reduce their use of alcohol or drugs. As brief motivational interventions are delivered in a broader array of treatment environments, it is important for social workers in all settings to become familiar with these strategies.

Acknowledgements We would like to thank Michelle Sanborn for her help preparing and editing this manuscript.

References

Amrhein, P. C., Miller, W. R., Yahne, C. E., Palmer, M., & Fulcher, L. (2003). Client commitment language during motivational interviewing predicts drug use outcomes. *Journal of Consulting and Clinical Psychology, 71*, 862–878.

Apodaca, T. R., & Longabaugh, R. (2009). Mechanisms of change in motivational interviewing: A review and preliminary evaluation of the evidence. *Addiction, 104*, 705–715.

Babor, T., & Grant, M. (1992). *Project on identification and management of alcohol related problems. Report on Phase II: A randomized clinical trial of brief interventions in primary health care.* Paper presented at the World Health Organization, Geneva.

Babor, T. F., McRee, B. G., Kassebaum, P. A., Grimaldi, P. L., Ahmed, K., & Bray, J. (2007). Screening, Brief Intervention, and Referral to Treatment (SBIRT): Toward a public health approach to the management of substance abuse. *Substance Abuse, 28*, 7–30.

Baker, A., Kochan, N., Dixon, J., Heather, N., & Wodak, A. (1994). Controlled evaluation of a brief intervention for HIV prevention among injecting drug users not in treatment. *AIDS Care, 6*, 559–570.

Baker, A., Lee, N. K., Claire, M., Lewin, T. J., Grant, T., Pohlman, S., et al. (2004). Brief cognitive behavioural interventions for regular amphetamine users: A step in the right direction. *Addiction, 100*, 367–378.

Bazargan-Hejazi, S., Bing, E., Bazargan, M., Der-Martirosian, C., Hardin, E., Bernstein, J., et al. (2005). Evaluation of a brief intervention in an inner-city emergency department. *Annals of Emergency Medicine, 461*, 67–76.

Ben-Ahron, V., White, D., & Phillips, K. (1995). Encouraging drinking at safe limits on single occasions: The potential contribution of protection motivation theory. *Alcohol and Alcoholism, 30*, 633–639.

Bernstein, E., Bernstein, J., & Levenson, S. (1997). Project ASSERT: An ED-based intervention to increase access to primary care, preventive services, and the substance abuse treatment system. *Annals of Emergency Medicine, 30*, 181–189.

Bernstein, J., Bernstein, E., Tassiopoulos, K., Heeren, T., Levenson, S., & Hingson, R. (2005). Brief motivational intervention at a clinic visit reduces cocaine and heroin use. *Drug and Alcohol Dependence, 77*, 49–59.

Bernstein, K. T., Bucciarelli, A., Piper, T. M., Gross, C., Tardiff, K., & Galea, S. (2007). Cocaine- and opiate-related fatal overdose in New York City, 1990–2000. *BMC Public Health, 7*, 31.

Blow F. C., Barry K. L., Walton M. A., Maio R.F., Chermack S. T., Bingham C. R., Ignacio R. V., Strecher V. J. (2006). The efficacy of two brief intervention strategies among injured, at-risk drinkers in the emergency department: impact of tailored messaging and brief advice. *Journal of Studies on Alcohol, 67*(4):568–78.

Booth, B. M., Walton, M. A., Barry, K. L., Cunningham, R. M., Chermack, S. T., Blow, F. C. (2011). Substance use, depression, and mental health functioning in patients seeking acute medical care in an inner-city ED. *The Journal of Behavioral Health Services and Research, 38*(3):358–72.

Bradley, K. A., Bush, K. R., Davis, T. M., Dobie, D. J., Burman, M. L., Rutter, C. M., et al. (2001). Binge drinking among female Veterans Affairs patients: Prevalence and associated risks. *Psychology of Addictive Behavior, 15*, 297–305.

Burke, B. L., Arkowitz, H., & Menchola, M. (2003). The efficacy of motivational interviewing: A meta-analysis of controlled clinical trials. *Journal of Consulting and Clinical Psychology, 71*, 843–861.

Center for Disease Control and Prevention. (2009). *Quick stats on binge drinking*. Retrieved 4/11/2009, http://www.cdc.gov/alcohol/quickstats/binge_drinking.htm.

Chick, J., Lloyd, G., & Crombie, E. (1985). Counselling problem drinkers in medical wards: A controlled study. *British Medical Journal, 290*, 965–967.

Cohen, E., Feinn, R., Arias, A., & Kranzler, H. R. (2007). Alcohol treatment utilization: Findings from the National Epidemiologic Survey on Alcohol and Related Conditions. *Drug and Alcohol Dependence, 86*, 214–221.

Compton, P., Monahan, G., & Simmons-Cody, H. (1999). Motivational interviewing: An effective brief intervention for alcohol and drug abuse patients. *Nurse Practitioner, 24*, 27–38.

Dawson, D. A., & Grant, B. F. (1998). Family history of alcoholism and gender: Their combined effects on DSM-IV alcohol dependence and major depression. *Journal of Studies on Alcohol, 59*, 97–106.

Dunn, C., Deroo, L., & Rivara, F. P. (2001). The use of brief interventions adapted from motivational interviewing across behavioral domains: A systematic review. *Addiction, 96*, 1725–1742.

Dunn, C. W., & Ries, R. (1997). Linking substance abuse services with general medical care: Integrated, brief interventions with hospitalized patients. *American Journal of Drug and Alcohol Abuse, 23*, 1–13.

Dyehouse, J. M., & Sommers, M. S. (1995). Brief intervention as an advanced practice strategy for seriously injured victims of multiple trauma. *American Association of Critical-Care Nurses, Clinical Issues, 6*, 53–62.

Edlund, M., Booth, B., & Feldman, Z. (2009). Perceived need for treatment for alcohol use disorders: Results from two national surveys. *Psychiatric Services, 60*, 1618–1628.

Fang, X., Stanton, B., Li, X., Feigelman, S., & Baldwin, R. (1998). Similarities in sexual activity and condom use among friends within groups before and after a risk-reduction intervention. *Youth & Society, 29*, 431–450.

Fleming, M. F., Barry, K. L., Manwell, L. B., Johnson, K., & London, R. (1997). Brief physician advice for problem alcohol drinkers: A randomized controlled trial in community-based primary care practices. *JAMA, 277*, 1039–1045.

Floyd, D. L., Prentice-Dunn, S., & Rogers, R. W. (2000). A meta-analysis of research on protection motivation theory. *Journal of Applied Social Psychology, 30*, 407–429.

Gentilello, L. M., Rivara, F. P., Donovan, D. M., Jurkovich, G. J., Daranciang, E., Dunn, C. W., et al. (1999). Alcohol interventions in a trauma center as a means of reducing the risk of injury recurrence. *Annals of Surgery, 230*, 473–480.

Glass, J. E., Perron, B. E., Ilgen, M. A., Chermack, S. T., Ratliff, S., & Zivin, K. (2010). Prevalence and correlates of specialty substance use disorder treatment for Department of Veterans Affairs Healthcare System patients with high alcohol consumption. *Drug and Alcohol Dependence, 112*, 150–155.

Gollwitzer, P. M. (1999). Implementation intentions—Strong effects of simple plans. *American Psychologist, 54*, 493–503.

Grant, B. F. (2000). Estimates of US children exposed to alcohol abuse and dependence in the family. *American Journal of Public Health, 90*, 112–115.

Grant, B. F., Hasin, D. S., & Dawson, D. A. (1996). The relationship between DSM-IV alcohol use disorders and DSM-IV major depression: Examination of the primary-secondary distinction in a general population sample. *Journal of Affective Disorders, 38*, 113–128.

Greber, R. A., Allen, K. M., Soeken, K. L., & Solounias, B. L. (1997). Outcome of trauma patients after brief intervention by a substance abuse consultation service. *American Journal on Addictions, 6*, 38–47.

Harris, K., & Miller, W. (1990). Behavioral self-control training for problem drinkers: Components of efficacy. *Psychology of Addictive Behavior, 4*, 82–90.

Harvard, S. S., Hill, W. D., & Buxton, J. A. (2008). Harm reduction product distribution in British Columbia. *Canadian Journal of Public Health. Revue Canadienne de Sante Publique, 99*, 446–450.

Hettema, J., Steele, J., & Miller, W. R. (2005). Motivational interviewing. *Annual Review of Clinical Psychology, 1*, 91–111.

Houlding, C., & Davidson, R. (2003). Beliefs as predictors of condom use by injecting drug users in treatment. *Health Education Research, 18*, 145–155.

Ilgen, M. A., Price, A. M., Burnett-Zeigler, I., Perron, B., Islam, K., Bohnert, A. S., et al. (2011). Longitudinal predictors of addictions treatment utilization in treatment-naive adults with alcohol use disorders. *Drug and Alcohol Dependence, 113*, 215–221.

Lang, E., Engelander, M., & Tracey Brooke, T. (2000). Report of an integrated brief intervention with self-defined problem cannabis users. *Journal of Substance Abuse Treatment, 19*, 111–116.

Longabaugh, R., Woolard, R. E., Nirenberg, T. D., Minugh, A. P., Becker, B., Clifford, P. R., et al. (2001). Evaluating the effects of a brief motivational intervention for injured drinkers in the emergency department. *Journal of Studies on Alcohol, 62*, 806–816.

Lundahl, B., & Burke, B. L. (2009). The effectiveness and applicability of motivational interviewing: A practice-friendly review of four meta-analyses. *Journal of Clinical Psychology, 65*, 1232–1245.

Lundahl, B. W., Kunz, C., Brownell, C., Tollefson, D., & Burke, B. L. (2010). A meta-analysis of motivational interviewing: Twenty-five years of empirical studies. *Research on Social Work Practice, 20*, 137–160.

McClendon, B. T., & Prentice-Dunn, S. (2001). Reducing skin cancer risk: An intervention based on protection motivation theory. *Journal of Health Psychology, 6*, 321–328.

McLellan, A., Carise, D., & Kleber, H. D. (2003). Can the national addiction treatment infrastructure support the public's demand for quality care. *Journal of Substance Abuse Treatment, 25,* 117–121.

McLellan, A. T., & Meyers, K. (2004). Contemporary addiction treatment: A review of systems problems for adults and adolescents. *Biological Psychiatry, 56,* 764–770.

Mello, M. J., Nirenberg, T. D., Longabaugh, R., Woolard, R., Minugh, A., Becker, B., et al. (2005). Emergency department brief motivational interventions for alcohol with motor vehicle crash patients. *Annals of Emergency Medicine, 45,* 620–625.

Midanik, L. T., & Greenfield, T. K. (2000). Trends in social consequences and dependence symptoms in the United States: The National Alcohol Surveys, 1984–1995. *American Journal of Public Health, 90,* 53–56.

Miller, W. R. (1998). Why do people change addictive behavior? The 1996 H. David Archibald Lecture. *Addiction, 93,* 163–172.

Miller, W. R., & Rollnick, S. (1991). *Motivational Interviewing: Preparing people to change addictive behaviors.* New York: Guilford Press.

Miller, W. R., & Rose, G. S. (2009). Toward a theory of motivational interviewing. *American Psychologist, 64,* 527–537.

Miller, W. R., Zweben, A., DiClemente, C. C., & Rychtarik, R. G. (1992). *Motivational-enhancement therapy manual: A clinical research guide for therapists treating individuals with alcohol abuse or dependence.* Rockville, MD: National Institute on Alcohol Abuse and Alcoholism.

Mulia, N., Ye, Y., Greenfield, T. K., Zemore, S. E. (2009). Disparities in alcohol-related problems among White, Black, and Hispanic Americans. *Alcoholism, Clinical and Experimental Research, 33*(4):654–62. Epub 2009 Jan 15.

National Institute on Alcohol Abuse and Alcoholism. (2005). *Helping patients who drink too much: A clinician's guide.* Bethesda, MD: National Institute on Alcohol Abuse and Alcoholism.

Project MATCH. (1993). Project MATCH (Matching Alcoholism Treatment to Client Heterogeneity): Rationale and methods for a multisite clinical trial matching patients to alcoholism treatment. *Alcohol Clinical and Experimental Research, 17,* 1130–1145.

Project MATCH Research Group. (1997). Matching alcoholism treatments to client heterogeneity: Project MATCH Posttreatment drinking outcomes. *Journal of Studies on Alcohol, 58,* 7–29.

Project MATCH Research Group. (1998). Matching alcoholism treatments to client heterogeneity: Project MATCH three-year drinking outcomes. *Alcohol Clin Exp Res, 22,* 1300–1311.

Reid, R. D., Tulloch, H., Kocourek, J., Morrin, L. I., Beaton, L. J., Papadakis, S., et al. (2007). Who will be active? Predicting exercise stage transitions after hospitalization for coronary artery disease. *Canadian Journal of Physiology and Pharmacology, 85,* 17–23.

Rogers, R. W. (1975). A protection motivation theory of fear appeals and attitude change. *Journal of Psychology: Interdisciplinary and Applied, 91,* 93–114.

Rogers, R. W., & Prentice-Dunn, S. (1997). Protection motivation theory. In D. Gochman (Ed.), *Handbook of health behavior research. Vol. 1: Determinants of health behavior: Personal and social* (Vol. 1, pp. 113–132). New York, NY: Plenum.

Runge, C., Prentice-Dunn, S., & Scogin, F. (1993). Protection motivation theory and alcohol use attitudes among older adults. *Psychological Reports, 73,* 96–98.

SAMHSA. (2007). *Results from the 2006 National Survey on Drug Use and health: National Findings.* Rockville: SAMHSA. Retrieved from http://www.oas.samhsa.gov/.

SAMHSA. (2010). *Results from the 2009 national Survey on Drug Use and health; SMA 10-4856.* Rockville, MD: SAMHSA.

Schober, R., & Annis, H. M. (1996). Barriers to help-seeking for change in drinking: A gender-focused review of the literature. *Addictive Behaviors, 21,* 81–92.

Schomerus, G., Lucht, M., Holzinger, A., Matschinger, H., Carta, M. G., & Angermeyer, M. C. (2011). The stigma of alcohol dependence compared with other mental disorders: A review of population studies. *Alcohol and Alcoholism, 46,* 105–112.

Smedslund, G., Berg, R. C., Hammerstrøm, K. T., Steiro, A., Leiknes, K. A., Dahl, H. M., & Karlsen, K. (2011). Motivational interviewing for substance abuse. *Cochrane Database Syst Rev, 11*(5):CD008063.

Smith, S. M., Dawson, D. A., Goldstein, R. B., & Grant, B. F. (2010). Examining perceived alcoholism stigma effect on racial-ethnic disparities in treatment and quality of life among alcoholics. *Journal of Studies on Alcohol and Drugs, 71*, 231–236.

Smith, M. J., Whitaker, T., & Weismiller, T. (2006). Social workers in the substance abuse treatment field: A snapshot of service activities. *Health and Social Work, 31*, 109–115.

Stotts, A. L., Schmitz, J. M., Rhoades, H. M., & Grabowski, J. (2001). Motivational interviewing with cocaine-dependent patients: A pilot study. *Journal of Consulting and Clinical Psychology, 69*, 858–862.

Vasilaki, E. I., Hosier, S. G., & Cox, W. M. (2006). The efficacy of motivational interviewing as a brief intervention for excessive drinking: A meta-analytic review. *Alcohol and Alcoholism, 41*, 328–335.

Wallace, P., Cutler, S., & Haines, A. (1988). Randomised controlled trial of general practitioner intervention in patients with excessive alcohol consumption. *British Medical Journal, 297*, 663–668.

Weaver, M. F., Jarvis, M. A., & Schnoll, S. H. (1999). Role of the primary care physician in problems of substance abuse. *Archives of Internal Medicine, 159*, 913–924.

Welte, J. W., Perry, P., Longabaugh, R., & Clifford, P. R. (1998). An outcome evaluation of a hospital-based early intervention program. *Addiction, 93*, 573–581.

Wood, M. E. (2008). Theoretical framework to study exercise motivation for breast cancer risk reduction. *Oncology Nursing Forum, 35*, 89–95.

World Health Organization. (2010). *World health statistics*. New York, NY: World Health Organization.

Wu, Y., Stanton, B. F., Li, X., Galbraith, J., & Cole, M. L. (2005). Protection motivation theory and adolescent drug trafficking: Relationship between health motivation and longitudinal risk involvement. *Journal of Pediatric Psychology, 30*, 127–137.

Chapter 7
Cognitive Behavioral Therapy with Substance Use Disorders: Theory, Evidence, and Practice

M. Teresa Granillo, Brian E. Perron, Christopher Jarman, and Sarah M. Gutowski

In the field of social work, whether one works specifically in a substance use disorder (SUD) treatment facility or in a hospital, child welfare agency, correctional services, employment assistance program, or in private practice, knowledge of SUDs and how to best treat them is necessary. Many treatment models are available for clients with SUDs (e.g., pharmacotherapy, motivational interventions, 12-step programs), some of which are described in this book. This chapter focuses on one of the most empirically supported interventions for the treatment of SUDs, cognitive behavioral therapy (CBT) (Carroll, 1998).

CBT is not a single discrete intervention, but a collection of interventions and strategies of complementary theories of learning. Interventions that comprise this collection include (but are not limited to) rational emotive therapy, multimodal therapy, cognitive therapy, behavioral therapy, contingency management, and applied behavioral analysis. While CBT represents many different intervention strategies, they are all unified by principles of learning. Specifically, CBT interventions take into account how learning processes are involved in the development and maintenance of maladaptive thought processes, emotional reactions, and behavioral responses. These learning processes are the foundation for interventions aimed at the reduction, replacement, or cessation of problematic behaviors.

M.T. Granillo (✉)
University of Texas at Austin, Austin, TX, USA
e-mail: mtgranillo@mail.utexas.edu

B.E. Perron • S.M. Gutowski
University of Michigan, Ann Arbor, MI, USA
e-mail: beperron@umich.edu

C. Jarman
Michigan State University, Lansing, MI, USA
e-mail: christja@med.umich.edu

M.G. Vaughn and B.E. Perron (eds.), *Social Work Practice in the Addictions*,
Contemporary Social Work Practice, DOI 10.1007/978-1-4614-5357-4_7,
© Springer Science+Business Media New York 2013

This chapter provides an overview of CBT, with specific descriptions of how it applies to SUDs. Within the following framework, we provide a basic discussion of the theory of CBT to promote an understanding of how people develop and maintain a SUD over time. We then highlight some of the empirical research on the effectiveness of CBT. The last section of the chapter covers the core components of CBT, with an emphasis on implementation of CBT for the treatment of SUDs. It should be noted that SUDs refers broadly to alcohol and drugs, nicotine is excluded from this chapter. Distinctions between alcohol and drugs will be made as needed.

Theoretical Underpinnings of CBT

The purpose of theory is to help describe, explain, and predict phenomena. For this chapter, we are centrally concerned with how people come to use and misuse drugs and alcohol. Understanding the theoretical background for substance use provides social workers with practical solutions for addressing problems directly or indirectly related to SUDs. CBT is not a single, monolithic theory but an integration of three different but complementary theoretical systems: behavioral theory, cognitive theory, and social cognitive theory. This section provides an overview of the major contributing theories, along with a description of how they are unified within the integrative CBT framework. For purposes of brevity, we provide a general overview of the theories. However a comprehensive understanding of CBT requires in-depth knowledge of the theories. Citations have been carefully selected to serve as key resources for the reader.

Behavioral Theory

Many researchers and theorists contributed to the early development of behavioral theory, of particular importance are the work of Pavlov and Skinner. Through experiments with animals, these researchers provided compelling evidence that behavior is a learned process influenced by the specific antecedents to Pavlov (1928) and consequences of behavior (Skinner, 1957). These learning processes evolved into two systems of thought referred to as *classical* and *operant conditioning*, respectively.

Classical Conditioning

From a classical conditioning approach, behavior is learned when it is associated or paired with a specific stimulus, which can be any anything that produces a response through any of the five senses. The strength of the association between the behavior and the stimulus largely depends on whether or not there are repeated pairings. With increased pairings the association can become so strong that the presence of the stimulus can elicit the behavior, even if the stimulus initially was unrelated to the behavior. A common example of this is Pavlov's original research in which he was able to produce a salivation response in a dog with the tone of a bell by simply repeatedly pairing the bell tone with food. Pavlov's research showed that these associations do not involve conscious processes, which is why behaviorists do not consider internal states—e.g., thoughts and feelings—to explain or modify behavior.

Classical conditioning is especially useful for understanding the significance of *triggers* to substance use. For example, cannabis produces a euphoric response when it is smoked or ingested. An individual who uses cannabis is also exposed to the aroma of the substance, both in a smokable and edible form. The smell of cannabis becomes associated with the euphoric response through repeated pairings. Thus, the smell of cannabis can elicit an anticipatory euphoric response among heavy users, which can then become a powerful cue for substance use. In fact, evidence suggests that such cue-induced responses to substances resemble the same conditioned appetitive responses that Pavlov found in his original work with dogs (see Niaura et al., 1988).

Treating persons with SUDs from this perspective involves careful attention to understanding and modifying environmental conditions that cue the use of substances. For example, cue exposure therapy treatments can involve repeatedly exposing clients to cues in a safe environment or practicing using coping skills in the presence of cues. In the treatment of alcohol-related problems, actual alcoholic beverages can be used as cues, whereas other substances may involve the use of pictures or mental imagery of the substance. Such interventions are theorized to work by habituating persons to cued exposures that are *not* followed by actual use. The purpose of this intervention is to extinguish the association between the cue and the response. Provide an excellent description of cue-exposure therapy, along with empirical evidence to support this treatment approach.

Operant Conditioning

From the perspective of operant conditioning, behavior is learned and maintained through three different processes: reinforcement, punishment, and extinction. Reinforcement is the process of increasing or maintaining the rate of a given behavior by presenting a stimuli or event after the emergence of a behavior. The stimuli or event is only a reinforcer if it increases or maintains a behavior. A punishment is an aversive stimulus or event that is presented following an undesirable behavior to decrease behavior. When no stimulus is presented after a given behavior, a behavior will likely disappear or become extinct.

These processes can be extended to understand the development and maintenance of substance-related problems. For example, consuming alcohol can involve a variety of reinforcements, such as increased sociability, feelings of relaxation, and even an enjoyable taste. These are considered positive reinforcements, as these add

	A →	B →	C
Example	John is a freshman at college and attends his first college party. He is pressured to participate in a drinking games.	John doesn't want to drink, but believes that others will not like him if he refuses.	John participates in the drinking game.

Fig. 7.1 ABC model applied to substance misuse

something to increase a response. Consumption of alcohol, or other substances, can also involve negative reinforcements, which is the elimination of a stimulus that increases the likelihood that behavior will be repeated. This could include tension release, temporarily forgetting about problems, decreased inhibitions, and minimizing pressures to use from peers. Of course, a variety of punishments can be associated with substance use, such as hangover and other consequences from bad decisions while under the influence. However, reinforcement has a stronger effect on behavior than punishment, which helps us understand the persistence of substance use.

Taken together, we can see that substance use is complex because it is influenced by so many different factors (e.g., environmental stimuli, reinforcers, punishments). Understanding the behavioral perspective on substance use is helpful in giving social workers important clues about the environmental conditions that may be modifiable to change problematic patterns of substance use.

Cognitive Theory

A fundamental assumption of cognitive theory is that our thoughts or beliefs—i.e., cognitions—influence how we feel, which subsequently influences how we respond or behave. Albert Ellis, who developed a system of cognitive therapy called rational emotive therapy represented this process with the *ABC model* (see Fig. 7.1) (Ellis, 1994). Ellis' model suggests that, an activating (A) event or situation triggers beliefs (B) about the event and/or the self in relation to the event. Then these beliefs determine how we feel and behave, which are regarded as the consequences (C) of the process.

Figure 7.1 provides a basic example of how this process is used to describe and explain problematic substance use. The beliefs that people hold are known as schemas, which are the "specific rules that govern information processing and behavior" (Beck et al., 1990, p. 8). In some instances our schemas are particularly effective at helping us navigate our way through the world. However, our schemas are also prone to errors, biases, and other distortions of reality, which can lead to irrational thoughts, emotional distress, and/or other types of problematic behaviors. Table 7.1 provides examples of cognitive errors and biases.

Treating a SUD from this perspective involves identifying and changing maladaptive schemas in order to minimize or eliminate the problems associated with substance use.

Table 7.1 Examples of common cognitive errors and distortions

Cognitive error or distortion	Description	Example
Personalization	Interpreting everything to be about oneself and one's own desires, often disregarding others	"The whole world revolves around me. If I want it, and can get away with it, I will do it"
Minimizing	Downplaying a thought and/or behavior to a degree that no longer reflects reality	"If it's the weekend, drinking alcohol in the morning isn't bad"
Assuming the worst	Expecting the worst possible outcome, usually without investigation	"If I stop drinking, I'll never have fun again"
Blaming others	Placing responsibility for one's own behavior and/or situation onto outside sources, often another person	"I get high because she ruined my life"
Selective abstraction	Forming a judgment based on particular information, while disregarding the remaining information	"I can't believe he gave me such a weird look, that dinner was awkward" [ignores hours of laughter]
Magnification	Exaggerating a thought and/or behavior to a degree that no longer reflects reality	"If I can't have a champagne toast at my wedding, I can't get married"
All-or-Nothing thinking	Categorizing thoughts into one of two extremes, e.g., always or never	"I hate Alcoholics Anonymous because everyone is boring"
Confirmation bias	Interpreting or seeking information in a way that confirms one's own perception	"I had so much fun last night, especially after talking with the cute bartender" [disregards vomiting in the bathroom and the hangover]
Fortune telling	Predicting negative and inflexible outcomes before they happen	"I'll be miserable after an entire year of sobriety"
Mind reading	Concluding negative intentions or thoughts of others	"That sales clerk is staring at me because he thinks I'm going to steal something"

The role of the social worker is to help the client identify alternative and more adaptive schemas. Belief questionnaires, such as the Dysfunctional Attitude Scale (Weissman & Beck, 1978; see also Young, 1990), can be used to help identify schemas. The client then collects data on the target schema, and the social worker engages the client in Socratic questioning to check the validity of a target schema. The goal is to weaken the maladaptive schemas and strengthen the adaptive ones (see Padesky, 1994). For example, Fig. 7.1 provides an example of a maladaptive schema—that is, "People won't like me if I don't drink." An adaptive and more desirable schema would be, "People will like me whether or not I drink." One way to bring about this shift in schemas is to have the client monitor social interactions that occur in absence of using substances. The social worker can help the client use these experiences (i.e., data) to check whether or not the schema is correct. This method can be quite effective in helping clients develop more adaptive schemas, which influences the way they feel and behave.

Social Cognitive Theory

Social cognitive theory is a learning theory that considers the interaction between social and cognitive factors that influence behavior. The theory is *social* because it posits that behavior is learned by observing what others do and do not do. The theory is *cognitive* because it posits that the observer evaluates the outcome of the observed behavior and depending on their level of self-efficacy—the belief in one's ability to act or perform in a particular manner, determines whether they will act in a similar fashion in the future. The theory also considers the environment as an important factor in providing the conditions for learning behavior.

Social cognitive theory has played an important role in guiding treatment for SUDs. From a social cognitive perspective, the risk of relapse increases when an individual has limited or ineffective coping skills in high-risk situations (e.g., social events with substances), expectations of pleasurable effects of substances, and a lack of confidence in ability to effectively cope (i.e., low self-efficacy) (Monti et al., 1999). In a treatment setting, social workers address these risks through focused skills training. One method is teaching-specific coping skills that are relevant to high-risk situations, such as refusal skills. Another strategy is to improve social skills in order to minimize conflicts, as substances are often used as an ineffective strategy for coping with conflict and stress. Improved social skills can also improve the quality of the client's social support system to promote abstinence (Monti et al., 1999). Both coping skills and social skills training can also enhance self-efficacy for managing high-risk situations.

CBT as an Integrative Framework

CBT is not a single unified theory, but rather a collection of learning processes informed by behavioral, cognitive, and social cognitive theories. Theories that make up CBT are generally unified under the idea that SUDs are the result of learned behaviors acquired through experience. Thus, treating SUDs from a CBT perspective involves identifying the specific needs of clients and providing skills training that address those needs (Kadden et al., 2002). Some interventions have a behavioral orientation, which emphasizes observable antecedents and consequences of behavior, and the cognitive orientation takes cognitions and emotions that precede or maintain behavior into consideration (Kadden et al., 2002). CBT offers the flexibility of drawing on both cognitive and behavioral approaches in order to provide the necessary skills training to achieve desired outcomes.

While CBT is heavily oriented toward skill development, this orientation does not take precedence over the therapeutic relationship. Rather, a major task of the social worker is to establish a balance between skills training and the development of the therapeutic relationship (Carroll, 1998). A positive therapeutic relationship is critical to establishing an environment that effectively engages the client in skills training processes (Carroll, 1998).

A number of general principles unify the practice of CBT, which helps distinguish CBT from other therapies. Therapies such as psychodynamic and insight-oriented therapies may work on uncovering unconscious processes and exploring the relationship between early childhood experiences and current problems. CBT, on the other hand, is problem-focused that gives priority to the *here* and *now*. It is also a time-limited and highly structured type of treatment. Although CBT sessions incorporate acute problems that client's experience, the overarching strategy is to facilitate the development of a generalizable skill set to help eliminate or reduce the severity of the problems. Successful treatment of SUDs involves achieving specific clinical goals with respect to the use of substances, as well as ensuring a highly definable skill set to minimize the risk of relapse.

Empirical Support for CBT with SUDs

The evidence for CBT can be considered from two different sources. One source includes the basic research on learning processes associated with each of the underlying theories. This provides good evidence for the validity of CBT theory, which gives us confidence in the interventions that are derived from this theoretical base. The reader is encouraged to review the extensive body of literature on the noted learning theories and their underlying empirical base.

The second source of evidence involves outcomes studies that specifically test the efficacy or effectiveness of CBT. As previously stated, CBT represents a large collection of different theories and intervention strategies, making it difficult to provide a coherent and comprehensive review of the evidence for CBT. Thus, provided below we try to highlight findings derived from key meta-analyses and systematic reviews specifically for SUDs. The reader is strongly encouraged to examine the other available evidence for CBT. We are confident that an independent assessment of this research will reveal that CBT is among the most well-supported approaches in the treatment of SUDs.

CBT as a Standalone Treatment

Magill and Ray (2009) conducted a meta-analysis of 53 randomized controlled trials of CBT to determine its efficacy for SUDs. Results showed that CBT was better than treatment as usual (i.e., supportive therapy or general counseling). Like many other psychosocial therapies, the strength of the positive outcomes of CBT interventions was evidenced to decrease over time (e.g., 12-month follow-up), which suggests the importance of booster sessions and long-term supports. CBT had the strongest effect when used to treat marijuana-related disorders or when compared to no treatment at all. The meta-analysis also identified that the effects of CBT may be slightly better for women than men, and when the intervention is delivered in a brief format (Magill & Ray, 2009).

McHugh, Hearon, and Otto (2010) summarize the results of a separate meta-analysis on the use of CBT to treat drug abuse or dependence, which included 34 randomized controlled trials. The treatment effects observed in this study were slightly stronger than the effects reported by Magill and Ray (2009). The effects of CBT were strongest in the treatment of cannabis, followed by cocaine, opioids, and polysubstance dependence.

Combination Treatments

Combination treatment is grounded in the idea that offering different types of treatment in a unified manner can enhance treatment outcomes. The enhancement occurs because the different treatments are thought to address separate aspects of a given problem. For example, pharmacotherapy can help regulate mood, which can also increase the effectiveness of coping skills. For the treatment of SUDs, a small number of studies have examined the combination of CBT with either pharmacotherapy or other psychosocial interventions.

Pharmacotherapy

Studies that examine the combination of CBT with pharmacotherapy for SUDs have found mixed results. For example, some studies provide support for CBT combined with naltrexone in the treatment of alcohol dependence (Carroll et al., 2004), as well as CBT combined with methadone for opioid dependence (Rawson, Huber, & McCann, 2002). However, a large multisite study, COMBINE (Anton et al., 2006) showed no additive effect of combined therapy relative to a single therapy.

Psychosocial Interventions

The combination of CBT and other psychosocial approaches has also produced mixed results (McHugh et al., 2010). For example, behavioral therapies (e.g., cue exposure) and contingency management combined with CBT did not reveal effects that exceeded the use of CBT as a standalone intervention (see McHugh et al., 2010). We are unaware of any research that has tested whether the combination of CBT and 12-step programs (e.g., Alcoholics Anonymous, Narcotics Anonymous) are more efficacious than either as a standalone treatment approach. More research is needed to determine what combination treatments may significantly increase the strength of CBT for SUDs. This is particularly important with respect to 12-step programs, given that 12-step programs are the most widely used treatments for SUDs (see Chap. XX of this book).

Key Ingredients of CBT

As described in the foregoing section, CBT is an important evidence-based practice available to social workers. A number of CBT treatment manuals exist to help guide treatment (e.g., Carroll, 1998; Kadden et al., 2002). Social workers are strongly encouraged to use high-quality treatment manuals whenever possible, as they provide important guidance on structure and content of treatment. However, a CBT treatment manual is hardly a *cookbook* approach to treatment. In fact, social workers retain considerable freedom in tailoring CBT to individual client needs. Through conscientious use of treatment manuals, we are confident that social workers will readily see that CBT treatment manuals provide guidelines, but the overall treatment must be tailored to the client's needs and values.

In this section, we provide an overview of how CBT is provided to persons with a SUD. We highlight characteristics of treatment that are common to many of the evidence-based treatment manuals that are freely available (e.g., Carroll, 1998; Kadden et al., 2002). Specifically, we summarize the major tasks and structural features of treatment and then discuss intervention strategies with a particular focus on functional analysis and skills training.

Major Treatment Tasks

A number of important treatment tasks provide the foundation for successful SUD treatment. Rounsaville and Carroll (1992) and Carroll (1998) propose a set of major tasks that are generalizable to treating different types of substances, SUDs (e.g., abuse, dependence), client populations, and unique client needs. These major tasks, summarized in Table 7.2, are grounded in both behavioral and cognitive theories.

Some tasks may be more relevant to certain clients than others. For example, some clients may be highly motivated to change their patterns of substance use, whereas others may be legally or socially coerced to treatment and have much lower levels of treatment motivation. Careful assessment is necessary in order to effectively tailor these treatment tasks to the unique needs of the client.

Table 7.2 Major treatment tasks for substance use disorders from a cognitive behavioral perspective

Treatment task	Description
Foster motivation for change	Stopping or reducing the use of substances requires a commitment to change. Social workers need to enhance the client's motivation for doing so. This is usually done through decisional balances, matching interventions to their level of motivation, and fostering a sense of self-efficacy
Enhance coping skills for managing risky situations	Clients need to be equipped with a variety of strategies for managing situations that involve exposure and pressures to use substances. This typically involves developing refusal skills that can be generalized to a wide range of situations
Modify reinforcement contingencies	Clients will need to spend considerable time addressing a range of problems associated with a SUD. In this process, it is important to help clients identify meaningful and rewarding activities that are substance free and can promote a substance free lifestyle
Manage emotional responses	Strong emotional responses can be problematic in managing substance use disorders. Anger and frustration are not uncommon, and ineffective responses can increase the likelihood of relapse. Clients should be equipped with the necessary skills to manage these responses
Improve social functioning	Long-term management of substance use disorders requires good social skills to elicit effective social support. Helping improve social skills can lead to improvement in social networks that support sobriety

Note: Adapted from Rounsaville and Carroll (1992) and Carroll (1998)

Structural Features of CBT

The length of CBT sessions are approximately one hour, although the length and number of sessions are determined by the treatment needs of the individual, payment mechanisms, and availability of social workers to provide treatment. As described by Carroll (1998), CBT for the treatment of SUDs involves approximately 12–16 sessions, although this is a general guide, as the actual number of sessions will be determined by the treatment needs of the individual and reimbursement mechanism.

CBT is a highly structured form of treatment, with an agenda guiding each session. The development of an agenda should be a collaborative effort between the social worker and client. Session topics can be predetermined, although they need to be tailored to the client's unique treatment needs and linked, whenever possible, to any acute problems.

When formulating an agenda, it is useful to divide the session into three different parts. The first part of the session reviews skills that were taught in the previous session, with an emphasis on addressing barriers to successful implementation. For example, a client may have learned a set of drinking refusal skills that are effective with friends and family, but the skills may not generalize to work-related social gatherings. This review allows the opportunity to further enhance skills when necessary. The second part of the session involves teaching new skills and information. The third part of the session involves planning for the use of the skills in real-world situations. This provides an opportunity to review potential barriers to successful implementation of skills, which is a critical and often under-recognized aspect of treatment.

Functional Analysis

As with most interventions, CBT for SUDs includes comprehensive assessment at the beginning of treatment. However, unlike other treatments assessment is an ongoing and essential process in CBT with SUDs. The particular type of assessment that plays such a crucial role in CBT with SUDs is the functional analysis. The purpose of functional analyses is to help the client identify and describe how a given behavior occurs in the real world. The functional analysis is driven by the A–B–C model. As previously described, the A–B–C model helps describe, explain, and even predict behavior through the linking of antecedents of the behavior to the consequences of the behavior. All three aspects of behavior are considered in formulating a clinical hypothesis, which is a working explanation of the *function* of behavior. Data is collected on the problem behavior in order to assess its response to treatment. The functional analysis helps determine the target of treatment, in addition to providing a framework for monitoring treatment outcomes.

Social workers must think carefully and creatively to help the client find the most reliable data to provide a valid summary of the *function* of behavior. One strategy involves the use of self-monitoring records, which are systematic data collection procedures for recording different aspects of their behavior over time. For example, clients may record the amount of substances they use each day for a selected period of time. Clients with higher levels of motivation and cognitive functioning can collect additional information that could be of potential value to the treatment process, including each aspect of the A–B–C model, triggers, location of substance use, persons present, emotional state, etc.

Systematic data collection can improve the reliability of data to inform the treatment process, given that retrospective account of substance use is subject to serious errors and biases in recall. Self-monitoring records are valuable at the beginning of treatment with respect to understanding patterns of substance use and targets of intervention. Self-monitoring records can also be an intervention, as such tools are often *reactive* (see Sobell, Bogardis, Schuller, Leo, & Sobell, 1989)—that is, such tools can help clients become more aware of problematic behavior and make adjustments. And, by systematically monitoring specific behaviors over time, the social worker can use the data for monitoring treatment progress and outcomes.

When using self-monitoring records, it is important that only data that is useful to treatment be collected. Social workers need to carefully think through how the data will specifically be used to inform treatment, otherwise requests for such data should not be made. Finally, a variety of existing self-monitoring records can be found in the literature, such as the Drinking Self-monitoring Log (available in Sobell & Sobell, 1993), which may be immediately amenable to treatment or modified in some fashion to meet unique treatment goals (see also Sobell et al., 1989).

Skills Training

Another important feature of CBT is teaching clients practical skills to help minimize the distress or consequences of thoughts and behaviors. Homework is an important way to facilitate the process of developing skills and generalizing their use to real-world situations. Social workers should construct assignments that are relevant to the information and skills taught in the session and promote generalizability. Thus, homework should be developed collaboratively with the client to ensure it is relevant to her or his interest and needs, which increases compliance. Completed assignments are typically discussed at the beginning of each session as part of the review process.

Structured Problem Solving

A general skill that can help clients respond more effectively to problems is to learn how to alter the nature of the problem (e.g., overcoming obstacles to a goal) or change the distress reaction to the problem (e.g., acceptance the goal cannot be reached) (Nezu & D'Zurilla, 2005). This process is known as structured problem solving. Clients are taught discrete steps that are involved in solving problems. These steps are considered highly generalizable to problems that are often encountered in treating SUDs.

The initial step is problem orientation, which involves introducing the client to the process of structured problem solving, its purpose and an overview of the method. This is a critical opportunity to help the client develop a sense of self-efficacy in problem solving, which can increase the likelihood of the client adopting structured problem solving as a primary coping strategy. This is especially important for clients with SUDs, as they often cope with problems by relying on substances. In fact, evidence suggests that a sense of self-efficacy is critical for the long-term management of SUDs (e.g., Hyde, Hankins, Deal, & Marteau, 2008). Other parts of the process involve problem definition and formulation, generation of alternatives, decision-making, and solution implementation and verification.

Refusal Skills

Given the ubiquity of substances in our society, it is unreasonable to expect a person with a SUD to avoid all situations in which substances might be present. Thus, it is important for clients to develop skills to effectively refuse substances. The development of refusal skills involves helping clients learn what to say, while also promoting self-efficacy in making refusals and integrating nonverbal skills to promote their effectiveness. The idea is to help clients develop refusal skills that will generalize to a wide-range of high-risk situations.

A recommended approach for teaching refusal skills, as well as other skills involving interpersonal interactions, is the three-step modeling sequence, comprised of modeling, rehearsal, and feedback (Rose-Colley, Eddy, & Cinelli, 1989). Modeling involves both a verbal overview and a physical demonstration of each step of the skill. After the verbal overview, the individual steps and the entire skills are demonstrated. Rehearsal or *coaching* is the process of guiding participants in the rehearsal, with prompts and cues offered to initiate the target behavior and promote accuracy. For example, clients may need coaching on effective nonverbal behaviors, such as maintaining good eye contact and speaking confidently. Feedback involves giving clients specific information on their rehearsal, focusing on both aspects that were done well and those that require further improvement.

Social Skills Training

From a CBT perspective, the use or maintenance of a SUD may be influenced, in part, by the client's social supports or network. For example, a client is at risk of using substances through exposure to substances within a social network and pressures to use. Negative interpersonal interactions can also be a trigger to using substances. Thus, enhancement of social skills can help establish a more effective social support system. Social workers need to carefully assess different aspects of the client's social skills and determine what can be effectively altered to meet a given goal.

Social skills training is often done using role play. Role play incorporates the different aspects of the modeling sequence, although they are structured to allow for role reversals. If the client is practicing the expression of feelings, the social worker might assume the role of the client, and the client would assume the role of an antagonist. This role reversal provides the opportunity for modeling the target behavior.

Revising Cognitive Errors and Distortions

A variety of cognitive errors and distortions (refer to Table 7.1) are commonly encountered among clients in treatment for SUDs. As previously described, such errors and distortions contribute to the maintenance and severity of SUD-related problems. CBT addresses these problems by helping the client identify and replace these biases and errors with adaptive schemas. Treatment involves learning to see other sources of data that can be used to help find support for adaptive schemas and refute maladaptive schemas.

Stress Management

Stress can be a *trigger* or a pre-cursor to cravings or urges to use substances. Thus, the development of stress management techniques is common to SUD treatment. Such strategies might involve diaphragmatic breathing, meditation practice, and progressive muscle relaxation. Social workers should work collaboratively with clients to find out whether they already have existing strategies that can be enhanced in the treatment setting.

Coping with Cravings and Urges

In the treatment of SUDs, significant attention is paid to eliminating various triggers or minimizing their consequences. For example, if a client has a cued response to substances, it is important that he or she has ways to manage subsequent cravings, urges, or negative emotions. This may involve relying on social supports or engaging in some type of mindfulness practice. The underlying idea is to help clients develop alternative responses to stimuli that are triggers for substance use (Kadden et al., 2002). From a CBT perspective, the role of the social worker is to help the client enhance or develop new coping skills that are highly generalizable to the client's daily routines.

Relapse Prevention

A focus of CBT in the treatment of SUDs involves preparing clients for setbacks in the treatment process, with relapse being one of the most serious. Relapse prevention involves helping clients anticipate challenges they expect to encounter in the treatment process and prepare what to do in advance. The advanced preparation provides a sort of menu of options for clients, which is particularly valuable in situations when options seem limited.

A relapse prevention plan typically includes the major coping strategies involved for managing urges, refusal skills, and contact information of persons who are supportive of their treatment. Furthermore, a relapse prevention plan can also outline how treatment will progress in case of a setback, including a relapse. Relapse prevention plans are always tailored around the client's needs, available resources, and skills. A plan should be in place to actively reengage or promote continued engagement in the treatment process following a relapse, which may be difficult when working in programs that have adopted *abstinent only* policies to treatment.

Conclusion and Future Directions

CBT represents a broad class of interventions that take into account how learning processes are involved in acquiring and maintaining maladaptive thoughts, emotional reactions, and behaviors. These learning processes provide the basis for various interventions targeting the reduction or cessation of substance use. The focus of CBT is on present symptoms and behaviors, as opposed to earlier life experiences. CBT sessions are highly structured, directive, solution-focused, and time-limited. A significant amount of research has been conducted to show the value in providing CBT to persons with SUDs. However, it is also important to consider the value of CBT in the context of some of the broader criticisms. Provided below is a brief summary of these criticisms, followed by additional suggestions for ongoing professional development to guide social workers in training.

Criticisms of CBT

CBT is arguably one of the most important psychosocial interventions available to social workers. However, it is necessary that our favor for CBT is contextualized in some of the broader criticisms about the popular therapeutic approach. One criticism that is not uncommon to hear is that CBT fails to address the *whole person* since treatment expressly targets symptoms. This is antithetical to many of the long-standing beliefs held in other forms of psychodynamic approaches. For example, the *symptom replacement* metaphor, also referred to as the *hydraulic model* of symptoms, is based on the idea that deeper-rooted problems are the source of the symptoms that present in the treatment context. From this, it is believed that removing a symptom simply opens the psychic space for new symptoms to emerge. Thus, from this perspective treating only the thoughts and behaviors associated with substance use, as is the focus of CBT, does not address the underlying source of the problem. This presumably leads to the emergence of other addictive behaviors (e.g., gambling, sex, exercise, and eating) or the misuse of other substances.

While the symptom replacement metaphor has tremendous intuitive appeal, the research does not actually provide support for its validity. Social workers may offer various clinical cases from their experience as support for the validity of the model. Clinical experience is regarded as a key part of the evidence-based practice framework (see Sacket, Rosenberg, Gray, & Haynes, 1996), but anecdotal evidence, especially retrospective interpretations, is subject to tremendous biases. Social workers who work in earnest to guide their practice decisions in the best available research should discover that the research conducted to date does not support the symptom replacement model.

Another criticism against CBT is that the high level of structure of CBT sessions, typified by the use and adherence to session agendas and use of homework, prevents the development of the therapeutic relationship. This criticism can be heard from social workers being guided by psychodynamic and person-oriented therapies that consider the relationship between the client and social worker as the basis for change. Again, this is a criticism that has not been supported in the existing research, given the relative success of CBT compared to other interventions. CBT does not discount the value of therapeutic alliance. Rather, therapeutic alliance remains critical to change, but it is not considered to be the primary mechanism in behavior change. In fact, the effectiveness of computer-delivered CBT further suggests that the actual tools and techniques are of primary value.

To date, we are aware of no research to suggest that agendas, homework, or other tools and techniques of CBT are detrimental to the therapeutic relationship. In fact, the accumulated evidence for CBT builds our confidence that tools and techniques like the use of agendas and homework can enhance the therapeutic relationship. As previously noted, agendas and homework are created collaboratively with the client. Not only does this provide opportunity of client engagement, but also ensures that ample time is allocated in each session to address issues that are of immediate concern to the client. Additionally, homework and related tools also provide the opportunity to apply skills in real-world situations. The effectiveness of the skills help build the confidence in clients that treatment is useful and beneficial, which is a necessary condition for therapeutic alliance.

Ongoing Professional Development

A historical review of CBT shows that the current system of treatment has evolved over many years, drawing on various strands of research, theory, and clinical experience. The overview of CBT provided in this chapter is merely a snapshot of its current place in social work. However, it is important to remain cognizant of the ongoing efforts to continually improve the effectiveness of CBT interventions for a wide range of problems, especially SUDs. Thus, social workers face the challenge of acquiring expertise with the major tenets, tools, and techniques of this therapeutic system, while updating their knowledge as new evidence becomes available. This is not easy, given the time constraints and limited resources that social workers commonly face in various treatment settings. Attending professional development trainings and seeking out high-quality supervision are important learning activities.

Social workers are also strongly encouraged to follow the scientific literature regarding CBT. This includes CBT-related research specifically for SUDs, as well as other disorders. A broad-based understanding of CBT can provide social workers with insights on how CBT may be tailored to meet the complex needs of persons with SUDs. Some journals that may be relevant include *Cognitive Behaviour Therapy, Cognitive and Behavior Practice, The Cognitive Behaviour Therapist*, and *The Journal of Cognitive and Behavioral Psychotherapies*. It is unlikely that social workers in routine practice settings will have subscriptions to these various journals. However, efforts are being made to increase the availability of articles to make them freely available via open access journals, especially research that has been supported by federal organizations. Professional associations, such as the *National*

Association of Cognitive-Behavioral Therapists and *Association for Behavioral and Cognitive Therapies*, can provide further opportunities for social workers to develop their professional networks. These associations can be useful in helping social workers in training identify high-quality supervision and other training opportunities to ensure their clients receive the best available treatment.

References

Anton, R. F., O'Malley, S. S., Ciraulo, D. A., Cisler, R. A., Couper, D., Donovan, D. M., et al. (2006). Combined pharmacotherapies and behavioral interventions for alcohol dependence: The combine study: A randomized controlled trial. *Journal of the American Medical Association, 295*, 2003–2017.

Beck, A. T., Freeman, A., Pretzer, J., Davis, D. D., Fleming, B., Ottavani, R., et al. (1990). *Cognitive therapy of personality disorders*. New York: Guildford Press.

Carroll, K. M. (1998). *A cognitive-behavioral approach: Treating cocaine addiction*. Rockville, MD: National Institute on Drug Abuse.

Carroll, K. M., Fenton, L. R., Ball, S. A., Nich, C., Frankforter, T. L., Shi, J., et al. (2004). Efficacy of disulfiram and cognitive behavior therapy in cocaine-dependent outpatients. *Archives of General Psychiatry., 61*(3), 264–272.

Ellis, A. (1994). *Reason and emotion in psychotherapy: Revised and updated*. Secaucus, NJ: Carol Publishing Group.

Hyde, J., Hankins, M., Deal, A., & Marteau, T. M. (2008). Interventions to increase self-efficacy in the context of addiction behaviours: A systematic literature review. *Journal of Health Psychology., 13*(5), 607–623.

Kadden, R., Carroll, K., Donovan, D., Cooney, N., Monti, P., Abrams, D., et al. (2002). *Cognitive-behavioral coping skills therapy manual*. Rockville, MD: National Institute of Health.

Magill, M., & Ray, L. A. (2009). Cognitive-behavioral treatment with adult alcohol and illicit drug users: A meta-analysis of randomized controlled trials. *Journal of Studies on Alcohol and Drugs, 70*(4), 516–527.

McHugh, R. K., Hearon, B. A., & Otto, M. W. (2010). Cognitive behavioral therapy for substance use disorders. *Psychiatric Clinics of North America, 33*(3), 511–525.

Monti, P. M., Rohsenow, D. J., Hutchison, K. E., Swift, R. M., Mueller, T. I., Colby, S. M., et al. (1999). Naltrexones effect on cue-elicited craving among alcoholics in treatment. *Alcoholism: Clinical and Experimental Research, 23*(8), 1386–1394.

Nezu, A., & D'Zurilla, T. (2005). Problem-solving therapy—General. In A. Freedman (Ed.), *Encyclopedia of Cognitive Behavioral Therapy* (VIII, pp. 301–304). New York: Springer Science+Business Media, Inc.

Niaura, R. S., Rohesnow, D. J., Binkoff, J. A., Monti, P. M., Abrams, D. A., & Pedraza, M. (1988). The relevance of cue reactivity to understanding alcohol and smoking relapse. *Journal of Abnormal Psychology, 97*, 133–152.

Padesky, C. A. (1994). Schema change processes in cognitive therapy. *Clinical Psychology and Psychotherapy, 1*(5), 267–278.

Pavlov, I. P. (1928). *Lectures on conditioned reflexes: Twenty-five years of objective study of the higher nervous activity (behavior) of animals*. New York: Liverwright Publishing Company.

Rawson, R. A., Huber, A., & McCann, M. (2002). A comparison of contingency management and cognitive-behavioral approaches during methadone maintenance treatment for cocaine dependence. *Archives of General Psychiatry, 59*, 817–824.

Rose-Colley, M. L., Eddy, J. M., & Cinelli, B. (1989). Relapse prevention: Implication for health promotion professionals. *Health Values, 13*(5), 8–13.

Rounsaville, B. J., & Carroll, K. M. (1992). Individual psychotherapy for drug abusers. In J. H. Lowinsohn, P. Ruiz, & R. B. Millman (Eds.), *Comprehensive textbook of substance abuse* (2nd ed., pp. 496–508). New York: Williams and Wilkins.

Sacket, D. L., Rosenberg, W., Gray, J. A., & Haynes, R. B. (1996). Evidence based medicine: What it is and what it isn't. *British Medical Journal, 13*(312), 71–72.

Skinner, B. F. (1957). The experimental analysis of behavior. *American Scientist, 45*(4), 343–371.

Sobell, M. B., Bogardis, J., Schuller, R., Leo, G. I., & Sobell, L. C. (1989). Is self monitoring of alcohol consumption reactive? *Behavioral Assessment, 11,* 447–458.

Sobell, M. B., & Sobell, L. C. (1993). *Problem drinkers: Guided self-change treatment.* New York: Guilford Press.

Weissman, A. N., & Beck, A. T. (1978). *Development and validation of the Dysfunctional Attitude Scale: A preliminary investigation.* Paper presented at the 62nd meeting of the American Educational Research Association, Toronto, Ontario, Canada.

Young, J. E. (1990). *Schema-focused cognitive therapy for personality disorders: A schema focused approach.* Sarasota, FL: Professional Resource Exchange.

Chapter 8
The Philosophy and Practice of Alcoholics Anonymous and Related 12-Step Programs

Joseph G. Pickard, Alexandre Laudet, and Ivana D. Grahovac

As documented throughout this book, substance use disorders (SUDs) are prevalent and highly significant problems that necessitate accessible and effective treatment and ongoing supports to achieve recovery. Although many different definitions of recovery exist, the Substance Abuse and Mental Health Services Administration (SAMHSA) offers the following working definition: "Recovery is a process of change whereby individuals work to improve their own health and wellness and to live a meaningful life in a community of their choice while striving to achieve their full potential" (SAMHSA, 2011). The core element of this definition is that recovery from SUDs is a process that involves improvements in the areas of functioning that are typically impaired by active SUDs (e.g., physical and mental health, social functioning, and employment).

Alcoholics Anonymous (AA) and its 12-step variants (e.g., Narcotics Anonymous, Cocaine Anonymous, Gambler's Anonymous — see later discussion) represent some of the most important nonclinical service options for people with a substance use disorder who seek recovery (Gossop et al., 2003). In fact, epidemiologic research shows that over 60 % of people with either a DSM-IV lifetime drug use disorder (i.e., abuse or dependence) or alcohol use disorder (i.e., abuse or dependence) have attended some type of 12-step program (Cohen, Feinn, Arias, & Kranzler, 2007; Perron et al., 2009).

J.G. Pickard (✉)
University of Missouri at St. Louis, St. Louis, MO, USA
e-mail: pickardj@umsl.edu

A. Laudet
National Development and Research Institutes, Inc., New York, NY, USA
e-mail: alexandrelaudet@gmail.com

I.D. Grahovac
The University of Texas at Austin, Austin, TX, USA

M.G. Vaughn and B.E. Perron (eds.), *Social Work Practice in the Addictions*, Contemporary Social Work Practice, DOI 10.1007/978-1-4614-5357-4_8,
© Springer Science+Business Media New York 2013

Twelve-step programs are voluntary, nonprofessional, self-directed programs that use peer support to promote recovery. They are often misunderstood by social workers and other treatment professionals, especially those who are not in recovery, which can result in a passive or dismissive view of a critical resource for people with SUDs (Davis & Jansen, 1998; Laudet, 2000). As social workers are the largest group of providers for people with SUDs, it is important that they have a strong understanding of 12-step programs and how to effectively engage clients who choose to use them. Toward this end, we first provide an overview of the history of 12-step fellowships followed by a description of the 12-steps and their underlying philosophy; we then review the evidence regarding the effectiveness and various types of 12-step programs. The chapter concludes with practical suggestions to guide social workers in utilizing this important resource among people with SUDs. It should be noted that our use of SUDs refers broadly to the different types of psychoactive substances used for purposes to get high (e.g., cocaine, heroin, and alcohol), as well as the different diagnosable disorders (i.e., abuse and dependence).

Brief History of 12-Step Programs

Twelve-step programs and their underlying philosophy have a rich history with many different sources of influence. The spiritual underpinnings of the 12-steps are often credited to an early twentieth century religious movement called the Oxford Group (Gross, 2010). Some individuals in the Oxford group reported being able to abstain from excessive consumption of alcohol by using some of the group's spiritual principles. They believed that this self-improvement was achieved through the practice of making personal assessments, admitting their wrongs, making restitution for harms done, praying and meditating, and carrying the message of their movement to others who might benefit (Alcoholics Anonymous General Service Office, 2011a, 2011b). Although the Oxford Group was not a program that was particularly focused on addressing alcohol issues, the principles and practices of the Oxford Group were the basis of the development of the spiritual principles of AA (Gross, 2010; Trice & Staudenmeier, 1989).

A second important contribution to the AA philosophy came from a physician from Townes Hospital in New York, Dr. William D. Silkworth, who changed the nature of the understanding of alcoholism from that of a moral weakness to a concept of disease. He described alcoholism as an illness consisting of an allergy of the body and compulsion of the mind (Alcoholics Anonymous World Services, 2001). Silkworth surmised that when an alcoholic ingests alcohol, it activates a craving, in turn causing the person to keep drinking despite great resulting harms.

Two men are credited with the founding of AA—William Wilson (often referred to as "Bill W") and Robert "Dr. Bob" Smith, both of whom were members of the Oxford Group. Wilson integrated the spiritual experience and group processes associated with the Oxford Group with the disease concept of alcoholism, thereby laying the following foundation for the 12-steps: (1) the nature of the problem consisting of an illness rather than moral weakness or lack of willpower; (2) the importance of a spiritual experience; and (3) the program of action adapted from the Oxford Group as it is applied specifically to alcohol problems.

Using this foundation, Alcoholics Anonymous was born in Akron, Ohio in 1935 when Bill W. and Dr. Bob met for the first time. The two soon realized the mutual benefits of helping each other stay sober. This was the foundation upon which the AA program was built, which states in its preamble: "Our primary purpose is to stay sober and help other alcoholics to achieve sobriety" (Alcoholics Anonymous General Service Office, 2011a, 2011b). Thus, the basic premise of AA is found in the power of one alcoholic helping another. AA is, therefore, an abstinence-based program of recovery that uses spiritual principles to help its members recover from alcoholism. Readers interested in a more detailed history of AA are encouraged to review the work of Kurtz (1979).

The 12 Steps and Their Underlying Philosophy

The 12-step program of recovery as initially formulated and outlined in AA's basic text, Alcoholics Anonymous (often called the *Big Book*) (Alcoholics Anonymous World Services, 2001), uses a 3-pronged approach consisting of unity (fellowship, traditions, and principles of the organization), recovery program (*working* the 12-step program), and service (chairing meetings, "qualifying," setting up the meeting space, and helping other alcoholics).

Fellowship

Fellowship is a key component of 12-step recovery; it is the community of members who gather at meetings and, importantly, socialize together before and after meetings as well as between meetings. Fellowship with other recovering persons is one of the cornerstones of 12-step recovery and is credited by recovering individuals as a critical source of support (Laudet, Savage, & Mahmood, 2002; Margolis, Kilpatrick, & Mooney, 2000; Nealon-Woods, Ferrari, & Jason, 1995). Rigorous recent studies have demonstrated that the formation of adaptive social networks is one of the key mechanisms of action through which AA helps reduce substance use among its members (Kelly, Hoeppner, Stout, & Pagano, 2011; Kelly, Stout, Magill, & Tonigan, 2011). Meeting attendance is the most popular and researched aspect of 12-step participation. At meetings, members share "their experience, strength and hope" with peers—individuals who all share a desire to stop their addictive behaviors—in a supportive environment; new members gain hope and learn coping strategies from more experienced "old-timers" who also come to be reminded of their pasts by listening to new members.

Twelve-step meeting attendance is an important activity for AA members and typically how new members are introduced to the fellowship. As for AA, it is important to note that there are usually different types of meetings indicated on meeting lists to assist newcomers (and any AA member looking for a meeting) locate a meeting that meets his/her needs. Above and beyond these specific types of meetings, most 12-step meetings worldwide are conducted according to a similar sequence that usually includes an opening group prayer, a reading of the 12 steps and other key elements of the program (e.g., How It Works, the Promises) followed by one of the several types of content/format (described in the next sentence), and a closing group prayer—generally prayers are either the Serenity prayer and/or the Lord's Prayer—to close the meeting. AA holds *open* meetings that any interested person is welcome to attend, whether or not they have an alcohol problem. *Closed* meetings are intended only for those people who are there for recovery purposes. In AA, for example, the only people welcome at a closed meeting are individuals who have a desire to stop drinking—AA's only requirement for membership per its third tradition (Alcoholics Anonymous World Services Inc., 1952, 2001).

In terms of the meeting content, in addition to the above standard practices to start and end the meeting, there are round robin or *sharing* meetings where each attendee may choose to share briefly following a speaker's short recounting of his or her *story*; Big Book meetings and Step meetings are among the more frequent formats. There are also meetings available for different subgroups of members including meetings for newcomers and for "old timers," meetings for women, gays and lesbians, Latinos, single parents, and veterans to name only a few. Some AA chapters (regional group of AA meetings often called intergroups or districts) also hold meetings for individuals who experience co-occurring mental health disorders. Finally in large cities, meetings held in languages other than English (e.g., Spanish) can be located to meet the needs of non-native English speaking members and foreign visitors. Similarly, large cities worldwide generally have one or more AA meetings held in English for visitors and expatriates.

Recovery Program

The 12-step recovery program is a set of suggested strategies that are based on a spiritual foundation whereby the individual is encouraged to rely on an external power greater than him/herself (Higher Power that many choose to call God), although no religious affiliation or belief is a requirement for 12-step membership (see discussion about Steps 2 and 3 below). The process of recovery in 12-step programs involves working through a series of tasks, behaviors, and reflective activities that comprise the 12-step philosophy. The 12-steps of AA (presented in Box 8.1 and reviewed later in this chapter) are the foundation for the many variations of 12-step programs subsequently developed to address problems with other substances of abuse as well as other issues (e.g., gambling, overeating, sexually compulsive behaviors).

Most members suggest that the addicted person should work through the steps with the guidance of a sponsor. A sponsor is someone who is also in recovery and

> **Box 8.1 The 12 Steps of Alcoholics Anonymous**
>
> *Source*: Alcoholics Anonymous World Services (2001). Note that *italics* are in original.
>
> 1. We admitted we were powerless over alcohol—that our lives had become unmanageable.
> 2. Came to believe that a Power greater than ourselves could restore us to sanity.
> 3. Made a decision to turn our will and our lives over to the care of God *as we understood Him.*
> 4. Made a searching and fearless moral inventory of ourselves.
> 5. Admitted to God, to ourselves, and to another human being the exact nature of our wrongs.
> 6. Were entirely ready to have God remove all these defects of character.
> 7. Humbly asked Him to remove our shortcomings.
> 8. Made a list of all persons we had harmed, and became willing to make amends to them all.
> 9. Made direct amends to such people wherever possible, except when to do so would injure them or others.
> 10. Continued to take personal inventory and when we were wrong promptly admitted it.
> 11. Sought through prayer and meditation to improve our conscious contact with God *as we understood Him,* praying only for knowledge of His will for us and the power to carry that out.
> 12. Having had a spiritual awakening as the result of these steps, we tried to carry this message to alcoholics, and to practice these principles in all our affairs.

has worked through the 12-steps. The sponsor provides a confidential and safe environment for discussion and spiritual growth in the context of working the steps, along with being a role model and offering meaningful guidance to new members (Whelan, Marshall, Ball, & Humphreys, 2009).

Before reviewing the steps, it is important to note two issues that are relevant to social work. First, the concept of *steps* implies a linear process with a terminal or end point. While a person works through the steps sequentially, it ultimately becomes a nonlinear and continuous process. In other words, completing the 12th step does not imply that a person has completely recovered. The process of recovery involves actively working to integrate and internalize the steps in order for them to serve as a set of principles for achieving a life of sobriety. For those with limited knowledge of the 12-steps, it is helpful to think of the steps as a group of related activities, as we have done in the following section.

Second, a social worker (or any other professional) cannot hold the dual role of sponsor and professional service provider. However, social workers can develop a deep understanding of how and why 12-step programs work and the role of the sponsor. This will aid helping professionals to make effective referrals to 12-step programs, integrate 12-step activities within the broader treatment plan, and support the client at various stages of the recovery process. This understanding serves as the foundation for guiding the social worker in delivering a Twelve-Step Facilitation (TSF) intervention, as described later in this chapter.

Surrendering the Fight

The first step represents the initial point of entry into the recovery process. The concept of *surrendering* involves admitting that a person is unable to control his or her substance use. The need to surrender is the keystone in recovery, although it is difficult for people with an addiction to achieve this in the absence, ignorance, or denial of serious life consequences. This process is akin to many of the tasks involved with professional treatment approaches. For example, motivational interviewing (see Chap. 4) involves helping clients become aware of their inability to control use and the associated consequences. It is not until awareness or insight is achieved that the individual can make a commitment to change.

Spiritual, Not Religious

Steps 2 and 3 deal with coming to the belief that there is a solution to one's problem (the unmanageability admitted to in step 1) that the solution lies outside of the self, and then in step 3, turning one's will and life over to the care of God or one's chosen conception of a higher power. The use of the word "God" and saying prayers (e.g., the Serenity Prayer and the Lord's Prayer) often gives the misguided impression that 12-step fellowships are religious organizations, which can be off-putting to many people with a SUD, as well as to many treatment professionals (Atkins & Howdon, 2007). Although the origins of AA were in the Oxford Group, a religious organization, AA founders felt it was important to emphasize the phrase, "…as we understood him" (refer to Box 1) by writing it in italics to stress that this portion of the principle is subject to individual interpretation (Alcoholics Anonymous World Services, 2001, p. 60). The AA founders specifically address the issue of religion in one of the early chapters of the *Big Book*,[1] *We Agnostics* (Alcoholics Anonymous World Services, 1939–2001), and the few empirical investigations of the association between religiosity and 12-step participation have found that extent of religious beliefs does not appear to affect the benefits derived from 12-step participation (Tonigan, Miller, & Schermer, 2002; Winzelberg & Humphreys, 1999). In AA it is understood and

---

[1] "Much to our relief, we discovered that we did not need to consider another's conception of God. Our own conception, however inadequate, was sufficient to make the approach and to effect a contact with Him. (…) To us, the Realm of Spirit is broad, roomy, all-inclusive; never exclusive or forbidding to those who honestly seek. It is open, we believe, to all men" (3rd Edition, p. 46).

respected that there may be as many different conceptions of "God" as there are persons in recovery. Indeed, AA's focus on spirituality rather than on (organized) religion has been a major factor in the fellowships' ability to reach people from various cultures and backgrounds where religious approaches to addressing treatments for alcoholism have been met with more limited successes (Gross, 2010).

As the term *God* is so closely connected with organized religions, it is common to hear people in recovery speak of their *higher power* (often referred to as: "*HP*"). Doing so further emphasizes the spiritual and personally defined nature of 12-step recovery. Ultimately, any manner in which a client is able to make sense of *God* is acceptable and even encouraged, as long as it is an entity outside the self, since the self is presumed to be among the chief causes of problems for the alcoholic. Overall the goal of Steps 2 and 3 is to help the individual in recovery infuse these spiritual principles in everyday life.

Personal Inventory

Steps 4 and 5 involve working with a sponsor to take stock of one's resentments, fears, and previous behaviors, including sexual behaviors. For this reason and others, it is suggested that females work with female sponsors and males with male sponsors, though this might not necessarily apply with LGBT members. This part of the 12-steps is where 12-step members begin to face their deepest truths—that is, the harm they have done to themselves and to others and the harm others have done to them—and the guilt, shame, and remorse they associate with their pasts. On the one hand, this can be a cathartic experience that liberates people from their previous experiences. On the other hand, it can have serious negative consequences for those who are not psychologically prepared to identify their innermost secrets and to share them aloud. Thus, it is imperative that sponsors be experienced, maintain strict confidentiality, guide their sponsees slowly through the process, and strive to help them feel accepted unconditionally while arming them with coping strategies to face the truths that are revealed through taking one's *searching and fearless moral inventory*.

Humility

Humility involves developing a deep understanding of one's strengths and weaknesses and of the need of relying on a power greater than—and outside of—oneself (the higher power—steps 2 and 3) to regain sanity (considered to be "soundness of mind") and healthy functioning, which are the basis of steps 6 and 7. Developing a sense of humility helps create a new identity that allows the repetition and practice of principles of recovery and fosters a healthy and sober lifestyle. This process replaces the negative character traits associated with a SUD, chief among them, according to the 12-step philosophy, self-centeredness. A basic ingredient of a successful AA program, according to the AA philosophy, is humility. Being humble is thought of not as thinking less of one's self, but thinking of one's self less often. Without encouraging servility, this principle places importance on being considerate and tactful toward others and abandoning the notion that one is *in charge* following the admission that one's attempts at control led directly to their current, painful situation (step 1). An individual who practices humility does not merely accept tangible or intangible resources or support from others in absence of showing genuine gratitude or appreciation. Rather, the genuine expression of gratitude and appreciation can begin to become a way of life among those in 12-step recovery.

Making Amends

In steps 8 and 9, the individual makes a list of people she or he has harmed and then makes amends, provided that the process does not cause any further harm. This restitution phase allows the start of a new life, or the continuance of the process of recovery, without being hindered by a sense of unfinished business.

These steps are best completed with the guidance of an experienced sponsor for two important reasons. First, in the exuberance of being new to recovery, it is possible for the person to go overboard in making amends, doing more harm than good to self or others (or both). The person needs to carefully consider what is an appropriate amend and the possible unintended consequences of making it. Second, many people in recovery (as well as those who are not in recovery) maintain a strong system of defense mechanisms that may prevent them from taking responsibility for their own actions.

While *denial* is considered a classic or hallmark defense mechanism among alcoholics, other defense mechanisms can also represent serious barriers to making amends. For example, Potter-Efron (1988) indicates that a common defense mechanism among people with an addiction is *rationalization*. Rationalization occurs when people convince themselves that their misbehavior, errors in judgment, or other transgressions are justified because of the wrongdoings of another person or because of a particular situation (Potter-Efron, 1988). Another dysfunctional defense mechanism involves cognitive distortions of the chain of events that minimize or eliminate a sense of accountability or personal responsibility. This process is readily apparent among people who speak openly about the wrongdoing of others without being open and honest about the part they played in the situation. Experienced sponsors can provide the wisdom and clarity to overcome these problems by challenging their sponsees on their lack of honesty and insincere self-appraisal. At the same time, sponsors can draw on their own experience to indicate that resistance to and difficulties in making amends is typical and even expected—but must be circumvented.

Maintenance and Carrying the Message

Steps 10–12 are similar to the maintenance phase in the stages of change model (see Chap. 4). That is, they are the critical steps that a person must take consistently on an ongoing basis to attain and maintain *spiritual well-being*, or a sense of equanimity and serenity in daily affairs. As part of step 10, members learn to complete regular personal inventories. This helps the individual to understand and accept a new identity, keeps the resurgence of old habits or thought patterns in check, and helps one to develop and practice new, healthy behaviors and thought patterns. Such efforts help integrate the work done in the earlier steps, while serving as a reminder that no single stage is ever complete; recovery is, indeed, a process. Step 11 helps integrate a spiritual perspective with the behavioral and cognitive work from the earlier steps, particularly the personal inventory. This is accomplished through the practice of daily prayer or meditation.

The final step involves sharing the philosophy of the 12-step program with those suffering from an addiction (see Alcoholics Anonymous World Services, 2001). As explained by those in recovery, the underlying value of sharing the 12-step program is that *by giving away what one has found, one is then able to keep it.* This is akin to Reissman's helper therapy principle (Riessman, 1965) whereby one is helped by helping others, especially similar others (e.g., other AA members). Some who are unfamiliar with the 12-step philosophy may consider this to be a form of religious zeal, proselytizing, or a pyramid scheme in order to grow membership. This last step involves nothing more and nothing less than an honest desire to share the benefits of a program that has helped one to enter a life of sobriety, and members of 12-step programs typically avoid discussing their programs with people who do not want or need them. Furthermore, as described in the *Big Book*, 12-step fellowships are programs of attraction, not promotion — that is, members share their experiences with other alcoholics, but they should never actively recruit others into the fellowship (Alcoholics Anonymous World Services, 2001).

Members of 12-step groups may bring meetings to various institutions (e.g., hospitals, various types of treatment facilities, jails) that want to hold onsite meetings but lack the experienced members to run a group. This is a form of service conducted as part of the 12th step. Other forms of service include chairing meetings, making coffee, setting up chairs, and holding positions of responsibility in the group (e.g., secretary or treasurer).[2]

Varieties of 12-Step Fellowships

Twelve-Step Fellowships

Alcoholics Anonymous is the oldest and the largest 12-step fellowship, with an estimated 100,000 AA groups worldwide and nearly 2 million members (Alcoholics Anonymous World Services Inc., 2011a). The popularity and success of AA and its 12-step program of recovery have led to extensive adaptations to other behaviors (e.g., drug use, gambling, overeating, sexual compulsions), belief systems

---

[2] Twelve-step groups also offer speakers to come to classes and other gatherings of professionals in order to educate the general public on their fellowships. They can be located through the local telephone directory or on the Internet.

(e.g., Christianity), and cultures (Humphreys, 2004; Makela et al., 1996); 258 fellowships use the 12-steps or the name "Anonymous" (Kurtz, 1997), and 94 "verified" 12-step fellowships exist (White & Madara, 1996).

Narcotics Anonymous (NA) is the second largest 12-step group in terms of membership size and number of meetings. This group stresses the importance of recovery from all mind-altering substances, including alcohol and marijuana (though many groups discourage direct discussion of alcohol), using a set of 12-steps that are only slightly different from the original 12-steps of AA.

Cocaine Anonymous (CA) is also modeled after AA, with a focus on cocaine; numerous other 12-step fellowships focusing on a specific illicit drug have emerged in the past 20 years (for discussion, see Laudet, 2008 and online resources such as the site of Faces and Voices of Recovery).[3] In addition to 12-step adaptations targeting problems with a specific substance or behavior, the 12-step program of recovery has also been adapted to mental health problems and co-occurring mental health and substance use disorders—i.e., dual diagnosis: Double Trouble in Recovery (DTR) and Dual Recovery Anonymous (DRA) provide a forum for discussing addiction, mental health problems, and use of prescribed medications (Laudet et al., 2004). These organizations are firmly grounded in peer support, relying on more experienced members to share their experience, strength, and hope with newcomers, in an effort to help each other overcome their problems, which is a core feature of 12-step recovery (see Laudet, Magura, Vogel, & Knight, 2000). While each of these fellowships centers around different problems, they all share the core principles of AA's 12-step program of recovery and its 12 traditions; thus generally, the same 12 steps are used, the only substantive adaptations being in steps 1 and 12 (see Box 1) where "alcohol" and "alcoholics" are replaced by the target problem substance or behavior. For example, NA's first step reads, "We admitted that we were powerless over our addiction, that our lives had become unmanageable" (Narcotics Anonymous, 2010).

Twelve-Step Inspired Recovery Supports

The 12-step philosophy has also been interpreted to inform the development of comprehensive recovery support services for addictive behaviors. For example, a growing number of college and university campuses with centralized health services are providing recovery-oriented services for students with addictive behaviors. The Center for Students in Recovery at the University of Texas at Austin is a model program that offers 12-step meetings, along with a comprehensive set of recovery-oriented activities to provide a supportive community and promote academic success among students in recovery (Perron et al., 2011; see also Perron, Grahovac, & Parrish, 2010). This Collegiate Recovery Community model of campus-based, peer-driven support for students in recovery is founded on the core

---

[3] http://www.facesandvoicesofrecovery.org

principles of 12-step recovery and has thus far been implemented in some 20 campuses nationwide with 3–5 institutions starting one every year (Harris, Baker, Kimball, & Shumway, 2008; U.S. Department of Education Higher Education Center for Alcohol and Other Drug Abuse and Violence Prevention, 2010).

Benefits of 12-Step Participation

Findings from numerous observational and quasi-experimental studies spanning over two decades suggest that participation in 12-step fellowships, both during and after treatment, is beneficial to sustaining reductions in drug and/or alcohol use initiated during treatment (Fiorentine & Hillhouse, 2000; Kelly, Dow, Yeterian, & Kahler, 2010; Laudet, Stanick, & Sands, 2007; McKay, Merikle, Mulvaney, Weiss, & Koppenhaver, 2001; Montgomery, Miller, & Tonigan, 1995; Morgenstern, Labouvie, McCrady, Kahler, & Frey, 1997; Project MATCH Research Group, 1997; Timko, Finney, Moos, & Moos, 1995; Timko, Moos, Finney, Moos, & Kaplowitz, 1999). Moreover, there is also evidence from quasi-experimental studies that by encouraging patients to participate in 12-step groups, one can provide a cost-effective post-treatment recovery resource that reduces professional health care utilization 1- and 2-years post-treatment while yielding abstinence rates that are superior to those of patients not encouraged to participate in 12 steps (Humphreys & Moos, 2001, 2007). While research has focused most on assessing the benefits of 12-step meeting attendance, other aspects of 12-step recovery, such as working the steps and having a home group, enhance the benefits of meeting attendance and are associated with more stable abstinence (Caldwell & Cutter, 1998).

One of a handful of long-term studies found that the most stable abstinence from alcohol over 10 years came from being a sponsor (Cross, Morgan, Mooney, Martin, & Rafter, 1990). Evidence suggests an association between a lack of additional 12-step suggested activities with high attrition and with the consequent loss of the potential benefits of affiliation (Walsh et al., 1991). In addition to the usefulness of attending meetings and engaging in other 12-step affiliated behaviors, embracing 12-step ideology (reliance on a Higher power, commitment to abstinence, recognizing the importance of needing to work the 12-step program, helping others) predicts subsequent abstinence independently of meeting attendance (Fiorentine & Hillhouse, 2000).

Note that there have been few randomized clinical trials (RCT) of 12-step participation because this community-based, peer-driven support resource does not lend itself to randomized assignment; thus while it is theoretically possible to assign a study group to attending 12-step meetings, doing so would be in direct violation of 12-step philosophy that emphasizes the completely voluntary and self-directed nature of 12-step participation. RCTs rely on investigator-controlled study conditions (i.e., a specific intervention or medication that is typically not available for non-study participants). Regarding 12-step programs, it would be unethical, and arguably impossible, to prevent members of the control group from attending community-based 12-step meetings on their own volition, as would making meeting attendance compulsory for members if they do not wish to do so. Thus, reviews and meta-analyses of 12-step RCTs have generally reported inconsistent results (Ferri, Amato, & Davoli, 2006; Kaskutas, 2009; Tonigan, Toscova, & Miller, 1996). Moreover, patients in these few studies are not representative of the population of 12-step participants, as they are most often legally or socially coerced to attend. From this perspective, inconsistent findings in these RCTs and related meta-analysis are not surprising (Kownacki & Shadish, 1999).

Practical Suggestions for Social Workers

The fact that 12-step programs are based upon voluntary participation and rely on peer-support may suggest that social workers cannot actively use this resource as part of their toolbox of recovery support strategies to give clients. Quite the contrary is true. Studies have concluded that clinicians' practices are critical to client outcomes (Luborsky, Barber, Siqueland, McLellan, & Woody, 1997; McLellan, Woody, Luborsky, & Goehl, 1988; Najavits, Crits-Christoph, & Dierberger, 2000; Project Match Research Group, 1998), and that not only whether—but also how—clinicians refer clients to 12-step groups significantly influences post-treatment outcomes (Sisson & Mallams, 1981; Timko & Debenedetti, 2007; Timko, Debenedetti, & Billow, 2006). Numerous online resources and published studies designed to help professionals inform clients about 12-step programs and to maximize the effectiveness of referrals are available. The following discussion provides an overview of these resources.

Twelve-Step Facilitation

Among the most practical and straightforward ways of incorporating 12-step programs in practice is the use of TSF, a manualized approach to help professionals prepare clients for, and facilitate a commitment to, attending a 12-step program, such as AA, NA, and CA (Nowinski, 2006). TSF is an individual-based therapy consisting of 12–15 sessions. The social worker or clinician guides the client in various didactic activities related to the behavioral, spiritual, and cognitive principles that form the core of 12-step philosophy. Part of the process also involves addressing barriers associated with attendance to a 12-step program. It is important to note that TSF is neither officially affiliated with nor endorsed by AA, nor does AA express any official opinion regarding the use of TSF.

Research has found TSF to be appropriate for people with either an alcohol or drug use disorder (Project Match Research Group, 1998). In a large-scale study comparing TSF with cognitive behavioral therapy (CBT) and motivational enhancement therapy (MET), TSF was most effective at promoting active membership in 12-step groups during and after treatment. Other formal and structured approaches to 12-step referrals include motivational enhancement (see Walitzer, Dermen, & Barrick, 2009) and Making Alcoholics Anonymous Easier (Kaskutas, Subbaraman, Witbrodt, & Zemore, 2008). To date, TSF is the oldest such intervention, has the strongest empirical support, and is the most widely available materials for clinicians. While most TSF materials must be purchased, solid descriptions of the approach can be found free of charge on the web including that prepared by SAMHSA's Addiction Technology Transfer Center (ATTC).[4]

Active Referrals and Promoting Engagement

One of the most important characteristics of TSF is that it establishes a way for the clinician to be active in supporting a client in 12-step programs, even though the social worker will not be a sponsor. This is in stark contrast to the common passive role of simply referring the client to a 12-step program without any meaningful follow-up. When TSF is not feasible, social workers can still actively engage clients in the 12-step process by conducting *active referrals*. Rather than merely telling the client to attend a 12-step meeting and giving him/her a meeting list, active referrals consists of working with the client before 12-step meeting attendance as well as over time, to follow-up on the referral, assess the client's experiences and guide him/her in maximizing fit between needs and program. This includes helping orient the client to the 12-step meeting process (what to expect at a meeting) and informing them in advance of the underlying philosophy.

Articles such as David and Jansen's "Making Meaning of Alcoholics Anonymous for Social Workers" (Davis & Jansen, 1998) and Caldwell's "Fostering Client Connections with Alcoholics Anonymous: A Framework for Social Workers in Various Practice Settings" (Caldwell, 1999) discuss how numerous aspects of the 12-step program are the cause of misinterpretation and controversy (also see Laudet, 2000)—and provide strategies that social workers can use to enhance 12-step participation and dispel misconceptions and myths about 12-step groups among their clients.

The handful of available studies assessing referral style generally support the usefulness of actively referring clients to 12-step groups. A small pilot study compared *simple referral* (i.e., clinician's suggestion that client attend SH groups and giving client a meeting list) with *intensive referral* whereby clinician and client arranged for an experienced 12-step member to accompany the client to a group meeting (Sisson & Mallams, 1981). While all clients in the intensive group affiliated with 12-step groups, none in the simple referral condition did, suggesting that the manner in which clinicians refer clients to 12-step groups may enhance clients' subsequent engagement.

Another study indirectly documented the importance of clinicians' role in engaging clients in 12-step groups. Investigating how treatment programs' theoretical

---

[4] http://www.nattc.org/userfiles/file/Vol.%2012,%20Issue%207.pdf

orientation influences clients' participation in—and benefits derived from—12-step participation, Humphreys and Moos (2007) found that clients in 12-step groups and eclectic programs (combined 12-step and cognitive-behavioral) had higher rates of subsequent 12-step participation than did clients in the cognitive-behavioral treatment programs. Moreover, program orientation (the degree to which the 12-steps are integrated) moderated the effectiveness of self-help participation: As the degree of programs' "12-stepness" increased, the positive relationship between 12-step participation and outcome (substance use and psychosocial) became stronger.

The most definitive evidence for the importance of clinicians' 12-step referral practices comes from a randomized controlled trial that assigned new clients entering outpatient treatment to either standard 12-step referral or to an intensive referral condition and assessed 12-step involvement and substance abuse outcomes 6-month and 12-months later (Timko et al., 2006; Timko & Debenedetti, 2007). Patients in the standard referral condition received a 12-step meeting list and were encouraged to attend. Intensive referral had the key elements of counselors linking patients to 12-step volunteers and using 12-step journals to check on meeting attendance. Compared to the standard referral condition, intensive referral yielded greater levels of 12-step attendance and involvement at both follow-ups and greater reductions in substance use over the year.

Being well informed about the philosophy of 12-step programs and how they operate effectively positions the social worker for addressing myths or prior negative experiences. For example, some clients may have attended 12-step meetings in the past, finding them to be unhelpful or unsuited for their needs. In such cases, it is important to emphasize the significant heterogeneity of meetings. No two meetings are ever the same in spite of the standardized format, because the meeting "flavor" is in part determined by its local membership (Montgomery, Miller, & Tonigan, 1993). Social workers can solicit feedback from other clients to understand the composition and styles of different meetings, which can then be used to help match a client with a particular meeting that may be more suitable.

Social workers can enhance their understanding and experience with 12-step programs by attending an *open* meeting (see earlier discussion), which is strongly recommended. While a social worker's initial reaction to an open meeting might be mixed, the experience can provide a new level of empathy to better understand the range of feelings a client might feel the first time she or he enters a meeting as well as useful information to impart to clients on what happens at a meeting and how to prepare.

Numerous other practical and creative opportunities exist for social workers to be active supporters with respect to 12-step programs. Resources that summarize these strategies include SAMHSA's, *Mutual Aid Resources: An Introduction to Mutual Support Groups for Alcohol and Drug Abuse* (Substance Abuse and Mental Health Services Administration Center for Substance Abuse Treatment, 2008) and AA's materials and webpage "Information for Professionals" (Alcoholics Anonymous World Services Inc., 2011b); note that other 12-step fellowships such as NA also have developed materials to inform professionals about their organizations.

Social workers are encouraged to actively seek out these opportunities and to work towards a deeper understanding of the underlying philosophies involved to help them become more active and understanding when working with addicted clients. It can also result in promoting and further engaging clients in this important resource that increases the maximum benefit possible to those with an addiction.

Conclusion

In summary, 12-step fellowships represent a potentially useful post-treatment recovery resource for patients with alcohol and/or drug problems. Key advantages of 12-step groups include their broad and consistent availability at no cost for as long as someone wishes to attend, compared to professional services that often have a wait list, may charge a fee, and are limited in time and intensity. Given that sustaining recovery is experienced as a process that unfolds over time and requires support (Laudet, 2007), the peer support provided by self-help groups—such as 12-step groups—can be critical to maintaining recovery. While 12-step groups are nonprofessional organizations, there are numerous opportunities for professionals to play an important role in informing patients about this resource, helping to redress misguided conceptions, addressing ambivalence, helping patients identify the elements of 12-step recovery that meet their needs, and to refer clients using proven strategies that maximize the likelihood that patients will give 12-step fellowships an honest try. Social workers would be wise to approach this with experience, an open mind, and sufficient knowledge of what to expect from 12-step participation.

References

Alcoholics Anonymous General Service Office. (2011a). *Origins*. Retrieved March 1, 2011, from http://www.aa.org/aatimeline/.

Alcoholics Anonymous General Service Office. (2011b). *A.A. preamble*. Retrieved March 1, 2011, from http://www.aa.org/lang/en/en_pdfs/smf-92_en.pdf.

Alcoholics Anonymous World Services. (1939–2001). *Alcoholics Anonymous: The story of how many thousands of men and women have recovered from alcoholism* (4th ed.). New York: Alcoholics Anonymous World Services Inc.

Alcoholics Anonymous World Services Inc. (1952). *Twelve steps and twelve traditions*. New York: Alcoholics Anonymous World Services Inc.

Alcoholics Anonymous World Services Inc. (2011a). *Estimates of A.A. groups and members*. Retrieved September 28, 2011, from http://www.aa.org/lang/en/subpage.cfm?page=74.

Alcoholics Anonymous World Services Inc. (2011b). *Information on AA: More information for professionals*. Retrieved September 28, 2011, from http://www.aa.org/lang/en/subpage.cfm?page=222.

Atkins, R. G., & Howdon, J. E. (2007). Religiosity and participation in mutual-aid support groups for addiction. *Journal of Substance Abuse Treatment, 33*, 321–331.

Caldwell, P. E. (1999). Fostering client connections with alcoholics anonymous: A framework for social workers in various practice settings. *Social Work and Health Care, 28*(4), 45–61.

Caldwell, P. E., & Cutter, H. S. (1998). Alcoholics anonymous affiliation during early recovery. *Journal of Substance Abuse Treatment, 15*(3), 221–228.

Cohen, E., Feinn, R., Arias, A., & Kranzler, H. R. (2007). Alcohol treatment utilization: Findings from the National Epidemiologic Survey on Alcohol and Related Conditions. *Drug and Alcohol Dependence, 86*, 214–221.

Cross, G. M., Morgan, C. W., Mooney, A. J., 3rd, Martin, C. A., & Rafter, J. A. (1990). Alcoholism treatment: A ten-year follow-up study. *Alcoholism: Clinical and Experimental Research, 14*(2), 169–173.

Davis, D. R., & Jansen, G. G. (1998). Making meaning of Alcoholics Anonymous for social workers: Myths, metaphors, and realities. *Social Work, 43*(2), 169–182.

Ferri, M., Amato, L., & Davoli, M. (2006). Alcoholics anonymous and other 12-step programmes for alcohol dependence. *Cochrane Database of Systematic Reviews, July(3)*, CD 005032

Fiorentine, R., & Hillhouse, M. P. (2000). Exploring the additive effects of drug misuse treatment and twelve-step involvement: Does twelve-step ideology matter? *Substance Use and Misuse, 35*(3), 367–397.

Gossop, M., Harris, J., Best, D., Man, L. H., Manning, V., Marshall, J., et al. (2003). Is attendance at alcoholics anonymous meetings after inpatient treatment related to improved outcomes? 6-month follow-up. *Alcohol & Alcoholism, 38*(5), 421–426.

Gross, M. (2010). Alcoholics anonymous: Still sober after 75 years. *American Journal of Public Health, 100*(12), 2361–2363.

Harris, K., Baker, A., Kimball, T., & Shumway, S. (2008). Achieving systems-based sustained recovery: A comprehensive model for collegiate recovery communities. *Journal of Groups in Addiction and Recovery, 2*(2–4), 220–237.

Humphreys, K. (2004). *Circles of recovery: Self-help organizations for addictions*. Cambridge: Cambridge University Press.

Humphreys, K., & Moos, R. (2001). Can encouraging substance abuse patients to participate in self-help groups reduce demand for health care? A quasi-experimental study. *Alcoholism: Clinical and Experimental Research, 25*(5), 711–716.

Humphreys, K., & Moos, R. H. (2007). Encouraging posttreatment self-help group involvement to reduce demand for continuing care services: Two-year clinical and utilization outcomes. *Alcoholism: Clinical and Experimental Research, 31*(1), 64–68.

Kaskutas, L. A. (2009). Alcoholics anonymous effectiveness: Faith meets science. *Journal of Addictive Disorders, 28*(2), 145–147.

Kaskutas, L. A., Subbaraman, M. S., Witbrodt, J., & Zemore, S. E. (2008). Effectiveness of making alcoholics anonymous easier: A group format 12-Step facilitation approach. *Journal of Substance Abuse Treatment, 37*, 228–239.

Kelly, J. F., Dow, S. J., Yeterian, J. D., & Kahler, C. W. (2010). Can 12-step group participation strengthen and extend the benefits of adolescent addiction treatment? A prospective analysis. *Drug and Alcohol Dependence, 110*(1–2), 117–125.

Kelly, J.F., Hoeppner, B., Stout, R.L., & Pagano, M. (2011). Determining the relative importance of the mechanisms of behavior change within Alcoholics Anonymous: A multiple mediator-analysis. *Addiction, 107*(2), 289–299.

Kelly, J. F., Stout, R. L., Magill, M., & Tonigan, J. S. (2011). The role of Alcoholics Anonymous in mobilizing adaptive social network changes: A prospective lagged mediational analysis. *Drug and Alcohol Dependence, 114*(2–3), 119–126.

Kownacki, R. J., & Shadish, W. R. (1999). Does alcoholics anonymous work? The results from a meta-analysis of controlled experiments. *Substance Use and Misuse, 9*, 1897–1916.

Kurtz, E. (1979). *Not-God: A history of Alcoholics Anonymous*. Center City, MN: Hazelden Educational Materials.

Kurtz, L. F. (1997). *Self help and Support Groups: A handbook for practitioners*. Thousand Oaks, CA: Sage.

Laudet, A. B. (2000). Substance abuse treatment providers' referral to self-help: Review and future empirical directions. *International Journal of Self-Help and Self-Care, 1*(3), 195–207.

Laudet, A. B. (2007). What does recovery mean to you? Lessons from the recovery experience for research and practice. *Journal of Substance Abuse Treatment, 33*(3), 243–256.

Laudet, A. B. (2008). The impact of Alcoholics Anonymous on other substance abuse related Twelve Step Programs. *Recent Development in Alcoholism., 18*, 71–89.

Laudet, A. B., Magura, S., Cleland, C. M., Vogel, H. S., Knight, E. L., & Rosenblum, A. (2004). The effect of 12-step based fellowship participation on abstinence among dually diagnosed persons: A two-year longitudinal study. *Journal of Psychoactive Drugs, 36*(2), 207–216 (PMCID: 1797895).

Laudet, A. B., Magura, S., Vogel, H. S., & Knight, E. (2000). Addictions services. Support, mutual aid and recovery from dual diagnosis. *Community Mental Health Journal, 36*, 457–474.

Laudet, A. B., Savage, R., & Mahmood, D. (2002). Pathways to long-term recovery: A preliminary investigation. *Journal of Psychoactive Drugs, 34*(3), 305–311.

Laudet, A., Stanick, V., & Sands, B. (2007). The effect of onsite 12-step meetings on post-treatment outcomes among polysubstance-dependent outpatient clients. *Evaluation Review, 31*(6), 613–646.

Luborsky, L., Barber, J. P., Siqueland, L., McLellan, A. T., & Woody, G. (1997). Establishing a therapeutic alliance with substance abusers. *NIDA Research Monograph, 165*, 233–244.

Makela, K., Arminen, I., Bloomfield, K., Eisenbach-Stangl, I., Bergmark, K. H., Kurube, N., et al. (1996). *Alcoholics Anonymous as a mutual help movement.* Madison, WI: The University of Wisconsin Press.

Margolis, R., Kilpatrick, A., & Mooney, B. (2000). A retrospective look at long-term adolescent recovery: Clinicians talk to researchers. *Journal of Psychoactive Drugs, 32*(1), 117–125.

McKay, J. R., Merikle, E., Mulvaney, F. D., Weiss, R. V., & Koppenhaver, J. M. (2001). Factors accounting for cocaine use two years following initiation of continuing care. *Addiction, 96*(2), 213–225.

McLellan, A. T., Woody, G. E., Luborsky, L., & Goehl, L. (1988). Is the counselor an "active ingredient" in substance abuse rehabilitation? An examination of treatment success among four counselors. *Journal of Nervous and Mental Disorders, 176*(7), 423–430.

Montgomery, H. A., Miller, W. R., & Tonigan, J. S. (1993). Differences among AA groups: Implications for research. *Journal of Studies on Alcoholism, 54*(4), 502–504.

Montgomery, H. A., Miller, W. R., & Tonigan, J. S. (1995). Does Alcoholics Anonymous involvement predict treatment outcome? *Journal of Substance Abuse Treatment, 12*(4), 241–246.

Morgenstern, J., Labouvie, E., McCrady, B. S., Kahler, C. W., & Frey, R. M. (1997). Affiliation with Alcoholics Anonymous after treatment: A study of its therapeutic effects and mechanisms of action. *Journal of Consulting and Clinical Psychology, 65*(5), 768–777.

Najavits, L. M., Crits-Christoph, P., & Dierberger, A. (2000). Clinicians' impact on the quality of substance use disorder treatment. *Substance Use and Misuse, 35*(12–14), 2161–2190.

Narcotics Anonymous. (2010). *Information about NA.* Retrieved March 1, 2011 from http://www.na.org/admin/include/spaw2/uploads/pdf/PR/Information_about_NA.pdf.

Nealon-Woods, M. A., Ferrari, J. R., & Jason, L. A. (1995). Twelve-step program use among Oxford House residents: Spirituality or social support in sobriety? *Journal of Substance Abuse, 7*(3), 311–318.

Nowinski, J. (2006). *The twelve step facilitation outpatient program.* Center City, MN: Hazelden Educational Materials.

Perron, B. E., Mowbray, O. P., Glass, J. E., Delva, J., Vaughn, M. G., & Howard, M. O. (2009). Differences in service utilization and barriers among Blacks, Hispanics, and Whites with drug use disorders. *Substance Abuse Treatment, Prevention, and Policy, 13*(4), 1–10.

Perron, B. E., Grahovac, I. D., & Parrish, D. (2010). Students for recovery: A novel approach to supporting students on campus. *Psychiatric Services, 61*, 633.

Perron, B. E., Grahovac, I. D., Uppal, J. S., Granillo, T. M., Shutter, J., & Porter, C. A. (2011). Supporting students in recovery on college campuses: Opportunities for student affairs professionals. *Journal of Student Affairs Research and Practice, 48*(1), 47–64.

Potter-Efron, R. T. (1988). Shame and guilt: Definitions, processes and treatment issues with AODA clients. In R. T. Potter-Efron & P. S. Potter-Efron (Eds.), *The treatment of shame and guilt in alcoholism counseling* (pp. 7–24). New York: Haworth Press.

Project MATCH Research Group. (1997). Matching alcoholism treatments to client heterogeneity: Project MATCH posttreatment drinking outcomes. *Journal of Studies on Alcohol, 58*, 7–29.

Project Match Research Group. (1998). Matching alcoholism treatments to client heterogeneity: Project MATCH three-year drinking outcomes. *Alcoholism: Clinical and Experimental Research, 22*(6), 1300–1311.

Riessman, F. (1965). The 'helper therapy' principle. *Social Work, 10*, 27–32.

Sisson, R. W., & Mallams, J. H. (1981). The use of systematic encouragement and community access procedures to increase attendance at Alcoholic Anonymous and Al-Anon meetings. *American Journal of Drug and Alcohol Abuse, 8*(3), 371–376.

Substance Abuse and Mental Health Services Administration. (2011). *Recovery defined—A unified working definition and set of principles*. Retrieved August 25, 2011, from http://blog.samhsa.gov/2011/05/20/recovery-defined-a-unified-working-definition-and-set-of-principles/.

Substance Abuse and Mental Health Services Administration Center for Substance Abuse Treatment. (2008). *Substance abuse in brief factsheet: An introduction to mutual support groups for alcohol and drug abuse*. Retrieved September 28 from: http://www.kap.samhsa.gov/products/brochures/pdfs/saib_spring08_v5i1.pdf.

Timko, C., & Debenedetti, A. (2007). A randomized controlled trial of intensive referral to 12-step self-help groups: One-year outcomes. *Drug and Alcohol Dependence, 90*(2–3), 270–279.

Timko, C., Debenedetti, A., & Billow, R. (2006). Intensive referral to 12-step self-help groups and 6-month substance use disorder outcomes. *Addiction, 101*(5), 678–688.

Timko, C., Finney, J. W., Moos, R. H., & Moos, B. S. (1995). Short-term treatment careers and outcomes of previously untreated alcoholics. *Journal of Studies on Alcohol, 56*(6), 597–610.

Timko, C., Moos, R. H., Finney, J. W., Moos, B. S., & Kaplowitz, M. S. (1999). Long-term treatment careers and outcomes of previously untreated alcoholics. *Journal of Studies on Alcohol, 60*(4), 437–447.

Tonigan, J. S., Miller, W. R., & Schermer, C. (2002). Atheists, agnostics, and Alcoholics Anonymous. *Journal of Studies on Alcohol, 63*(5), 534–541.

Tonigan, J. S., Toscova, R., & Miller, W. R. (1996). Meta-analysis of the literature on alcoholics anonymous: Sample and study characteristics moderate findings. *Journal of Studies on Alcoholism, 57*, 65–72.

Trice, H. M., & Staudenmeier, W. J. (1989). A sociocultural history of alcoholics anonymous. *Recent Developments in Alcoholism, 7*, 11–35.

U.S. Department of Education Higher Education Center for Alcohol and Other Drug Abuse and Violence Prevention. (2010). *Meeting the needs of students in recovery*. Retrieved March 1, 2011 from http://www.higheredcenter.org/files/prevention_updates/august2010.pdf.

Walitzer, K. S., Dermen, K. H., & Barrick, C. (2009). Facilitating involvement in alcoholics anonymous during outpatient treatment: A randomized clinical trial. *Addiction, 104*, 391–401.

Walsh, D. C., Hingson, R. W., Merrigan, D. M., Cupples, L. A., Levenson, S. M., & Coffman, G. A. (1991). Associations between alcohol and cocaine use in a sample of problem-drinking employees. *Journal of Studies on Alcohol, 52*(1), 17–25.

Whelan, P. J., Marshall, E. J., Ball, D. M., & Humphreys, K. (2009). The role of AA sponsors: A pilot study. *Alcohol and Alcoholism, 44*(4), 416–422.

White, B. J., & Madara, E. J. (1996). *The self-help sourcebook* (5th ed.). Denville, NJ: American Self-Help Clearinghouse.

Winzelberg, A., & Humphreys, K. (1999). Should patients' religiosity influence clinicians' referral to 12-step self-help groups? Evidence from a study of 3,018 male substance abuse patients. *Journal of Consulting and Clinical Psychology, 67*(5), 790–794.

Part III
Culture, Diversity, and Special Populations

Part III builds on the knowledge covered in Parts I and II by examining culture, diversity, and special populations. The first chapter in this section provides a framework for thinking critically about issues of culture, diversity, and social justice vis-à-vis addiction. The next chapter focuses on the empirical validity of culturally competent practices particularly as it relates to prevention. Adolescents are the first of the three special populations that receive focus in this volume. Adolescence is a period marked by the experimental use of substances, and this chapter evaluates the empirical knowledge based on prevention and treatment of addictive behaviors during adolescence. Social workers in the addictions and mental health fields frequently encounter substance abusing women who have the added pressures such as care giving and trauma. This provides a comprehensive overview of these issues for effectively intervening with this special population. The last chapter examines addiction among older persons, an often overlooked population. Demographic shifts will necessitate increased social work practice with older persons with addiction problems. Accordingly, this chapter provides critical information and principles for the effective practice with older persons whose medical and psychosocial needs are often unique compared to other age groups.

Chapter 9
A Framework for Integrating Culture, Diversity, and Social Justice in Addictions

Felipe González Castro and Natalie J. Gildar

Overview of Core Concepts and Elements of Culture

Introduction

Issues of culture and human diversity that exist between and within cultural groups can be perplexing as research investigators and health service providers alike attempt to understand the "real-world" complexities inherent in the study of culture. In this chapter we will examine cultural variables and dimensions of culture, as applied to the study of addictive behaviors. No one model fully captures this rich diversity, and thus we will examine select models which serve as frameworks for organizing and understanding how "culture" influences human behavior, including addictive behaviors. We will complete our analysis with commentaries on methodological approaches for conducting more integrative analyses that can inform our understanding of these complex cultural effects. The aim is to do so with sensitivity to complex cultural processes, yet also with rigorous research designs for conducting scientific studies that "do justice" to the analysis of cultural influences on human behavior.

F.G. Castro (✉)
Department of Psychology, University of Texas, El Paso, TX, USA
e-mail: fcastro4@utep.edu

N.J. Gildar
Counseling Psychology Program, School of Letters and Sciences,
Arizona State University, Tempe, AZ, USA
e-mail: ngildar@asu.edu

M.G. Vaughn and B.E. Perron (eds.), *Social Work Practice in the Addictions*,
Contemporary Social Work Practice, DOI 10.1007/978-1-4614-5357-4_9,
© Springer Science+Business Media New York 2013

Concepts of Culture and Race and Ethnicity

Concepts and Definitions of Culture

"Culture" is a multifaceted and pervasive construct which is as old as human civilization. Culture is a human construction—a product of human experience. Culture emerged when humans organized their perceptions of the environment, recorded their observations and used language to communicate to others their thoughts and feelings about the world (Roberts, 2003). "Culture" consists of beliefs, practices, values and other "world views." Ostensibly, the beliefs, practices, and values that were most adaptive for survival were preserved and passed along from parents to children (Shiraev & Levy, 2010).

Culture has been defined in over 100 ways (Baldwin & Lindsley, 1994), although collectively these definitions echo certain core themes. These themes are that: (a) culture is constructed by a people and emerges from the social and ecological environment in which people live; (b) cultural knowledge and skills are transmitted from elders to children; (c) culture confers people with a sense of "peoplehood" and of belonging; (d) culture provides norms and expectations regarding socially acceptable behaviors; (e) culture is a distinctive human capacity for adapting to life's circumstances; (f) culture evolves across time; (g) cultural practices include traditions and customs that emerge when a community develops adaptive coping responses to environmental challenges; and (h) cultural adaptations to a new environment include *changes* in beliefs, attitudes, values, and norms that promote a group's survival within the new environment. Thus, culture consists of a system of communications—shared symbols and meanings that are utilized by members of a given ethnic group or community. Given its complexity, often the deepest facets of a culture are captured through folk art, music, and drama (McGoldrick & Giordano, 1996). A fitting metaphor for culture is that: "Culture is an ocean that shelters the diverse creatures of the sea—it exists everywhere around them, yet they seldom notice it. Nonetheless, were this ocean to disappear, all of these creatures would die." And so it is with people and their culture.

Race and Ethnicity in Cultural Formulations Within the USA

The constructs of race and ethnicity are typically measured as categorical variables based on a respondent's self-classification (U.S. Census Bureau, 2008). As one important distinction, the U.S. Census distinguishes "racial" categories from "ethnic" categories, i.e. being Hispanic (U.S. Census Bureau, 2008). However, considerable variation exists in the conceptualization and measurement of race and ethnicity (Bonham, 2005). Scholars have argued that race is *not* a biological construct, but rather, a sociocultural one (Smedley & Smedley, 2005). In many epidemiological studies, race is utilized as a categorical grouping variable for conducting group comparisons (Karasz & Singelis, 2010), as for example to examine health-related disparities across racial/ethnic groups (i.e., in comparing Hispanics/ Latinos and Blacks/African Americans with non-Hispanic White Americans). Such group comparisons, however, *do not explain* the underlying mechanisms that produce these differences. To further examine within-group variations, relevant cultural variables such as *level of acculturation* have been used as more refined indicators of within-group variability. As contrasted with the construct of race, *ethnicity* is primarily a cultural variable, and refers to "a common ancestry through which individuals have evolved shared values and customs. It is deeply rooted to the family to which it is transmitted" (McGoldrick & Giordano, 1996, p. 1).

Aptly describing "culture" is not a simple task, although scholars have attempted to create relevant and meaningful conceptualizations to promote a better understanding of culture. For example, Chao and Moon (2005) introduced a cultural framework that they call the "cultural mosaic." Under this organizing framework, a given person's identity consists of a unique combination of discrete elements (cultural tiles), such as *demographic elements* (e.g., age, race, ethnicity, gender), *geographic elements* (e.g., urban–rural status, region or country), and *associative elements* (e.g., family, religion, profession). As an extension of this framework, an *ethnic group* consists of a collective of individuals who share many common elements (e.g., a common heritage, religion or ethnic identity). This mosaic may appear quite intricate, although on closer inspection it exhibits a coherent and identifiable structure. Thus, this integrative systemic approach captures in part the complexities of culture, as these exist within their natural ecological context.

Ecodevelopmental Models and Conditions

Bronfenbrenner (1986) proposed a systems model that describes a hierarchy of social systems, including family systems, as these systems directly or indirectly affect child development. This model emphasizes various levels of ecological influences that range from macro-level societal factors, such as social policies and community norms, to micro-level individual factors, such as a child's temperament. In a contemporary elaboration of Bronfenbrenner's systems model, Pantin and collaborators proposed a modified *ecodevelopmental model* (Pantin et al., 2003; Szapocznik & Coatsworth, 1999). These investigators present additional ideas about the role of cultural factors, such as immigration stressors, as well as ecological factors, as these influence the development of minority-culture families and their children.

In a similar ecological analysis, Wandersman and Nation (1998) introduced an *environmental stress model* that examines the influences on psychological wellbeing of four types of environmental stressors that occur within urban neighborhoods. These are types of environmental stressors are: (a) cataclysmic events, (b) stressful life events, (c) daily hassles, and (d) ambient stressors. Higher levels of exposure to these stressors are "associated with negative effects on mental and physical health" (Wandersman & Nation, 1998). Within this model, *ambient stressors* consist of environmental stressors that, "interfere with important goals or affect physical or psychological health," e.g., noise and crowding (Wandersman & Nation, 1998). Chronic ambient stressors can deplete a person's coping resources, leading to psychological problems, such as youth behavioral problems.

From a family strengthening perspective, one may ask, "What factors promote *resilience* and *survival* in the midst of ongoing exposures to such toxic neighborhood stressors?" Wandersman and Nation (1998) identified these *resource factors* within two domains: (a) *individual factors,* such as resourcefulness in new situations and school achievement and (b) *community factors,* such as supportive relationships with other community members, e.g., church leaders and teachers. In particular, community-based supportive relationships involve the presence of: (a) caring adults and role models who "have made it;" (b) the presence of social bonding and social supports; (c) exposure to positive influences such as adult–child connections that create a safe setting in which a child can develop and achieve (Wandersman & Nation, 1998).

In summary, ecodevelopmental models such as these highlight the effects of environmental and interpersonal contexts on human behavior. One of the several environmental "surrounding" conditions may be regarded as a *contextual factor.* A contextual factor can operate as *moderator* of effects, as for example, in the differential effect of *gender norms* on the onset of a disease that differs in prevalence rates by gender, e.g., rates of depression, where it is well established that women, as compared with men, experience higher rates of depression.

Cultural Factors and Dimensions of Culture

Castro and Hernández-Alarcón (2002) have identified and described a set of cultural variables or factors that are mentioned frequently within the literature on Hispanic/Latino[1] health, and also regarding the health of other racial/ethnic minority populations of the USA. Table 9.1 presents these variables. In cross-cultural psychology, some of these cultural variables have been described as dimensions of culture (Shiraev & Levy, 2010). The analysis of these dimensions aids in describing core features of a cultural or subcultural group. Here we examine three of these

---

[1] In the year 2009, the US population numbered 307.01 million. For 2009, the Hispanic/Latino population of the United States numbered 48.42 million, which constituted 15.77% of the US population, thus making Hispanics/Latinos the largest racial/ethnic population of the USA (U.S. Census Bureau, 2011). Also in 2009, Blacks/African Americans numbered 39.64 million, constituting 12.91% of the US population, and constituting the second largest racial/ethnic population. We will use the terms "Latino" and "Hispanic" interchangeably, based on the dual usage that occurs within the contemporary literature. Similarly, we will also use the terms "Black" and "African American," interchangeably. Unless specified, "Latinos" will refer to people living in the USA, primarily Mexican Americans, Chicanos or Chicanas who live in the Southwestern United States, as well as Puerto Ricans (both from the Island of Puerto Rico and from the mainland United States), and Cubans, as well as other Hispanics/Latinos which include: Colombians, Guatemalans, Nicaraguans, and other immigrants and naturalized persons from Central America and South America.

Table 9.1 Cultural variables

Cultural factor/variable	Description
Acculturation	Lifeways including beliefs and behaviors that conform to the mainstream U.S. American way of life
Afrocentricity (or Africentricity)	Cultural orientation and pride towards being Black/African American
Biculturalism	A well-developed capacity to function effectively within two distinct cultures based on the acquisition of the norms, values, and behavioral routines of the dominant culture as well as those of one's own group
Cultural flex	Capacity to function effectively and to "shuttle" adaptively between two cultures
Enculturation	An orientation towards learning about one's ethnic culture
Ethnic affirmation and belonging	An expression of personal identification as a member of an ethnic minority group
Ethnic identity	Personal identification with one's ethnic cultural group or group of origin
Ethnic pride	The expression of a positive attitude, a sense of belonging, and gratification from belonging to one's ethnic, cultural, or national group
Familism	Strong family orientation, involvement, and loyalty
Field independence	A "self-oriented" preference or style in ways of thinking and in ways of approaching work and tasks
Field sensitivity	An "others oriented" preference or style in ways of thinking and ways of relating to others
Individualism–collectivism	A cognitive and behavioral orientations involving a tendency to prefer an individualistic, self-oriented style, or conversely, to prefer a group-oriented collectivistic interpersonal style
Machismo	A traditional Latino gender role orientation that accepts male dominance as a proper or acceptable form of male identity and conduct
Marianismo	A traditional Latino female role orientation that accepts motherly nurturance, and the demure and pure identity of a virgin (Virgin Mary) as a proper form of female identity and conduct
Modernism	An emphasis on innovation and accepting change and modern beliefs and behaviors as being better and preferred ways to live one's life
Personalismo	Preference for personalized attention and courtesy in relating to others
Respeto	Emphasis on respect and attention to issues of social position in interpersonal relations, as for example, respect for elders
Simpatia	A deferential posture towards family members, and other in efforts to maintain harmony in family and in interpersonal relations. Traits of agreeableness, respect, and politeness are core aspects of *simpatia*
Spirituality	A belief in a higher source of strength and well being, and a related appreciation for natural and beneficial aspects of the world

(continued)

Table 9.1 (continued)

Cultural factor/variable	Description
Tiu lien (loss of face)	Among Asian Americans, especially among those who are more traditional, "loss of face" involves the shame of improper behavior or a failing to live up to social obligations. Engaging in proper conduct helps to "save face'" and avoid this loss of face
Traditionalism	An emphasis and value for maintaining and adhering to established and often conservative beliefs and behaviors. These customs and traditions are seen as appropriate and preferred ways to live life

Modified from Castro and Hernández-Alarcón (2002)

dichotomous dimensions: (a) individualism–collectivism, (b) modernism–traditionalism, and (c) acculturation–enculturation (levels of acculturation).

Individualism Vs. Collectivism

Many Latinos and other racial/ethnic minority groups value certain relational styles, such as family unity, i.e., familism/*familismo*, and harmony in interpersonal relationships, i.e., *simpatia*. These values regarding interpersonal relations are associated with the cultural dimension of: interdependence (collectivism) (Oyserman, Coon, & Kemmelmeier, 2002) vs. personal autonomy (individualism). To this dimension of individualism–collectivism, Triandis (1996) added the dimension of "vertical–horizontal," to describe distinct types of *cultural syndromes*. The vertical dimension (e.g., vertical collectivist vs. a vertical individualist) refers to variations in types of *power*, while the horizontal dimension refers to variations in types of *equity*. In research on variations of individualism and collectivism as observed among certain countries, the vertical–horizontal dimension provides a more detailed framework for understanding national cultural attitudes and practices that involve individualism and collectivism (Shiraev & Levy, 2010).

Modernism Vs. Traditionalism

Traditionalism refers to an individual's or group's adherence to conservative "old world" familial norms and values. This typically involves an acceptance of "old-fashioned lifeways" that have survived across generations based partly on their utility for promoting group survival and in maintaining the cultural group's sense of "peoplehood" (Castro & Coe, 2007; McGoldrick & Giordano, 1996). In addition, traditionalism often consists of conservative cultural norms that emphasize a strict adherence to restrictive cultural beliefs, behaviors and norms, including a resistance to change (Castro & Coe, 2007). However, expressions of traditionalism can vary across cultural groups, as in the use of alcohol and drugs, where in some traditional subcultural groups alcohol use is strictly forbidden or highly discouraged. For instance, alcohol use is strictly forbidden among devout Muslims, whereas among some Native American tribes in the Southwest, the ceremonial and nonaddictive use of peyote, a psychoactive drug, is a core aspect of cultural rituals and allowed among male members of these tribal communities (Julien, Advokat, & Comaty, 2008; McKim, 2003).

Traditionalism also sanctions prescribed gender role expectations of behaviors that are considered appropriate based on gender. Such traditional expectations, norms and behaviors are usually more salient within agrarian societies, which also typically endorse collectivistic forms of familial and social relations. Traditional gender norms tend to be *prescriptive* and also *restrictive*, as contrasted with modernistic open-ended and more *permissive* gender role expectations that are observed within modern Westernized societies (Castro & Garfinkle, 2003; Costa, Terracciano, & McCrae, 2001; Schwartz, Montgomery, & Briones, 2006). Perhaps due to this restrictiveness, these conservative traditional norms when directed from parents to their children tend to confer protection against antisocial behaviors, including the early use of tobacco, alcohol and drugs, so long as the youth obeys and adheres to these conservative traditional norms (Cuadrado & Lieberman, 1998; Gil, Wagner, & Vega, 2000).

For this dimension of traditionalism–modernism, among specific subcultural groups and within a society, an abiding tension exists between the cultural norms that favor change, i.e., *modernism,* as contrasted with the norms that favor adherence to long-standing traditions, i.e., *traditionalism.* Individual members of a family, community and nation may thus disagree among themselves regarding which of these norms are best in order to live "the good life." Accordingly, among most minority people and their families, variations exist in their acceptance of these conservative beliefs, attitudes and norms that favor preserving traditions, relative to those that favor modernistic change.

Acculturation, Enculturation, and Biculturalism

Acculturation is a worldwide phenomenon that occurs when individuals and families migrate from one sociocultural environment to another, usually in quest of better living conditions and opportunities (Lopez-Class, Castro, & Ramirez, 2011). Often, acculturation into a new ecological environment covaries with upward socioeconomic mobility, although in some cases it covaries with downward sociocultural mobility. These differences in socioeconomic upward mobility may result from exposure to specific opportunities or to specific barriers, such as racial or other forms of discrimination, including xenophobia, an "attitudinal, affective, and behavioral prejudice towards immigrants and those perceived to be foreign" (Yakushko, 2009, p. 43). In the USA, and primarily among immigrating groups or individuals, acculturation refers to a process of sociocultural learning, change, and adaptation. Within the USA this includes the acquisition of mainstream American cultural norms, values, behaviors, and skills, including leaning to speak English

(Trimble, 1995). It is noteworthy that *acculturative change* does not only occur during cross-national migration, but also during migration *within* a nation's geographic boundaries, such as in migration from rural to urban environments (Portes & Rumbaut, 1996).

At the individual and group levels, cultural adaptation and integration into a new society or to a new environment typically involves the acquisition of new *cultural traits* or *competencies*. These include: (a) acquiring *new knowledge* about local and regional laws and social customs; (b) learning *new skills* including occupational and linguistic skills; (c) establishing *new networks* of neighbors, acquaintances, friends, and other sources of social support; and (d) acquiring *new values, norms,* and *behaviors* that are prevalent or valued within the new cultural environment. For immigrant children, the acquisition of these competencies typically occurs as a natural part of their youth development, and often occurs at a faster rate than among their parents. These parent–child generational differences that occur during the process of acculturation have been described as "differential acculturation" (Szapocznik & Kurtines, 1989). Moreover, this change can be stressful, i.e., *acculturative stress*, depending on the ecological environment and the available opportunities or barriers under which this change occurs. Acculturation stress occurs when a person faces threats to their well-being within the new community or environment (Farver, Narang, & Bhadha, 2002; Yakushko, 2009).

How May Racial and Ethnic Factors Be Associated with Addictive Behaviors?

Addictive Behaviors in Minority Youth Development

As with many complex human behaviors, addictive behaviors occur and develop within the *context* of a person's environmental ecology. Thus, the meaning of a compulsive, repetitive, and destructive behavior depends in part on the local community's acceptance or prohibition of that pattern of behavior. Based on DSM-IV diagnostic criteria, there are two forms of addictive behaviors, (a) substance abuse, and (b) substance dependence. *Substance abuse* refers to a, "maladaptive pattern of substance use, leading to clinically significant impairment or distress" (American Psychiatric Association, 1994, p. 182). Substance abuse includes a failure to fulfill major role obligations, substance use in hazardous situations, the occurrence of legal problems, and continued use despite the occurrence of social or occupational problems.

Beyond substance abuse, *substance dependence* refers to, the presence of these criteria for abuse, with the addition of three or more of seven other symptoms: tolerance, withdrawal, use of larger amounts than intended, persistent desire for the substance along with unsuccessful attempts to cut down, considerable time spent pursuing the substance of choice, a reduction or impairment in social or occupational activities, and continued use despite the occurrence of physical or psychological problems (American Psychiatric Association, 1994). Thus, relative to substance abuse, substance dependence is a more extreme form of addiction. This conception of addiction provides a medical psychiatric view of the adverse consequences resulting from behaviors that involve excessive substance use, and thus which is considered to be an "addictive behavior." From these definitions, as a basis of maladaptive substance use, a major question is "How do cultural factors operate as antecedents, mediators or moderators of these forms of addictive behavior?"

Changing Concepts of Addiction

In May of 2013 the fifth edition of the DSM will be published, and within this latest edition significant changes to the diagnostic criteria of substance use and addictive behaviors are expected. For example in the fifth edition, the addictions will include not only substance-related disorders but also non-substance related addictions, such as gambling, which is currently listed as an "Impulse Control Disorder—Not Elsewhere Classified" (American Psychiatric Association, 2010). The DSM classification of substance-related diagnoses is anticipated to change from "Substance-Related Disorders," to "Substance Use and Addictive Disorders." Moreover, it is anticipated that the DSM will move away from the terms substance abuse and dependence and towards a more singular diagnosis of a "Substance Use Disorder." In other words, the DSM's conceptualization of *additive behaviors* will no longer be limited to substance abuse and will include a broader diagnostic lens from which addictions will be viewed. In fact, it is interesting to point out that the current edition of the DSM does not include any diagnostic section with the term "addiction."

Discrimination/Oppression/Barriers

Among racial/ethnic minority individuals and groups, perceived discrimination has been associated with psychological distress and with emotional responses that include anger and anxiety (Clark, Anderson, Clark, & Williams, 1999; Yakushko, 2009). Responses to this emotional distress can include coping via the use of alcohol, legal and illegal drugs (Castro, Brook, Brook, & Rubenstone, 2006; Felix-Ortiz & Newcomb, 1995; Nieri, Kulis, & Marsiglia, 2007; Vega, Gil, & Zimmerman, 1993). Coping with discrimination to reduce stress via the use of alcohol and other drugs has been described as an "escapist" form of substance use (Martin, Tuch, & Roman, 2003). Under a stress-coping paradigm such behavior may be regarded as *maladaptive*, where a more adaptive form of coping with the stressors of discrimination involves seeking social support from family and friends. These findings suggest that minority parents and members of the family can and should communicate actively and often with their children, while offering them social support as one form of parental influence that can prevent substance use in response to distress (Kelly, Comello, & Hunn, 2002). A more complete understanding of the associations of youth emotional distress and substance use can aid in the development of more efficacious prevention interventions. Such interventions may provide parents with insights on how discrimination and acculturation-related conflicts can be stressful, and how parents can support their child in ways that discourage substance use.

Social Justice Issues: Racial/Ethnic Disparities in Arrests and Incarceration

It is often noted that minorities comprise a disproportionate percentage of prison inmates and convicted criminals. However, what percentage do racial and ethnic minorities actually represent among convicted felons, and what are possible explanations for any observed race-related disparities? First, according to U.S. Census, 72.4% of the US population is non-Hispanic white, i.e., Caucasian. In addition, in 2003 it was estimated that 3.2% of America's adults (age 18 and above) were incarcerated, or were still involved with the criminal justice system, such being on probation. Although racial/ethnic minorities, i.e., nonwhites, only constitute about 25% of the total US population, studies have shown that the majority of individuals in jails or prisons are racial/ethnic minorities, at a rate between 62–57% (Primm, Osher, & Gomez, 2005). Moreover, researchers have also described the racial breakdown of this incarcerated nonwhite population: African Americans (46%), Hispanics (16%), Whites (36%), American Indians or Alaskan Natives (1%), and Asian Americans or Pacific Islanders (1%) (Primm et al., 2005). Thus, African Americans and Hispanics are overrepresented among those who are committed to jails or prisons.

It has also been documented that racial/ethnic minorities are more likely to be unfairly treated within the criminal justice system. For instance, close to 75% of men that have been wrongfully convicted of a crime are either African American or Hispanic, and minorities represent the bulk of individuals, 55%, on death row (Porter, 2009). Such findings may lead one to wonder how and why minority status would be associated with criminal behavior. Among various explanations, it is possible that higher rates of criminality are associated with a biased and prejudiced legal system. For example, Keen and Jacobs (2009) found that racial arrests and imprisonments were higher in states where there was a smaller than average African-American population. Keen and Jacobs (2009) assert, along with other researchers, that these racial disparities in rates of arrests and imprisonments may be influenced by the "minority threat" effect, which occurs when members of the dominant culture group believe they have special privileges and that they must protect these from growing groups of minorities. This form of racial intolerance is difficult to address, although many people of color are observant and sensitive to these social inequalities.

Frameworks for Understanding Culture and Context in the Addictions

Models of Acculturation with Implications for Substance Use and Abuse

The construct of acculturation has a long history in the study of immigrant and minority populations. The process of acculturation appears important in the occurrence of substance use and abuse among Hispanic/Latino, African American, Asian American, and Native American youths and families. Acculturative change towards mainstream American culture has been associated with increased risks of alcohol, tobacco, and illegal drug use (Vega, Alderete, Kolody, & Aguilar-Gaxiola, 1998). In several studies, higher levels of acculturation to the mainstream US American culture and society have been associated with: more frequent substance use, greater quantities of use, and higher rates of lifetime use of hard drugs (Amaro, Whitaker, Coffman, & Heeren, 1980; Gil et al., 2000; Brook, Whiteman, Balka, Win, & Gursen, 1998; Felix-Ortiz, & Newcomb, 1995). Accordingly, we will examine aspects of acculturation, with implications for substance use among racial/ethnic minority populations.

Unidimensional Model of Acculturation

Acculturation was originally formulated by anthropologists as a group-level phenomenon involving a cultural group's change and adaptation (Redfield, Linton, & Herskovitz, 1936). As noted previously, acculturation consists of a sociocultural process in which members of one cultural group adopt the beliefs and behaviors of another group, where this includes changes in language, socioeconomic status, and/or cultural orientation, and including changes in values and attitudes (Berry, 2005). During the 1980s, the measurement-focused approach to acculturation pursued by psychologists (Cuellar, Arnold, & Gonzalez, 1995; Cuellar, Harris, & Jasso, 1980), introduced a change in the conceptualization of acculturation by conceptualizing and measuring it as a *personal trait* that relates to individual changes upon migration to a new host culture or environment (Farver et al., 2002; Lopez-Class et al., 2011).

Early conceptions of acculturation described it as a linear, unidirectional process involving the eventual loss of elements of the immigrant's original culture, i.e., language, customs, and traditions, upon adopting the lifeways of the new host culture or society (Ryder, Alden, & Paulhus, 2000). In this regard, the term *assimilation* has been used to refer to the final outcome, with this being the complete loss of ethnic identity resulting from a total immersion into the new host culture, i.e., a "melting pot" model.

Two-Factor Models of Acculturation

More recently, an *orthogonal acculturation model* was proposed that describes variations in acculturation and related cultural identity formation that would occur along two dimensions: (a) an orientation towards a new host culture, i.e., *acculturation*, and (b) an orientation towards the culture of origin, i.e., *enculturation* (Cuellar et al., 1995; Marin & Gamboa, 1996; Oetting & Beauvais, 1991). It is now well recognized that the acquisition of elements of a new culture does not necessarily produce an automatic loss of elements from the culture of origin (Rogler, 1994; Rogler, Cortes, & Malgady, 1991), thus challenging the major premise of the "melting pot" model. For example, a Spanish-speaking 12-year-old child whose family migrates from Mexico to the USA will not necessarily lose his or her ability to speak Spanish after several years of living within the USA and as they learn to speak English. Any reduction in Spanish-speaking skills or behaviors, if occurring, may instead be the consequence of other identity-related issues, such as suppressing their use of Spanish to avoid discrimination.

Berry (1994, 1997, 2005) is the major proponent of this two-factor (orthogonal) model that describes four acculturation outcomes: (a) *marginalization* (low affiliation with both cultures); (b) *separation* (high origin-culture affiliation, low new-culture affiliation); (c) *assimilation* (high new-culture affiliation, low origin-culture affiliation); and (d) *integration* (high affiliation with both cultures). Despite its improvement over the original unidimensional model of acculturation, this orthogonal model has also been criticized, with one concern being that these four forms of acculturative change do not actually occur as postulated (Rudmin, 2003).

Today, more advanced conceptions of acculturation acknowledge the role of *context* as an important determinant of the acculturation process (Lara, Gamboa, Kahramanian, Morales, & Hayes Bautista, 2005). Contextual factors, such as one's place of residence, the size and form of a family unit, the school system, can affect the manner and course in which the process of acculturation occurs and progresses. This consideration has prompted studies that utilize various factor mixture model analyses, e.g., latent class or latent profile analyses (Flaherty, 2010; Lubke & Muthen, 2005) to detect latent *acculturation groups* and their differential trajectories of acculturative change across time (Castro, Marsiglia, Kulis, & Kellison, 2010).

From this perspective, the occurrence of variations in trajectories of sociocultural and socioeconomic mobility across time has been described as *segmented assimilation* (Abraido-Lanza et al., 2005; Castro, Marsiglia, et al., 2010). Segmented assimilation refers to the differential assimilation trajectories that are experienced by diverse immigrant individuals and groups. *Segmented Assimilation Theory* (Portes & Zhou, 1993) postulates three outcomes from this process of assimilation: (a) acculturation change towards the mainstream White American culture, coupled with upward socioeconomic mobility (upward assimilation); (b) acculturation change albeit with downward socioeconomic mobility into an underclass (downward assimilation); and (c) resistance to acculturation and to assimilation into the mainstream society subsequently leading to some degree of downward assimilation

(Portes & Rumbaut, 1996). Downward assimilation is believed to occur among immigrant groups that migrate to a new environment while having low levels of *social capital* (few sources of social support), and/or low levels of *human capital* (low levels of education, income and other professional resources) (Portes & Rumbaut, 2001). Thus as a result of having low levels of "marketable" skills and resources, these immigrants are less competitive within the new cultural environment and society.

Ethnic Identity with Implications for Substance Use

Overview of Identity Issues

In America during this first decade of the twenty-first century, the construct of *ethnic identity* has become more complex and diversified. One consequence of the Civil Rights Movement of the 1960s and the reduction in overt racial segregation, was an increase in racially mixed marriages beginning in the 1970s (McGoldrick & Giordano, 1996). This cultural change in the USA produced children of mixed racial and ethnic backgrounds who today may face more complex issues in their identity formation (Marks, Flannery, & Garcia Coll, 2011).

Ethnic identity refers to ways in which a youth identifies with his or her ethnic group, which involves a process of exploration and commitment (Erickson, 1968). Phinney (1990, 1993) proposed a three-stage model of ethnic identity development, which involves the three stages of: (a) *unexamined ethnic identity*, (b) *ethnic identity search*, and (c) *ethnic identity achievement*. In Stage 1, *unexamined ethnic identity*, the adolescent has an unexplored identity, and accepts without question the values and attitudes communicated by the mainstream culture, including negative views of the youth's own ethnic group. In Stage 2, *ethnic identity search*, the ethnic youth develops an awareness of own ethnic identity, along with a sense of dissonance when experiencing a discriminatory personal or social event. This includes a sense of anger from an awareness that certain values that are espoused by the dominant culture group are discriminatory towards one's own racial/ethnic group. This stage is followed by Stage 3, *ethnic identity achievement*, in which the youth develops a more defined and confident sense of their own ethnicity.

Today, ethnic identity formation may involve an identification with multiple groups including: (a) with one's own ethnic group, (b) with the mainstream group, and (c) in some instances with a generic *pan-ethnic group*, such as being an "Asian American" or an "Hispanic" (Chung, Kim, & Abreu, 2004; Marks et al., 2011). Some evidence has accrued which suggests that mixed racial/ethnic youth face greater obstacles in youth development, and as a group they may also experience higher rates of some psychiatric disorders, although the evidence for this is mixed (Shih & Sanchez, 2005).

In this regard, adolescents having low self-worth, unclear value orientations, and undefined or ambiguous life goals may experience *identity confusion* and related feelings of emptiness, worthlessness, and alienation. Some theories of youth development have postulated that a diffuse and marginalized personal identity prompts adolescents to affiliate with deviant peers (Andrews & Hops, 2010; Lettieri, Sayers, & Pearson, 1980). Such peer affiliations have been associated subsequently with experimentation in early adolescence with alcohol and cigarettes, which may later progress to regular and heavier use of alcohol and tobacco, and subsequently progressing to the use of illegal drugs (Castro et al., 2007).

In examining the process of acculturation as it may influence identity formation, Schwartz et al. (2006) conceptualized identity as a *complex construct* that consists of several components including: (a) *personal identity*—personal goals, values, and beliefs, (b) *social identity*—group identification and affiliation, and (c) *cultural identity*, which is a subset of social identity. Cultural identity refers to a youth's solidarity and connectedness with their own cultural or ethnic group. These investigators assert that personal identity, "anchors" the person. For immigrant and minority youths, the development of a stable personal, social, and cultural identity, *identity integration*, appears characterized by the capacity for effective coping with cultural conflicts. Ostensibly, a stable and integrated *bilingual/bicultural identity* likely promotes the development of certain skills for coping with *dialectical cultural conflicts*, i.e., for resolving conflicts involving individualism vs. collectivism, or traditionalism vs. modernism (La Fromboise, Coleman, & Gerton, 1993).

Bicultural Identity, Ethnic Pride, and Resilience

A dual-cultural identity, that is, *bicultural competence* (La Fromboise et al., 1993) has been described as the capacity for *cultural flex*—the ability to "shuttle" or transition between majority and minority cultures (La Fromboise et al., 1993; Ramirez, 1999). This bicultural orientation includes positive skills and attitudes towards both cultures, ostensibly fostering positive emotions and a positive self-concept (Izard, 2002; Tugade & Frederickson, 2004). From a *cultural strengths* perspective, ethnic minority youth who develop a well-defined *ethnic identity schema* (Alvarez & Helms, 2001) along with *ethnic pride* are regarded to have a greater *intercultural competency* (Torres & Rollock, 2007), the capacity for active problem solving, including adaptive ways to avoid risk behaviors, including early alcohol and tobacco use (Brook et al., 1998). Racial/ethnic minority youth who recognize their ethnic identity and express a positive self-appraisal, i.e., *ethnic pride*, despite their minority status, may be expressing *resiliency* (Klohnen, 1996; Masten, 2001), and *self-confidence*, forms of *personal agency* that operate as a resources that can strengthen a youth's resolve to refuse or to avoid offers or temptations to use tobacco, alcohol, and illegal drugs. As one example, research with American Indian youth has shown that ethnic pride is associated with stronger antidrug norms (Kulis, Napoli, & Marsiglia, 2002).

Despite experiencing psychological distress and conflict, mixed-racial identity youth can develop adaptive ways of coping with temptations to use drugs. Effectively resolving conflicts involving acculturation stress, complex identity issues, and discrimination may lead to the development of a unique and complex yet integrated personal identity, one that transcends struggle and evolves towards personal growth based on a full appreciation for the richness and complexity of one's dual racial–ethnic heritage. In this regard, an abiding question is, "What aspects of ethnic identity formation may operate as potent *protective factors* for youth, as these factors can protect them against negative developmental outcomes?"

The Risk and Protective Factor Paradigm

Substance use often begins in adolescence, and thus research studies have examined factors that may constitute risk and protective factors for the onset of substance use in early adolescence (Hawkins, Catalano, & Miller, 1992). Researchers have identified several risk and protective factors for substance use. Taylor defines a risk factor as a variable that increases the likelihood that a person will initiate the use a substance such as marijuana (Taylor, 2010, p. 604). Numerous studies have identified several life conditions as risk factors for substance use, and these include: a chaotic home life, parents who use or abuse substances or suffer with mental disorders, poor parenting, children having irritable temperaments (impulsivity, attention deficit disorder), oppositional and defiant behaviors, aggressive conduct, shy or aggressive behavior at school, poor academic performance, lack of social coping skills, associating with deviant peers, and approval of drug use that is communicated from significant others within their social environments (Taylor, 2010). Similarly, risk factors associated with alcohol consumption include alcohol use to reduce negative affect, being from a family that has a history of alcoholism, and being in a family in which alcohol is consumed to reduce negative affect, i.e., to feel better when under stress (Patrick, 2010).

In contrast to risk factors, *protective factors* are those that safeguard an individual from substance use, either currently or in the long term (Taylor, 2010, p. 605). Protective factors include cultural factors such as family support and familial norms that discourage the use of alcohol, tobacco, and other drugs. For instance, high levels of familism (called *familismo* in Spanish) appear to protect Hispanic youths from substance use perhaps in relation to the value placed on *simpatia* and *respeto*, relational styles that emphasize the importance of maintaining harmony in relations to parents and other family members. Similarly, in Asian cultures the tradition of respect for elders appears to protect Asian adolescents from substance use, because these adolescents may be disinclined to disobey rules and expectations that are set by their parents. Nonetheless, cultural values do not always operate as protective factors. For example, among substance users in drug abuse treatment, Wong and Longshore (2008) postulate that high *familismo*, which emphasizes the importance of family cohesiveness, can also make it more difficult for adult Hispanics to separate from their drug-using family and friends (Wong & Longshore, 2008). Thus, risk and protective factors need to be considered within the context of specific social and familial situations and ecological environments (Warner et al., 2006).

Shih, Miles, Tucker, Zhou, and D'Amico (2010) examined racial and ethnic differences in substance use among middle-school students. Using a sample from 16 different middle schools in Southern California ($n = 5,500$), these researchers examined differences in alcohol, cigarette, and marijuana use, and how they may be related to race and ethnicity. Their multiethnic sample included: White Americans (Caucasians), Hispanics, African Americans, and Asian/Pacific Islanders. Mixed-race adolescents were not included in this study. These investigators assessed lifetime and past-month use of several substances. Other measures addressed other important factors, such as individual, family, and school (Shih et al., 2010). Using path analytic models, these researchers found that the Hispanic students exhibited a *higher* likelihood of using drugs, as compared with their White American (Caucasian) peers (an odds ratio, OR = 1.58 for the past year). By contrast, Asian youths exhibited a *lower* likelihood of using any substance during the past year, when compared with White American youths (OR = 0.25). Additionally, this study found no statistically significant difference between the White American and African-American students (Shih et al., 2010).

In this regard, one emerging question from this study is why the Hispanic youths were *more* likely to use, whereas the Asian youths were *less* likely to use, when compared with the White American youths? First, it was found that drug use among Hispanic and Asian youths was significantly mediated by *resistance self-efficacy* (the belief they could resist drugs if given the opportunity to use), and by *negative expectancies* towards the use of a given substance (Shih et al., 2010). Additionally, for the Asian youths lower substance use was also mediated by family factors, which included *parental respect* and less substance use by older siblings. In other words, among Asian youths, the family unit operated as a protective factor against substance use. This study is just one of the many that attempt to explain variations in substance use among different racial and ethnic groups. Clearly, understanding the factors that influence youth substance use is not a simple endeavor, given that this involves a complex process that includes several interacting factors.

From 25 years of data as observed for several cohorts of adolescents, Johnson and colleagues have indicated that two of the most potent *protective factors*, those that are negatively correlated with the use of a particular substance are: (a) *perceived risks*, youth perceptions regarding impairments to own health that are associated with the use of a particular drug such as cocaine, and (b) *perceived disapproval*, youth perceptions of the disapproval they would receive from parents or peers as a consequence of their use of a particular substance (Bachman, O'Malley, Schulenberg, Johnson, Bryant, & Merline, 2002). Similarly, *negative youth attitudes* towards the use of alcohol, tobacco and illegal drugs, and *expectations of harm* from substance use may contribute to a preparedness to avoid the use of these substances. Such attitudes when coupled with *self-efficacy* for refusing these substances portend a low risk of developing an addiction to these substances (Hecht et al., 2003; Sturges & Rogers, 1996). Moreover, among racial/ethnic minority adolescents, the motivational effects of *ethnic pride enhancement* and of *cultural traditions* are cultural processes that may offer "value added" competencies that would be protective in resisting the use alcohol, tobacco, or illegal drugs (Castro et al., 2007; Torres & Rollock, 2007).

Towards a Framework for Integrating Culture into Research and Interventions on the Addictions

Considerations for More Culturally Informed Research

The prior research suggests that the effects of culture on the behavior or racial/ethnic minority youth manifests itself via a process that exerts its influences within three domains: (a) the *individual domain* of the person (beliefs, attitudes, values, expectations, norms); (b) the *interpersonal domain* involving social relations with siblings, parents, other family, and peers; and (c) the *environmental domain* (community factors including ambient stressors, community norms, civic rules, and sociopolitical effects, including racial discrimination) (Wandersman & Nation, 1998). An examination of the aforementioned multilevel relationships, as informed by the complex effects of culture, will require novel research designs that allow a deep-structure analysis (Resnicow, Soler, Braithwait, Ahluwalia, & Butler, 2000) of cultural effects on the initiation and development of substance use, abuse, and other addictive behaviors. Regarding this approach, we offer a few observations about research approaches that are needed for the design and conduct of culturally responsive and also scientifically rigorous research with racial/ethnic populations.

Community-Based Participatory Research

Culturally responsive research can be developed by using a community-based participatory approach in which a planned research study requests input and advice from members of the local cultural community to ensure proper conceptualization, operationalizations and interpretation of research constructs and variables, as grounded within the local community (Dickens & Watkins, 1999; Minkler & Wallerstein, 2003). These approaches have been used successfully in several drug use research studies (e.g., Gosin, Dustman, Drapeau, & Harthun, 2003). The inclusion of community leaders, *key informants* and *stakeholders,* in the design and development of a research study that is also scientifically rigorous, gives voice to the local community, while also informing the proposed study of "real-world" considerations as voiced by local community residents (Parsai, Castro, Marsiglia, Harthun, & Valdez, 2011).

Qualitative and Mixed Methods Designs

As noted previously, the use of novel yet rigorous research designs will aid in examining the rich and complex effects of culture and cultural factors in the study of addictive behaviors, as these occur among diverse racial/ethnic minority populations.

This section presents methodological issues in the use of qualitative and mixed methods methodologies to conduct more probing and informative research studies.

Qualitative Approaches

Qualitative approaches emphasize the need for depth of analysis in the study of culture, as it affects the lives of diverse subcultural groups. Such depth of analysis is necessary to, "tell the full story" of these peoples' complex and intriguing lives. The in-depth study of persons' lives within the context of their local community and culture is facilitated by the well-planned use of various qualitative research methods. Among these, *focus groups* allow the analysis of group process that confers a deeper-level of analysis on a given a topic, e.g., parenting conflicts among Mexican heritage parents. Informative discussions can be elicited from group members' responses to a specific focus question, such as, "What issues do you face in communicating with your adolescent child about the use of alcohol?" Collective parental narratives obtained from a *purposive sample* of focus group participants can provide key ideas as perceived by representatives from a specific demographic group. Such responses aid in inductively discovering themes which can be derived from answers to a given focus question. Similarly, *in-depth interviews* that include open-ended questions provide the opportunity for a one-to-one, face-to-face dialogue that aids in understanding, "why people do what they do" (Karasz & Singelis, 2010, p. 911). From a more in-depth perspective, classical anthropological *ethnographies* provide the most comprehensive "real-world" analysis of the lives of actors as they operate within their native environments (Page & Singer, 2010). As this work is conducted via participant observation within participants' community or dwellings, such analyses are "fully contextualized" within these environments.

Some qualitative investigators have asserted that qualitative researchers, "stress the *socially constructed* nature of reality and also emphasize," "the value-laden nature of inquiry" (Denzin & Lincoln, 1994, p. 4). However, this approach which emphasizes the *constructionist* and *interpretive perspectives* may be at odds with the scientific approach which emphasizes *objectivity* and the avoidance of bias in the measurement and interpretation of research data. *Grounded theory* offers a more balanced approach that aims to capture the richness of qualitative inquiry, with a theory-driven, organized, and systematic qualitative approach that typifies scientific research. When using *grounded theory* the investigator organizes and encodes textual information via the use of *open coding, axial coding,* and *selective coding* (Straus & Corbin, 1998). These grounded theory procedures aid in giving form and structure to recorded text narratives, thus helping to conceptualize and interpret the contents from the narratives obtained, while also contributing towards theory building. In this regard, the in-depth analyses of life story narratives can offer deep insights into the mental and emotional lives of selected cases of participants, an approach that can "do justice" to the study of culture and its complexities. In contrast to conventional questionnaire studies, "qualitative approaches emphasize an in-depth understanding of the experiences and perspectives of research participants,

… [and such] discovery-oriented data from qualitative studies can creatively disrupt pat assumptions and provide a basis for the development of new culturally appropriate theories of psychological phenomenon" (Karasz & Singelis, 2010, p. 914).

Qualitative approaches, however, also present some distinct limitations. For example, in many qualitative studies it is difficult to conduct an unequivocal and specific synthesis and integration of textual evidence across cases or units of analysis. It has also been argued that scientifically oriented objective, reliable, and valid conclusions *cannot* be obtained from qualitative text analysis, due to its subjectivity and putative bias in data gathering and interpretation. In addition, it has also been argued that much qualitative analysis is affected by investigator bias, especially under an interpretive approach to inquiry, data gathering, and analysis (Karasz & Singelis, 2010).

Mixed Methods Approaches

Combined Qual-Quant (mixed methods) designs aim to capture the "best of both" forms of data/evidence, which, if well designed, can yield reliable and informative research results. Qual and Quant "data" or "evidence" can offer *complementary* information, the property of *complementarity*, whereby each form of data can offer unique and important types of information that can enrich a research study (Jick, 1979). If Qual-Quant data can be reliably integrated within studies of culture, this can offer the capacity for generating important outcomes that include: (a) the confirmatory testing of research hypotheses using conventional scientific deductive methodology, as well as offering, (b) an in-depth descriptive and discovery analyses via a qualitative inductive methodology. However, the reliable integration of text data and numeric data has posed perhaps the greatest challenge in the conduct of generative mixed methods research (Bryman, 2007).

Two basic approaches in mixed methods design methodology are to: (a) examine Qual-Quant data in phases, that is, *sequentially*, or (b) within a single phase, that is *concurrently*. Indeed, the major mixed methods research designs consist of variations on two dimensions: (a) *concurrent* vs. *sequential*, and (b) *exploratory* vs. *confirmatory*. From this framework, six major mixed methods research designs have been identified (Hanson, Creswell, Clark, Petska, & Creswell, 2005).

One criticism of the Mixed Methods Research approach (MMR) is described by the "Incompatibility Hypothesis," which asserts that it is *not* feasible to reliably synthesize verbal (textual) and quantitative (numeric) evidence because both forms of evidence are fundamentally incompatible (Karasz & Singelis, 2010). Conversely, the "Compatibility Hypothesis" argues that the objective scope and nature of inquiry remains consistent across paradigms (Karasz & Singelis, 2010). Thus, a central question is, "Is the compatibility hypothesis stronger than the incompatibility hypothesis?," where if so, then this supports the viability of conducting integrative mixed methods research. If a fully integrative mixed methods design can be developed which allows for a reliable and rigorous integration of text narrative data/evidence and numeric data, then this would form the basis for generating a rich and informative dataset that allows the exchange and integration of both forms of data (Castro, Kellison, Boyd, & Kopak, 2010). That is, with this integration as a core design feature, data gathering and data analytic methods can be synchronized to allow for this complete integration. Gelo and colleagues have asserted that the field of mixed methods research (MMR) has now advanced to the stage in which, "MMR may reasonably overcome the limitations of purely quantitative and purely qualitative approaches…[thus] providing a fruitful context for a more comprehensive psychological research" (Gelo, Braakman, & Benetka, 2008, p. 266).

Concluding Comments

Integrative approaches to theory, research design, data analysis, and interpretation can aid in understanding the influences of "culture" on human behavior, and in particular, on addictive behaviors. We recognize that culture is a complex multidimensional construct which is difficult to capture via simple numeric measures. Accordingly, by *deconstructing* the actual experience of culture into its core dimensions and cultural elements, we can begin to examine in depth the influences of specific cultural factors on targeted health-related outcomes. We can also do so by incorporating these factors into theoretically driven models that can test hypotheses and generate new knowledge about the unified effects of several of these cultural factors. Multivariate quantitative methods provide a powerful tool for confirmatory analysis of certain cultural effects. As a complement to these multivariate quantitative analyses, well-designed qualitative research study and data analyses can aid in capturing the rich complexity of culture, although significant challenges arise in reliably integrating evidence that is derived from both forms of data/evidence. Today mixed methods research designs and methodologies provide new and more rigorous approaches for the study of cultural influences (Gelo et al., 2008), with methods that allow the integration of qualitative and quantitative data into a unified research approach. Research investigators may now use theory-driven and well-designed integrative mixed methods methodologies, to aid in concurrently generating both confirmatory and explanatory outcomes, to better inform the study of cultural influences on addictive behaviors among racial/ethnic minority populations.

References

Abriado-Lanza, A. F., Chao, M. T., & Florez, K. R. (2005). Do healthy behaviors decline with greater acculturation?: Implications for the Latino mortality paradox. *Social Science & Medicine, 61,* 1243–1255.

Alvarez, A. N., & Helms, J. E. (2001). Radical identity and reflected appraisals as influences on Asian Americans' racial adjustment. *Cultural Diversity and Ethnic Minority Psychology, 7,* 217–231.

Amaro, H., Whitaker, R., Coffman, G., & Heeren, T. (1980). Acculturation and marijuana and cocaine use: Findings from HHANES 1982–84. *American Journal of Public Health, 80*(Suppl.), 54–60.

American Psychiatric Association. (1994). *Diagnostic and statistical manual of mental disorders* (4th ed.). Washington, DC: American Psychiatric Association.

American Psychiatric Association. (2010). *Substance use and addictive disorders.* Retrieved from dsm5.org.

Andrews, J., & Hops, H. (2009). The influence of peers in substance use. In L. M. Sheier (Ed.), *Handbook of drug use etiology: Theory, methods and empirical findings* (pp. 403–420). Washington DC: American Psychological Association.

Bachman, J. G., O'Malley, P. M., Schulenberg, J. E., Johnston, L. D., Bryant, A. L., Merline, A. C. (2002). *The decline of substance use in young adulthood: Changes in social activities, roles, and beliefs.* Lawrence Erlbaum, Mahwah, NJ.

Baldwin, J. R., & Lindsley, S. L. (1994). *Conceptualizations of culture.* Tempe, AZ: Urban Studies Center, Arizona State University.

Berry, J. W. (1994). Acculturative stress. In W. Lonner & R. Malpass (Eds.), *Psychology and culture* (pp. 211–215). Boston, MA: Allyn and Bacon.

Berry, J. W. (1997). Immigration, acculturation, and adaptation. *Applied Psychology: An International Review, 46*(1), 5–68.

Berry, J. W. (2005). Acculturation: Living successfully in two cultures. *International Journal of Intercultural Relations, 29,* 697–712.

Bonham, V. L. (2005). Race and ethnicity in the genome era: The complexity of the constructs. *American Psychologist, 60,* 9–15.

Bronfenbrenner, U. (1986). Ecology of the family as a context for human development: Research perspectives. *Developmental Psychology, 22,* 723–724.

Brook, J. S., Whiteman, M., Balka, E. B., Win, P. T., & Gursen, M. D. (1998). Drug use among Puerto Ricans: Ethnic identity as a protective factor. *Hispanic Journal of Behavioral Sciences, 20*(2), 241–254.

Bryman, A. (2007). Barriers to integrating quantitative and qualitative research. *Journal of Mixed Methods Research, 1,* 8–22.

Castro, F. G., Brook, J. S., Brook, D. W., & Rubenstone, E. (2006). Paternal, perceived maternal, and youth risk factors as predictors of your stage of substance use: A longitudinal study. *Journal of Addictive Diseases, 25,* 65–75.

Castro, F. G., & Coe, K. (2007). Traditions and alcohol use: A mixed-methods analysis. *Cultural Diversity and Ethnic Minority Psychology, 13,* 269–284.

Castro, F. G., & Garfinkle, J. (2003). Critical issues in the development of culturally relevant substance abuse treatments for specific minority groups. *Alcoholism: Clinical and Experimental Research, 27,* 1–8.

Castro, F. G., Garfinkle, J., Naranjo, D., Rollins, M., Brook, J. S., & Brook, D. W. (2007). Cultural traditions as "protective factors", among Latino children of illicit drug users. *Substance Use and Misuse, 42,* 621–642.

Castro, F. G., & Hernández-Alarcón, E. (2002). Integrating cultural variables into drug abuse prevention and treatment with racial/ethnic minorities. *Journal of Drug Issues, 32,* 783–810.

Castro, F. G., Kellison, J. G., Boyd, S. J., & Kopak, A. (2010). A methodology for conducting integrative mixed methods research and data analyses. *Journal of Mixed Methods Research, 4*(4), 342–360.

Castro, F. G., Marsiglia, F., Kulis, S., & Kellison, J. (2010). Lifetime segmented assimilation trajectories and health outcomes in Latino and other community residents. *American Journal of Public Health, 100*(4), 669–676.

Chao, G. T. & Moon, H. (2005). The cultural mosaic: A metatheory for understanding the complexity of culture. *Journal of Applied Psychology, 90,* 1128–1140.

Chung, R. H. G., Kim, B. S. K., & Abreu, J. M. (2004). Asian American Multidimensional Acculturation Scale: Development, factor analysis, reliability and validity. *Cultural Diversity and Ethnic Minority Psychology, 10,* 66–80.

Clark, R., Anderson, N. D., Clark, V. R., & Williams, D. R. (1999). Racism as a stressor for African Americans. *American Psychologist, 54,* 805–816.

Costa, P. T., Terracciano, A., & McCrae, R. R. (2001). Gender differences in personality traits across cultures: Robust and surprising findings. *Journal of Personality and Social Psychology, 81*, 322–331.

Cuadrado, M., & Lieberman, L. (1998). Traditionalism in the prevention of substance misuse among Puerto Ricans. *Substance Use and Misuse, 33*, 2737–2755.

Cuellar, I., Arnold, B., & Gonzalez, G. (1995). Cognitive referents of acculturation: Assessment of cultural constructs in Mexican Americans. *Journal of Community Psychology, 23*, 339–356.

Cuellar, I., Harris, L. C., & Jasso, R. (1980). An acculturation rating scale for Mexican American normal and clinical populations. *Hispanic Journal of Behavioral Sciences, 2*, 199–217.

Denzin, N. K., & Lincoln, Y. S. (1994). Entering the field of qualitative research. In N. K. Denzin & Y. S. Lincoln (Eds.), *Handbook of qualitative research* (pp. 1–17). Thousand Oaks, CA: Sage.

Dickens, L., & Watkins, K. (1999). Action research: Rethinking Lewin. *Management Learning, 30*, 127–140.

Erickson, E. (1968). *Identity: Youth and crisis*. New York: Norton.

Farver, J. A., Narang, S. K., & Bhadha, B. R. (2002). East meets West: Ethnic identity, acculturation, and conflict in Asian Indian families. *Journal of Family Psychology, 16*, 338–350.

Felix-Ortiz, M., & Newcomb, M. D. (1995). Cultural identity and drug use among Latino adolescents. In G. Botvin, S. Schinke, & M. Orlandi (Eds.), *Drug abuse prevention with multi-ethnic youth* (pp. 147–165). Newbury Park: Sage.

Flaherty, B. P. (2009). The role of latent class and mixture models in substance use theory. In L. M. Scheier (Ed.), *Handbook of drug use etiology: Theory, method and empirical findings* (pp. 513–523). Washington DC: American Psychological Association.

Gelo, O., Braakmann, D., & Benetka, G. (2008). Quantitative and qualitative research: Beyond the debate. *Integrative Psychology and Behavioral Science, 42*, 266–290.

Gil, A., Wagner, E., Vega, W. (2000). Acculturation, familism and alcohol use among Latino adolescent males: Longitudinal relations. *Journal of Community Psychology . 28*, 443–458.

Gosin, M. N., Dustman, P. A., Drapeau, A. E., & Harthun, M. L. (2003). Participatory action research: Creating an effective prevention curriculum for adolescents in the Southwest. *Health Education Research: Theory and Practice, 18*, 363–379.

Hanson, W. E., Creswell, J. W., Clark, V. L. P., Petska, K. S., & Creswell, J. D. (2005). Mixed methods research designs in counseling psychology. *Journal of Counseling Psychology, 52*, 224–235.

Hawkins, J. D., Catalano, R. F., & Miller, J. Y. (1992). Risk and protective factors for alcohol and other drug problems in adolescence and early adulthood: Implications for substance abuse prevention. *Psychological Bulletin, 112*, 64–105.

Hecht, M. L., Marsiglia, F. F., Elek, E., Wagstaff, D., Kulis, S., Dustman, P., et al. (2003). Culturally grounded substance use prevention: An evaluation of the keepin' it REAL curriculum. *Prevention Science, 4*(4), 233–248.

Izard, C. E. (2002). Translating emotion theory and research into preventive interventions. *Psychological Bulletin, 128*, 796–824.

Jick, T. D. (1979). Mixing qualitative and quantitative methods: Triangulation in action. *Administrative Science Quarterly, 24*(4), 602–611.

Julien, R. M., Advokat, C. D., & Comaty, J. E. (2008). *A primer of drug action: A comprehensive guide to the action, uses, and side effects of psychoactive drugs* (11th ed.). New York, NY: Worth.

Karasz, A., & Singelis, T. M. (2010). Qualitative and mixed methods research in cross-cultural psychology. *Journal of Cross-Cultural Psychology, 40*, 909–916.

Keen, B., & Jacobs, D. (2009). Racial threat, partisan politics, and racial disparities in prison admissions: A panel analysis. *Criminology: An Interdisciplinary Journal, 47*(1), 209–238. doi:10.1111/j.1745-9125.2009.00143.x.

Kelly, K. J., Comello, M. L. G., & Hunn, L. C. P. (2002). Parent–child communication, perceived sanctions against drug use, and youth drug involvement. *Adolescence, 37*, 775–787.

Klohnen, E. C. (1996). Conceptual analysis and measurement of the construct of ego-resiliency. *Journal of Personality and Social Psychology, 70*, 1067–1079.

Kulis, S., Napoli, M., & Marsiglia, F. F. (2002). Ethnic pride, biculturalism, and drug use norms of urban American Indian adolescents. *Social Work Research, 26*(2), 101–112.

La Fromboise, T., Coleman, H. L. K., & Gerton, J. (1993). Psychological impact of biculturalism: Evidence and theory. *Psychological Bulletin, 114*, 395–412.

Lara, M., Gamboa, C., Kahramanian, M. I., Morales, L. S., & Hayes Bautista, D. E. (2005). Acculturation and Latino health in the United States: A review of the literature and its sociopolitical context. *Annual Review of Public Health, 26*, 367–397.

Lettieri, D. J., Sayers, M., & Pearson, H. W. (1980). *Theories on drug abuse: Selected contemporary perspectives.* NIDA Research Monograph No. 30. Rockville, MD: National Institute on Drug Abuse.

Lopez-Class, M., Castro, F. G., & Ramirez, A. G. (2011). Conceptions of acculturation: A review and statement of critical issues. *Social Science and Medicine, 72*, 1555–1562.

Lubke, G. H., & Muthen, B. (2005). Investigating population heterogeneity with factor mixture models. *Psychological Methods, 10*, 21–39.

Marin, G., & Gamboa, R. J. (1996). A new measurement of acculturation for Hispanics: The Bidimensional Acculturation Scale for Hispanics (BAS). *Hispanic Journal of Behavioral Sciences, 18*, 297–316.

Marks, A. K., Flannery, P., & Garcia Coll, C. (2011). Being bicultural: A mixed-methods study of adolescents' implicitly and explicitly measured ethnic identities. *Developmental Psychology, 47*, 270–288.

Martin, J. K., Tuch, S. A., & Roman, P. M. (2003). Problem drinking patterns among African Americans: The impacts of reports of discrimination, perceptions of prejudice, and "risky" coping strategies. *Journal of Health and Social Behavior, 44*, 408–425.

Masten, A. S. (2001). Ordinary people: Resilience process in development. *American Psychologist, 56*, 227–238.

McGoldrick, M., & Giordano, J. (1996). Overview: Ethnicity and family therapy. In M. McGoldrick, J. Giordano, & J. K. Pearce (Eds.), *Ethnicity and family therapy* (2nd ed., pp. 1–27). New York: Guilford Press.

McKim, W. A. (2003). *Drugs and behavior: An introduction to behavioral pharmacology* (5th ed.) Upper Saddle River, NJ: Prentice Hall.

Minkler, M., & Wallerstein, N. (2003). *Community-based participatory research for health.* San Francisco, CA: Jossey-Bass.

Nieri, T., Kulis, S., & Marsiglia, F. F. (2007, May). *Acculturation stress or perceived ethnic discrimination? Assessing their relative influences on substance use among Latino elementary students.* Poster session presented at the annual meeting of the Society for Prevention Research, Washington, DC.

Oetting, E. R., & Beauvais, F. (1991). Orthogonal cultural identification theory: The cultural identification of minority adolescents. *International Journal of the Addictions, 25*, 655–685.

Oyserman, D., Coon, H. M., & Kemmelmeier, M. (2002). Rethinking individualism and collectivism: Evaluation of theoretical assumptions and meta-analyses. *Psychological Bulletin, 128*, 3–72.

Page, J. B., & Singer, M. (2010). *Comprehensive drug use: Ethnographic research at the social margins.* New Brunswick, NJ: Rutgers University Press.

Pantin, H., Coatsworth, J. D., Feaster, J. D., Newman, F. L., Briones, E., Prado, G., et al. (2003). Familias Unidas: The efficacy of an intervention to increase parental investment in Latino immigrant families. *Prevention Science, 4*, 189–201.

Parsai, M. B., Castro, F. G., Marsiglia, F. F., Harthun, M., & Valdez, H. (2011). Using community based participatory research to create a culturally grounded intervention for parents and youth to prevent risky behaviors. *Prevention Science, 12*, 34–47.

Patrick, M. E., Schulenberg, J. E., O'Malley, P. M., Johnston, L. D., & Bachman, J. G. (2011). Adolescents' reported reasons for alcohol and marijuana use as predictors of substance use and problems in adulthood. *Journal of Studies on Alcohol and Drugs, 72*(1), 106–116.

Phinney, J. (1990). Ethnic identity in adolescents and adults: Review and research. *Psychological Bulletin, 108*, 499–514.

Phinney, J. S. (1993). A three-stage model of ethnic identity development in adolescence. In M. E. Bernal & G. P. Knight (Eds.), *Ethnic identity: Formation and transmission among Hispanics and other minorities* (pp. 61–79). Albany, NY: State University of New York Press.

Porter, N. (2009). *Racial and ethnic disparities in incarceration: Criminal justice or economic servitude?* Santa Barbara, CA: Praeger/ABC-CLIO.

Portes, A., & Rumbaut, R. G. (1996). *Immigrant America: A portrait* (2nd ed.). Berkeley, CA: University of California Press.

Portes, A., & Rumbaut, R. G. (2001). *Legacies: The story of the immigrant second generation.* Berkeley, CA: University of California Press.

Portes, A., & Zhou, M. (1993). The new second generation: Segmented assimilation and its variants. *Annals of the American Academy of Political and Social Science, 530,* 74–96.

Primm, A. B., Osher, F. C., & Gomez, M. B. (2005). Race and ethnicity, mental health services and cultural competence in the criminal justice system: Are we ready to change? *Community Mental Health Journal, 41*(5), 557–569. doi:10.1007/s10597-005-6361-3.

Ramirez, M. (1999). *Multicultural psychotherapy: An approach to individual and cultural differences* (2nd ed.). Boston, MA: Allyn & Bacon.

Redfield, R., Linton, R., & Herskovitz, M. (1936). Memorandum for the study of acculturation. *American Anthropologist, 38,* 149–152.

Resnicow, K., Soler, R., Braithwait, R. L., Ahluwalia, J. S., & Butler, J. (2000). Cultural sensitivity in substance abuse prevention. *Journal of Community Psychology, 28,* 271–290.

Roberts, J. M. (2003). *The new history of the world.* New York: Oxford.

Rogler, L. H. (1994). International migrations: A framework for directing research. *American Psychologist, 49,* 701–708.

Rogler, L. H., Cortes, D. E., & Malgady, R. G. (1991). Acculturation and mental health status among Latinos. *American Psychologist, 46,* 585–597.

Rudmin, F. W. (2003). Critical history of the acculturation psychology of assimilation, separation, integration, and marginalization. *Review of General Psychology, 7,* 3–37.

Ryder, A. G., Alden, L. E., & Paulhus, D. L. (2000). Is acculturation unidimensional or bidimensional? A head-to-head comparison in the prediction of personality, self-identity, and adjustment. *Journal of Personality and Social Psychology, 79,* 49–65.

Schwartz, S. J., Montgomery, M. J., & Briones, E. (2006). The role of identity in acculturation among immigrant people: Theoretical propositions, empirical questions, and applied recommendations. *Human Development, 49,* 1–30.

Shih, R. A., Miles, J. N. V., Tucker, J. S., Zhou, A. J., & D'Amico, E. J. (2010). Racial/ethnic differences in adolescent substance use: Mediation by individual, family, and school factors. *Journal of Studies on Alcohol and Drugs, 71,* 640–651.

Shih, M., & Sanchez, D. (2005). Perspectives and research on the positive and negative implications of having multiple racial identities. *Psychological Bulletin, 131,* 569–591.

Shiraev, E. B., & Levy, D. A. (2010). *Cross-cultural psychology: Critical thinking and contemporary applications.* Boston, MA: Allyn & Bacon.

Smedley, A. S., & Smedley, B. D. (2005). Race as biology is fiction, racism as a social problem is real: Anthropological and historical perspectives on social construction of race. *American Psychologist, 60,* 16–26.

Straus, A., & Corbin, J. (1998). *Basics of qualitative research: Techniques and procedures for developing grounded theory* (2nd ed.). Thousand Oaks, CA: Sage.

Sturges, J. W., & Rogers, R. W. (1996). Preventive health psychology from a developmental perspective: An extension of prevention motivation theory. *Health Psychology, 15,* 158–166.

Szapocznik, J., & Coatsworth, J. D. (1999). An ecodevelopmental framework for organizing the influences on drug abuse: A developmental model of risk and protection. In M. Glanz & C. Hartel (Eds.), *Drug abuse: Origins & interventions* (pp. 331–366). Washington, DC: American Psychological Association.

Szapocznik, J., & Kurtines, W. M. (1989). *Breakthroughs in family therapy with drug abusing and problem youth.* New York: Springer.

Taylor, O. D. (2010). Predictors and protective factors in the prevention and treatment of adolescent substance use disorders. *Journal of Human Behavior in the Social Environment, 20*(5), 601–617. doi:10.1080/10911351003673369.

Torres, L., & Rollock, D. (2007). Acculturation and depression among Hispanics: The moderating effect of intercultural competence. *Cultural Diversity and Ethnic Minority Psychology, 13*, 10–17.

Trimble, J. E. (1995). Toward an understanding of ethnicity and ethnic identity, and their relationship to drug use research. In G. Botvin, S. Schinke, & M. Orlandi (Eds.), *Drug abuse prevention with multiethnic youth* (pp. 3–27). Thousand Oaks, CA: Sage.

Triandis, H. C., (1996). The psychological measurement of cultural syndromes. *American Psychologist, 51*, 407–415.

Tugade, M. M., & Frederickson, B. L. (2004). Resilient individuals use positive emotions to bounce back from negative emotional experiences. *Journal of Personality and Social Psychology, 86*, 320–333.

U.S. Census Bureau. (2008). *2006 American Community Survey*. Downloaded on 1/13/08 from http://factfinder.census.gov/servlet/DTTable?_bm=y&-geo_id=01000US&-ds_name= ACS_2006_EST_G00_&-mt_name=ACS_2006_EST_G2000_B02001.

U.S. Census Bureau. (2011). *Table 6. Resident population by sex, race, and Hispanic origin status: 2000 to 2009.* Downloaded on 8/31/2011 from http://www.census.gov/compendia/statlab.2011/tables/11s0006.pdf.

Vega, W. A., Alderete, E., Kolody, B., & Aguilar-Gaxiola, S. (1998). Illicit drug use among Mexicans and Mexican Americans in California: The effects of gender and acculturation. *Addiction, 93*, 1839–1850.

Vega, W. A., Gil, A. G., & Zimmerman, R. S. (1993). Patterns of drug use among Cuban-American, African-American and white, non-Latino boys. *American Journal of Public Health, 83*, 257–259.

Wandersman, A., & Nation, M. (1998). Urban neighborhoods and mental health: Psychological contributions to understanding toxicity, resilience, and interventions. *American Psychologist, 53*, 648–649.

Warner, L. A., Valdez, A., Vega, W. A., de la Rosa, M., Turner, R. J., & Canino, G. (2006). Hispanic drug abuse in an evolving cultural context: An agenda for research. *Drug and Alcohol Dependence, 84S*, S8–S16.

Wong, E. C., & Longshore, D. (2008). Ethnic identity, spirituality, and self-efficacy influences on treatment outcomes among Hispanic American methadone maintenance clients. *Journal of Ethnicity in Substance Abuse, 7*(3), 328–340. doi:10.1080/15332640802313478.

Yakushko, O. (2009). Xenophobia: Understanding the roots and consequences of negative attitudes towards immigrants. *The Counseling Psychologist, 37*, 36–66.

Chapter 10
Empirical Status of Culturally Competent Practices

Flavio F. Marsiglia and Jaime Booth

Effective prevention and treatment programs are rooted in a deep understanding of the etiology of substance abuse and integrate the strengths inherent in each individual client, their families, and their larger social and cultural networks. Culture of origin can be a source of resiliency, protecting individuals against substance abuse, and at the same time social minority statuses can be a source of stress and risk (Davis & Proctor, 1989; Marsella & Yamada, 2007). Because culture impacts the nature and expression of substance use and misuse, substance abuse treatment and prevention interventions are more effective when they are grounded in the clients' culture (La Roche & Christopher, 2009). Cultural specific interventions tend to be more efficacious in recruiting and retaining participants and in attaining prevention and treatment goals (Coatsworth, Santisteban, McBride, & Szapocznik, 2001; Kandel, 1995).

Although there is a shared awareness of the importance of culture of origin in the prevention and treatment of substance abuse, empirically supported interventions have been traditionally developed and tested with middle class white Americans. White middle class interventions typically are applied to members of diverse ethnic and racial groups under the assumption that evidence of efficacy with one group is transferable to other groups with similar needs (Miller, 2004). More recently, the prevention and treatment fields have recognized that individuals, to varying degrees, retain many aspects of their culture of origin, and that their values, beliefs, and behavior systems influence substance use choices and behaviors (Cheung, 1991; La Roche & Christopher, 2009).

Integrating culture into interventions is not an easy task. As humans we are beautifully complex beings and as such we are the product of intersecting identities (Collins, 1995). NASW defines culture as "the integrated pattern of human behavior that includes thoughts, communication, actions, customs, beliefs, values,

F.F. Marsiglia (✉) • J. Booth
Arizona State University, Southwest Interdisciplinary Research Center,
School of Social Work, Tempe, AZ, USA
e-mail: marsiglia@asu.edu; jmbooth2@asu.edu

M.G. Vaughn and B.E. Perron (eds.), *Social Work Practice in the Addictions*,
Contemporary Social Work Practice, DOI 10.1007/978-1-4614-5357-4_10,
© Springer Science+Business Media New York 2013

and institutions of a racial, ethnic, religious, or social group" (NASW, 2000, p. 61). This definition includes aspects of deep culture, such as thought patterns and value systems, as well as surface characteristics, such as language and customs (Resnicow, Baranowski, Ahluwalia, & Braithwaite, 1999). In addition to ethnicity and race, other key factors to consider when designing culturally competent interventions are socioeconomic status, gender, sexual orientation, and ability status (Abrams & Moi, 2009).

Ecological systems theory helps us understand that individuals are simultaneously influenced by several dimensions of their social system (Bronfenbrenner, 1977). Culture is a key factor affecting individual beliefs and behaviors (micro level), family norms and values (mezzo level), and how the person interacts with larger structures (macro level) such as the school system or local law enforcement (Szapocznik & Coastworth, 1999). Social work approaches culture of origin, cultural identities, and the individual client's social context not as something to be changed or suppressed, but as factors to be recognized and integrated into practice (Marsiglia & Kulis, 2009). This chapter presents specific strategies on how to apply cultural competency principles while identifying and adopting evidence-based culturally competent prevention and treatment interventions. The premise behind the chapter is that communities deserve to have access to the best available science without having to sacrifice cultural competency. Culture of origin is approached here as a source of resiliency and as a possible determinant of health.

Evidence-Based Prevention and Treatment Interventions

The evidence-based practice movement has radically influenced the social work profession, including the drug abuse prevention and treatment specialization (Grinnell & Unrau, 2011). In addition to its strong support for culturally competent practice, social workers advocate for empirically validated or science-based practice (Nathan & Gorman, 2002). There is a growing expectation that drug abuse prevention and treatment interventions be validated through Randomized Control Trials (RCTs) and through other rigorous evaluation methods and designs. Evidence-based interventions also incorporate empirical knowledge about the mechanisms that lead to addiction and other factors that might protect individuals from substance abuse. The design and testing of efficacious prevention and treatment is informed by a deeper understanding of the social and cultural processes that create and maintain certain desired or undesired behaviors.

Although empirically tested treatment and prevention interventions are the gold standard in prevention and treatment, many innovative culturally competent approaches are not rigorously tested because of the lack of research capacity to conduct RCTs. In fact, there is a large gap between science and practice in the substance use prevention and treatment field (Glasner-Edwards & Rawson, 2010; Merrell, 2010). Available interventions often lack empirical evidence of efficacy while treatment and prevention interventions that have been shown to be efficacious are rarely implemented in the field (Sorensen & Midkiff, 2000; Torrey & Gorman, 2005).

In part, researchers' strong reliance on scholarly journals to disseminate their findings about efficacious interventions limits the translation of findings into the field (Sobell, 1996). On the other hand, practitioners feel overwhelmed by the ever-expanding choices of prevention and treatment modalities and have limited time for evaluation and research-related activities (Levinson, Schaefer, Sylvester, Meland, & Haugen, 1982).

The existence of efficacy does not automatically translate into outcomes in the field because evidence-based interventions are often implemented without consideration for fidelity (Backer, 2001; Gottfredson & Gottfredson, 2002). Fidelity is the act of verifying that an intervention is being implemented in a manner consistent with the treatment or prevention model and matches the research that produced the practice. Fidelity is achieved when implementers can demonstrate that there is consistency in the manner in which the treatment is delivered to all participants and that it follows the underlying theory and goals of the research (Dumas, Lynch, Laughlin, Phillips-Smith, & Prinz, 2001). Several reasons have been cited for the lack of fidelity, including poor training and inadequate resource, low morale, and high levels of burn out (Botvin, 2004). Regardless of the intervention or the setting, practitioners naturally make explicit and implicit adaptations (Backer, 2001). In order for treatment or prevention interventions to be implemented with fidelity, the staff implementing the program must be trained to administer the treatment and be aware of what elements of the program are essential for effectiveness and what elements are more flexible (Bridge, Massie, & Mills, 2008).

The divide between research and practice is even more pronounced for culturally specific interventions (Cross et al., 2011). Funding sources are increasingly requiring the implementation of evidence-based practices and expect agencies to only adopt interventions included in approved lists of evidence-based interventions (Gira, Kessler, & Poertner, 2004). In order to oblige, some agencies might rush to select an evidence-based program without considering if it is culturally appropriate (Willis, 2007).

Identifying, Evaluating, and Implementing Culturally/ Empirically Supported Interventions

The process of selecting and implementing evidence-based empirically supported interventions has been summarized by Rycroft-Malone et al. (2004) into an easy to use three step review process:

1. *Evidence.* Does the evidence exist? Has the research been conducted rigorously?
2. *Context.* Is the intervention appropriate for my community or my organization?
3. *Facilitation.* How will it be implemented with fidelity?

In order to insure that this process is culturally competent, it has been suggested that even before a intervention is selected the practitioner should consider: the clients being served, are they culturally homogeneous, what are the key components of their culture that interacts with their substance use behaviors, and whether or not treatment or prevention programs need to reflect their cultural values, norms and identity to be effective (Bridge et al., 2008).

Once the culture of origin and identities of the clients to be served are identified attention is given the repertoire of available interventions. This process also follows a set of standards to assess empirically supported treatment and prevention interventions (SAMHSA, 2009):

1. Rigor of evaluation design (use of intervention and control or comparison group; appropriateness of assignment to groups; control for other explanatory factors. Did the researchers conduct a RCT?).
2. Rigor and appropriateness of methods used to collect and analyze data (use of measures that match desired outcomes).
3. Magnitude and consistency of effects of the intervention on desired outcomes (it is agreed that evidence becomes stronger when it is replicated).
4. The extent to which the findings can be applied to other populations in other settings.

The most reliable sources of empirically supported treatment and prevention interventions are national registries and peer-reviewed journal articles. Registries often offer a rating system that judges the quality of the evidence offered, but the level of evidence required and the rating system utilized varies by registry. While national registry's of empirically tested substance abuse interventions are helpful, when possible it is important to find the original article and examine the study design, in order to critically evaluate the strength of the findings. Most lists of empirically tested interventions include the citations of the studies, as well as information regarding the availability of program materials and training.

Two examples of national registries that include culturally specific substance abuse prevention and treatment interventions are: (1) SAMHSA Nation Registry of Evidence Based Programs and Practices (NREPP) www.nrepp.samhsa.gov and (2) OJJDP Model Programs Guide www.ojjdp.gov/mpg. Both lists are a very helpful resource for practitioners. Peer-reviewed journals/articles reporting on the results of RCTs are also a reliable source of information about the efficacy of interventions. In order for an intervention to be considered to have strong evidence it should be shown to be efficacious in two or more studies (Roth & Fonagy, 2004). Finding and reviewing evidence for interventions in journals can be very labor intensive and requires a certain level of expertise to discern quality evidence from flawed studies.

This process of discernment can have many different outcomes depending on the characteristics of the targeted population and the availability of efficacious interventions. If concerns persist about the cultural appropriateness of existing evidence-based interventions, certain strategies can be considered:

1. The most basic strategy is providing cultural competency training to the service providers delivering the treatment without changing the intervention.
2. Adapting the evidence-based practice to reflect cultural values and norms, and
3. Creating and testing original cultural-specific interventions (Santisteban, Vega, & Suarez-Morales, 2006).

Each of these strategies promotes cultural competent practice to a varying degree, from surface to deep culture (Castro, Barrera, & Martinez, 2004) and will result in cultural competence training, program adaptation, or the design and evaluation of a new culturally specific intervention.

Cultural Competency Training

Cultural competency training often gives clinicians a general overview of specific cultures and culturally based norms and behaviors that may affect the clients' engagement and treatment process without addressing specific skills or practices (Santisteban et al., 2006). While cultural competency training is helpful and may lead to more culturally sensitive practice, it cannot address the larger structural factors that are impacting substance abuse; in other words it might not go deep enough. It requires an in-depth knowledge of how culture of origin impacts the family process, adolescent development, couple decision-making, and interaction with the community at large, and a variety of other factors (Santisteban, Muir-Malcolm, Mitrani, & Szapocznik, 2002). Cultural competency training has been added to interventions that have been originally shown to be efficacious with majority populations and then have later been applied with ethnic and racial minority clients (Turner, 2000). While culturally competency training is positive and helpful, one cannot presume that training the interventionist alone will make a treatment more effective for minority clients. In the absence of culturally specific interventions, applying an evidence-based practice validated with a different population in a culturally competent way is a move in the right direction but may not adequately address the deeper cultural norms and beliefs that drive substance use behavior or that protect individuals from it.

Cultural Adaptation

Cultural adaptation is an ongoing phenomenon often informally conducted by practitioners or facilitators who identify a mismatch between aspects of the intervention and the population they are serving (Botvin, 2004; Castro et al., 2004). There have been efforts to provide practitioners and/or agencies with the tools necessary to systematically modify interventions for specific groups rather than creating and testing cultural-specific intervention from the ground-up (Kazdin, 1993). If evidence-based interventions lack cultural appropriateness or cultural fit, they will benefit from cultural adaption in order to assure that they are relevant to the population being served (Kumpfer & Kaftarian, 2000). While culturally tailoring interventions to better match the norms and behaviors of a population increases program efficacy (Jackson & Hodge, 2010), if the modifications are not part of a specific adaptation protocol, they may compromise the integrity of the original intervention and affect the overall efficacy (Bridge et al., 2008; Castro et al., 2004). Two basic steps proposed to conduct such an adaptation and to protect the integrity of the program (La Roche & Christopher, 2009) include: (1) identifying the core ideas and theories of the mechanism for change within the original curriculum and (2) partnering with the cultural group to assure their involvement in making the necessary changes that would make the intervention more relevant to the population (Castro et al., 2004; Castro, Barrera, & Holleran Steiker, 2010).

When adapting an intervention, a deep understanding is needed for both the theoretical underpinnings of the intervention and the cultural norms and values of the culture that it is being adapted for. Frequently adaptations change surface aspects of the intervention like the cultural contexts of stories or the identity of actors in a film. This allows the individual in the treatment or the prevention program to identify themselves in the curriculum but fails to address the larger cultural norms that may be impacting their use or decision-making process. While modifications that change certain surface aspects of an intervention might work, it runs the risk of continuing to communicate dominant cultural values on which the intervention was designed, undermining the cultural groups experience (Frable, 1997). Another challenge that arises with adaptation is the tendency for providers to pick and choose aspects of several programs and combine them into one intervention impacting the integrity of the program and negating the empirical evidence of the original intervention (Kumpfer & Kaftarian, 2000). Programs that are implemented as they were written, with little variation from the original curriculum, are more effective (Elliott & Mihalic, 2004).

Culturally Specific Interventions

Evidence has shown that substance prevention and treatment programs are more successful when they are grounded in the participant's culture (Kandel, 1995; Kulis, Nieri, Yabiku, Stromwall, & Marsiglia, 2007; Shadish et al., 1993). In addition, treatments that are tailored to meet specific cultural needs have been shown to have high program retention rates, which is crucial for success (Santisteban et al., 1996). An intervention is cultural-specific when it begins with the culture and builds the program around that culture's experiences with drug use and related cultural norms, attitudes, and beliefs. Cultural-specific interventions not only incorporate cultural symbols and language but also core values that influence how a person, their support systems, and their community perceive their substance use. A culturally specific approach accounts for deeper aspects of culture such as norms and values by considering the cultural context at every level of program development.

Different providers and agencies may be at different levels of readiness and capacity to implement one or more of these strategies at the same time. The ideal situation would be to identify an existing evidence-based intervention that is also culturally appropriate for the targeted population. There are a growing number of empirically tested substance abuse prevention and treatment interventions to consider. The following summary of selected interventions specifically designed and tested with adolescents serve as an example of such a review. Although this section focuses on adolescents, the process for selecting and evaluating prevention and treatment intervention is similar for adult programs.

American Indians

Prevention

Bicultural Competence Skills Approach (Schinke, Tepavac, & Cole, 2000) has been identified by the Office of Juvenile Justice and Delinquency as an effective program. This intervention is designed to prevent substance use among American Indian youth by teaching social skills within the context of both the American Indian and mainstream American culture. The intervention is administered by American Indian facilitators and focuses on communication skills and coping skills, in order to enhance a participant's ability to resist substances both in his/her native community and in the dominant culture as well. Every intervention session included native values, legends, and stories. This intervention does not necessarily focus on substance abuse but rather on the more general subject of holistic health. Its Bicultural Competence Skills Approach includes a community component that is unique from other substance abuse prevention with American Indians. This intervention was evaluated in two separate studies using an experimental design. The first study found a statistically significant difference in the reported attitudes and substance use of the youth in the treatment group versus the control condition, and these results remained at the 6-month follow-up (Schinke et al., 1988). In the second RCT, the use of alcohol, tobacco, and marijuana was significantly lower in schools that received the cultural-adapted life skills training rather than the control at the three-year follow-up (Schinke et al., 2000).

Critical assessment of evidence: Strengths of this study include the incorporation of a bicultural approach identified as protective in the literature, large sample size, random assignment of schools to treatment and control groups and study sites ten different reservations in five different states.

Project Venture (Carter, Straits, & Hall, 2007) is an outdoor program for 5–8th grade American Indian youth. Project Ventures seeks to enhance antidrug norms and facilitate personal development through the incorporation of traditional American Indian values. The intervention consists of a minimum of 20 one-hour sessions in the classroom and weekly after school and weekend and summer activities such as hiking and camping trips. Project Venture emphasizes service learning, spiritual awareness, and the importance of family. This intervention was assessed using a quasi-experimental design. When this intervention was tested, rates of drinking increased for both the intervention and control group, but leveled off for the intervention group and continued to rise in the control group at the 6- and 18-month follow-up. When this study was replicated, rates of drinking for the intervention group remained the same while they continued to increase in the control group. The same pattern was observed for the use of illicit drugs, with the intervention group remaining the same and the control groups use increasing.

Critical assessment of evidence: While the strength of the evidence is supported by multiple studies and longitudinal data (several follow ups over time) because of the use of a quasi-experimental design rather than a randomized control trial, we cannot be sure that the effects observed were due to the intervention and not on baseline differences in the two groups.

Treatment

There is a limited number of culturally specific treatment interventions designed with and for American Indian youth and even less that can be considered evidence-based (Goodkind et al., 2011). Cultural adaptation such as the White Bison, a cultural competent version of the traditional 12 step program, has been designed introducing traditional healing practices, such as sweat lodges, but their efficacy has not been tested (Moore & Coyhis, 2010). While some studies have shown that treatment program incorporating traditional healing improves retention, no studies have been done testing their efficacy in treating substance abuse problems (Fisher, Lankford, & Galea, 1996).

Latinos

Prevention

Families Unidas (Coatsworth, Pantin, & Szapocznik, 2002; Pantin et al., 2003) is a substance use prevention program designed for Latino families with children between the ages of 12–17 and is guided by ecological systems theory. This intervention is administered in 2 h once-a-week groups for 3–5 months. Families Unidas focuses on increasing effective parenting skills though psychosocial education, participatory exercises, and group discussion and is administered in three stages. Facilitators were Spanish speaking, bicultural, and trained to implement the intervention with fidelity. This program was tested using an experimental design, where participants were randomly assigned to Families Unidas or a variety of other interventions (ESOL classes, HeartPower, PATH) and adolescences were surveyed at several time periods after the completion of the intervention. When testing Families Unidas, no difference was found between the intervention and the control group on measures of alcohol use; however significant decreases in cigarette and illicit drug use were shown. Like many other interventions for adolescence, substance use is not the primary target of this intervention, but is included in a bundle of other problem behaviors being targeted.

Critical assessment of evidence: Strengths of this study include a lengthy discussion of theoretical foundation, use of a randomized control trials, and a great deal of attention has been paid to implementing this intervention with fidelity; however, lack of outcomes for alcohol should be considered when selecting this intervention.

Storytelling for Empowerment (Nelson & Arthur, 2003) is a school-based bilingual intervention based on combination of narrative therapy and empowerment theory. It is designed to address substance abuse, HIV and other behaviors of at risk teenagers. Storytelling for Empowerment was created for Latino/Latina youth and is rooted in the development of positive cultural identity and resiliency models of prevention. The intervention guides youth through a Storytelling PowerBook that includes an exploration of physiology, decision making, multicultural stories, identification of historical figures, defining culture, identifying cultural symbols, identifying role models and setting goals. This intervention was tested using a quasi-experimental design with one group participating in the program and the other serving as an assessment only comparison group. When tested this program was shown to significantly decrease alcohol and marijuana use at post test and 1 year follow-up relative to the no treatment control group. The dosage of the treatment seemed to be significant in the outcome with student who received 28 h or more of contact showing significantly greater decreases in substance use outcome than those that experienced less. While there was no significant decrease in marijuana usage, the same interaction with contact hours was observed, with those who received more contact hours reporting significantly less usage than those who had less.

Critical assessment of evidence: While this prevention program is solidly based on theory and showed positive outcomes, the differential effect based on dosage suggest that it may be the amount of time spent with the adolescents rather than the prevention program that is having an effect on the adolescents' outcomes.

Treatment

Brief Strategic Family Therapy (Santisteban et al., 1997, 2003) has been developed to prevent, reduce and treat a wide variety of problem behaviors in adolescents including substance use and has been tested in several quasi-experimental designs with Latino youth and found effective. This intervention was designed to be administered in 12–16 sessions but can take as little as 8 depending on the communication patterns and functioning within the family. These sessions are 1 h, 1 day a week in an office setting. BSFT is grounded in the theory that substance use and misuse in adolescences is rooted in dysfunctional family interactions, alliance and boundaries, and is based on the assumption that if the overall functioning of the family improves then adolescence substance use will be addressed as well (Dishion & Andrews, 1995; Santisteban & Szapocznik, 1994). When conducting Brief Strategic Family Therapy the therapist works to improve functioning by joining the family system, diagnosing repetitive patterns in relationships that reinforce the problem and then finally restructuring the family system (Santisteban et al., 1997). Brief Strategic Family Therapy has been shown to be more effective than controls (including group, individual and family therapy) at engaging and retaining families in treatment and reducing substance use in adolescences (Santisteban et al., 1997, 2003).

Critical assessment of evidence: Comparison groups were used rather than randomized control groups opening results up to threats to internal validity; however, the researchers in these studies conducted statistical tests on the two groups at pre-test to ensure they were comparable. Brief Strategic Family Therapy has also been adapted and tested with African-American adolescents. It should be noted that substance abuse treatment is not the sole goal of this intervention with conduct disorder, socialized aggression, and over all family functioning as concurrent outcomes.

African Americans

Prevention

Hip-Hop 2 prevent substance abuse and HIV (Turner-Musa, Rhodes, Harper, & Quinton, 2008) is a school-based prevention program designed for African-American youth, 12- to 16-year years of age and incorporates hip-hop culture into prevention messages. This intervention consists of ten sessions in which students developed self-efficacy, clarity of norms and values, and conflict resolution skills. The first four session occur in an after-school program and the remaining 6 are implemented in a 4-day camp. A randomized control trial of this intervention was conducted at the same school for two consecutive years to test the treatment effectiveness of increasing the perceived risk of using drugs and overall disapproval of drug use. In both groups there was a significant increase in the perception of risk associated with using marijuana, but there were no other significant differences between treatment and control group. At post test, a significantly higher percentage of students who participated in H2P reported believing that it is wrong for youth to drink alcohol, smoke cigarettes, or smoke marijuana regularly, but only the negative beliefs about marijuana remained at the 6-month follow-up.

Critical assessment of evidence: While this study used a randomized control trial to test the intervention, the use of only one school, and the study small sample size with 135 students total (68 in the control and 67 in the treatment) with only 68 participants completing the 6-month follow-up, weaken the strength of the evidence.

Treatment

Healer Women Fighting Disease: Integrated Substance Abuse and HIV Program for African American Woman (HWFD) (Nobles, Goddard, & Gilbert, 2009) is in intervention designed to target both substance abuse and HIV risk in woman age 13–55. The program curriculum is based on the idea that understanding African-American culture is central to behavior and must be incorporated when discussing behavioral change. In HWFD women are presented pro-health values rooted in traditional African culture in the hopes that adapting these attitudes and beliefs will counteract negative main stream messaging that promote unsafe sex and substance abuse in a 16 weekly 2 h sessions. The program is implemented by trained professionals and paraprofessionals in a fixed format that may be modified with input from participants in an urban community setting. To test this intervention effectiveness African-American women were recruited from a community agency and were assigned to two different groups, half participating in HWFD and the other half receiving treatment as usual. Although improvements across all areas were observed in both the treatment and comparison group, HWFD was shown to be more effective than treatment as usual when addressing safer sex attitudes, feeling of self-efficacy, and motivation and depression symptoms, but not in attitudes toward drug use and self-esteem (Nobles et al., 2009).

Critical evaluation: It should be recognized that this study used a comparison group rather than a control group, had high rates of attrition, and while this intervention was shown to be better than treatment as usual in some areas it did not improve outcome in attitudes toward drug use. A strength of this intervention is that it has been outlined in detail in a manual and training for facilitators is available.

Multiethnic Prevention

Keepin' it REAL (Hecht et al., 2003; Marsiglia & Hecht, 2005) is a multicultural substance abuse prevention program designed to be implemented with adolescents. This intervention is presented in 10, 45-min classroom sessions and is administered by teachers who have been trained in the curriculum. Based on communication competency theory and a resilience model, *keepin' it REAL*'s curriculum focuses on helping students assess risk, enhance resistance skills, increase antidrug belief and attitudes and ultimately reduce substance use. *keepin' it REAL*'s is culturally grounded, with culturally specific and multicultural versions available. Using an experimental design, 30-day substance use was measured at 2, 8, and 14 months after the intervention was completed. Adolescents that received the intervention reported significantly lower levels of alcohol, marijuana and tobacco use through the 8-month follow-up. A higher percentage of students in the treatment group reported a reduction or discontinuation of alcohol use from baseline when compared to the control group.

Critical assessment of evidence: Strengths of this study include teacher training and attention to implementation with fidelity, the use of an experimental design, assessment at multiple time points and a large sample size. Weaknesses include differing dosages and use of measure of resistance strategies that had not been assessed from reliability prior to the intervention.

Treatment

Alcohol Treatment Targeting Adolescents in Need (Gil, Wagner, & Tubman, 2004), or ATTAIN, is a randomized controlled trial of a guided self-change treatment that is brief and focuses on skills building and motivation enhancement. The authors argue that guided self-change treatment is appropriate for a cultural diverse population due to the emphasis on individual treatment goal setting based on the clients personal experience, making it more flexible and culturally. Sensitive ATTAIN was implemented in juvenile detention facilities with both Latino and African American offenders. Materials were adapted to be culturally and developmentally appropriate, including material about other problem behaviors that often co-occur with substance use in adolescents and were provided in both English and Spanish. The staff implementing the intervention was both multiethic and multilingual and focus groups were used to address cultural and language preference in the creation of the manual. Study participants were randomly assigned into the individual intervention, family involved format, a condition where they were given their choice between the two formats or a wait list control group. Surveys were completed at baseline and after the intervention (3-, 6-, and 9-month follow-up were done but the results have not been published). A significant decrease in 30-day substance use was observed in all three treatment conditions, with the most dramatic decrease occurring among African-American participants. In addition this study found that participants with more ethnic mistrust benefited less from the treatment and those with higher reported levels of ethnic pride and orientation reported fewer days of alcohol consumption post-treatment when controlling for reported use at baseline. This program has been shown to be efficacious in reducing the number of days participants using in the past 30 days but no analysis was done comparing the treatment group with the control group due to a small sample size.

Critical assessment of evidence: Some of the strengths of this study include the use of a control group, the inclusion of clients in the curriculum development, the use of a manual and the analysis of treatment effects considering different levels of acculturation, mistrust, and ethnic pride. This study is, however, limited due to the absences of analysis comparing the treatment to the control group, the lack of females in the sample and exclusion of the analysis of follow-up data.

Discussion

While it has been widely accepted that services provided by social workers must be culturally competent, researchers designing and testing cultural-specific intervention and practitioners implementing them are challenged and enriched by the complexity of culture, heterogeneity among cultural groups, issues of fidelity and implementation and lack of evidence-based practice specifically designed for some populations. A common misunderstanding in both research and practice is approaching culture, ethnicity, race, non-western, and minority as interchangeable ideas; when in reality, culture embodies concepts separate from race and some so-called minority groups have cultures deeply rooted in Western civilization (McAdoo, 1997; Phillips, 2007). Even in the presence of a concrete definition of culture, it can be difficult to distinguish the edges and boundaries of culture as they mix together with other cultures; they change over time, and they are affected by individual and generational differences and sociopolitical factors. A culturally competent social worker acknowledges that each individual is unique within his/ her cultural group and remembers that individuals identify with their community cultural norms at different degrees (La Roche & Christopher, 2009; McGoldrick, Giordano, & Garcia-Preto, 2005).

There is a paucity of research on culturally specific drug use and abuse prevention and treatment interventions for some groups. For example, it is difficult to locate control randomized trials testing the efficacy of substance abuse treatment-specific to Latinas (Amaro & Cortés, 2003) or American Indian adolescents in general (Goodkind et al., 2011). While some culturally specific research exists about substance abuse within the Asian American communities, no rigorous prevention or treatment programs have been developed to meet this very heterogeneous population needs.

Evaluating Your Culture Specific Intervention, Adding to the Evidence Base

Communities have been addressing the substance abuse needs of their members within their culture for hundreds of years. While these treatments or methods may not have been scientifically tested for efficacy, they have benefited from the wisdom that comes with time. In the same way, social workers that have been working with substance abusing clients for several years may have found techniques and interventions that they believe work, but do not have the evidence to support their claim. Historically, researchers at the university level have been primarily responsible for generating and disseminating empirically supported substance abuse treatment; in many cases without fully incorporating the rich experiences of the community members and community-based treatment professionals' experience. In the absence of empirical support, practitioners may be required to implement treatment and prevention programs that have been found to be efficacious in place of interventions that have been reined over the years. So that this wisdom is not lost, researchers, practitioners, and communities need to begin a conversation about what works within a given culture, so that traditional practices can be scientifically tested for efficacy. In addition to partnering with researchers, an effort can be made to train communities and social workers to rigorously evaluate their practices and disseminate their findings adding to the literature of culturally competent empirically supported substance abuse prevention and treatment.

Practitioners and agencies are increasingly being asked to provide services that are not only culturally relevant but also that have been shown to be efficacious in rigorous studies. Many of the substance abuse treatment and prevention interventions that have been used for years have not yet been tested. They are not necessarily ineffective; we simply do not know. While social workers are briefly taught in both the BSW and MSW programs to evaluate their practice, the practitioner–researcher role often does not emerge due to the large case loads, increases in documentation and reporting, or a lack of confidence in their own research abilities. Single subject research designs have been suggested as a viable technique for evaluating social work practice on a small scale (Thyer, 2004). To execute a single subject research design, the social worker assesses the client at intake and then repeatedly throughout treatment using a valid measure so that any change in the outcome can then be attributed to the treatment. These types of research designs can produce the preliminary findings needed for follow-up adaptation or development studies and randomized control trials. Agencies can also evaluate their practice by administrating valid pre- and post-test measures of efficacy. By partnering with universities and evaluating treatment and prevention outcomes social workers can empirically validate programs, not only insuring the success of their clients but also adding to the existing knowledge about culturally specific evidence-based prevention and treatment interventions.

References

Abrams, L. S., & Moi, J. A. (2009). Critical race theory and the cultural competence dilemma in social work education. *Journal of Social Work Education, 45*, 245–261.

Amaro, H., & Cortés, D. E. (2003). *National strategic plan on Hispanic drug abuse research: From the molecule to the community*. Boston: Northeastern University.

Backer, T. (2001). *Finding the balance: Program fidelity and adaptation in substance abuse prevention: A state-of-the-art review*. Rockville, MD: Center for Substance Abuse Prevention.

Botvin, G. J. (2004). Advancing prevention science and practice: Challenges, critical issues, and future directions. *Prevention Science, 5*, 69–72.

Bridge, T. J., Massie, E. G., & Mills, C. S. (2008). Prioritizing cultural competence in the implementation of an evidence-based practice model. *Children and Youth Services Review, 30*, 1111–1118.

Bronfenbrenner, U. (1977). Toward an environmental ecology of human development. *American Psychologist, 32*, 513–531.

Carter, S., Straits, K. J. E., & Hall, M. (2007). Project Venture: Evaluation of an experiential culturally based approach to substance abuse prevention with American Indian Youth. *Journal of Experiential Education, 29*, 397–400.

Castro, F. G., Barrera, M., Jr., & Holleran Steiker, L. K. (2010). Issues and challenges in the design of culturally adapted evidence-based interventions. *Annual Review of Clinical Psychology, 6*, 213–239.

Castro, F. G., Barrera, M., & Martinez, C. R. (2004). The cultural adaptation of prevention interventions: Resolving tensions between fidelity and fit. *Prevention Science, 5*, 41–45.

Cheung, Y. W. (1991). Ethnicity and alcohol/drug use revisited: A framework for future research. *Substance Use & Misuse, 25*, 581–605.

Coatsworth, J. D., Pantin, H., & Szapocznik, J. (2002). Familias Unidas: A family-centered ecode-velopmental intervention to reduce risk for problem behavior among Hispanic adolescents. *Clinical Child and Family Psychology Review, 5*, 113–132.

Coatsworth, J. D., Santisteban, D. A., McBride, C. K., & Szapocznik, J. (2001). Brief strategic family therapy versus community control: Engagement, retention, and an exploration of the moderating role of adolescent symptom severity. *Family Process, 40*, 313–332.

Collins, R. L. (1995). Issues of ethnicity in research on prevention of substance abuse. In G. J. Botvin, S. Schinke, & M. A. Orlandi (Eds.), *Drug abuse prevention with multiethnic youth* (pp. 28–45). Thousand Oaks, CA: Sage.

Cross, T. L., Friesen, B. J., Jivanjee, P., Gowen, L. K., Bandurraga, A., Mathew, C., & Maher, N. (2011). Defining youth success using culturally appropriate community-based participatory research methods. *Best Practices in Mental Health, 7*, 94–114.

Davis, L. E., & Proctor, E. K. (1989). *Race, gender, and class: Guidelines for practice with individuals, families, and groups*. Boston, MA: Allyn & Bacon.

Dishion, T., & Andrews, D. (1995). Preventing escalation in problem behaviors with high-risk young adolescents: Immediate and 1-year-outcomes: Prediction and prevention of child and adolescent antisocial behavior. *Journal of Consulting and Clinical Psychology, 63*, 538–548.

Dumas, J. E., Lynch, A. M., Laughlin, J. E., Phillips-Smith, E., & Prinz, R. J. (2001). Promoting intervention fidelity: Conceptual issues, methods, and preliminary results from the EARLY ALLIANCE prevention trial. *American Journal of Preventive Medicine, 20*(Suppl.), 38–47.

Elliott, D. S., & Mihalic, S. (2004). Issues in disseminating and replicating effective prevention programs. *Prevention Science, 5*, 47–53.

Fisher, D. G., Lankford, B. A., & Galea, R. P. (1996). Therapeutic community retention among Alaska Natives 1: Akeela house. *Journal of Substance Abuse Treatment, 13*, 265–271.

Frable, D. E. S. (1997). Gender, racial, ethnic, sexual, and class identities. *Annual Review of Psychology, 48*, 139–162.

Gil, A. G., Wagner, E. F., & Tubman, J. G. (2004). Culturally sensitive substance abuse intervention for Hispanic and African American adolescents: Empirical examples from the Alcohol Treatment Targeting Adolescents in Need (ATTAIN) project. *Addiction, 99*, 140–150.

Gira, E. C., Kessler, M. L., & Poertner, J. (2004). Influencing social workers to use research evidence in practice: Lessons from medicine and the allied health professions. *Research on Social Work Practice, 14*, 68–79.

Glasner-Edwards, S., & Rawson, R. (2010). Evidence-based practices in addiction treatment: Review and recommendations for public policy. *Health Policy, 97*, 93–104. doi:10.1016/l. healthpol.2010.05.013 (Downloaded on 04-01-11).

Goodkind, J. R., Ross-Toledo, K., John, S., Hall, J. L., Ross, L., Freeland, L., et al. (2011). Rebuilding trust: A community, multiagency, state, and university partnership to improve behavioral health care for American Indian youth, their families, and communities. *Journal of Community Psychology, 39*, 452–477.

Gottfredson, D. C., & Gottfredson, G. D. (2002). Quality of school-based prevention programs: Results from a national survey. *Journal of Research in Crime and Delinquency, 39*, 3–35.

Grinnell, R. M., & Unrau, Y. A. (2011). *Social work research and evaluation: Foundation for evidence-based practice*. Oxford: New York.

Hecht, M. L., Marsiglia, F. F., Elek, E., Wagstaff, D. A., Kulis, S., Dustman, P., et al. (2003). Culturally grounded substance use prevention: An evaluation of the keepin' it REAL curriculum. *Prevention Science, 4*, 233–248.

Jackson, K. F., & Hodge, D. R. (2010). Native American youth and culturally sensitive interventions: A systematic review. *Research on Social Work Practice, 20*, 260–271.

Kandel, D. B. (1995). Ethnic differences in drug use: Patterns and paradoxes. In G. Botvin, S. Schinke, & M. Orlandi (Eds.), *Drug abuse prevention with multi-ethnic youth* (pp. 81–104). Newbury Park, CA: Sage.

Kazdin, A. E. (1993). Adolescent mental health: Prevention and treatment programs. *American Psychologist, 48*, 127–141.

Kulis, S., Nieri, T., Yabiku, S., Stromwall, L., & Marsiglia, F. F. (2007). Promoting reduced and discontinued substance use among adolescent substance users: Effectiveness of a universal prevention program. *Prevention Science, 8,* 35–49.

Kumpfer, K. L., & Kaftarian, S. J. (2000). Bridging the gap between family-focused research and substance abuse prevention practice: Preface. *The Journal of Primary Prevention, 21,* 169–184.

La Roche, M. J., & Christopher, M. S. (2009). Changing paradigms from empirically supported treatment to evidence-based practice: A cultural perspective. *Professional Psychology: Research and Practice, 40,* 396–402.

Levinson, D., Schaefer, J. M., Sylvester, R., Meland, J. A., & Haugen, B. (1982). Information dissemination and overload in the alcoholism treatment field. *Journal of Studies on Alcohol, 43,* 570–575.

Marsella, A. J., & Yamada, A. M. (2007). Culture and psychopathology: Foundations, issues, directions. In S. Kitayama & D. Cohen (Eds.), *Handbook of cultural psychology* (pp. 797–818). New York, NY: Guilford.

Marsiglia, F. F., & Hecht, M. L. (2005). *Keepin' it REAL: An evidence-based program.* Santa Cruz, CA: ETR Associates.

Marsiglia, F. F., & Kulis, S. (2009). *Diversity, oppression, and change: Culturally grounded social work.* Chicago, IL: Lyceum Books.

McAdoo, H. P. (1997). Upward mobility across generations in African American families. In H. P. McAdoo (Ed.), *Black families* (3rd ed., pp. 139–162). Thousand Oaks, CA: Sage.

McGoldrick, M., Giordano, J., & Garcia-Preto, N. (2005). *Ethnicity and family therapy.* New York: The Guilford Press.

Merrell, K. W. (2010). Linking prevention science and social and emotional learning: The Oregon Resiliency Project. *Psychology in the Schools, 47,* 55–70.

Miller, G. A. (2004). *Learning the language of addiction counseling.* Hoboken, NJ: Wiley.

Moore, D., & Coyhis, D. (2010). The multicultural wellbriety peer recovery support program: Two decades of community-based recovery. *Alcoholism Treatment Quarterly, 28,* 273–292.

Nathan, P. E., & Gorman, J. M. (2002). *A guide to treatments that work.* London: Oxford University Press.

National Association of Social Workers. (2000). Cultural competence in social work profession. In *Social work speaks: NASW policy statements* (pp. 59–62). Washington, DC: NASW Press.

Nelson, A., & Arthur, B. (2003). Storytelling for empowerment: Decreasing at-risk youth's alcohol and marijuana use. *The Journal of Primary Prevention, 24,* 169–180.

Nobles, W. W., Goddard, L. L., & Gilbert, D. J. (2009). Culture-ecology, women, and African-centered HIV prevention. *Journal of Black Psychology, 35,* 228–246.

Pantin, H., Coatsworth, J. D., Feaster, D. J., Newman, F. L., Briones, E., Prado, G., et al. (2003). Familias Unidas: The efficacy of an intervention to promote parental investment in Hispanic immigrant families. *Prevention Science, 4,* 189–201.

Phillips, A. (2007). *Multiculturalism without culture.* Princeton: Princeton University Press.

Resnicow, K., Baranowski, T., Ahluwalia, J. S., & Braithwaite, R. L. (1999). Cultural sensitivity in public health: Defined and demystified. *Ethnicity & Disease, 9,* 10–21.

Roth, A., & Fonagy, P. (2004). *What works for whom? A critical review of psychotherapy research* (2nd ed.). New York: Guilford.

Rycroft-Malone, J., Seers, K., Titchen, A., Harvey, G., Kitson, A., & McCormack, B. (2004). What counts as evidence in evidence-based practice? *Journal of Advanced Nursing, 47,* 81–90.

SAMHSA. (2009). *Identifying and selecting evidence-based interventions: Revised guidance document for the strategic prevention framework state incentive grant program.* Rockville, MD: Center for Substance Abuse Prevention, Substance Abuse and Mental Health Services Administration.

Santisteban, D. A., Coatsworth, J. D., Perez-Vidal, A., Mitrani, V., Jean-Gilles, M., & Szapocznik, J. (1997). Brief structural/strategic family therapy with African and Hispanic high-risk youth. *Journal of Community Psychology, 25,* 453–471.

Santisteban, D. A., Muir-Malcolm, J. A., Mitrani, V. B., & Szapocznik, J. (2002). Integrating the study of ethnic culture and family psychology intervention science. In H. Liddle, R. Levant, D. A. Santisteban, & J. Bray (Eds.), *Family psychology: Science based interventions* (pp. 331–352). Washington, DC: American Psychological Association.

Santisteban, D. A., Perez-Vidal, A., Coatsworth, J. D., Kurtines, W. M., Schwartz, S. J., LaPerriere, A., et al. (2003). Efficacy of brief strategic family therapy in modifying Hispanic adolescent behavior problems and substance use. *Journal of Family Psychology, 17*, 121–133.

Santisteban, D. A., & Szapocznik, J. (1994). Bridging theory, research and practice to more successfully engage substance abusing youth and their families into therapy. *Journal of Child & Adolescent Substance Abuse, 3*, 9–24.

Santisteban, D. A., Szapocznik, J., Perez-Vidal, A., Kurtines, W. M., Murray, E. J., & LaPerriere, A. (1996). Efficacy of intervention for engaging youth and families into treatment and some variables that may contribute to differential effectiveness. *Journal of Family Psychology, 10*, 35–44.

Santisteban, D., Vega, R. R., & Suarez-Morales, L. (2006). Utilizing dissemination findings to help understand and bridge the research and practice gap in the treatment of substance abuse disorders in Latino populations. *Drug and Alcohol Dependence, 84*, 94–101.

Schinke, S. P., Orlandi, M. A., Botvin, G. J., Gilchrist, L. D., Trimble, J. E., & Locklear, V. S. (1988). Preventing substance abuse among American-Indian adolescents: A bicultural competence skills approach. *Journal of Counseling Psychology, 35*, 87–90.

Schinke, S. P., Tepavac, L., & Cole, K. C. (2000). Preventing substance use among native American youth: Three-year results. *Addictive Behaviors, 25*, 387–397.

Shadish, W. R., Montgomery, L. M., Wilson, P., Wilson, M. R., Bright, I., & Okwumabua, T. (1993). Effects of family and marital psychotherapies: A meta-analysis. *Journal of Consulting and Clinical Psychology, 61*, 992–1002.

Sobell, L. C. (1996). Bridging the gap between scientists and practitioners: The challenge before us. *Behavior Therapy, 27*, 297–320.

Sorensen, J. L., & Midkiff, E. E. (2000). Bridging the gap between research and drug abuse treatment. *Journal of Psychoactive Drugs, 32*, 379–382.

Szapocznik, J., & Coatsworth, J. D. (1999). An ecodevelopmental framework for organizing the influences on drug abuse: A developmental model of risk and protection. In M. D. Glantz & C. R. Hartel (Eds.), *Drug abuse: Origins & interventions* (pp. 331–366). Washington, DC: American Psychological Association.

Thyer, B. A. (2004). What is evidence-based practice? *Brief Treatment and Crisis Intervention, 4*, 167–176.

Torrey, W., & Gorman, P. (2005). Closing the gap between what services are and what they could be. In R. E. Drake, M. R. Merrans, & D. W. Lynde (Eds.), *Evidence-based mental health practice* (pp. 167–188). New York: W.W. Norton.

Turner, W. L. (2000). Cultural considerations in family-based primary prevention programs in drug abuse. *The Journal of Primary Prevention, 21*, 285–303.

Turner-Musa, J. O., Rhodes, W. A., Harper, P. T. H., & Quinton, S. L. (2008). Hip-hop to prevent substance use and HIV among African American youth: A preliminary investigation. *Journal of Drug Education, 38*, 351–365.

Willis, D. (2007). Evidenced-based practice implementation issues. Panel Presentation presented at the University of Michigan Conference: Solving problems in society: Ideas and people, Ann Arbor, MI.

Chapter 11
Adolescents

Kimberly Bender, Stephen Tripodi, and Jacoba Rock

Substance use and abuse during adolescence is a serious concern with substantial consequences for adolescents and their families. Several risk factors have been shown to predict adolescents' substance involvement, informing development of interventions to address these concerns. As the field of adolescent addictions has grown, several intervention approaches have been tested, and certain interventions show promising effects in reducing substance use. This chapter reviews what is known about adolescent substance use, its prevention and treatment, and adolescent resiliency in the presence of risk. Finally, the chapter concludes with a look forward to young adulthood and substance abuse trends as adolescents move on to this next developmental period.

Prevalence and Trends for Adolescent Substance Use and Abuse

According to the Monitoring the Future survey, an annual national survey of self-reported adolescent drug use in the USA, drug use rates have fluctuated over the past 20 years (Johnston, O'Malley, Bachman, & Schulenberg, 2010). Figure 11.1 shows changes in lifetime prevalence rates of use of different substances from 1991 to 2009. Rates of use declined in the early 1990s followed by increases in use in late 1990s. Since then, adolescents' use of most substances has demonstrated slow but

K. Bender(✉) • J. Rock
University of Denver, Denver, CO, USA
e-mail: Kimberly.Bender@du.edu

S. Tripodi
Florida State University, Tallahassee, FL, USA
e-mail: stripodi@fsu.edu

M.G. Vaughn and B.E. Perron (eds.), *Social Work Practice in the Addictions,* Contemporary Social Work Practice, DOI 10.1007/978-1-4614-5357-4_11, © Springer Science+Business Media New York 2013

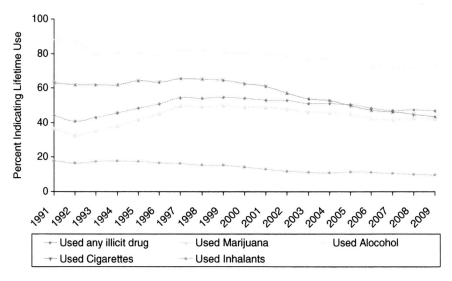

Fig. 11.1 Lifetime prevalence of illicit drug use by 12th graders (1991–2009). Data from: Monitoring the Future, 2010, Volume II; 2009 Data Collection

steady declines. Recent data, however, indicate use of certain substances, such as alcohol and marijuana, have stopped declining in the past few years, causing concern. While use of substances is common among adolescents, addiction rates are less so; results from a nationally representative sample of 4,175 adolescents indicate 3% meet criteria for substance abuse or dependence disorders (Roberts, Roberts, & Chan, 2009).

Substance use generally increases with age during the adolescent years, with high school seniors reporting greater use than adolescents in the 8th and 10th grades. Figure 11.2 depicts the prevalence rates of use during the past 30 days for different substances. While rates of use of illicit drugs in general, and alcohol and marijuana use specifically, are lower in earlier grades and highest among 12th graders, inhalant use follows a different pattern, most commonly used among younger adolescents and declining in later adolescence.

Alcohol is the drug used most by adolescents. In 2009, substantial proportions of 12th graders reported being drunk in the past 30 days (46%) and binge drinking (12%), generally defined as having at least five consecutive drinks (Johnston et al., 2010). Similar rates have been reported by Simons-Morton, Pickett, Boyce, Ter Bogt, and Vollebergh (2010), with monthly drinking reported by 34% of 10th grade boys and 20% of 10th grade girls in the USA; 28% of the boys and 24% of the girls report frequent drunkenness. Marijuana is the second most commonly used drug by adolescents and the most commonly used illicit drug. In 2009, 33% of 12th graders, 24% of 10th graders, and 11% of 8th graders reported using marijuana (Johnston et al., 2010). The trends for marijuana and alcohol use have been parallel over the years. Inhalants, the third most commonly used drug, have demonstrated increased rates for 8th graders from 2001 to 2004 and again in 2007. The most commonly

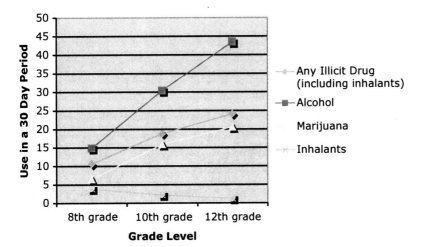

Fig. 11.2 Prevalence of substance use during the past 30 days for 8th grade, 10th grade, and 12th grade students. Data from: Monitoring the Future, 2010, Volume II; 2009 Data Collection

used inhalants are glue, shoe polish, toluene, lighter fluid, and gasoline. There appears to be a strong association between inhalant use and juvenile delinquency. Among 723 incarcerated adolescents in Missouri, for example, 37% participated in inhalant use, much higher rates than reported in the general adolescent population (Howard, Balster, Cottler, Wu, & Vaughn, 2008).

Research documents some significant gender and ethnic differences for substance use and abuse. Males have higher rates of illicit drug use and binge drinking compared to their female counterparts. However, gender differences are reduced in regards to alcohol use; while 8th grade males traditionally report higher rates of use, girls demonstrated higher rates starting in 2002 and this has continued through 2009. African-American students have lower rates of illicit drug use and alcohol use than Whites. Hispanic students' substance use rates fall between the rates for African Americans and Whites but closer to rates reported by White adolescents (Johnston et al., 2010).

Risk Factors for Adolescent Substance Use and Abuse

There are many risk factors that increase the chances adolescents will use and abuse substances. In fact, risk factors are stronger predictors of substance use outcomes than protective factors, regardless of grade level or type of substance (Cleveland, Feinberg, Bontempo, & Greenberg, 2008). Individual factors associated with risk for adolescent substance abuse, include several social and emotional problems (Cleveland et al., 2008), such as low self-esteem and poor body image (particularly among girls) (Roberts et al., 2009), Attention Deficit Hyperactivity Disorder

(ADHD) and conduct disorders (Gau et al., 2007; Lynskey, Fergusson, & Horwood, 1998), and sensation-seeking behavior (Gunning, Sussman, Rohrbach, Kniazev, & Masagutov, 2009). Furthermore, youth who experience school stress (Roberts et al., 2009), spend time in counterproductive after-school settings (Schinke, Fang, & Cole, 2008), and experience poor academic performance are at increased risk for use and abuse (Gau et al., 2007; Gunning et al., 2009).

Family can also be source of risk for adolescent substance use; parents play an especially influential role (Jones, Hussong, Manning, & Sterrett, 2008). Youth are particularly at risk if they have poor relationships with their parents (Roberts et al., 2009) or if their parents hold low expectations for their child's success (Nash, McQueen, & Bray, 2005). Youth from families characterized by authoritarian parenting styles (Castro, Brook, Brook, & Rubenstone, 2006), poor family management practices (Tobler, Komro, & Maldonado-Molina, 2009), poor communication, and low family cohesion (Szapocznik, Prado, Burlew, Williams, & Santisteban, 2007) are at increased risk. Moreover, parents' own use of substances significantly predicts their adolescents' use (Castro et al., 2006; Gunning et al., 2009), especially maternal drug use, parental drug use with a child (Castro et al., 2006), and parental alcoholism (Poelen, Scholte, Willemsen, Boomsma, & Engels, 2007; Scholte, Poelen, Willemsen, Boomsmsa, & Engels, 2007).

Among social context variables, peer substance use is the strongest predictor of alcohol use (Gunning et al., 2009). Several peer group risk factors are associated with adolescent substance use, including peer influence (Nash et al., 2005), peer alcohol use (Poelen et al., 2007; Scholte et al., 2007), best friend's substance use for female adolescents (Schinke et al., 2008), and gang involvement (Ryan, Miller-Loessi, & Nieri, 2007).

Finally, community and environmental risk factors include: economic stress; neighborhood effects (Kulis, Marsiglia, Sicotte, & Nieri, 2007); and disorganized neighborhood structure (Lambert, Brown, Phillips, & Ialongo, 2004). Neighborhood perceptions are associated with substance use particularly among African Americans (Lambert et al., 2004).

Consequences of Substance Abuse

Adolescent alcohol use disorders are associated with serious psychosocial problems both in adolescents and later in life as adults (Rowe, Liddle, Greenbaum, & Henderson, 2004). Substance abusers demonstrate greater risk for cognitive deficits (Tapert, Brown, Myers, & Granholm, 1999), reduced motivation to succeed academically (Baer, Garrett, Breadnell, Wells, & Peterson, 2007), and increased risk for subsequent adult alcohol abuse and related problems (D'Amico, Miles, Stern, & Meredith, 2008).

Despite popular perception, there are many physical, mental, and social consequences associated with marijuana use for adolescents (Volkow, 2005), including but not limited to the following: impairment to coordination and reaction time

(Degenhardt, Hall, & Lynskey, 2001); poor school performance and reduced likelihood of graduating from high school (Brook, Balka, & Whiteman, 1999; Lynskey & Hall, 2000); delinquent and sexually risky behaviors (Brook et al., 1999); and disruptions in transitions to young adulthood, including unemployment, increased rebelliousness, and increased risks of teenage pregnancies (Brook, Adams, Balka, & Johnson, 2002).

Finally, recurrent inhalant use is associated with conditions such as Parkinsonism, cerebellar ataxia, encephalopathy, trigeminal neuropathy, hepatoxicity, heptorenal syndrome, delayed neurological recovery, and deaths due to drug actions and accidents. Adolescents who use inhalants are frequently more likely to experience adverse consequences than adolescents who moderately or rarely use inhalants. Common related consequences include committing acts of violence and vandalism, committing property crimes, driving under the influence, having unprotected sex, suffering serious injury while high, having suicidal thoughts, and disrupting friendships (Howard et al., 2008).

Treatment Modalities

Many of the risk factors described below have informed development of interventions to address adolescent substance use and abuse. Interventions for adolescent substance use include several individual and family-based approaches. Individual treatments are often behavioral and/or cognitive in nature and often utilize motivational interviewing. The goal of behavioral approaches is to first identify internal and external stimuli that trigger use and then to learn and practice techniques for refusal, relaxation, coping, and behavior management. Often treatment is structured with the therapist modeling behaviors, youth rehearsing skills, and then youth having assignments between sessions; praise for progress is considered essential. Planners are used to structure time and keep track of behaviors in each environment. Significant others (family, partners, friends) are invited to attend sessions to promote safe activities and support avoidance of risky situations (Azrin et al., 1994) often by providing positive reinforcements for desired behavior.

Cognitive behavioral treatment (CBT) is often provided in an didactic format. It is based on the concept that thoughts affect feelings, and feelings are connected to particular substance use behaviors. Clients are encouraged to identify and challenge distorted thoughts and maladaptive perceptions that lead to negative feelings connected to the desire to use substances. With practice, the goal is for youth to accurately assess problems, evaluate their own thoughts related to the problem, and find a balanced interpretation that results in more productive and healthy behaviors. Thus, cognitive approaches rely greatly on problem solving.

Motivational Interviewing (MI) is a therapeutic technique for recognizing a problem behavior and building internal motivation toward behavioral change. It is considered to be a low-demand intervention that can be provided in a brief format. Aimed at increasing the individual's motivation to use services and reduce substance use, the approach is non-confrontational and nondirective for substance users. The therapist works with the client to explore his or her own thoughts about substance use and readiness for change (Baer et al., 2007).

Family and multi-systemic approaches move beyond individual interventions with youth to also include reduction of risk factors in youths' families and other important systems, including schools, peers, and communities. Multi-systemic approaches with empirical support include Multi-systemic Therapy (MST), Integrated Family and Cognitive Behavioral Therapy (IFCBT), Multidimensional Family Therapy (MDFT), and Brief Strategic Family Therapy (BSFT); each is briefly described below.

MST is performed with youth in the context of their homes, schools, and neighborhoods, to reduce substance use and associated risk factors. MST provides services in the natural environment (home and community) around the clock, with therapists on-call to respond to crises in the home. The therapist is goal-oriented and offers pragmatic interventions to change risk factors across systems and reduce substance use. For example, MST may focus on: (1) changing family dynamics (empowering the parent to set rules and structure, and improve discipline techniques), (2) reducing deviant peer associations, and (3) helping teachers to encourage greater academic success (Henggeler, Smith, & Melton, 1992). The MST model also focuses on strengths and available support systems (Timmons-Mitchell, Bender, Kishna, & Mitchell, 2006).

IFCBT integrates family therapy with peer group therapy, using a cognitive-behavioral approach. This therapy is informed by neuroscience evidence that demonstrates youth who use substances have deficits in certain executive functions such as response inhibition, planning, concept formation, cognitive flexibility, and language that might prevent engagement and success in drug treatment. IFCBT aims to help youth develop skills in problem solving. Like other approaches, IFCBT also aims to address and reduce risk factors in various ecological systems (Latimer, Winters, D'Zurilla, & Nichols, 2003).

Multidimensional Family Therapy (MDFT) is a family-focused treatment that includes four domains: adolescent, parent, interactional, and extra-familial. The goal of the adolescent domain is to engage the youth in treatment and help the youth to effectively communicate their thoughts and feelings to parents and other important adults in their lives, develop methods of coping and regulating difficult emotions, develop problem-solving skills, increase social skills and functioning in school and work environments, and participate in alternative behaviors to substance use. MDFT also works in the parent domain to engage parental figures in the treatment process, develop and improve parenting strategies, increase parental monitoring, help parents to establish clear limits and expectations (and follow through with consequences), and help parents to enhance their own psychosocial functioning as to be a better support in the youth's life. MDFT therapists also work in the interactional domain, where they aim to decrease conflicts and increase bonding and attachment through improvements to communication and family problem solving. Finally, the MDFT therapists aim to address the extra-familial domain by helping the family interact competently with other systems involved in the youth's life, such as school, recreational agencies, or the juvenile justice system (Liddle, Dakof, Turner, Henderson, & Greenbaum, 2008).

Brief Strategic Family Therapy (BSFT) was initially developed as a treatment for addressing family conflict among Latino immigrant families, but has since expanded to address family issues, including youth substance use, across a range of ethnic/ racial backgrounds. BSFT changes family interactions in the context of cultural factors that influence youth substance use. The family is seen as the base of development where youth learn how to think and feel and respond to their environment. BSFT, like many of the other family interventions above, recognizes the impact other social systems can have on the family and the individual, and aims to help families, and parents in particular, to reduce risk factors inherent in the broader social systems. The primary goal of BSFT is to improve relationships within and outside of the family. To do so, BSFT uses planed interventions that are pragmatic and problem-focused. The family problems and patterns that most directly affect the youths' substance use are addressed first, and then other interaction problems are addressed subsequently. In implementing planned interventions, the therapist focuses on joining the family, reducing resistance, and engaging them as active partners in treatment. Specifically, the treatment focuses on the family hierarchy, making sure the parents are most powerful in the family, are engaging in behavior control, are nurturing, are aligned with one another, and have healthy boundaries (Winters & Leitten, 2007).

Although each multi-systemic approach may address substance use with a unique framework, several commonalities are seen across multi-systemic approaches to adolescent substance abuse. Multi-systemic approaches often focus on addressing risk and protective factors associated with the substance use; involve important individuals from a variety of other systems influencing youth behaviors (parents, schools, peers, etc.); and often include a common intervention emphasis on problem solving and parental skill development.

Synthesis of Intervention Effectiveness

With the proliferation of studies examining the effects of substance abuse prevention and intervention approaches, researchers have conducted several meta-analyses and systematic reviews to synthesize findings across studies, enabling them to make broader claims about overall effectiveness and to identify approaches most successful in reducing substance use and abuse. A meta-analysis is a kind of study of studies that attempts to arrive at a statistical conclusion regarding the status of research in a given area. Several meta-analyses have focused on prevention programs provided to youth before substance use has been initiated or problem use has occurred. Meta-analytic results indicate variation in the effectiveness of substance use prevention programs (Tobler et al., 2000). Tobler et al.'s (2000) meta-analysis of substance use prevention programs found prevention programs demonstrating the greatest effects are those that employ interactive methods where youth are given the opportunity to exchange ideas, communicate with other students and with facilitators, and practice refusal skills. These approaches demonstrate better effects than knowledge-based, noninteractive methods in which youth are merely taught about substances and encouraged to clarify their own values and feelings related to use. Research suggests that the more interactive programs utilized a social influence approach that combated peer pressure by helping youth develop assertiveness, coping and communication skills (Tobler et al., 2000).

Other meta-analyses of substance use prevention programs, specifically implemented in school-based settings, found small yet positive effects across programs with greatest support for programs that utilize behavior and cognitive behavioral interventions (Wilson, Gottfredson, & Najaka, 2001). School-based prevention programs providing more general, noncognitive behavioral counseling or social work showed negative effects, and alternative programs such as mentoring, tutoring, and recreational programs were not associated with significant reductions in use. It is also important to note that prevention programs are not equally effective for all types of students. Prevention programs targeting higher risk youth had larger effects than those provided to general school samples (Wilson et al., 2001). It appears that teaching specific behavioral or cognitive behavioral skills is an important part of effective in school-based substance use prevention programming; methods in skill building should include repeatedly exposing students to new skills, providing ample opportunities for practice and rehearsal, and provision of feedback to refine skill development (Wilson et al., 2001). In addition, programs should include booster sessions in which students are reminded of skills learned several months after the program ends (White & Pitts, 1998).

Meta-analyses have also examined the effectiveness of treatment programs aimed at reducing substance use and abuse among youth with established substance use problems or addictions. Vaughn and Howard (2004) reviewed controlled trials of adolescent substance abuse across various types of substances. Although several interventions demonstrated reductions in substance use, their review found the greatest levels of support for Multidimensional Family Therapy and Cognitive Behavioral Therapy provided in a group format. With growing pressure to provide substance abuse treatment in abbreviated formats, Tait and Hulse (2003) focused their synthesis of the literature more narrowly on brief interventions (four or fewer treatment sessions) for their effectiveness in reducing adolescent substance use. The authors found brief treatments to be beneficial, but benefits differed by the substance targeted. Interventions targeting tobacco use had very small effects; alcohol interventions had small but significant effects; and interventions to reduce multiple substances showed medium effects (Tait & Hulse, 2003). These findings suggest adolescents may respond differently to treatment depending on the type of substance they are using. To investigate this further, recent meta-analyses have examined the effects of treatments for specific commonly abused substances.

A recent meta-analysis synthesized the evidence of rigorously controlled studies of interventions to reduce adolescent alcohol use (Tripodi, Bender, Litschge, & Vaughn, 2010). After a thorough search of existing studies, Tripodi et al. (2010) identified 16 random clinical trials, and, synthesis across these findings indicated interventions were successful in significantly reducing alcohol use and had medium effects. Specific interventions highlighted for producing particularly large effects included several brief interventions such as Cognitive Behavioral Therapy integrated with a 12-step approach, Brief Motivational Interviewing and Multidimensional Family Therapy. It is important to note that the evidence base is still growing, so few interventions have been tested in multiple studies; this prevents clear conclusions regarding the most effective intervention approach. Also important, the effects of interventions begin to wane after treatment is over. Youth may reduce their use of skills learned in therapy and may reengage with risk factors such as negative peer groups, resulting in reduced effects after treatment. Of interventions tested for long-term effects, behaviorally oriented treatments appear the best at sustaining outcomes up to 1 year after treatment ends.

Similar efforts to synthesize the effects of interventions to reduce adolescent marijuana use through meta-analytic techniques similarly found significant yet moderate effects (Bender, Tripodi, Sarteschi, & Vaughn, 2011). Youth who received marijuana interventions did 67% better in reducing their marijuana use compared to youth in control conditions. Cognitive Behavioral approaches were again highlighted for particularly large effect sizes, including Cognitive Behavioral Therapy provided individually and when integrated with family therapy. Other interventions, including Multidimensional Family Therapy, Behavioral Treatment, and Motivational Interviewing also reported large effects. Similar to evidence on alcohol treatment, marijuana treatment effects appear to decrease over time post-treatment (Bender et al., 2011). Although not surprising, these waning treatment effects are still of clinical concern. Clinicians working with adolescent substance users are encouraged to provide booster sessions to reinforce skills learned in treatment several months after treatment ends. They should also consider involving parents or other professionals (at school or other community organizations) who can continue to help youth practice skills and avoid risk factors.

To summarize, efforts to synthesize the substance abuse intervention literature reveal that many different interventions may be effective in preventing or reducing adolescent substance use. Yet, certain approaches have stronger support, including behavioral, cognitive-behavioral, and skill-building interventions. Brief interventions may be effective when settings require it, but post-treatment follow-up or booster sessions are recommended.

Comorbidity

A primary challenge of treating adolescent substance use is addressing comorbid psychiatric mental health problems. Approximately 50–90% of adolescents abusing substances also report other psychiatric mental health problems (Rounds-Bryant, Kristiansen, & Hubbard, 1999), leading some scholars to assert dually diagnosed adolescents are not a special subpopulation but are the norm in substance abuse treatment (Roberts & Corcoran, 2005). Youth with co-occurring disorders often present with more severe symptoms and serious disorders; they begin using substance earlier and use more frequently and chronically than youth with only substance use disorders (Rowe et al., 2004). Dually diagnosed adolescents are often difficult to engage in treatment, have poor compliance rates, and end treatment early; this is of concern as poor treatment retention is associated with poor prognosis (Crome, 2004). Relapse is a major concern for youth with comorbid disorders, and gains made in treatment may be lost for youth struggling with both types of disorders (Dakof, Tejeda, & Liddle, 2001).

A systematic review by Bender, Springer, and Kim (2006) examined interventions for dually diagnosed adolescents. Several interventions produced large reductions in substance use, such as cognitive-behavioral therapy and family-based therapy, and youth continued to show these effects at follow up. Preliminary guidelines for treating dually diagnosed adolescents mirror components of effective treatments mentioned above, including multipronged, ongoing assessment; strategic engagement and retention; flexible treatment plans; integrated treatment to address mental health and substance use disorders concurrently; developmental and cultural sensitivity; ecological (systems-oriented) foundation; problem-solving, decision-making, affect regulation, communication skills, and family relations; and goal-directedness (Bender et al., 2006).

Resiliency Processes

Parents can play an important role in protecting their adolescents from developing substance use problems. Showing affection and developing a close parent–child bond is important in protecting adolescents from substance abuse (Cohen, Richardson, & LaBree, 1994). Bonds can be developed through providing parental support and encouragement and effective communication patterns (Castro et al., 2006). Such bonds may allow adolescents to talk to their parents about their problems which is, in turn, associated with lower levels of use (Stronski, Ireland, Michaud, Narring, & Resnick, 2000). Adolescents alienated from their parents are less likely to adopt conventional norms of behavior, and subsequently, more likely to abuse substances. Parents should also establish clear rules and discipline, monitor their adolescent's behavior, and send a message of intolerance for their substance use to buffer against substance use risks (Castro et al., 2006; Ryan et al., 2007).

The school environment is also a strong source of resiliency to adolescent substance use. High academic performance is a protective factor for risky adolescent behavior in general (Ryan et al., 2007) and a protective factor for binge drinking more specifically (Piko & Kovacs, 2010). Youth who report being attached to their teachers, enabling them to talk comfortably with their teachers about problems, are less likely to abuse substances (Fitzpatrick, Piko, Wright, & LaGory, 2005).

Culturally specific protective factors have been noted in the literature. For African-American adolescents, strong racial identity, including endorsement of positive attitudes toward being African American, has been found to be associated with antidrug attitudes and less substance use (Sellers, Copeland-Linder, Martin, & Lewis, 2006; Szapocznik et al., 2007). For Hispanic adolescents, acculturation is negatively associated with substance use (Szapocznik et al., 2007), such that youth born in the USA, youths who have lived more years in the USA, and youths with higher levels of acculturation exhibit higher rates of substance use (Turner, Lloyd, & Taylor, 2006). Discrepancies in acculturation (i.e., when adolescents from immigrant families are more likely than are their parents to master English and to adopt U.S. values) promotes risk for drug abuse in Hispanic immigrants because it creates additional familial conflict that undermines adolescent bonding to the family and erodes parental authority (De La Rosa, Vega, & Radisch, 2000). Thus, for Hispanic adolescents, family cohesion, effective parenting, family communication, and low family drug problems all increase resiliency against drug use.

Transitions to Adulthood

Though researchers have historically given less consideration to young adulthood (ages 18–25) than adolescence (Osgood, Foster, Flanagan, & Ruth, 2005), this life stage is increasingly seen as its own entity, requiring its own unique considerations and services. Many life changes prevalent in young adulthood are generally considered to reduce risk for substance use, including completing education, beginning careers, advancing relationships (often to marriage and parenthood), and renting or even purchasing independent housing; these roles may protect young adults because they require increased responsibility-taking behavior (Maggs & Schulenberg, 2004). However, young adults are taking on these roles with more hesitancy and ambivalence than ever before. Emerging adulthood is increasingly a stage of experimenting before making life commitments. During this time, young adults express uncertainty about taking on the freedoms and responsibilities of adult roles, and often carry unrealistic expectations about life (Arnett, 2007). Those who have used substances and engaged in other at-risk behaviors during adolescence are less likely to experience the positive role changes characteristics of emerging adulthood (Baer & Peterson, 2002).

Figure 11.3 depicts substance use rates during young adulthood from the national Monitoring the Future survey. While most illicit drugs, including marijuana decrease into young adulthood, alcohol use shows increases in early adulthood before tapering off in the late twenties. Although most young adults will consistently engage in light drinking for all or most of young adulthood, a smaller subgroup will binge drink—an indicator of problem use (Maggs & Schulenberg, 2004). Dishion and Owen (2002) suggest that use of 'heavier' drugs during young adulthood may greatly predict the chronic usage of those drugs later in life, unlike alcohol use.

Problems with substance use during young adulthood are predicted by early use of substances in adolescence (DiClemente, 2006) and poor achievement in high school (Schulenberg, Bachman, O'Malley, & Johnston, 1994). However, high-school students who attend college increase alcohol use for a limited period of time, as alcohol

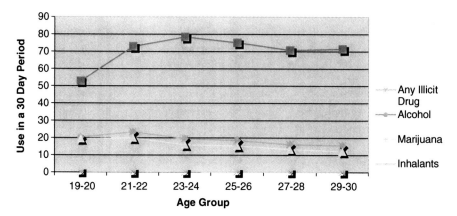

Fig. 11.3 Thirty-day prevalence of substance use for young adults. Data from: Monitoring the Future, 2010, Volume II; 2009 Data Collection

is considered normative and drinking is considered a "rite of passage" (Miller, Turner, & Marlatt, 2001). A survey of college students across 140 universities found 44% engage in binge drinking during young adulthood (Miller et al., 2001). Like in adolescence, peer influence continues to be a predictor of substance use and abuse in young adulthood; friends influence drug use, and drugs influence friendship selection (Dishion & Owen, 2002). Though there may be significant impact such as health risk, academic failure, and motor vehicle accidents, research shows that for young adult college students, alcohol abuse is most often not chronic. Yet, young adulthood is a pivotal time in which successful milestones in college predict better paid employment down the road; likewise, having difficulty during this time period including abusing drugs and alcohol can predict further difficulties (Osgood et al., 2005). Because of the diverse trajectories substance use takes during young adulthood, various approaches are required for this population. Those interventions that are brief, focused on reducing harm (instead of abstinence-only), and incorporate the peer group seem to be most applicable and beneficial for the young adult population (Baer & Peterson, 2002).

Conclusion

Adolescence is a developmental period characterized by increased experimentation with substances. Prevention programs, particularly skill building interventions provided in school-based settings, have been successful in preventing substance use. For some youth, those with elevated levels of individual, family, and societal risk factors, experimentation with substances may result in substance addiction. Several individual and family-based interventions are effective in treating adolescent addiction. Interventions that use behavioral, cognitive-behavioral, and motivational enhancing approaches are particularly effective, as are interventions that ameliorate risks across multiple systems (home, school, community). Despite heightened risk during adolescence, many youth, especially those with supportive parents and teachers, avoid substance use problems, and most will reduce use naturally as they transition to young adulthood. Although findings from intervention studies are promising, further research is needed to rigorously test potentially effective interventions in order to identify methods for reducing adolescent substance abuse and its detrimental social consequences.

References

Arnett, J. J. (2007). Emerging adulthood: What is it, and what is it good for? *Society for Research in Child Development, 1*, 68–73.

Azrin, N. H., McMahon, P. T., Donohue, B., Besalel, V. A., Lapinski, K. J., Kogan, E. S., et al. (1994). Behavior therapy for drug abuse: A controlled treatment outcome study. *Behavior Research and Therapy, 32*, 857–866.

Baer, J. S., Garrett, S. B., Breadnell, B., Wells, E. A., & Peterson, P. (2007). Brief motivational intervention with homeless adolescents: Evaluating effects on substance use and service utilization. *Psychology of Addictive Behaviors, 21*, 582–586.

Baer, J. S., & Peterson, P. L. (2002). Motivational interviewing with adolescents and young adults. In W. R. Miller & S. Rollnick (Eds.), *Motivational interviewing: Preparing people for change* (pp. 320–332). New York: Guilford Press.

Bender, K., Springer, D. W., & Kim, J. S. (2006). Treatment effectiveness with dually diagnosed adolescents: A systematic review. *Brief Treatment and Crisis Intervention, 6*, 177–205.

Bender, K., Tripodi, S. J., Sarteschi, C., & Vaughn, M. G. (2011). A meta-analytic review of interventions to reduce adolescent cannabis use. *Research on Social Work Practice, 21*, 153–164.

Brook, J. S., Adams, R. E., Balka, E. B., & Johnson, E. (2002). Early adolescent marijuana use: Risks for the transition to young adulthood. *Psychological Medicine, 32*, 79–91.

Brook, J. S., Balka, E. B., & Whiteman, M. (1999). The risks for late adolescence of early adolescent marijuana use. *American Journal of Public Health, 89*, 1549–1554.

Castro, F. G., Brook, J. S., Brook, D. W., & Rubenstone, E. (2006). Paternal, perceived maternal, and youth risk factors as predictors of youth stage of substance use: A longitudinal study. *Journal of Addictive Diseases, 25*, 65–75.

Cleveland, M. J., Feinberg, M. E., Bontempo, D. E., & Greenberg, M. T. (2008). The role of risk and protective factors in substance use across adolescents. *Journal of Adolescent Health, 43*, 157–164.

Cohen, D. A., Richardson, J., & LaBree, L. (1994). Parenting behaviors and the onset of smoking and alcohol use: A longitudinal study. *Pediatrics, 94*, 368–375.

Crome, I. B. (2004). Comorbidity in youth people: Perspectives and challenges. *Acta Neuropsychiatrica, 16*, 47–53.

D'Amico, E. J., Miles, J. V., Stern, S. A., & Meredith, L. S. (2008). Brief motivational interviewing for teens at risk of substance use consequences: A randomized pilot study in a primary care clinic. *Journal of Substance Abuse Treatment, 35*, 53–61.

Dakof, G. A., Tejeda, M., & Liddle, H. A. (2001). Predictors of engagement in adolescent drug abuse treatment. *Journal of the American Academy of Child & Adolescent Psychiatry, 40*, 274–281.

De La Rosa, M., Vega, R., & Radisch, M. A. (2000). The role of acculturation in the substance abuse behavior of African-American and Latino adolescents: Advances, issues, and recommendations. *Journal of Psychoactive Drugs, 32*, 33–42.

Degenhardt, L., Hall, W., & Lynskey, M. (2001). The relationship between cannabis use, depression and anxiety among Australian adults: Findings from the National Survey of Mental Health and Well-Being. *Social Psychiatry and Psychiatric Epidemiology, 36*, 219–227.

DiClemente, C. C. (2006). Natural change and the troublesome use of substances: A life-course perspective. In W. R. Miller & K. M. Carroll (Eds.), *Rethinking substance abuse: What the science shows, and what we should do about it* (pp. 81–96). New York: Guilford Press.

Dishion, T. J., & Owen, L. D. (2002). A longitudinal analysis of friendship and substance use: Bidirectional influence from adolescence to adulthood. *Developmental Psychology, 38*, 480–491.

Fitzpatrick, K. M., Piko, B. F., Wright, D. R., & LaGory, M. (2005). Depressive symptomatology, exposure to violence, and the role of social capital among African American adolescents. *American Journal of Orthopsychiatry, 75*, 262–274.

Gau, S. S., Chong, M., Yang, P., Yen, C., Liang, K., & Cheng, A. T. (2007). Psychiatric and psychosocial predictors of substance use disorders among adolescents: Longitudinal study. *British Journal of Psychiatry, 190*, 42–48.

Gunning, M., Sussman, S., Rohrbach, L. A., Kniazev, V., & Masagutov, R. (2009). Concurrent predictors of cigarette and alcohol use among U.S. and Russian adolescents. *Journal of Drug Education, 39*, 385–400.

Henggeler, S. W., Smith, L. A., & Melton, G. B. (1992). Multisystemic therapy with violent and chronic juvenile offenders and their families: The role of treatment fidelity in successful dissemination. *Journal of Consulting and Clinical Psychology, 60*, 953–961.

Howard, M. O., Balster, R. L., Cottler, L. B., Wu, L., & Vaughn, M. G. (2008). Inhalant use among incarcerated adolescents in the United States: Prevalence, characteristics, and correlates of use. *Drug and Alcohol Dependence, 93*, 197–209.

Johnston, L. D., O'Malley, P. M., Bachman, J. G., & Schulenberg, J. E. (2010). *Monitoring the future national survey results on drug use, 1975–2009. Vol. 1: Secondary school students.* NIH Publication No. 10-7584. Bethesda, MD: National Institute on Drug Abuse.

Jones, D. J., Hussong, A. M., Manning, J., & Sterrett, E. (2008). Adolescent alcohol use in context: The role of parents and peers among African American and European American youth. *Cultural Diversity and Ethnic Minority Psychology, 14*, 266–273.

Kulis, S., Marsiglia, F. F., Sicotte, D., & Nieri, T. (2007). Neighborhood effects on youth substance use in a Southwestern city. *Sociological Perspectives, 50*, 273–301.

Lambert, S. F., Brown, T. L., Phillips, C. M., & Ialongo, N. S. (2004). The relationship between perceptions of neighborhood characteristics and substance use among urban African American adolescents. *American Journal of Community Psychology, 34*, 205–218.

Latimer, W. W., Winters, K. C., D'Zurilla, T., & Nichols, M. (2003). Integrated family and cognitive-behavioral therapy for adolescent substance abusers: A stage I efficacy study. *Drug and Alcohol Dependence, 71*, 303–317.

Liddle, H. A., Dakof, G. A., Turner, R. M., Henderson, C. E., & Greenbaum, P. E. (2008). Treating adolescent drug abuse: A randomized trial comparing multidimensional family therapy and cognitive behavior therapy. *Addiction, 103*, 1660–1670.

Lynskey, M., Fergusson, D. M., & Horwood, L. J. (1998). The origins of the correlations between tobacco, alcohol, and cannabis use during adolescence. *Journal of Child Psychology and Psychiatry, 39*, 995–1105.

Lynskey, M., & Hall, W. (2000). The effects of adolescent cannabis use on educational attainment: A review. *Addiction, 95*, 1621–1630.

Maggs, J. L., & Schulenberg, J. (2004). Trajectories of alcohol use during the transition to adulthood. *Alcohol Research and Health, 28*, 195–201.

Miller, E. T., Turner, A. P., & Marlatt, G. A. (2001). The harm reduction approach to the secondary prevention of alcohol problems in adolescents and young adults. In P. M. Monti, S. M. Colby, & T. A. O'Leary (Eds.), *Adolescents, alcohol, and substance abuse: Reaching teens through brief interventions* (pp. 58–79). New York: Guilford Press.

Nash, S. G., McQueen, A., & Bray, J. H. (2005). Pathways to adolescent alcohol use: An examination of mediating and moderating effects. *Journal of Child and Family Studies, 9*, 509–528.

Osgood, D. W., Foster, E. M., Flanagan, C., & Ruth, G. R. (2005). Why focus on the transition to adulthood for vulnerable populations? In D. W. Osgood et al. (Eds.), *On your own without a net: The transition to adulthood for vulnerable populations* (pp. 1–26). Chicago: University of Chicago Press.

Piko, B. F., & Kovacs, E. (2010). Do parents and school matter? Protective factors for adolescent substance use. *Addictive Behaviors, 35*, 53–56.

Poelen, E. A., Scholte, R. H., Willemsen, G., Boomsma, D. I., & Engels, C. M. (2007). Drinking by parents, siblings, and friends as predictors of regular alcohol use in adolescents and young adults: A longitudinal twin-family study. *Alcohol & Alcoholism, 42*, 362–369.

Roberts, A. R., & Corcoran, K. (2005). Adolescents growing up in stressful environments, dual diagnosis, and sources of success. *Brief Treatment and Crisis Intervention, 5*, 1–8.

Roberts, R. E., Roberts, C. R., & Chan, W. (2009). One-year incidence of psychiatric disorders and associated risk factors among adolescents in the community. *Journal of Child Psychology and Psychiatry, 50*, 4405–4415.

Rounds-Bryant, J. L., Kristiansen, P. L., & Hubbard, R. L. (1999). Drug abuse treatment outcome study adolescents: A comparison of client characteristics and pretreatment behaviors in three treatment modalities. *American Journal of Drug and Alcohol Abuse, 25*, 573–591.

Rowe, C. L., Liddle, H. A., Greenbaum, P. E., & Henderson, C. E. (2004). Impact of psychiatric comorbidity on treatment of adolescent drug abusers. *Journal of Substance Abuse Treatment, 26*, 129–140.

Ryan, L. G., Miller-Loessi, K., & Nieri, T. (2007). Relationships with adults as predictors of substance use, gang involvement, and threats to safety among disadvantaged urban high-school adolescents. *Journal of Community Psychology, 35*, 1053–1071.

Schinke, S. P., Fang, L., & Cole, K. C. (2008). Substance use among early adolescent girls: Risk and protective factors. *Journal of Adolescent Health, 43*, 191–194.

Scholte, R. H., Poelen, E. A., Willemsen, G., Boomsmsa, D. I., & Engels, R. C. (2007). Relative risks of adolescent and young adult alcohol use: The role of drinking fathers, mothers, siblings, and friends. *Addictive Behaviours, 33*, 1–14.

Schulenberg, J., Bachman, J. G., O'Malley, P. M., & Johnston, L. D. (1994). High school educational success and subsequent substance use: A panel analysis following adolescents into young adulthood. *Journal of Health and Social Behavior, 35*, 45–62.

Sellers, R. M., Copeland-Linder, N., Martin, P. P., & Lewis, R. L. (2006). Racial identity matters: The relationship between racial discrimination and psychological functioning in African American adolescents. *Journal of Research on Adolescence, 16*, 187–216.

Simons-Morton, B., Pickett, W., Boyce, W., Ter Bogt, T. F., & Vollebergh, W. (2010). Cross-national comparison of adolescent drinking and cannabis use in the United States, Canada, and the Netherlands. *International Journal of Drug Policy, 21*, 64–69.

Stronski, S. M., Ireland, M., Michaud, P., Narring, F., & Resnick, M. D. (2000). Protective correlates of stages in adolescent substance use: A Swiss national study. *Journal of Adolescent Health, 26*, 420–427.

Szapocznik, J., Prado, G., Burlew, A. K., Williams, R. A., & Santisteban, D. A. (2007). Drug abuse in African American and Hispanic adolescents: Culture, development, and behavior. *Annual Review of Clinical Psychology, 3*, 77–105.

Tait, R. J., & Hulse, G. K. (2003). A systematic review of the effectiveness of brief interventions with substance using adolescents. *Drug and Alcohol Review, 22*, 337–346.

Tapert, S. F., Brown, S. A., Myers, M. G., & Granholm, E. (1999). The role of neurocognitive abilities in coping with adolescent relapse to alcohol and drug use. *Journal of Studies on Alcohol and Drugs, 60*, 500–508.

Timmons-Mitchell, J., Bender, M. B., Kishna, M. A., & Mitchell, C. C. (2006). An independent effectiveness trial of multisystemic therapy with juvenile justice youth. *Journal of Clinical Child and Adolescent Psychology, 35*, 227–236.

Tobler, A. L., Komro, K. A., & Maldonado-Molina, M. M. (2009). Relationship between neighborhood context, family management practices and alcohol use among urban, multi-ethnic, young adolescents. *Prevention Science, 10*, 313–324.

Tobler, N. S., Roona, M. R., Ochshorn, P., Marshall, D. G., Streke, A. V., & Stackpole, K. M. (2000). School-based adolescent drug prevention programs: 1998 meta-analysis. *The Journal of Primary Prevention, 20*, 275–336.

Tripodi, S. J., Bender, K., Litschge, C., & Vaughn, M. G. (2010). Interventions for reducing adolescent alcohol abuse: A meta-analytic review. *Archives of Pediatric and Adolescent Medicine, 164*, 85–91.

Turner, R. J., Lloyd, D. A., & Taylor, J. (2006). Stress burden, drug dependence and the nativity paradox among U.S. Hispanics. *Drug and Alcohol Dependence, 83*, 79–89.

Vaughn, M. G., & Howard, M. O. (2004). Adolescent substance abuse treatment: A synthesis of controlled evaluations. *Research on Social Work Practice, 14*, 325–335.

Volkow, N. D. (2005). *Marijuana abuse: National Institute on Drug Abuse research report series.* NIH Publication No. 05-3859. Washington, D.C: NIDA Drug Abus Research Dissemination Center.

White, D., & Pitts, M. (1998). Educating young people about drugs: A systematic review. *Addiction, 93*, 1475–1487.

Wilson, D. B., Gottfredson, D. C., & Najaka, S. S. (2001). School-based prevention of problem behaviors: A meta-analysis. *Journal of Quantitative Criminology, 17*, 247–271.

Winters, K. C., & Leitten, W. (2007). Brief intervention for drug-abusing adolescents in a school setting. *Psychology of Addictive Behaviors, 21*, 249–254.

Chapter 12
Women and Families

Bonnie Carlson

Abuse and dependence on alcohol and other drugs (AOD) is so pervasive, including among women, that it is imperative that social workers understand the implications of substance use and abuse. Despite their greater frequency in men, alcohol and drug use problems are significant among women. Until the late 1980s, addiction to drugs and alcohol was viewed primarily as a male disease, and women's addiction was regarded in much the same way as men's chemical dependency (Finkelstein, 1994). In response to the crack cocaine epidemic of the 1980s, concern developed about female crack users, especially those who were mothers or pregnant. For the past couple decades, women substance abusers have been typically viewed differently by society as compared to their male counterparts—sicker and more deviant— especially women who abuse illicit drugs (Finkelstein, 1994).

Substance Use and Abuse Patterns for Women

Alcohol

The National Survey on Drug Use and Health (NSDUH) is an annual, national survey based on in-person interviews with over 67,000 Americans age 12 and over [Substance Abuse and Mental Health Services Administration (SAMHSA), 2010]. This ongoing survey, and research in general, has consistently shown that men are more likely than women to consume alcohol. The NSDUH found that in 2009, 58% of males over age 12 were current drinkers, compared to 47% of females. However, among adolescents the percentages of male and female drinkers were quite comparable: 15% and 14%, respectively.

B. Carlson (✉)
Arizona State University, Tempe, AZ, USA
e-mail: bonnie.carlson@asu.edu

M.G. Vaughn and B.E. Perron (eds.), *Social Work Practice in the Addictions*,
Contemporary Social Work Practice, DOI 10.1007/978-1-4614-5357-4_12,
© Springer Science+Business Media New York 2013

Although alcohol is a legal substance, a major concern for women is drinking during pregnancy. Research has accumulated that alcohol consumption during pregnancy can be harmful to the fetus, especially heavy drinking and binge drinking [Center for Substance Abuse Treatment (CSAT), 2009]. The NSDUH found that although pregnant women were much less likely to drink than nonpregnant women, 10% versus 54%, respectively, 4.4% of pregnant women reported binge drinking and 0.8% reported heavy drinking. Alarmingly, during the first trimester when the central nervous system is starting to develop, 12% of pregnant women reported binge drinking (SAMHSA, 2010).

Drugs

As is the case with alcohol, consumption of illicit drugs is higher among males age 12 and older than females, 10.8% versus 6.6%, respectively, in particular marijuana and cocaine. However, the usage rates for non-prescribed tranquilizers and methamphetamines are comparable for males and females. Among youths, females had higher rates of non-prescribed psychotherapeutic drugs and pain relievers (SAMHSA, 2010). Methamphetamine (MA) use and abuse among women is a particular concern in some regions of the country such as the Southwest and Midwest, where MA use in general is more common (e.g., Brecht, O'Brien, von Mayrhauser, & Anglin, 2004; Brown & Hohman, 2006;). For example, more than 40% of women admitted for drug treatment in five Western states identified MA as their primary substance of abuse (SAMHSA, 2005). Among pregnant women, use of illicit drugs is lower than among nonpregnant women, 4.5% in contrast to 10.6%, and this rate has remained stable over the past few years, according to the NSDUH.

Prevalence of Substance Use Disorders Among Women

Rates of substance abuse and dependence, based on criteria of the *Diagnostic and Statistical Manual IV-TR* (American Psychiatric Association, 2000) criteria, are approximate half for females age 12 and older (6.1%) as they are for males (11.9%). However, among youths age 12–17, substance abuse or dependence rates are actually slightly higher for girls, 7.4% versus 6.7% (SAMHSA, 2010).

Among treatment admissions, based on the most recent (2007) federal data, women were about half as likely to be admitted to treatment for drug or alcohol problems, although the relative proportion of male-to-female admissions varies considerable by specific type of substance. Men were about three times as likely as women to be admitted for alcohol only, but twice as likely to be admitted for opiates, only slightly more likely to be admitted for smoked cocaine and methamphetamine, and equally likely to be admitted for tranquilizer dependence (Table 2a, SAMHSA, 2009). By numbers alone and similar to men, the primary substance for which women were most likely to be admitted to treatment was alcohol alone (105,937), followed by alcohol with another drug (87,910) and heroin (77,753). Female MA-users have been found to constitute the largest group of those mandated to treatment by the child welfare system in several states (Grella, Hser, & Huang, 2006), and national treatment admissions data from 2007 indicated that the majority of those entering treatment programs for MA use were women (SAMHSA, 2009).

Risk Factors for Substance Use and Abuse in Women

A strong consensus has emerged in the field of addictions that some risk factors for chemical dependency differ in important ways as a function of gender. Women begin to use alcohol and drugs for a wide variety of reasons, often beginning in conjunction with a male partner (CSAT, 2009), and generally at somewhat older ages than males.[1] Women share many common risk factors with men, such as exposure to substance use in the family and genetic predisposition, but there are also some noteworthy differences. A recent CSAT Treatment Improvement Protocol observed that "exposure to chaotic, argumentative, and violent households, or being expected to take on adult responsibilities as a child, are other factors associated with initiation and prevalence of substance use disorders (SUDs) among the female population" (CSAT, 2009, p. xvii). Women's chemical dependency is more often initiated in response to a stressful life event, in the aftermath of abuse by an intimate partner, and in conjunction with a romantic partner, in contrast to men (CSAT, 2009; Nelson-Zlupko, Dore, Kauffman, & Kaltenbach, 1996). Many who start to use MA cite the desire to lose weight or have more energy to complete multiple responsibilities they have (Brecht et al., 2004). Peer use of substances is a well-established correlate of initiation in drug and alcohol use, but what is unique for women is the importance of partner substance use as an influence on use of both alcohol and illegal drugs (e.g., Amaro & Hardy-Fanta, 1995). Having a substance-using partner is also more common among women and can make it more difficult for women to enter and complete treatment (CSAT, 2009; Tuten & Jones, 2003). Sexual orientation can also be a risk factor for alcohol problems, use of marijuana, and abuse of prescription drugs, with some studies showing that lesbians more likely to use these substances than heterosexual women (see CSAT, 2009, Chap. 2).

Researchers have consistently found that women entering treatment for drug or alcohol dependence are likely to have experienced childhood and/or adult interpersonal victimization (e.g., Brown, Stout, & Mueller, 1996; Hien, Nunes, Levin, & Fraser, 2000; Kang, Magura, Laudet, & Whitney, 1999). Thus, exposure to traumatic experiences can lead to the initiation of substance use or its progression, such as an adolescent who has been sexually abused starting to drink to self-medicate the painful feelings associated with her maltreatment. Abuse of substances can also

---

[1] However, for some substances such as non-prescribed pain killers, adolescent girls are initiating their use at about the same age or even younger ages than males (SAMHSA, 2010).

elevate a women's risk of traumatic exposure, for example a women using illegal drugs that associates with violent male drug users and purchases drugs in dangerous neighborhood. Because traumatic exposure and substance use are so often associated there has been much discussion of the causal pathway between the two. At least one longitudinal study has found that circular causality may be operating wherein traumatic exposure heightens the risk for substance use, which in turn increases the likelihood of future traumatic experiences (Kilpatrick, Acierno, Resnick, Saunders, & Best, 1997).

A related risk factor for substance use and abuse is co-occurring mental disorders. There is high comorbidity between SUDs and other mental disorders in women, most commonly mood disorders and anxiety disorders, including posttraumatic stress disorder. As is the case with trauma and SUDs, there has been debate about which comes first—the comorbid disorder or the SUD. It appears that in the majority of cases mental disorders precede SUD: "the overwhelming majority of drug dependence cases (79 percent for both men and women) are temporally secondary to at least one other psychiatric disorder" (Kandel, Warner, & Kessler, 1998, p. 116). The National Comorbidity Study found that 86% of women who were diagnosed with alcohol abuse had another lifetime mental disorders (Kessler et al., 1997).

In some cases there are biological differences between women and men that affect how substances are metabolized that have implications for risk of addiction. A 2005 SAMHSA report summarized research showing that alcohol is absorbed and eliminated differently in women compared to men. Women have been found to achieve higher concentrations of alcohol in the bloodstream than men after consuming equivalent amounts of alcohol and get "sicker quicker" (Brady & Ashley, 2005).

Consequences of Substance Use and Abuse for Women and Families

To some extent, consequences vary depending on which specific substances are abused, especially with regard to the physical and mental health effects as well as legal implications. For example, use of illicit substances is by definition illegal, but also due to the high cost of illicit drugs often eventually leads to other illegal behavior to obtain these substances, including theft and prostitution. The latter in turn can lead to adverse physical health consequences for women. Chronic stimulant use is often associated with paranoid ideation, physical aggression, and child maltreatment (Connell-Carrick, 2007). In general, research shows that adverse consequences of drug and alcohol use often occur more quickly in women,[2] the medical and social consequences for women are more severe (Greenfield et al., 2007), and women experience unique effects, for example due to menstruation, pregnancy, and menopause, compared to men. More is known about the effects of alcohol on women than

[2] See Chap. 3 in *Substance abuse treatment: Addressing the Specific Needs of Women* (CSAT, 2009) for an excellent summary of research on gender differences in effects of drugs and alcohol.

illicit drugs. Alcohol consumption has been shown to increase the risk for liver and cardiac problems as well as breast cancer and osteoporosis (CSAT, 2009). More research needs to be conducted on the effects of licit and illicit drugs such as stimulants and opioids on women before firm conclusions can be drawn about their effects relative to men.

A growing body of research has investigated birth outcomes in relation to consumption of alcohol and drugs. Much more is known about alcohol's effects on the developing fetus than the effects of illicit drugs such as cocaine and heroin. Consumption of alcohol during pregnancy can result in a range of effects on the fetus, the most serious being fetal alcohol syndrome (FAS). FAS is associated with cognitive impairments and other central nervous system problems, growth deficiencies, attention deficit and hyperactivity, and socioemotional problems (CSAT, 2009). FAS is the major preventable form of mental retardation. Alcohol-related birth defects is the term used to describe less severe adverse birth outcomes associated with drinking during pregnancy. Prenatal exposure to cocaine has been found to be associated with a range of poor birth outcomes, including low birth weight and irritability. Opioid exposure during pregnancy can lead to birth complications such as lower birth weight, irritability, premature labor and delivery, and high blood pressure, some of which may be related to lack of prenatal care as much as opioid exposure (CSAT, 2009). Much less is known about the effects of exposure to marijuana, amphetamine, and MA on the developing fetus. Special concerns with injection drug use are sexually transmitted diseases, including HIV, which can be transmitted to the fetus and hepatitis C, the major cause of cirrhosis and liver cancer (CSAT, 2009).

One major consequence of substance abuse for women is impaired parenting. Evidence has accumulated that abuse and dependence on AOD play a major role in child maltreatment (e.g., Magura & Laudet, 1996). The relationship between substance abuse and child maltreatment is complex as both of these conditions are connected to other intractable social problems. It is difficult to disentangle the effects of parents' drug abuse on children from the larger high-risk context in which parents abuse drugs (McMahon & Luthar, 1998). These families tend to have a plethora of co-occurring life difficulties that are also known to be associated with poor developmental outcomes in children, including poverty; early childbearing; single parenthood; intergenerational maltreatment; numerous other stressors, such as substandard housing; homelessness; criminal involvement, such as prostitution; and inadequate health care (Conners et al., 2004; Reid, 1996).

Cultural Diversity

An in-depth consideration of ethnic and cultural diversity is beyond the scope of this review. Chapter 6 of CSAT's (2009) Treatment Improvement Protocol (TIP) 51 on women addresses special populations in detail, including Latina/Hispanic, African-American, Asian American, and Native American women. General points for clinicians to be aware include (1) there is great diversity within each of these broad subgroups that should be taken into account with working with clients; and (2) across groups, immigration, and acculturation greatly affect risk for substance use and abuse, with more acculturated women at higher risk. Chapter 6 offers excellent advice to clinicians as well as administrators regarding best practices for working with women from diverse groups.

Implications for Social Work Practice

Service Needs of Women with SUDs

Women are now regarded as having unique substance abuse treatment needs as well as more complex problems and needs, as compared to men (Brady & Ashley, 2005; Wechsberg, Luseno, & Ellerson, 2008). Traditional substance abuse treatment approaches that were designed for men have failed to take into account women's roles as mothers. Research indicates that most women entering treatment for SUDs are mothers, and many, if not most, are or have been involved with the child welfare system (e.g., Conners et al., 2004) and are motivated to retain custody of their children or have their children returned to their custody. Furthermore, many will not enter treatment if it means putting their children in foster care because they fear, often with good reason, permanently losing custody (Finkelstein, 1994; Wechsberg et al., 2008). Thus, a pressing service need for substance-abusing women is childcare.

Because women entering substance abuse treatment have many co-occurring problems, such as unemployment, low educational attainment, pending legal cases, and poor physical and mental health, treatment services must be comprehensive and take into account gender-related risk factors for AOD use and abuse. A comprehensive package of services would include either provided directly or through referral: prenatal care; child care; parenting education; drug and alcohol education; case management; relapse prevention; individual counseling provided by therapists qualified to address co-occurring mental disorders; family counseling; HIV education; after care; transportation; GED classes; and vocational education.

Barrier to Treatment

Women, especially pregnant women and those with young children are regarded as having more barriers to receipt of SUD treatment than men (Brady & Ashley, 2005; Shannon & Walker, 2008). These barriers can be intrapersonal, interpersonal, sociocultural, structural, or systemic (CSAT, 2009). *Personal barriers* include the greater stigma associated with chemical dependency in women (CSAT, 2009). Women struggling with addiction, especially those who are mothers, have tremendous guilt, shame, and embarrassment that contribute to denial and can serve as barriers to entering treatment (Brady & Ashley, 2005; Finkelstein, 1994). Women, especially poor women who are most vulnerable to addiction, single parent women, and women who resort to prostitution to support their drug habits, already are socially marginalized. Society continues to have a double standard regarding parenting, with women held to a higher standard in terms of expectations for care of children. Every substance-exposed infant also has a father, who is in many cases often a drug or alcohol abuser, and yet the mother is typically held solely or primarily responsible for and penalized for this condition. Having a co-occurring disorder can also be a service barrier in that some programs are not equipped to address mental health issues beyond substance use, and some women may seek help for their psychiatric issue rather than their substance abuse issue (Greenfield et al., 2007). All of these factors can contribute to women's denial of their problems with AOD and a greater reluctance to enter treatment unless mandated.

Other personal barriers include role and relationship issues, such as parenting responsibilities. Having children or being pregnant can also be a barrier to treatment entry because relatively few programs can accommodate the needs of pregnant or parenting women (Greenfield et al., 2007). In order to enter treatment women may be put in the position of having to relinquish custody of their children temporarily or make other arrangements for their care (Wechsberg et al., 2008), a dilemma rarely faced by men and especially problematic for single parent women. Worries include how well their children will be cared for while they are in treatment as well as how much difficulty they will have regaining custody of their children once they are substance-free (Finkelstein, 1994). Another obstacle to entering treatment can be a substance-abusing partner who does not want the woman to enter treatment (Amaro & Hardy-Fanta, 1995).

Sociocultural barriers include the relative paucity of culturally responsive treatment and greater stigma sometimes experienced by women from ethnic minority groups (CSAT, 2009). In some ethnic groups such as Latinos and Native Americans, it is not normative to seek help from strangers outside the family, and distrust of professional service providers is high (CSAT, 2009). Structural barriers include limited access to services specifically tailored to the special needs of women. Such services would provide childcare or allow women to bring their children to treatment with them, but according to SAMHSA (2004), as of 2003 fewer than 10% of SUD treatment services provided child care or treatment beds for children to accompany their mothers. Another structural limitation is treatment slots for pregnant women (CSAT, 2009). *Systems barriers* are those that occur because of the involvement of female clients in multiple systems of care that require coordination so that services are neither missed nor duplicated. Often women receiving substance abuse treatment services are involved in the child welfare and/or criminal justice systems and may also be receiving services from the mental health and medical systems. Case management is necessary to ensure proper coordination of such services.

Retention and treatment completion have been universally identified in the substance abuse treatment literature as major challenges but also critical to achieving effective outcomes. This has been particularly problematic for women with children with regard to entering detoxification or other residential treatment settings that do not allow children; retention rates have been found to be higher in residential programs where women can bring their children (Szuster, Rich, Chung, & Bisconer, 1996). A recent thorough and carefully performed review of gender and treatment outcomes concluded that the research on treatment retention and completion has shown mixed findings, but on the whole it cannot be concluded that women have lower retention or completion rates than men. Gender responsive programming may enhance retention for certain subgroups of women (Greenfield et al., 2007).

Three major federal initiatives targeting women's substance abuse were developed starting in the late 1980s and into the mid-1990s: NIDA's Perinatal-20 demonstration projects, SAMHSA's Pregnant and Postpartum Women's and their infants demonstration programs, and SAMHSA's Residential Women and Children demonstration grant program. Broadly, these initiatives were designed to both expand treatment slots for women and develop comprehensive service delivery approaches that responded to women's unique treatment needs, as service providers and those studying women's addiction began to realize that there were important differences between men and women that had implications for treatment of SUDs.

Gender-sensitive treatment for women is becoming more common in the USA, defined as incorporating program components that address women's unique needs, including child care, transportation, treatment of co-occurring disorders, and treatment of physical health problems such as HIV screening and referral (Wechsberg et al., 2008). The National Survey of Substance Abuse Treatment Services found that 35% of facilities surveyed offered special programming for women, and 14% offered special programming for pregnant of postpartum women (SAMHSA, 2004). Specialized programming for women was found to be most commonly at programs that combined residential and outpatient services.

Screening, Diagnosis, and Treatment

In general, research suggests that women are underrepresented in treatment, compared to their male counterparts (Greenfield et al., 2007). CSAT's TIP 51, "Substance Abuse Treatment: Addressing the Special Needs of women," is an excellent, up-to-date resource for clinicians on screening, assessment and treatment of substance-abusing women. Treatment of women's substance abuse needs to take into account the context of women's lives, in particular their unique socioeconomic circumstances and family factors such as responsibility for children (CSAT, 2009). The purpose of screening is to identify women who have an AOD problem that requires more detailed assessment. In contrast, the purpose of assessment is to provide sufficient in-depth information, including a diagnosis, to formulate a treatment plan that addresses a client's specific needs.

Effective assessments are comprehensive and culturally responsive. Numerous evidence-supported assessment instruments are available, including a number that are gender-sensitive. Chapter 4 in TIP 51 discusses screening and assessment instruments that are both gender- and culture sensitive, such as the Alcohol Use Disorder Identification Test (Babor & Grant, 1989) and the Texas Christian University Drug Screen II (Knight, Simpson, & Hiller, 2002), which is available at www.ibr.tcu.edu. Because of the serious adverse consequences of AOD use during pregnancy, best practices indicate the need to screen all women for AOD use during pregnancy, using a screening tool such as the 5-item TWEAK (Russell, 1994).

Clinicians should be aware that the assessment interview initiates and sets the tone for the therapeutic relationship (CSAT, 2009). Clients should be informed at the outset why the assessment is being performed. Domains that should be evaluated in comprehensive assessment include: (1) AOD use history, with particular attention to recent use to determine if withdrawal is a risk that would call for detoxification; (2) prior treatment for AOD problems or other mental health issues; (3) mental health symptoms and disorders, due to high comorbidity between SUDs and other mental disorders, in particular mood, anxiety, and eating disorders; (4) risk of harm to self or others; (5) family relationships and responsibilities; (6) living arrangements; (7) interpersonal victimization history, in particular physical or sexual abuse in childhood, adolescence or adulthood; (8) educational and employment history; (9) legal issues; and (10) health status and medical problems, including information on pregnancies. A model for a comprehensive interview can be found in the 300-item Psychosocial History interview protocol developed by Comfort and Kaltenbach (1996). The appendix provides excerpts from the protocol.

Untreated co-occurring mental disorders can complicate the recovery process and undermine a woman client's ability to avoid relapse and achieve abstinence. It is common for women in early recovery to experience intense negative feelings that they have been self-medicating through the use of drugs and alcohol. If substances are no longer available to cope with such feelings but new, healthier coping skills have not yet been developed, the risk of relapse is high. Therefore, it is essential to assess trauma history and provide opportunities at appropriate time to deal with that history.

Treatment

Treatment planning involves taking the results of a comprehensive client assessment and utilizing them to make decisions about the appropriate level of care and treatment goals to pursue. The American Society of Addiction Medicine (ASAM) has guidelines (Patient Placement Criteria; found at: www.asam.org/pdf/Publications/PPC2R_TOC.pdf) that are widely used and apply regardless of gender to decide which level of care is appropriate and whether detoxification should be pursued prior to formal initiation of treatment. ASAM has articulated five levels of care ranging from standard outpatient (Level I, individual or group treatment once or twice weekly) to intensive outpatient (Level II, more intensive service than outpatient but not residential) to residential and inpatient treatment (Level III, for clients who need a safe, residential environment staffed around the clock and clinically managed) to medically managed intensive inpatient (Level IV, for clients with complex medical problems and/or withdrawal complications who need hospital care).

Despite the fact that women often enter SUD treatment with more risk factors and life stressors than do male clients, a recent review concluded that, in general, treatment outcome studies have found that outcomes for women are comparable to those of men (Greenfield et al., 2007). This finding is surprising in light of the greater problems that women enter treatment with, such as co-occurring mental disorders. A strong consensus has emerged that substance abuse treatment services for women need to be comprehensive to ensure that their needs are met and they are given the best chances to achieve long-term recovery. What this means in practical terms is that not only must we provide treatment to achieve abstinence from drugs and alcohol in the short run but also provide services that allow substance-abusing women to achieve self-sufficiency, address co-occurring disorders, and become effective parents. The common mistaken belief that recovery must come first and that women cannot focus on their recovery with children present (Finkelstein, 1994) should be replaced by a recognition that women cannot concentrate on recovery when they are distracted by concerns about their children's well-being and relationships with children are important to women's recovery (CSAT, 2009). At the same time, "for the alcoholic or drug-abusing mother, the task of combining early recovery and parenting can be overwhelming. Quite often in early stages of sobriety women experience unrealistic expectations for themselves as parents and believe that they must instantly become 'perfect' mothers" (Finkelstein, 1994, p. 11). Thus, women's treatment should fully address parenting concerns and children's needs, either directly or through referral (CSAT, 2009).

CSAT's (2009) Comprehensive Treatment Model, which grew out of the demonstration model experience in the 1990s and is considered an "evolving paradigm," includes three broad categories of services: (1) clinical treatment services ("those services necessary to address the medical and biopsychosocial issues of addiction"); (2) clinical support services ("services that assist clients in their recovery"); and (3) community support services ("those services and community resources outside of treatment but within a community that serve as an underpinning or support system for the recovering individual"). Examples of *clinical treatment services* are detoxification, assessment, treatment planning, and mental health services. *Clinical support services* include housing services, parenting services and preparation for employment, whereas *community support services* include "recovery management, recovery community support services, housing services, family strengthening, child care, transportation, Temporary Assistance for Needy Families (TANF) linkages, employer support services, vocational and academic education services, and faith-based organization support" (CSAT, 2009, p. 278).

This approach recognizes that there is no single road to long-term recovery for women but rather numerous different paths that might include a variety of different treatment modalities as well as or in addition to assistance from a self-help and/or faith community. Effective engagement and treatment retention are the first steps toward effective treatment for substance-abusing women, recognizing that many of the barriers to women entering treatment, such as stigma, family responsibilities and pressures from romantic partners, can also interfere with treatment retention. Treatment success is directly linked to retention and length of stay, and women's retention rates and length of stay are comparable to those of men (see Greenfield et al., 2007 for a review). Thus, like men, women who do not complete treatment are less likely to achieve or maintain abstinence or accomplish other important goals such as learning to deal with a trauma history, complete education, find employment of permanent housing, or learn to be more effective parents. Although limited research has been conducted on the efficacy of women-only versus mixed gender treatment, for example in groups, the limited research, cited in Chap. 7 of TIP 51, suggests women-only approaches may be more effective in retaining women and addressing their specific needs and such groups are perceived by women as more effective (SAMHSA, 2009). In addition, women clients often express a preference for female staff.

Family and relationships issues are often central to the development of women's AOD problems are important to their recovery and should be addressed directly in treatment. This can take the form of parenting education, addressing childhood physical or sexual abuse, or addressing adult abuse and other relationship issues. On the other hand, many women in treatment lack partners, especially non-using partners, and are lacking close relationships and social support. Treatment should address these issues; women-only groups and regular attendance at 12-step meetings in the community can be effective in helping women to connect with others in a meaningful way. An evidence-supported, manualized group intervention targeted to women can be useful in addressing trauma histories and teaching coping skills to women at any stage of recovery is Najavits (2002b) Seeking Safety intervention. Her *Women's Addiction Workbook* (Najavits, 2002a) may also be useful. The Center for Substance Abuse Treatment has numerous free resources such as *Helping yourself heal: A recovering woman's guide to coping with childhood abuse issues* (CSAT, 2003) that can be helpful to clinicians and clients that are available at http://www.samhsa.gov/about/csat. aspx. Covington's (2008) *Helping Women Recover* curriculum also addresses issues specific to women such as relationships, boundaries, and finding healthy support.

Because of the centrality of family relationships to women in recovery, treatment should include family members, broadly defined, if at all possible (CSAT, 2009). This would include not only spouses and children, but also parents and extended family members, especially in the case of women from ethnic minority groups that include in their definition of "family" a broader array of individuals than simply nuclear family members such as siblings, grandparents, aunts, and uncles. Disconnections from family members have often occurred due to the woman's AOD use and often can be repaired. TIP 51 notes that "family therapy is a more essential approach in substance abuse treatment for women" (CSAT, 2009, p. 144). Most women enter treatment unmarried and often without romantic partners, but others have partner relationships they wish to continue. In many cases these are unhealthy and/or abusive relationships, sometimes with partners who continue to use AOD and do not support a woman's recovery. Treatment providers can perform an important role in helping such women examine the advantages and disadvantages of maintaining such relationships as they work toward abstinence and recovery. CSAT has a useful resource that providers might find helpful in this regard, TIP 25, *Substance Abuse Treatment and Domestic Violence* (CSAT, 1997).

Although there is a strong rationale for gender-specific programming and it is now often considered a best practice, there is limited research comparing woman only to mixed gender treatment. A recent review concluded that "while the current body of evidence comparing women-only versus mixed-gender treatment does not provide strong support for differential outcomes…a subgroup of women with substance abuse disorders may perceive women-only treatment more positively than mixed-gender treatment" (Greenfield et al., 2007, p. 14).

Summary and Conclusions

Women suffer from SUDs, albeit in smaller numbers than men, and families figure prominently in both the risks for and consequences of women's AOD use. Interpersonal victimization in childhood and adulthood as well as life stressors of all types has been found in the histories of women who abuse alcohol and drugs. Because most substance-abusing women are parents, their SUDs also affect their family members, especially young children. Pregnancy is a particular concern for women who abuse substances because of the adverse consequences of substance use on the developing fetus. Women's special circumstances such as very low educational attainment, low employment rates, and the likelihood of being parents translate to additional service needs and barriers to services, and women are considered to be underserved by AOD treatment programs. In particular, substance-abusing women are more stigmatized than men who abuse substances and more often suffer from co-occurring disorders that require treatment. As a result, best practices for social workers require comprehensive screening, diagnosis, and assessment as well as clinical treatment services, clinical support services and community support services. Social workers are ideally suited to be treatment providers for substance abusing women due to social work's ecological approach to treatment.

References

Amaro, H., & Hardy-Fanta, C. (1995). Gender relations in addiction and recovery. *Journal of Psychoactive Drugs, 27*, 325–337.

American Psychiatric Association. (2000). *Diagnostic and statistical manual of mental disorders, IV-TR*. Washington, DC: APA.

American Society of Addiction Medicine. (2001). *Patient placement criteria for the treatment of substance-related disorders: ASAM PPC-2R* (2nd revised ed.). Chevy Chase, MD: American Society of Addiction Medicine.

Babor, T. F., & Grant, M. (1989). From clinical research to secondary prevention: International collaboration in the development of the Alcohol Use Disorders Identification Test (AUDIT). *Alcoholism and Health Research World, 13*, 371–374.

Brady, T. M., & Ashley, O. S. (Eds.). (2005). *Women in substance abuse treatment: Results from the Alcohol and Drug Services Study (ADSS)*. DHHS Publication No. SMA 04-3968, Analytic Series A-26. Rockville, MD: U.S. Department of Health and Human Services, Substance Abuse and Mental Health Services Administration, Office of Applied Studies.

Brecht, M., O'Brien, A., von Mayrhauser, C., & Anglin, M. D. (2004). Methamphetamine use behaviors and gender differences. *Addictive Behaviors, 29*, 89–106.

Brown, J. A., & Hohman, M. (2006). Impact of methamphetamine use on parenting. *Journal of Social Work Practice in the Addictions, 6*, 63–88.

Brown, P., Stout, R., & Mueller, T. (1996). Post-traumatic stress disorder and substance abuse relapse among women: A pilot study. *Psychology of Addictive Behaviors, 10*, 124–128.

Center for Substance Abuse Treatment. (1997). *Substance abuse treatment and domestic violence.* Treatment Improvement Protocol (TIP) Series 25. HHS Publication No. SMA 97-3163. Rockville, MD: U.S. Department of Health and Human Services, Substance Abuse and Mental Health Services Administration.

Center for Substance Abuse Treatment. (2003). *Helping yourself heal: A recovering woman's guide to coping with childhood abuse issues.* HHS Publication No. (SMA) 03-3789. Rockville, MD: U.S. Department of Health and Human Services, Substance Abuse and Mental Health Services Administration.

Center for Substance Abuse Treatment. (2009). *Substance abuse treatment: Addressing the specific needs of women.* Treatment Improvement Protocol (TIP) Series 51. HHS Publication No. (SMA) 09-4426. Rockville, MD: U.S. Department of Health and Human Services, Substance Abuse and Mental Health Services Administration. Found at http://www.ncbi.nlm.nih.gov/books/NBK26118/.

Comfort, M., & Kaltenbach, K. A. (1996). The psychosocial history: An interview for pregnant and parenting women in substance-abuse treatment and research. In E. Rahdert (Ed.), *Treatment for drug-exposed women and children: Advances in research methodology.* NIDA Research Monograph 165. Rockville, MD: National Institute of Drug Abuse.

Connell-Carrick, K. (2007). Methamphetamine and the changing face of child welfare: Practice principles for child welfare workers. *Child Welfare, 86*, 125–141.

Conners, N. A., Bradley, R. H., Mansell, L. W., Liu, J. Y., Roberts, T. J., Burgdorf, K., et al. (2004). Children of mothers with serious substance abuse problems: Accumulation of risks. *The American Journal of Drug and Alcohol Abuse, 30*(1), 85–100.

Covington, S. S. (2008). *Helping women recover: A program for treating addiction.* San Francisco: Jossey-Bass.

Finkelstein, N. (1994). Treatment issues for alcohol- and drug-dependent pregnant and parenting women. *Health and Social Work, 19*, 7–15.

Greenfield, S. F., Brooks, A. J., Gordon, S. M., Green, C. A., Kropp, F., McHugh, K., et al. (2007). Substance abuse treatment entry, retention, and outcome in women: A review of the literature. *Drug and Alcohol Dependence, 86*, 1–21.

Grella, C. E., Hser, Y., & Huang, Y. (2006). Mothers in substance abuse treatment: Differences in characteristics based on involvement in child welfare services. *Child Abuse & Neglect, 30*, 55–73.

Hien, D. A., Nunes, E., Levin, F. R., & Fraser, D. (2000). Posttraumatic stress disorder and short-term outcome in early methadone treatment. *Journal of Substance Abuse Treatment, 19*, 31–37.

Kandel, D. B., Warner, L. A., & Kessler, R. C. (1998). The epidemiology of substance use and dependence among women. C. L. Wetherington, & A. B. Roman (Eds.), *Drug addiction research and the health of women* (pp. 105–130). Washington, DC: National Institute of Drug Abuse.

Kang, S.-Y., Magura, S., Laudet, A., & Whitney, S. (1999). Adverse effect of child abuse victimization among substance-using women in treatment. *Journal of Interpersonal Violence, 14*, 657–670.

Kessler, R. C., Crum, R. M., Warner, L. A., Nelson, C. B., Schulenberg, J., & Anthony, J. C. (1997). Lifetime co-occurrence of DSM-III-R alcohol abuse and dependence with other psychiatric disorders in the National Comorbidity Survey. *Archives of General Psychiatry, 54*, 313–321.

Kilpatrick, D. G., Acierno, R., Resnick, H. S., Saunders, B. E., & Best, C. L. (1997). A 2-year longitudinal analysis of the relationships between violent assault and substance use in women. *Journal of Consulting and Clinical Psychology, 65*, 834–847.

Knight, K., Simpson, D. D., & Hiller, M. L. (2002). Screening and referral for substance abuse treatment in the criminal justice system. In C. G. Leukefeld, F. M. Tims, & D. Farabee (Eds.), *Treatment of drug offenders: Policies and issues* (pp. 259–272). New York: Springer.

Magura, S., & Laudet, A. (1996). Parental substance abuse and child maltreatment: Review and implications for intervention. *Child and Youth Services Review, 18*, 193–220.

McMahon, T. J., & Luthar, S. S. (1998). Bridging the gap for children as their parents enter substance abuse treatment. In R. L. Hampton, V. Senatore, & T. P Gullotta (Eds.), *Substance abuse, family violence, and child welfare: Bridging perspectives* (pp. 143–187). Thousand Oaks, CA: Sage.

Najavits, L. M. (2002a). *A woman's addiction workbook: Your guide to in-depth healing*. Oakland, CA: New Harbinger.

Najavits, L. M. (2002b). *Seeking safety: A treatment manual for PTSD and substance abuse*. New York: Guilford Press.

Nelson-Zlupko, L., Dore, M. M., Kauffman, E., & Kaltenbach, K. (1996). Women in recovery: Their perceptions of treatment effectiveness. *Journal of Substance Abuse Treatment, 13*(1), 51–59.

Reid, J. (1996). *Substance abuse and the American woman*. New York: The National Center on Addiction and Substance Abuse at Columbia University.

Russell, M. (1994). New assessment tools for risk drinking during pregnancy: T-ACE, TWEAK, and others. *Alcohol Health and Research World, 18*, 55–61.

Shannon, L., & Walker, R. (2008). Increasing the recognition of barriers for pregnant substance abusers seeking treatment. *Substance Use & Misuse, 43*, 1266–1267.

Substance Abuse and Mental Health Services Administration, Office of Applied Studies. (2004). *National Survey of Substance Abuse Treatment Services (N-SSATS): 2003. Data on substance abuse treatment facilities*. DASIS Series: S-24, DHHS Publication No. (SMA) 04-3966. Rockville, MD: Substance Abuse and Mental Health Services Administration, Office of Applied Studies.

Substance Abuse and Mental Health Services Administration, Office of Applied Studies. (2005). *Treatment episode data set (TEDS)—Highlights, 2003. National admissions to substance abuse treatment services*. DASIS Series S-27, DHHS Publication No. (SMA) 05-4043, Rockville, MD: Substance Abuse and Mental Health Services Administration, Office of Applied Studies.

Substance Abuse and Mental Health Services Administration, Office of Applied Studies. (2009). *Treatment episode data set (TEDS)—Highlights, 2007. National admissions to substance abuse treatment services*. DASIS Series S-45, DHHS Publication No. (SMA) 09-4360, Rockville, MD: Substance Abuse and Mental Health Services Administration, Office of Applied Studies.

Substance Abuse and Mental Health Services Administration. (2010). *Results from the 2009 National Survey on Drug Use and Health: Vol. I. Summary of national findings*. Office of Applied Studies, NSDUH Series H-38A, HHS Publication No. SMA 10-4586 Findings. Rockville, MD: Substance Abuse and Mental Health Services Administration.

Szuster, R. R., Rich, L. L., Chung, A., & Bisconer, S. W. (1996). Treatment retention in women's residential chemical dependency treatment: The effect of admission with children. *Substance Use & Misuse, 31*, 1001–1013.

Tuten, M., & Jones, H. E. (2003). A partner's drug-using status impacts women's drug treatment outcome. *Drug and Alcohol Dependence, 70*, 327–330.

Wechsberg, W. M., Luseno, W., & Ellerson, R. M. (2008). Reaching women substance abusers in diverse settings: Stigma and access to treatment 30 years later. *Substance Use & Misuse, 43*, 1277–1279.

Chapter 13
Older Adults

Paul Sacco and Alexis Kuerbis

Throughout the next century, social workers will be challenged to meet the needs of a burgeoning population moving into late life. The median age of the worldwide population is projected to increase from 26.6 years old to 37.3 years old by 2050 (Lutz, Sanderson, & Scherbov, 2008). These changes mean social workers will need to integrate an understanding of aging into their practice, so they can better serve a graying population.

The field of addiction services is no exception. Substance abuse providers will be treating an aging clientele in coming decades, and treatment providers are already taking note of aging among help seekers. Recent projections suggest that prevalence rates of substance use disorders among people over 50 will rise from an average of 2.8 million from 2002 to 2006 to 5.7 in 2020 (Han, Gfroerer, Colliver, & Penne, 2009), and the number of older adults needing substance abuse treatment will increase from 1.7 million (2000–2001) to 4.4 million in 2020 (Gfroerer, Penne, Pemberton, & Folsom, 2003). Shifts in the need for treatment are not simply about increasing numbers of older adults, but also, generational shifts in attitudes about alcohol and drugs; societal attitudes about substance use have changed over the last 50 years bringing increases in the prevalence of alcohol and drug use.

A complex relationship exists between health and substance use among older adults. These issues need to be considered when discussing substance use with clients, diagnosing substance use disorders, and in our understanding of substance use as a public health problem. Prescription medications are dispensed to older adults at

P. Sacco (✉)
School of Social Work, University of Maryland-Baltimore, Baltimore, MD, USA
e-mail: psacco@ssw.umaryland.edu

A. Kuerbis
Research Foundation for Mental Hygiene, Inc, New York, NY, USA

Department of Psychiatry, Columbia University College of Physicians & Surgeons,
New York, NY, USA
e-mail: Kuerbis@pi.cpmc.columbia.edu

M.G. Vaughn and B.E. Perron (eds.), *Social Work Practice in the Addictions*,
Contemporary Social Work Practice, DOI 10.1007/978-1-4614-5357-4_13,
© Springer Science+Business Media New York 2013

very high rates, but use of multiple medications (even addictive ones) by older adults is not necessarily a problem. Alcohol consumption is not necessarily a sign of increased risk for older adults; moderate alcohol use can be a part of, and contribute to, healthy aging including lowering mortality (McCaul et al., 2010), improving cardiovascular health (Mukamal et al., 2006), and lowering risk of dementia (Mukamal et al., 2003) and disability (Karlamangla, Zhou, Reuben, Greendale, & Moore, 2006). Even illicit drugs, such as marijuana, are being used by older adults to alleviate pain (Jaret, 2010). Substance use among older adults exists along a continuum, and social workers need to think holistically and collaboratively about the role of addictive substances among older adults.

Addiction social workers must be mindful of the unique aspects of substance abuse among older adults, while recognizing commonalities with addictive behaviors at earlier points in the life course. This chapter explores the unique aspects of substance use, abuse, and dependence in older adults including the following areas: epidemiology, definitional issues, high-risk subgroups, etiology, assessment and screening, treatments, and generic approaches that social workers may use in practice settings.

Epidemiology of Substance Abuse in Older Adults

Epidemiologic studies suggest that on average, alcohol and drug use decline as people age (Moore et al., 2005). Older adults on average drink, smoke cigarettes, and use drugs at lower levels than their younger counterparts. Among individuals age 65 and older, 45% have used alcohol in the past 12-months, 14% have used tobacco, and 1% have used drugs (nonmedical) (Moore et al., 2009). Still, there is a great deal of variability among individuals with many maintaining substance use, or increasing over time (Brennan, Schutte, & Moos, 2010).

Currently, the vast majority of substance use by older adults involves alcohol and misuse of medications, although evidence suggests the use of other substances may increase in coming years (Blazer & Wu, 2009b). For instance, data on substance-related treatment admissions from 1995 and 2002 found more than a 100% increase in non-alcohol-related admissions among those over age 55 (Office of Applied Studies, 2005). Prescription drugs used by older adults include benzodiazepines, sedative-hypnotics, opioid analgesics, and stimulants. In part, the prevalence of prescription drug misuse may be a function of the fact that older adults have the highest rates of medication use (Kaufman, Kelly, Rosenberg, Anderson, & Mitchell, 2002). Although rare, illicit drugs such as cannabis, cocaine, heroin, and hallucinogens are other drugs used by older adults (Simoni-Wastila & Yang, 2006). Prevalence of DSM-IV (American Psychiatric Association (APA), 2000) substance abuse and dependence are lower among older adults than younger age groups. For men (age 65+), the 12-month prevalence rate of alcohol abuse is 2.38%, and for women, 0.36%. Alcohol dependence rates are lower, at less than 1% for both men and women. Rates of any drug abuse and drug dependence among individuals age 65 and older are 0.2% (Compton, Thomas, Stinson, & Grant, 2007).

Challenges to Classification

The use of diagnostic measures as a means of assessing the problem of drug and alcohol use among older adults has been criticized for a number of reasons. First, the applicability of DSM-IV diagnostic criteria in older adults has been questioned (Atkinson, 1990). Due to the biological aspects of aging, older adults are less likely to report physical dependency and tolerance to drugs and alcohol, and may therefore be less likely to meet DSM-IV criteria. Interrupted social and vocational roles or other consequences may be less likely to occur or less noticeable in old age. For many older adults, aging is associated with a winnowing of these roles (Moody, 2006, p. 21), through retirement or social isolation due to the mortality of age group peers.

Broadly stated, prescription medication issues can be seen ranging from inappropriate use (because of medications that cause over sedation), to misuse (taking extra medication above the prescribed dose), or abuse (the nonmedical use of a prescription drug). Inappropriate use (Beers, 1997) may represent a serious risk to the health of an older adult, even though the threshold for DSM-IV abuse or dependence is not met. Normal side effects of medication may seem like abuse even though the older adult is taking medication appropriately. Problematic drug use in older adults may arise during the course of medical care and represent a process where use drifts from serving as a solution to a problem to becoming the problem itself (Simoni-Wastila & Yang, 2006).

Similarly, changes in body composition and function in old age may lead to greater risk of use of alcohol and drugs, even at levels deemed safe for younger persons, making simple classifications of addiction difficult. This may be a challenge for clients who may not recognize that their normal drinking patterns at 40 may be problematic at 70. Older adults have lower lean body mass, which leads to higher blood alcohol levels even at the same alcohol dose (Vestal et al., 1977). Changes in liver functioning in old age lessen the ability of the body to metabolize drugs and alcohol (Durnas, Loi, & Cusack, 1990). In sum, alcohol, medication, and drug use may be a medical concern in the absence of the hallmarks of addiction.

To address the issue of risk among older drinkers, the National Institute on Alcohol Abuse and Alcoholism (NIAAA) (1995) has developed alcohol consumption guidelines for older adults which can be used to assess risk. These limits on drinking include no more than one drink per day, seven drinks per week, and no more than three drinks on any given occasion; guidelines for women are lower. Using this broader concept of drinking risk, rates of "at-risk" use are higher than rates of diagnoses. Blazer and Wu (2009a) identified at-risk drinking in 17% (men) and 11% (women) in a nationally representative sample of middle-aged and older adults. A longitudinal survey of adults maturing into their 70s and 80s found that 27.1% of women and 48.6% of men qualified as at-risk drinkers according to these guidelines (Moos, Schutte, Brennan, & Moos, 2009).

Because of these unique factors in drinking and substance abuse among older adults, specialists in this area have advocated for an even broader conceptualization of alcohol risk in this population (Moore et al., 1999). By including medical and psychiatric comorbidity, medication use, and psychosocial functioning, it is possible to identify risk among drinkers who fall below criteria and/or consumption thresholds. It is important to remember that alcohol and drug use in older adults needs to be understood in the context of overall health and functioning.

Who is at Risk?

While definitions of risk vary, much is known about who can be considered the most vulnerable. In terms of alcohol, some of the main determinants of risk for older adults is a previous history of alcohol or other substance-related problems (Sacco, Bucholz, & Spitznagel, 2009), male gender (Grant et al., 2004), being divorced or never married (Karlamangla et al., 2006), having friends who approved of drinking, relying on substances to deal with stress, and those individuals with more financial resources (Moos, Schutte, Brennan, & Moos, 2010). The picture of who is at risk for prescription drug use is somewhat different. Overall, health problems, female gender, daily alcohol use, and older age are risk factors for problem medication use (Simoni-Wastila & Yang, 2006). The least is known about older adults who use illicit drugs. A study by Rosen, Smith and Reynolds (2008) of older adults in methadone maintenance found that individuals were mostly male and in late middle age (50–59), had mental health comorbidity (57%) and significant disability. Rivers et al. (2004) found that elders testing positive for cocaine in the emergency department were significantly younger, more likely to be male, and more likely to have a substance use disorder than those who did not test positive for cocaine.

Polysubstance comorbidity is common among older adults (Oslin, 2000). Nicotine and prescription medications are commonly used by older adult problem drinkers (Nakamura et al., 1990). In a study of older problem drinkers, Brennan, Moos, and Kim (1993) found that females were more likely to use psychoactive (e.g., tranquilizers) medications than their male counterparts. Severity of alcohol use is also associated with the likelihood of nonmedical use of prescription drugs (McCabe, Cranford, & Boyd, 2006).

Why Do Older Adults Use Substances?

To help older adults who may struggle with alcohol and drug use, it is important to understand factors that may contribute to use. Many of the causal factors at play in late life alcohol and substance use are the same ones present in early adulthood or even childhood. Genetic predisposition, at-risk personality features, physiologic vulnerability, and substance-related expectancies, which may promote problems with alcohol and drugs, remain important in later life. These risk factors may be amplified or suppressed based on contextual factors in older adulthood (Zucker, 1998, p. 5), and work in concert with create problems.

In combination with known risk factors from early life, the presence of stressful life events and limited coping among some older adults has been theorized as proximal risk factor for substance abuse (Finney & Moos, 1984). Similar to the transition to adulthood, the passage into late life entails new roles and stresses, including retirement, changes in health status, changes in income, potentially changes in mobility, and bereavement (Hunter & Gillen, 2006). Stress itself may not cause substance abuse problems, but may interact with individuals' vulnerabilities leading to alcohol or drug problems. For example, a history of alcohol related coping in earlier in life might lead to continued alcohol-related coping or a resumption of alcohol use in late life (Lemke, Brennan, Schutte, & Moos, 2007).

Assessment and Screening of Older adults

Late life context is also important in assessment and screening of older adults. When social workers assess older adults for addiction, the first challenge is to overcome stereotyped thinking about aging. If a clinician does not believe aging persons have the potential to exhibit a problem, he or she may not recognize the signs and symptoms of a substance use disorder and will not gather the information necessary to intervene. Research suggests that older adults are less likely to be screened for problem drinking (D'Amico, Paddock, Burnam, & Kung, 2005; Duru et al., 2010). In one study, 400 primary care physicians were provided with a list of symptoms related to problematic substance abuse by a hypothetical older female patient, only 1% considered the possibility of a substance abuse (National Center on Addiction and Substance Abuse, 1998).

Unfortunately, published data on rates of screening by social workers are nonexistent. Many social workers outside the field of addiction have indicated they either fail to consider, or feel uncomfortable asking about substance use. Given the vast majority of older adults with substance use disorders never seek formal addiction treatment, having a routine brief substance use assessment regardless of the agency context or setting is important.

Asking About Substance Use: General Considerations

Although there are some different ways of asking about substance use, some general issues apply. Discussions of alcohol and other substance use should occur in the context of an overall assessment. This is crucial for two reasons. First, older adults may be more likely to provide information about potentially stigmatizing behavior if they feel the social worker is interested in their overall well-being. Drug and alcohol use should be evaluated in light of older adults' biopsychosocial functioning. The social worker should bring up alcohol use in reference to the presenting problem and in a matter-of-fact manner. The technique of "Gentle Assumption" should be considered (Shea, 1998, pp. 401–402). Using this approach, the person is asked about how much they drink under the assumption that they drink. Given the rarity of other drug use, this approach is more applicable for alcohol.

It is reasonable to start conversations about drinking, and then discuss medication use, and finally illicit substances. Rather than questioning the person's judgment (e.g., do you have a drinking or drug use problem?) about their use of substances, the focus should be on the facts of their use. The social worker should ask detailed questions medications (prescription and over-the-counter) under the assumption that this information is important, whether the older adults' use is a problem or not. During this discussion, questions about overuse and misuse can be included in a nonjudgmental way, akin to the "not knowing posture" popularized in Solution Focused Brief Psychotherapy (Anderson & Goolishian, 1992).

For instance, the person could be asked whether they sometimes take an extra pill to fall asleep or to cope with pain. The social worker can ask about potential signs of prescription misuse such as running out of medication early, and losing or borrowing medication. Frequently, older adults see multiple doctors, and may not be aware of the potential dangers of medication interactions. It is key for the conversation to be based on assessing overall health, and not separating "drug abusers" out from a population, because this approach is likely to stigmatize older adults, may engender defensiveness, and is inconsistent with the idea that alcohol or drug use can be problematic in the absence of abuse or dependence.

As practitioners, it is tempting to focus on telltale signs of alcohol or drug problems among older adults as is included in this chapter (see Table 13.1). Be aware that many signs of substance use in older adults can often be attributed to aging or other problems. Heavy alcohol use can cause severe memory problems such as Wernicke–Korsakoff Syndrome, short-term memory impairment due to insufficient Thiamine, but Alzheimer's type dementia is much more common in this population. Similarly, assessing for risk of falls is important in older adults, but only a limited number of older adults fall because of substance abuse. Social workers should conduct a complete assessment and consider overall biopsychosocial functioning.

Brief Screening Instruments

For social workers in nonaddiction settings, screening instruments are a convenient option for assessing level of risk due to alcohol and drugs, as they are less burdensome than obtaining a blood test or drug screen, and they can be administered without impinging on other agency demands. Some screening tools are adaptations of instruments created for younger cohorts, and others have been designed with older adults in mind. Unfortunately, there are no screening instruments for assessing prescription or illicit drug use designed for older adults. The use of biological screening (i.e., lab tests) has limited utility for social workers and can be problematic in older adults.

Table 13.1   Signs of potential alcohol or drug problems

Somatic	Psychological	Social
Sleep problems	Cognitive impairment/ memory loss/ disorientation	Family problems
Headaches	Unexplained persistent irritability	Financial problems
Frequent unexplained falls, bruises, or burns	Anxiety	Social isolation (including changes in social habits, withdrawal from social activities)
Poor nutrition or changes in eating habits	Depressed mood	Legal difficulties
Unexplained seizures		Neglecting responsibilities (e.g., to a plant, pet, or friend)
Slurred speech		Engaging in secretive behaviors
Tremor		
Shuffling gait		
Unexplained vomiting or gastrointestinal distress		
Complaints of blurred vision or dry mouth		
Unusual restlessness or agitation		
Unexplained pain or other somatic complaints		
Headaches		
Incontinence		
Blackouts/dizziness		
Poor hygiene		

Adapted from Blow (1998).

CAGE

The most recognizable screening test in substance abuse treatment is the CAGE questionnaire; the four-question acronym includes the following: (1) Have you ever felt that you should *C*ut down on your drinking? (2) Have people *A*nnoyed you by criticizing your drinking? (3) Have you ever felt bad or *G*uilty about your drinking? And (4) have you ever had a drink first thing in the morning to steady your nerves or to get rid of a hangover (*E*ye opener)? Two positive responses are considered a cutoff for alcoholism (O'Connell et al., 2004). The screening test can be administered through an interview or self-administered. The CAGE has been used clinically since the 1970s and has been studied extensively in adult populations. The CAGE does not distinguish between current and lifetime use, an especially difficult issue among the aging, who may have a history of problematic use without having a current problem. Furthermore, the CAGE questions offer brevity at the expense of a more thorough collection of data about such issues as consumption levels, consequences of use and functional deficits.

Michigan Alcohol Screening Test-Geriatric

Unlike the CAGE, the Michigan Alcohol Screening Test-Geriatric (MAST-G) (Blow et al., 1992) was developed for elderly populations as a modification of the MAST. The instrument contains 24 questions with yes/no responses. Five or more positive responses indicate problematic use. The measure encompasses five symptom domains: Loss and Loneliness, Relaxation, Dependence, Loss of Control with Drinking, and Rule Making. It is also administered in a short form, the Short Michigan Alcoholism Screening Test-Geriatric Version (SMAST-G), which has ten questions, with two positive responses indicating a problem with alcohol. The MAST-G focuses more on potential stressors and behaviors relevant to alcohol use in late life, as opposed to the MAST, which directs questions toward family, vocational, and legal consequences of use. This screen has many of the advantages of the CAGE, such as ease of administration, low cost, and familiarity to substance abuse researchers and clinicians. It is also more specific than the CAGE in identifying problematic use. While useful as an indicator of lifetime problem use, it lacks information about frequency, quantity, and current problems important in research.

Alcohol Use Disorders Identification Test

The Alcohol Use Disorders Identification Test (AUDIT) was developed by the World Health Organization to assess for current alcohol problems in adult populations (Babor, Higgins-Biddle, Saunders, & Monteiro, 2001). Like the CAGE, the AUDIT was validated in adults to detect problematic or hazardous use (Beullens & Aertgeerts, 2004). The test consists of ten questions, pertaining to amount and frequency of use, alcohol dependency and the consequences of alcohol abuse. The screening test can be administered through an interview or self-administered. Each of the ten questions is scored on a four-point continuum with total scores ranging from 0 to 40. A score of above eight indicates problem drinking.

Intervention with Older Adults

Depending on the setting and the severity of problems indicated by screening tools, there is a continuum of treatment options available for older adults (see Table 13.2). Contrary to common perceptions of older substance users as stuck in permanent patterns of use, older adults have demonstrated treatment outcomes as good, or better, than those seen in younger groups (Brennan, Nichol, & Moos, 2003); however, few older adults have access to specialized services for the elderly. A national survey of substance abuse treatment programs found that only about 18% were specifically designed for older adults (Schultz, Arndt, & Liesveld, 2003). Rates of mental health utilization are lower among older adults than any other age group

Table 13.2   The continuum of older adult substance use[†]

Continuum of severity	Continuum of care
Abuse/dependence	*Specialized treatment approaches*
Tolerance and withdrawal	Medically monitored detoxification
Unsuccessful attempts to cut down	Inpatient psychiatric care
Decline in normal activities	Elder-specific inpatient rehabilitation
Larger amounts and for longer period than intended	Elder-specific intensive outpatient rehabilitation
Use in risky situations	Outpatient substance abuse treatment
Legal problems	Alcoholics or narcotics anonymous
Continued use despite social consequences	Case management
Decline in personal functioning	*Care management models*
Misuse	Case management
Hoarding or excess medication use	Co-location of services in medical offices
Use of medications for purposes other than indications	*Brief advice models*
Alcohol/medication/illicit drug co-use	Physician advice
At-risk use	Brief intervention
Use in spite of health/mental health comorbidity	*Prevention models*
Use in presence of potential medication interaction	Outreach/education initiatives Substance abuse screening
Use of alcohol in excess of NIAAA guidelines	

(Left column marked "Level of risk" as an upward arrow; right column marked "Level of intensity" as an upward arrow.)

[†]Adapted from Center for Substance Abuse Treatment (1998). Substance abuse among older adults. (Treatment Improvement Protocol (TIP) Series, No. 26). Rockville, MD: Substance Abuse and Mental Health Services Administration

(Bartels et al., 2004). Stigma and shame surrounding substance use and related problems, geographical isolation, inability to pay, or difficulties with transportation are just some of the barriers to specialized treatment for older adults (Blow, 1998; Fortney, Booth, Blow, Bunn, & Cook, 1995). For these reasons, several interventions for prevention of and treatment for substance abuse have been created for implementation in nontraditional settings, such as emergency rooms, senior centers, and primary care offices (Schonfeld et al., 2009).

Screening, Brief Intervention, and Referral to Treatment

The majority of brief interventions in nontraditional settings have focused on alcohol and prescription medication misuse or abuse, and they vary in length from one to five sessions (Barry, 1999; Barry, Oslin, & Blow, 2001). Their purpose is to enhance motivation for change in nondependent drinkers, and connect more severe users with more intensive treatment programs (Blow & Barry, 2000). Most of these interventions use Motivational Interviewing (MI) (Miller & Rollnick, 2002), which encourages a client-centered, nonjudgmental approach to discussing substance use and encouraging positive, healthy changes to the individual's life. MI aims to reduce ambivalence by assisting the client to identify in his or her own words the pros and cons perceived as relevant to making a change versus maintaining the status quo. For older adults, reasons for change often include maintaining independence, optimal health, and mental capacity (Blow & Barry, 2000). In addition, social workers should provide individualized feedback about how the quantity and frequency of the client's drinking or substance use behavior compares to norms in their age group. Finally, social workers providing brief interventions should also provide guidelines to healthy drinking for individuals in their age group: one or fewer drinks per day and no more than seven in 1 week, and even less for older women (National Institute on Alcohol Abuse and Alcoholism, 1995).

Like brief interventions, case and care management models (hereafter referred to as CMM) also take advantage of nontraditional settings to engage older adults in reducing their use or connecting them to treatments. Often offered in primary care settings or community agencies focused on senior health, CMM interventions take a systems approach, attempting to address the complexity of medical and psychiatric comorbidities common in this population (Blow, 1998), while also connecting isolated individuals to needed community resources. There have been a number of program evaluations focused on case management strategies with older adult problem drinkers, which supports the notion that case management is an important tool in working with this population (D'Agostino, Barry, Blow, & Podgorski, 2006). While some CMM have proven to be marginally more effective than traditional treatment, they may be better at engaging and maintaining older at-risk drinkers in treatment (Oslin et al., 2006). Another advantage of CMM is that substance use interventions are imbedded in a broad approach to addressing health, lessening stigma, and also working towards a likely common goal among older adults: overall better health (Blow, 1998). Because older adults may have medical or mental health comorbidities, efforts should be made to work with the individual's primary medical provider regardless of modality of intervention. This will help address some of the unique needs of older adults such as pain management.

Common Formats for Treating Older Adults

Like for other populations, formal substance abuse treatment for older adults is provided on a continuum of intensity depending on severity of need, ranging from detoxification to outpatient. Due to the unique issues facing older adults, it is recommended that older adults be provided the opportunity for both individual and group treatment, and that all treatment plans be individualized and flexible according to the specific needs of the client. Assuming there is no cognitive impairment, older adults must be able to exercise client choice and be actively involved in the treatment decisions. While group treatment is often the preferred method of providing substance abuse treatment and is often a cornerstone in reducing isolation and shame, the lack of elder specific treatment available in the community may actually enhance feelings of isolation and shame in group context if they do not easily relate to the other group members or feel uncomfortable discussing their problems with a younger generation. Individual therapy provides a private and confidential forum for older adults to explore their unique issues, without these same risks.

Within the context of formal treatment, regardless of modality, there are numerous approaches to treatments. Two modalities have been explored specifically in the context of older adults: supportive therapy models (STM) and cognitive-behavioral treatments (CBT). STM represent a traditional treatment with age-specific modifications. These approaches arose out of concern about whether older adults could effectively engage in standard treatment (Kofoed, Tolson, Atkinson, & Toth, 1987). Specifically, there was concern that confrontational approaches were ill-suited and disrespectful to older adults, and the unique issues faced by older individuals including health conditions, depression comorbidity, and social isolation went unaddressed (Blow, 1998). Indeed, confronting "denial" in any individual about their drug or alcohol use has proven ineffective in helping individuals modify their behavior to be more healthy (Miller & Rollnick, 2002). STM were designed, therefore, to focus on developing a culture of support and successful coping for older adult substance abusers; supportive therapies concentrate on building social support, improving self-esteem, and taking a global approach to treatment planning through addressing multiple biopsychosocial arenas in the client's life.

CBT focus on identifying and altering sequences of thinking, feeling, and behaving that lead to problem drinking or drug use (Rotgers, 2003). CBT can be delivered individually or in group settings, and there is strong evidence for positive outcomes across populations and age groups (Morgenstern & McKay, 2007). In addition, evidence exists for the effectiveness of CBT with older adults (Dupree, Broskowski, & Schonfeld, 1984; Schonfeld et al., 2000), and the Substance Abuse and Mental Health Services Association (SAMHSA) published a CBT-based treatment manual specific to aging (Dupree & Schonfeld, 1996). The highly structured, didactic approach taken in CBT may be particularly helpful to older adults, because of the tendency to present with memory difficulties (Blow, 1998).

Self-Help Groups

Alcoholics or Narcotics Anonymous and their related groups can also be useful to older adults in reducing isolation, shame, and stigma. Specific meetings may be more or less suited to older adults given variation in the pace of meetings and the general focus of the group. Some experts have recommended traditional self-help groups be modified for older adults, such as slowing the pace of the meeting to reflect cognitive changes in aging, and devoting attention to handling losses and extending social support (Schonfeld & Dupree, 1997). Social workers should be aware of elder-friendly meetings in their geographic area and encourage their older adult clients to try more than one meeting, prior to deciding whether it is a good fit.

Overall Approach or Guiding Principles to Working with Older Adults

Regardless of treatment setting or modality, older adults must be viewed from a client-centered perspective where their wishes and needs are respected and addressed. Social workers working with older adults will find taking a holistic approach to intervention will provide the most ample opportunities for older adults to engage in the process. For example, inquire about individual values and how changing substance use will enhance those values. According to well-established approaches, potential for personal enhancement should include health, hobbies, social networks or relationships and financial stability (Blow & Barry, 2000, p. 118). As with any client, one should work to instill hope.

References

American Psychiatric Association (APA). (2000). *Diagnostic and statistical manual of mental disorders* (revised 4th ed.). Washington, DC: APA.

Anderson, H., & Goolishian, H. (1992). The client is the expert: A not-knowing approach to therapy. In *Therapy as social construction* (pp. 25–39). London: Sage.

Atkinson, R. M. (1990). Aging and alcohol use disorders: Diagnostic issues in the elderly. *International Psychogeriatrics, 2*(1), 55–72.

Babor, T. F., Higgins-Biddle, J., Saunders, J. B., & Monteiro, M. G. (2001). *The alcohol use disorders identification test: Guidelines for use in primary care* (2nd ed.). Geneva: World Health Organization.

Barry, K. L. (1999). *Brief interventions and brief therapies for substance abuse*. U.S. Department of Health and Human Services, Public Health Service, Substance Abuse and Mental Health Services Administration, Center for Substance Abuse Treatment.

Barry, K. L., Oslin, D. W., & Blow, F. C. (2001). *Alcohol problems in older adults: Prevention and management*. New York: Springer Publishing Company.

Bartels, S. J., Coakley, E., Zubritsky, C., Ware, J. H., Miles, K. M., Arean, P. A., et al. (2004). Improving access to geriatric mental health services: A randomized trial comparing treatment engagement with integrated versus enhanced referral care for depression, anxiety and at-risk alcohol use. *American Journal of Psychiatry, 161*(8), 1455–1462.

Beers, M. H. (1997). Explicit criteria for determining potentially inappropriate medication use by the elderly: An update. *Archives Internal Medicine, 157*(14), 1531–1536.

Beullens, J., & Aertgeerts, B. (2004). Screening for alcohol abuse and dependence in older people using DSM criteria: A review. *Aging and Mental Health, 8*(1), 76–82.

Blazer, D. G., & Wu, L.-T. (2009a). The epidemiology of at-risk and binge drinking among middle-aged and elderly community adults: National Survey on Drug Use and Health. *American Journal Psychiatry, 166*(10), 1162–1169.

Blazer, D. G., & Wu, L.-T. (2009b). The epidemiology of substance use and disorders among middle aged and elderly community adults: National Survey on Drug Use and Health. *American Journal of Geriatric Psychiatry, 17*(3), 237–245.

Blow, F. C. (1998). *TIP 26: Substance abuse among older adults*. Rockville, MD: National Library of Medicine.

Blow, F. C., & Barry, K. (2000). Older patients with at-risk and problem drinking patterns: New developments in brief interventions. *Journal of Geriatric Psychiatry and Neurology, 13*, 115–123.

Blow, F. C., Brower, K. J., Schulenberg, J. E., Demo-Dananberg, L. M., Young, K. J., & Beresford, T. P. (1992). The Michigan Alcohol Screening Test: Geriatric Version (MAST-G): A new elderly specific screening instrument. *Alcoholism: Clinical and Experimental Research, 16,* 172.

Brennan, P. L., Moos, R. H., & Kim, J. Y. (1993). Gender differences in the individual characteristics and life contexts of late-middle-aged and older problem drinkers. *Addiction, 88*(6), 781–790.

Brennan, P. L., Nichol, A. C., & Moos, R. H. (2003). Older and younger patients with substance use disorders: Outpatient mental health service use and functioning over a 12-month interval. *Psychology of Addictive Behaviors, 17*(1), 42–48.

Brennan, P. L., Schutte, K. K., & Moos, R. H. (2010). Patterns and predictors of late-life drinking trajectories: A 10-year longitudinal study. *Psychology of Addictive Behaviors, 24*(2), 254–264.

Compton, W. M., Thomas, Y. F., Stinson, F. S., & Grant, B. F. (2007). Prevalence, correlates, disability, and comorbidity of DSM-IV drug abuse and dependence in the United States: Results from the National Epidemiologic Survey on Alcohol and Related Conditions. *Archives of General Psychiatry, 64*(5), 566–576.

D'Agostino, C. S., Barry, K., Blow, F. C., & Podgorski, C. (2006). Community interventions for older adults with comorbid substance abuse: The Geriatric Addictions Program (GAP). *Journal of Dual Diagnosis, 2*(3), 31–43.

D'Amico, E. J., Paddock, S. M., Burnam, A., & Kung, F. Y. (2005). Identification of and guidance for problem drinking by general medical providers: Results from a national survey. *Medical Care, 43*(3), 229–236.

Dupree, L. W., Broskowski, H., & Schonfeld, L. (1984). The Gerontology Alcohol Project: A behavioral treatment program for elderly alcohol abusers. *The Gerontologist, 24*(5), 510–516.

Dupree, L. W., & Schonfeld, L. (1996). *Manual developed for UPBEAT (Unified Psychogeriatric Behavioral Evaluation, Assessment and Treatment) Project for the Department of Veterans Affairs and Center for Substance Abuse Treatment (CSAT).* Tampa, FL: University of South Florida.

Durnas, C., Loi, C. M., & Cusack, B. J. (1990). Hepatic drug metabolism and aging. *Clinical Pharmacokinetics, 19*(5), 359–389.

Duru, O. K., Xu, H., Tseng, C.-H., Mirkin, M., Ang, A., Tallen, L., et al. (2010). Correlates of alcohol-related discussions between older adults and their physicians. *Journal of the American Geriatrics Society, 58*(2), 2369–2374.

Finney, J. W., & Moos, R. H. (1984). Life stressors and problem drinking among older adults. *Recent Developments in Alcoholism, 2,* 267–288.

Fortney, J. C., Booth, B. M., Blow, F. C., Bunn, J. Y., & Cook, C. A. L. (1995). The effects of travel barriers and age on utilization of alcoholism treatment aftercare. *American Journal of Drug and Alcohol Abuse, 21*(3), 391–407.

Gfroerer, J., Penne, M., Pemberton, M., & Folsom, R. (2003). Substance abuse treatment need among older adults in 2020: The impact of the baby-boom cohort. *Drug and Alcohol Dependence, 69,* 127–135.

Grant, B. F., Dawson, D. A., Stinson, F. S., Chou, S. P., Dufour, M. C., & Pickering, R. P. (2004). The 12-month prevalence and trends in DSM-IV alcohol abuse and dependence: United States, 1991–1992 and 2001–2002. *Drug and Alcohol Dependence, 74*(3), 223–234.

Han, B., Gfroerer, J., Colliver, J. D., & Penne, M. A. (2009). Substance use disorder among older adults in the United States in 2020. *Addiction, 104*(1), 88–96.

Hunter, I. R., & Gillen, M. C. (2006). Alcohol as a response to stress in older adults: A counseling perspective. *Adultspan, 5*(2), 114–126.

Jaret, P. (2010). Older adults increasingly use medical marijuana for nausea, pain. *AARP Bulletin* Retrieved October 29, 2010.

Karlamangla, A., Zhou, K., Reuben, D., Greendale, G., & Moore, A. (2006). Longitudinal trajectories of heavy drinking in adults in the United States of America. *Addiction, 101*(1), 91–99.

Kaufman, D. W., Kelly, J. P., Rosenberg, L., Anderson, T. E., & Mitchell, A. A. (2002). Recent patterns of medication use in the ambulatory adult population of the United States: The Slone Survey. *Journal of the American Medical Association, 287*(3), 337–344.

Kofoed, L. L., Tolson, R. L., Atkinson, R. M., & Toth, R. L. (1987). Treatment compliance of older alcoholics: An elder-specific approach is superior to "mainstreaming". *Journal of Studies on Alcohol, 48*(1), 47–51.

Lemke, S., Brennan, P. L., Schutte, K. K., & Moos, R. H. (2007). Upward pressures on drinking: Exposure and reactivity in adulthood. *Journal of Studies on Alcohol and Drugs, 68*(3), 437–445.

Lutz, W., Sanderson, W., & Scherbov, S. (2008). The coming acceleration of global population ageing. *Nature, 451*(7179), 716–719.

McCabe, S. E., Cranford, J. A., & Boyd, C. J. (2006). The relationship between past-year drinking behaviors and nonmedical use of prescription drugs: Prevalence of co-occurrence in a national sample. *Drug and Alcohol Dependence, 84*(3), 281–288.

McCaul, K. A., Almeida, O. P., Hankey, G. J., Jamrozik, K., Byles, J. E., & Flicker, L. (2010). Alcohol use and mortality in older men and women. *Addiction, 105*(8), 1391–1400.

Miller, W., & Rollnick, S. (2002). *Motivational interviewing: Preparing people for change* (2nd ed.). London: Guilford Press.

Moody, H. R. (2006). *Aging: Concepts and controversies* (5th ed.). Thousand Oaks, CA: Pine Forge.

Moore, A. A., Gould, R., Reuben, D. B., Greendale, G. A., Carter, M. K., Zhou, K., et al. (2005). Longitudinal patterns and predictors of alcohol consumption in the United States. *American Journal of Public Health., 95*(3), 458–465.

Moore, A. A., Karno, M. P., Grella, C. E., Lin, J. C., Warda, U., Liao, D. H., et al. (2009). Alcohol, tobacco, and nonmedical drug use in older U.S. adults: Data from the 2001/02 National Epidemiologic Survey of Alcohol and Related Conditions. *Journal of the American Geriatrics Society, 57*(12), 2275–2281.

Moore, A. A., Morton, S. C., Beck, J. C., Hays, R. D., Oishi, S. M., Partridge, J. M., et al. (1999). A new paradigm for alcohol use in older persons. *Medical Care, 37*(2), 165–179.

Moos, R. H., Schutte, K. K., Brennan, P. L., & Moos, B. S. (2009). Older adults' alcohol consumption and late-life drinking problems: A 20-year perspective. *Addiction, 104*(8), 1293–1302.

Moos, R. H., Schutte, K. K., Brennan, P. L., & Moos, B. S. (2010). Late-life and life history predictors of older adults' high-risk alcohol consumption and drinking problems. *Drug and Alcohol Dependence, 108*(1–2), 13–20.

Morgenstern, J., & McKay, J. R. (2007). Rethinking the paradigms that inform behavioral treatment research for substance use disorders. *Addiction, 102*(9), 1377–1389.

Mukamal, K. J., Chung, H., Jenny, N. S., Kuller, L. H., Longstreth, W. T., Jr., Mittleman, M. A., et al. (2006). Alcohol consumption and risk of coronary heart disease in older adults: The cardiovascular health study. *Journal of the American Geriatrics Society, 54*(1), 30–37.

Mukamal, K. J., Kuller, L. H., Fitzpatrick, A. L., Longstreth, W. T., Jr., Mittleman, M. A., & Siscovick, D. S. (2003). Prospective study of alcohol consumption and risk of dementia in older adults. JAMA: *The journal of the American Medical Association, 289*(11), 1405–1413.

Nakamura, C. M., Molgaard, C. A., Stanford, E. P., Peddecord, K. M., Morton, D. J., Lockery, S. A., et al. (1990). A discriminant analysis of severe alcohol consumption among older persons. *Alcohol and Alcoholism, 25*(1), 75–80.

National Center on Addiction and Substance Abuse. (1998). *Under the rug: Substance abuse and the mature woman.* New York: Columbia University

National Institute on Alcohol Abuse and Alcoholism. (1995). *The physicians' guide to helping patients with alcohol problems.* NIH Pub. No. 95-3769. Rockville, MD: Public Health Service.

O'Connell, H., Chin, A.-V., Hamilton, F., Cunningham, C., Walsh, J. B., Coakley, D., et al. (2004). A systematic review of the utility of self-report alcohol screening instruments in the elderly [review]. *International Journal of Geriatric Psychiatry, 19*, 1074–1086.

Office of Applied Studies. (2005). *Older adults in substance abuse treatment: Update.* Arlington, VA: Substance abuse and Mental Health Services Administration.

Oslin, D. W. (2000). Alcohol use in late life: Disability and comorbidity. *Journal of Geriatric Psychiatry and Neurology, 13*(3), 134–140.

Oslin, D. W., Grantham, S. J., Coakley, E. J., Maxwell, J. J., Miles, K., Ware, J., et al. (2006). PRISM-E: Comparison of integrated care and enhanced specialty referral in managing at-risk alcohol use. *Psychiatric Services, 57*(7), 954–958.

Rivers, E., Shirazi, E., Aurora, T., Mullen, M., Gunnerson, K., Sheridan, B., et al. (2004). Cocaine use in elder patients presenting to an inner-city emergency department. *Academic Emergency Medicine, 11*(8), 874–877.

Rosen, D., Smith, M. L., & Reynolds, C. F., III. (2008). The prevalence of mental and physical health disorders among older methadone patients. *American Journal of Geriatric Psychiatry, 16*(6), 488.

Rotgers, F. (2003). Cognitive-behavioral theories of substance abuse. In F. Rotgers, J. Morgaenstern, & S. T. Walters (Eds.), *Treating substance abuse: Theory and technique* (2nd ed., pp. 166–189). New York: Guilford Press.

Sacco, P., Bucholz, K. K., & Spitznagel, E. L. (2009). Alcohol use among older adults in the National Epidemiologic Survey on Alcohol and Related Conditions: A latent class analysis. *Journal of Studies on Alcohol and Drugs, 70*(6), 829–838.

Schonfeld, L., & Dupree, L. (1997). Treatment alternatives for older adults. In A. M. Gurnack (Ed.), *Older adults' misuse of alcohol, medicine, and other drugs* (pp. 113–131). New York: Springer.

Schonfeld, L., Dupree, L. W., Dickson-Fuhrmann, E., Royer, C. M., McDermott, C. H., Rosansky, J. S., et al. (2000). Cognitive-behavioral treatment of older veterans with substance abuse problems. *Journal of Geriatric Psychiatry and Neurology, 13*(3), 124–129.

Schonfeld, L., King-Kallimanis, B. L., Duchene, D. M., Etheridge, R. L., Herrera, J. R., Barry, K. L., et al. (2009). Screening and brief intervention for substance misuse among older adults: The Florida BRITE Project. *American Journal of Public Health, 100*(1), 108–114.

Schultz, S. K., Arndt, S., & Liesveld, J. (2003). Locations of facilities with special programs for older substance abuse clients in the US. *International Journal of Geriatric Psychiatry, 18*, 839–843.

Shea, S. (1998). *Psychiatric interviewing: The art of understanding: A practical guide for psychiatrists, psychologists, counselors, social workers, nurses, and other mental health professionals* (2nd ed.). Philadelphia: Saunders.

Simoni-Wastila, L., & Yang, H. K. (2006). Psychoactive drug abuse in older adults. *The American Journal of Geriatric Pharmacotherapy, 4*(4), 380–394.

Vestal, R. E., McGuire, E. A., Tobin, J. D., Andres, R., Norris, A. H., & Mezey, E. (1977). Aging and ethanol metabolism. *Clinical Pharmacology & Therapeutics, 21*(3), 343–354.

Zucker, R. A. (1998). Developmental aspects of aging, alcohol involvement, and their interrelationship. In E. L. Gomberg, A. M. Hegedus & R. A. Zucker (Eds.), *Alcohol Problems and Aging (NIAAA Research Monograph No. 33)* (Vol. 33, pp. 3–26). Bethesda, MD: U.S. Department of Health and Human Services.

Part IV
Addiction and Social Policy

Understanding the policy context in which practice takes place is an important aspect of effective training in the addictions. As such, the final two chapters provide a critical appraisal of policies surrounding the use, abuse, and dependence on alcohol and other drugs. Some of the topics that impinge on social work practice such as marketing and regulation in various settings, the biomedicalization of alcohol and drug use disorders, harm reduction and prevention policies, and social welfare issues related to treatment are discussed. When reading these chapters it is useful to think about the range of policy choices available and the empirical support for various drug control strategies that occur at the national, state, and local levels and how this effects client services.

Chapter 14
Alcohol Policy

Jennifer Price Wolf and Lorraine T. Midanik

Alcohol abuse can cause a variety of harms to the drinker (i.e., health, occupational, or social problems), to their families, and to society in general (i.e., drunk driving, alcohol-related violence, or alcohol-related crime) (Greenfield et al., 2009). Alcohol use has been linked to approximately 60 different negative health outcomes, and causes an estimated 4% of the global disease burden (Rehm et al., 2009; Room, Babor, & Rehm, 2005). In 2009, almost one-third of all traffic-related fatalities in the USA were alcohol related, resulting in nearly 11,000 deaths (National Highway Traffic Safety Administration, 2010). Many other incidents of alcohol impaired driving go without arrest; an estimated 1.1% of women and 3.4% of men in the U.S. report driving under the influence of alcohol in the last 30 days (Shults, Beck, & Dellinger, 2010). Between 1997 and 2008, alcohol was involved in 19–37% of violent crimes (Bureau of Justice Statistics, 2010). Alcohol abuse is also a significant problem on college campuses; in 2005, 1,825 college students died in alcohol-related incidents (excluding suicides), while in 2001, 97,000 students experienced an alcohol-related sexual assault (Hingson, Heeren, Winter, & Wechsler, 2005; Hingson, Wenxing, & Weitzman, 2009). Overall, 60% of Americans report that they have experienced negative effects from someone else's drinking during their lifetime, ranging from family or financial problems to vehicular accidents, assaults, or vandalized property (Greenfield et al., 2009).

Although those with alcohol dependence are more likely to have alcohol-related problems, most alcohol-related social harms are caused by alcohol abuse in the much larger non-alcohol-dependent population. This "prevention paradox" suggests that alcohol policies must be designed to regulate a wide spectrum of alcohol consumption in order to best protect public health (Holder, 2009; Kreitman, 1986). While intensive treatment can be effective for those with alcohol dependence

J.P. Wolf (✉) • L.T. Midanik
University of California at Berkeley, Berkeley, CA, USA
e-mail: jpwolf@berkeley.edu; lmidanik@berkeley.edu

M.G. Vaughn and B.E. Perron (eds.), *Social Work Practice in the Addictions*,
Contemporary Social Work Practice, DOI 10.1007/978-1-4614-5357-4_14,
© Springer Science+Business Media New York 2013

(Weisner, Matzger, & Kaskutas, 2003), policies must also address moderate or heavy drinking by nondependent individuals in environments or contexts in which problems are most likely to occur.

The majority of social work practice dealing with alcohol-related problems is influenced by these large-scale social policies and regulations. There is little understanding, however, of how specific policies filter down to social work practice even though these policies directly, and sometimes indirectly, affect treatment and prevention efforts.

The purpose of this chapter is to provide a bridge between policy and practice for social workers. First, this chapter will delineate specific policy arenas that directly influence drinking practices. While these policies can and have been organized in several ways, we will focus on two major groupings: prevention and harm reduction. Second, we will discuss specific social welfare issues that are impacted by alcohol abuse and dependence: child welfare; welfare and disability; co-occurring disorders; screening, brief intervention and referral to treatment (SBIRT); and health care reform. We will conclude with a discussion of how social work practice in the alcohol field is influenced by larger health trends, e.g., biomedicalization, that encourage alcohol problems to be identified and handled on an individual level with less emphasis on social and environmental factors.

Key Policies

In general, alcohol policy seeks to decrease alcohol consumption and alcohol-related problems (Holder, 2009) and can be generally classified into two types: *prevention* or *harm reduction*. Prevention policies attempt to minimize or stop drinking and related problems at the population level (Edwards, 1997), while harm reduction policies seek to specifically decrease the harms associated with drinking but not necessarily the amount of alcohol being consumed (Nadelmann et al., 1994). There is significant conceptual overlap between these two types of policies, as the ultimate goal of most prevention policies is to reduce harms caused by alcohol. However, prevention and harm reduction policies typically use different approaches to reaching this goal, and may have different underlying philosophies.

Prevention Policies

Primary prevention policies seek to stop or reduce drinking, either for specific groups or the general population. Instead of addressing problems as they arise, prevention policies aim to improve individual and societal health and well-being by preventing them from happening in the first place. Prevention policies are consequently concerned with removing risks instead of just reducing them. This can be achieved through limiting the economic or physical availability of alcohol or prohibiting alcohol for targeted populations. Prevention policies can also try to educate individuals about alcohol's risks before they drink through warning labels or other programs.

Economic Accessibility

The price of alcohol appears to be directly related to alcohol consumption; as the monetary price of alcohol goes up, consumption generally goes down (Holder, 2009). The price sensitivity of alcohol appears to differ by the substance (with wine and liquors being more price sensitive than beer) (Chaloupka, Grossman, & Saffer, 2002) and the segment of the population. For example, those dependent on alcohol may be less likely to decrease consumption when prices rise than those who drink more moderately. In addition, those with lower incomes, including adolescents, may be more likely to reduce consumption than adults or those with higher incomes (Grossman, Chaloupka, Saffer, & Laixuthai, 1994). While beer is less price sensitive than wine or liquor for the general population, it appears that for adolescents, who drink more beer than other substances, beer is highly price sensitive (Chaloupka et al., 2002). However, to truly understand the cost of alcohol to adolescents, both the economic and opportunity costs (i.e., obtaining alcohol illegally, the potential negatives of illegal drinking) need to be considered (Laixuthai & Chaloupka, 1993). Consequently, in more regulated environments, including those with minimum drinking age laws (Laixuthai & Chaloupka, 1993) or state monopolies on alcohol distribution (Ponicki, Gruenewald, & LaScala, 2007), alcohol consumption may be less price sensitive because those who would be deterred from drinking by higher prices are already deterred by more restrictive regulation.

Raising alcohol prices to decrease consumption can have an effect on several negative consequences of alcohol use (Chaloupka et al., 2002). One study found that increases in state taxes on alcohol led to reductions in motor vehicle accident fatalities in youth (Saffer & Grossman, 1987). Increasing the price of beer may be one of the most helpful ways of preventing drinking and driving in the USA, as some authors have estimated that raising alcohol taxes to their 1951 levels would reduce alcohol-related vehicular fatalities by 11.5% overall, and by 32.1% among those between 18 and 20 years of age (Chaloupka, Saffer, & Grossman, 1993). Increasing the price of alcohol could also reduce child abuse rates (Markowitz & Grossman, 1998), particularly by women perpetrators (Markowitz & Grossman, 2000), spousal violence (Markowitz & Grossman, 2000), and violence on college campuses (Grossman & Markowitz, 2001).

Since supply and demand markets and alcohol distributors set the commercial price of alcohol, policy makers typically manipulate alcohol prices through raising alcohol excise taxes. Taking inflation into account, U.S. taxation of alcoholic beverages is significantly lower than in the past, causing declines in the "real price" of alcohol (Chaloupka et al., 2002). In addition, the goal of small tax increases that have occurred have been to increase government revenue, and not specifically to reduce alcohol consumption (Chaloupka et al., 2002). Significantly raising these taxes would likely be controversial, as the alcohol industry has a powerful lobbying presence (Jernigan & DeMarco, 2011), and excise taxes are considered by some to be both an infringement on individual liberty and disproportionately discriminatory against those with low-incomes (Chapman, 2003). In 2010, 23 states made an attempt to raise alcohol excise taxes; none of which succeeded (Jernigan & DeMarco, 2011). State budget crises, however, may result in governments looking for additional revenue. For example, Maryland successfully raised alcohol taxes by 3% in 2011 (Jernigan & DeMarco, 2011). Consequently, while prevention of alcohol problems through reducing economic availability remains primarily unrealized, it is a potential policy option for the future.

Physical Accessibility

Community factors such as the drinking culture of a neighborhood (Ahern, Galea, Hubbard, Midanik, & Syme, 2008) or the qualities of its built environment (Bernstein, Galea, Ahern, & Vlahov, 2007) have been shown to affect individual drinking levels. Policies that limit alcohol's physical accessibility draw on this phenomenon by regulating where and how alcohol can be purchased. Studies have shown that limiting the number of retail outlets selling alcohol reduces alcohol consumption (Gruenewald, Ponicki, & Holder, 1993), and could in turn reduce the rates of alcohol-related harms such as violence (Gruenewald & Remer, 2006), and youth driving under the influence (Treno, Grube, & Martin, 2003).

Other policies limiting alcohol's physical accessibility create government monopolies on alcohol sales. Under this regulation, alcohol is only sold through government-owned stores, often with limited hours of operation (Holder, 2009). Changing from a government monopoly to privately owned alcohol retail has been linked to increased alcohol consumption (Wagenaar & Holder, 1996). Limiting the hours of sale for alcohol has also been shown to reduce consumption (Holder, 2009). Consequently, restricting the physical accessibility of alcohol to the general population may be an effective way of reducing alcohol consumption and alcohol-related problems, although these efforts may be challenged by those against market regulation.

Alcohol Prohibitions

One of the most widely known alcohol prevention policies is the Uniform Drinking Age Act of 1984, which tied federal transportation funding to a minimum drinking age of 21 (O'Malley & Wagenaar, 1991). States that maintain a lower minimum drinking age receive less funding, creating a significant incentive to follow the federal guideline. Research has demonstrated that the minimum drinking age law is effective in reducing alcohol-related problems among those under age 21, most significantly through lower rates of vehicular injury and fatalities (Jones, Pieper, & Robertson, 1992; Wagenaar, 1993). Despite these lower rates, approximately 40% of U.S. 12th graders drank alcohol in the last month in 2010 (Johnston, O'Malley, Bachman, & Schulenberg, 2010). Thus while the institution of a minimum drinking age law likely has reduced alcohol consumption and related problems in this population (Holder, 2009), it has not prevented all alcohol use nor all alcohol-related problems. This could be the result of inadequate enforcement, as policies increasing regulation and compliance with this law can result in decreased consumption (Dent, Grube, & Biglan, 2005; Wagenaar et al., 2000). This policy has also been challenged by those who argue that the minimum drinking age should be lower, coinciding with the onset of legal adulthood at age 18, or that prohibiting alcohol for the young leads to unhealthy drinking patterns (see http://www.chooseresponsibility. org; McCardell, 2004).

In addition to the minimum age drinking law, other policies prohibit alcohol use for certain populations. For example, Native Alaskan villages have used several prevention policies to decrease alcohol consumption and related problems in their communities. Alcohol is the primary substance of choice for Alaska Natives (Brems, 1996; Namyniuk, Brems, & Kuka-Hindin, 2001) and approximately one-half of Native Alaskan men and one-quarter of Native Alaskan women may be problem drinkers (Searle, Shellenberger, & Spence, 2006), a rate far above that of the general U.S. population. In 1981, Alaska state law passed the "local option" referendum, which allowed individual communities to control how and if alcohol entered their area (Berman, Hull, & May, 2000). If they choose to regulate alcohol, communities are given three options: (1) to prohibit both the sale and importation of alcohol for personal use ("dry" communities); (2) prohibit the sale of alcohol but allow personal importation; and (3) allow both personal importation and the selling of alcohol in one licensed private or government store ("damp" communities). All citizens are entitled to vote in these referendums, but since nonnative Alaskans generally do not support prohibition, only primarily Alaska Native communities have passed prohibition. One study estimated that becoming a "dry" community prevented approximately 1/5 of alcohol-related injury deaths as compared to unregulated communities, more than the moderately regulated "damp" communities (Berman et al., 2000). "Dry" communities with alcohol prohibition also have lower rates of vehicular and assault injuries than communities without alcohol prohibition (Landen et al., 1997; Wood & Gruenewald, 2006). Other Native American populations in the contiguous USA, however, have attempted alcohol prohibitions with little success (Landen et al., 1997), even demonstrating a rise in injury rates after becoming "dry" (Berman et al., 2000). It could be that the unique geographic isolation of Alaska native communities makes prevention policies more effective than in other areas, where those interested in obtaining alcohol can drive out of Native lands to purchase it (thereby potentially increasing alcohol-related vehicular injuries). In addition, by making the policies local and determined by referendum, the local policy option in Alaska ensures that community members support alcohol prohibition or regulation in their communities, potentially leading to greater enforcement and compliance.

Educational Prevention Policies

In 1989, the federal government mandated that all alcoholic beverages contain a warning label stating that women should not drink alcohol during pregnancy, alcohol impairs driving ability, and alcohol can cause negative health effects. This label was designed to prevent alcohol use, particularly among pregnant women and those operating machinery, by educating them of the dangers and risks involved. In addition to warning on beverages themselves, other regulations have been passed calling for warning messages posted at alcohol retail outlets (MacKinnon & Nohre, 2006). While initially these warnings appeared to change adolescent's attitudes towards drinking alcohol, these effects faded fairly quickly (MacKinnon, Nohre, Pentz, & Stacy, 2000). Evidence also suggests that the labels do not decrease alcohol consumption (MacKinnon, Nohre, Cheong, Stacy, & Pentz, 2001). This is contrary to tobacco warning labels, which have been found to be effective internationally (Hammond, Fong, Borland, & Cummings, 2007). However, since the alcohol warnings are generally smaller, less informative, and less graphic than tobacco warnings, it is unknown whether more prominent display or more detail would increase their efficacy (Center for Science in the Public Interest, 2001).

Harm Reduction Policies

For many years, the dominant substance abuse treatment paradigm has been the disease model (Bigler, 2005; Frans, 1994), which argues that alcoholism is a progressive, chronic disease for which total abstinence is the only method to stop its progression (Jellinek, 1960). While abstinence might be a helpful goal for many who are dependent on alcohol, the disease model offers little alternatives for those who wish to cut down on their drinking or whose main problem is alcohol abuse, not alcohol dependence. Following this ideology, most substance abuse treatment providers view abstinence as the ultimate goal of treatment, although social workers are more likely to accept other strategies than nonsocial workers (Burke & Clapp, 1997). This is in line with recommendations emphasizing the use of a variety of treatment strategies to best meet an individual client's needs (Council on Social Work Education, 1994), embodying the field's emphasis on strengths-based and client centered treatment (MacMaster, 2004).

Harm reduction is a strategy that has gained increasing attention in the alcohol abuse treatment and policy fields. The harm reduction paradigm emphasizes minimizing the risks that accompany unhealthy behaviors (Des Jarlais, 1995; MacMaster, 2004). Harm reduction recognizes that substance use is a well-established practice in many societies, and does not regard intoxication, in and of itself, as negative (Des Jarlais, 1995). Instead of prohibiting use, harm reduction strategies aim to identify and prevent situations where substance use and intoxication lead to ill effects. Traditionally, harm reduction has been associated with policies designed to reduce the negative consequences of illicit drug use, such as safe needle exchange (Des

Jarlais, 1995). This approach is also relevant to alcohol abuse, as there are many avenues for the minimization of alcohol's harms, both in populations who are legally allowed to drink and those younger than the minimum drinking age.

Since they emphasize the reduction of risk instead of direct prohibition, harm reduction policies have been criticized as condoning alcohol use among populations for whom it is illegal to drink, such as adolescents (MacCoun & Caulkins, 1996), and for populations for whom drinking any alcohol might be perceived as risky, such as pregnant women (NIAAA, 2011) or those who take alcohol-interactive prescription medications (Adams, 1995). Despite these concerns, harm reduction policies are increasingly being used to address alcohol abuse (Anderson, Chisholm, & Fuhr, 2009). These include efforts to minimize the drinking patterns that are most likely to lead to harm, such as binge and chronic heavy drinking (British Medical Association Board of Science, 2008), and the drinking environments where hazardous drinking is more likely to occur (Brocato & Wagner, 2003). While harm reduction policies have been utilized in several areas, including social marketing and public information campaigns, traffic safety measures, and responsible alcohol serving trainings, there is little systematic knowledge about their efficacy.

Social Marketing, Public Information, and Social Norms Campaigns

Social marketing and public information campaigns are designed to impart information about the negative consequences of alcohol abuse (Anderson et al., 2009). Social norms campaigns, which are commonly used on college campuses, aim to alter students' alcohol expectations and perceptions of drinking norms (Toomey, Lenk, & Wagenaar, 2007). Students commonly overestimate the amount of alcohol that their peers drink (Larimer & Cronce, 2007). Proponents of social norms campaigns hypothesize that knowing the dangers of drinking, and that heavy drinking is not as common as they expect, will lead individuals to reconsider heavy drinking in the future. Campaigns can include posters, media messages, warning labels, and other local or national efforts. While social norms-based efforts have demonstrated effectiveness in individual or small-group interventions (Larimer & Cronce, 2007), few large-scale social norms campaign have been found effective, with some potentially increasing drinking in targeted college campuses (Toomey et al., 2007). In general, reviews of public information campaigns have found little positive effect, particularly in the long term (Anderson et al., 2009).

Traffic Safety Measures

Many harm reduction policies are designed to improve road safety by limiting the amount of alcohol consumed by drivers. The creation of a legal threshold for blood alcohol concentration (BAC) is a harm reduction policy that does not prohibit driving after any alcohol consumption, but establishes a level above which driving is more likely to cause accidents and injury (Mann et al., 2001). Sobriety checkpoints, where drivers are stopped and asked to provide breathalyzer readings of their BAC, have been found to reduce alcohol-related accidents (Elder et al., 2002; Shults et al., 2001). The BAC limit and sobriety checkpoints are designed to deter heavy drinkers from driving, or prevent drivers from drinking heavily, to avoid legal consequences and risk of injury. Another promising intervention, alcohol ignition interlocks, prevent repeat DUI offenders from driving their cars without providing a legal limit breathalyzer reading (Willis, Lybrand, & Bellamy, 2004). The relative success of these policies suggests that policies that limit the amount of acceptable drinking for drivers effectively make roads safer.

Environmental Measures

Other harm reduction policies are designed to alter drinking environments. Some are designed to reduce worker and patron injuries at bars by replacing regular glassware with less breakable material, train workers on responsible serving strategies (i.e., how to detect when customers are intoxicated and should be denied further drinks), or prevent "bar hopping" (i.e., frequent movement of groups between different drinking establishments) (Ker & Chinnock, 2008). Although the majority of alcohol-related crimes occur in personal residences (Bureau of Justice Statistics, 2010), these policies are designed to prevent aggression, injury, and other harms by limiting intoxication and creating a moderate drinking environment. The overall evidence for these policies is mixed, as there have been limited studies, few of which used rigorous methodologies (Ker & Chinnock, 2008).

Alcohol's societal harms are significant. Harm reduction policies offer opportunities to lessen these negative impacts without prohibiting alcohol use for responsible drinkers. While more rigorous research evaluating these policies is needed, they allow social workers in policy and practice to consider practical and potentially effective alternatives to the disease model.

Social Welfare Issues

Alcohol policy and treatment have traditionally been an understudied area in the social work curriculum, even though most social workers will encounter clients who have problems with alcohol (Corrigan, Bill, & Slater, 2009). Alcohol abuse has a complicated and interconnected relationship with a myriad of social problems, including domestic violence (Humphreys, Regan, River, & Thiara, 2005), child maltreatment, and mental health issues (Woodcock & Sheppard, 2002). As a result, even social workers that do not specialize in alcohol or substance abuse need to be aware of how alcohol regulation and prevention policies relate to their clients. In addition, social workers need to understand how alcohol-related policies and requirements within other social welfare systems, such as the child welfare, welfare, and health-care systems, might help their clients succeed or fail in their goals.

Child Welfare Alcohol Policies

Although there is mixed evidence about the causal relationships between alcohol and child abuse (Widom & Hiller-Sturmhofel, 2001), research has indicated that an alcoholic parent can have negative consequences on a young child's emotional, social, and cognitive development (Fitzgerald & Das Eiden, 2007). In many areas, child welfare system social workers are required to assess whether substance abuse treatment is warranted in cases where child abuse has been substantiated and alcohol or substance abuse is alleged (Social Service Manual, 2006). This assessment includes questioning of the children and observation of current intoxication or withdrawal symptoms, indicating that in less severe or "hidden" cases of alcohol abuse, this problem may be missed. However, some states, such as Maine, have developed universal screening for substance-related disorders in all families referred to the child welfare system (State of Maine, 2007). When alcohol or substance abuse is identified, a number of child welfare agencies have developed funding streams to help get parents treatment and speed family reunification (Young, Gardner, Whitaker, Yeh, & Otero, 2003). Other states, such as New York, have developed partnerships between the chemical dependency treatment facilities and child welfare systems and courts, to encourage interdepartmental efforts to bring families together (New York State Department of Children and Family Services, 2008). While many states have not developed integrated systems to deal with this issue, the strict timelines placed on family reunification by the Adoption and Safe Families Act of 1997, and the high frequency of relapse and readmission to treatment make close monitoring of treatment goals and progress crucial, in order to prevent permanent loss of custody and ensure the safety of children. The diversity and complexity of child welfare systems across the USA require that social workers in this field understand the resources and regulations of their local agencies.

Welfare and Disability Alcohol Policies

Alcohol abuse-related problems are also evident in welfare systems for the poor and disabled, perhaps partly because long-term heavy alcohol use can lead to reduced wages (Bryant, Samanayake, & Wilhite, 1993). Heavy drinking may be more prevalent in Temporary Aid for Needy Families (TANF) recipients than in women not receiving welfare (Cheng & Lo, 2010; Zabkiewicz & Schmidt, 2007), with an estimated 31% of recipients in Washington state needing alcohol or drug treatment (Shah et al., 2010). Some states mandate screening for alcohol abuse in TANF applicants, with research indicating that this screening does not impact their welfare involvement (Cheng & Lo, 2010). While qualitative research has indicated that substance use could cause premature exit from the welfare system due to resulting limited ability to obtain employment or contextual factors such as substance using social networks and involvement in the child welfare or criminal justice systems (Mulia & Schmidt, 2003), there is no clear evidence that alcohol dependence or at-risk drinking significantly affect the transition between welfare and work (Zabkiewicz & Schmidt, 2007). Despite this uncertainty, TANF recipients are required to attend alcohol or drug treatment if it is part of their case plan and accessible. With the expansion of Medicaid services under health-care reform, more treatment options may become available, allowing more individuals to obtain care and potentially saving states money in the long term (Shah et al., 2010).

In addition to creating TANF, the Personal Responsibility and Work Opportunity Reconciliation Act of 1996 eliminated substance-related disability as a criterion for SSI eligibility (Hogan, Unick, Speiglman, & Norris, 2008). Previously, individuals diagnosed with alcohol- or drug-related disabilities were eligible for Supplemental Security Income. In one study, approximately half of those who lost substance-related SSI payments remained unemployed 3.5 years after losing their benefits, indicating that instead of acting as a "moral hazard" (i.e., keeping able individuals out of work), the benefits were helping individuals stay out of poverty (Hogan et al., 2008). The loss of SSI disability payments for those with significant alcohol problems leaves social workers with one less safety net option for clients with few resources.

Co-occurring Disorders

Social workers should also be aware of disparities in substance abuse treatment access, as individuals with developmental disabilities and serious mental illness may be less likely to receive substance abuse treatment (Slayter, 2010). These populations with co-occurring disorders often require long-term treatment stays, and may benefit the least from policies or managed care treatment approaches that are time-limited (Slayter, 2010).

Emphasis of Brief Treatment for Alcohol Problems

Although some clients require intensive, long-term care, government and policy focus has shifted to providing brief interventions in a variety of setting. SBIRT programs have been embraced in trauma centers and emergency rooms, where many visits are related to alcohol abuse (American College of Surgeons Committee on Trauma, 2006; Cherpitel, 2007). SBIRT begins with screening, where standardized screening instruments are use to determine a client's level of risk. Those who screen as mildly at-risk, or above, receive a brief intervention, based on motivational interviewing and typically emphasizing harm reduction rather than abstinence goals. In cases where it is indicated, referrals to treatment are then made. Social workers are involved in SBIRT administration in a variety of settings, from hospitals, criminal justice settings, and mental health clinics to college campuses and maternity settings (NIAAA, 2005). However, these interventions are not solely administered by behavioral health workers, and can be utilized by medical staff, police officers, and other professionals (Moyer & Finney, 2004/2005). Due to their apparent effectiveness with alcohol abusing populations (Moyer, Finney, Swearingen, & Vergun, 2002) and relatively low cost, SBIRT interventions are increasingly being covered by both private and public insurers (APA, 2008). However, it remains unclear whether brief intervention results can be maintained long-term, and whether they are effective in alcohol-dependent or chronic heavy drinking clients (McQueen, Howe, Allan, & Mains, 2009; Moyer et al., 2002). The current emphasis on SBIRT treatment consequently might take the focus away from more expensive longer-term treatment needed by those with the worst alcohol problems.

Health Care Reform and Alcohol Problems

The pending reforms under the Patient Protection and Affordable Care and Health Care and Education Reconciliation Acts of 2010 (otherwise known as the Affordable Care Act), most of which are due to occur in 2014, are anticipated to bring significant changes in alcohol-related treatment funding, delivery, and provision of services. Due to expansions in Medicaid eligibility and coverage mandates, approximately 94% of the U.S. population is expected to have medical coverage (Substance Abuse and Mental Health Services Administration (Producer), 2010). This will provide coverage to most of the 61% of individuals receiving treatment from State Substance Abuse Agencies who previously had no insurance, primarily through Medicaid (O'Brien, Ingoglia, & Jarvis, 2010). As a result of the Wellstone/ Domenici Parity Act of 2008, Medicaid and other insurers that provide mental health and substance abuse treatment benefits must maintain parity between these benefits and other medical benefits. Insurers consequently cannot place treatment limitations or cost-sharing measures (i.e., large co-pays) specifically on mental health or substance abuse services. While this bill will help many obtain treatment for alcohol problems, it does not require that insurers cover substance use treatment, and allows cost exemptions (SAMSHA, 2010). Although not yet implemented, the Affordable Care Act is designed to close this gap by requiring all insurance plans on health exchange markets to include behavioral health coverage, including substance abuse treatment coverage (Office of National Drug Control Policy, 2010). In conjunction with the Wellstone/Domenici Parity Act, the Affordable Care Act will potentially greatly expand the availability of substance abuse treatment in the USA.

While the long-term implications of health-care reform are yet unknown, social workers will likely play a significant role in providing behavioral and mental health care for alcohol abusing clients (O'Brien et al., 2010; Ofosu, 2011). Improvements in social worker recruitment and training, such as those proposed in the Social Work Reinvestment Act (Social Work Reinvestment Initiative, n.d.), should emphasize the important role of policy analysis and advocacy in fully completing the person-in-environment perspective.

Social Work Practice in the Twenty First Century

As a field, social work is uniquely defined by its emphasis on the person-in-environment perspective, which includes examining the micro-, mezzo-, and macro-level factors that impact and alter a client system (Frankel, 1990). The policy environment, which dictates how the social welfare system operates, is a crucial component of the person-in-environment system. Policies determine the eligibility criteria, benefits, administration, and financing of the social welfare programs that social workers work for and with to serve clients. Unfortunately, policy and advocacy work have sometimes received less emphasis than individually oriented work (Lens & Gibelman, 2000). Policy work and the person-in-environment system, however, remain a fundamental element of the social work curricula (Council on Social Work Education, 1994). As a result, all social workers need to understand how policy impacts clients and treatment systems, as well as how changes in treatment systems can impact policy. Additionally, social workers need to be aware of the larger trends occurring on a national or global level that can determine how health and social problems are framed.

One of these trends is biomedicalization, which some have argued has dominated the ways in which medicine and health are framed since the mid-1980s (Clarke, Shim, Mamo, Fosket, & Fishman, 2003, 2010). The technoscientific changes that make up the foundation of biomedicalization can be characterized by five processes:

1. a new biopolitical economy of medicine, health, illness, living, and dying which forms an increasingly dense and elaborate arena in which biomedical knowledges, technologies, services, and capital are ever more co-constituted;
2. a new and intensifying focus on health (in addition to illness, disease, injury), on optimization and enhancement by technoscientific means, and on the elaboration of risk and surveillance at individual, niche group, and population levels;
3. the technoscientization of biomedical practices where intervention for treatment and enhancement are progressively more reliant on sciences and technologies, are conceived in those very terms, and are ever more promptly applied;
4. transformations of biomedical knowledge production, information management, distribution, and consumption; and
5. transformations of bodies and the production of new individual, collection, and population (or niche group) level technoscientific identities (Clarke, Mamo, Fosket, Fishman, & Shim, 2010, pp. 1–2).

A major theme of this biomedicalization movement has been to move away from societal or collective concerns and towards the improvement of an individual's life.

Within the overall health arena, there are many examples to illustrate how this process of biomedicalization has deeply impacted several fields including aging (Estes & Binney, 1989; Lyman, 1989); psychiatry and mental health (Cohen, 1993; Gomory, Wong, Cohen, & Lacasse, in press; Orr, 2010), sexual dysfunction (Fishman, 2010) and surgical interventions for weight loss (Boero, 2010). In each case, biomedical techniques are used to define both the problem and its solution with little or no regard for societal processes that affect individuals identified as having a "problem."

Within the alcohol field, biomedicalization has been approached from an institutional perspective which has implications for how alcohol problems are framed for political constituencies, the public and researchers: which aspects of alcohol use and alcohol-related problems are deemed important and which are not? For example, it is noted in Midanik (2004) that five of the seven goals of the National Institute on Alcohol Abuse and Alcoholism (2001–2005) reflect the dominance of biomedical issues. This focus on biomedical factors is strongly evident in other data provided by NIAAA. First, the vast majority of content areas covered by NIAAA's publication, entitled "Alcohol & Health," since 1983 has been devoted to biomedical issues. These publications were designed to provide the latest updates in the alcohol field to congress and to the public. The emphasis on the biomedical as "cutting edge" suggests the lesser importance of social and psychological issues in the alcohol field. Second, the number and amount of grant awards over time are dominated by the biomedical and neuroscience branches. Thus, fewer research grants and dollars are designated to research projects that are not biomedical in nature such as prevention, underage drinking, and policy analysis (Midanik, 2006). Once again, the message is clear that there appears to be a hierarchy of importance in the alcohol field and more significantly, in research on alcohol issues.

There are several implications of biomedicalization for social work practice. First, a key element of social work practice is working in the environment to enact changes that will benefit vulnerable clients. Social workers must understand that this focus on environment is in sharp contrast to the prevailing trend in the health and alcohol fields. Second, social workers should fully understand the biopsychosocial model that includes biomedical processes that influence behavior. Thus, a better knowledge of biomedical and medical factors is needed primarily to be able to accurately assess the interaction between medical, biomedical, and psychosocial issues. Training for social workers needs to include information on how the physical, psychological, and social world interact and influence assessment and treatment. Third, social work needs to be more closely aligned with the intersection of psychosocial and biomedical factors by expanding its knowledge base and being part of research teams that assess a wider range of outcomes. Traditionally, federally funded research is categorized as either biomedical or behavioral (Midanik, 2006). The result of this bifurcation is that there is little incentive to combine efforts. Hopefully, future social work researchers will bypass this boundary and find more ways to delineate the crucial functions of social work to a larger audience.

References

Adams, W. (1995). Interactions between alcohol and other drugs. *International Journal of the Addictions, 30*(13–14), 1903–1923.

Ahern, J., Galea, S., Hubbard, A., Midanik, L. T., & Syme, S. L. (2008). "Culture of drinking" and individual problems with alcohol use. *American Journal of Epidemiology, 167*(9), 1041–1049.

American College of Surgeons Committee on Trauma. (2006). *Resources for optimal care of injured patients.* Chicago, IL: American College of Surgeons.

American Psychological Association. (2008). Screening, brief intervention now common in insurance plans. *Psychiatric News, 43*(10), 4–4.

Anderson, P., Chisholm, D., & Fuhr, D. C. (2009). Effectiveness and cost-effectiveness of policies and programmes to reduce the harm caused by alcohol. *The Lancet, 373*, 2234–2246.

Berman, M., Hull, T., & May, P. (2000). Alcohol control and injury death in Alaska Native communities: Wet, damp, and dry under Alaska's local option law. *Journal of Studies on Alcohol, 61*(2), 311–319.

Bernstein, K. T., Galea, S., Ahern, J., & Vlahov, D. (2007). The built environment and alcohol consumption in urban neighborhoods. *Drug and Alcohol Dependence, 91*(2–3), 244–252.

Bigler, M. O. (2005). Harm reduction as a practice and prevention model. *The Journal of Baccalaureate Social Work, 10*(2), 69–86.

Boero, N. (2010) Bypassing blame. Bariatric surgery and the case of biomedical failure. In A. E. Clarke, L. Mamo, J. R. Fosket, J. R. Fishman, & J. K. Shim (Eds.), *Biomedicalization. Technoscience, health and illness in the U.S.* Durham, NC: Duke University Press (Chapter 11).

Brems, C. (1996). Substance use, mental health, and health in Alaska: Emphasis on Alaska Native peoples. *Arctic Medical Research, 55*, 135–147.

British Medical Association Board of Science. (2008). *Alcohol misuse: Tackling the UK epidemic.* London, UK: British Medical Association.

Brocato, J., & Wagner, E. F. (2003). Harm reduction: A social work practice model and social justice agenda. *Health & Social Work, 28*(2), 117–125.

Bryant, R. R., Samanayake, V. A., & Wilhite, A. (1993). The influence of current and past alcohol use on earnings: Three approaches to estimation. *Journal of Applied Behavioral Science, 29*(1), 9–31.

Bureau of Justice Statistics. (2010). *Alcohol and crime: Data from 2002 to 2008.* 2010, from http://bjs.ojp.usdoj.gov/content/acf/ac_conclusion.cfm.

Burke, A. C., & Clapp, J. D. (1997). Ideology and social work practice in substance abuse settings. *Social Work, 42*(6), 552–562.

Center for Science in the Public Interest. (2001). *Alcohol warning labels go unnoticed, poll finds.* Retrieved May 23, 2011, from http://www.cspinet.org/booze/batf_labels2001_press.htm.

Chaloupka, F., Grossman, M., & Saffer, H. (2002). *The effects of price on alcohol consumption and alcohol-related problems.* Bethesda, MD: National Institute on Alcohol Abuse and Alcoholism.

Chaloupka, F., Saffer, H., & Grossman, M. (1993). Alcohol-control policies and motor-vehicle fatalities. *Journal of Legal Studies, 22*(1), 161–186.

Chapman, C. J., Jr. (2003). The new sumptuary laws: How Massachusetts consumption taxes keep the poor poor. In *BHI policy study.* Boston, MA: The Beacon Hill Institute at Suffolk University.

Cheng, T. C., & Lo, C. C. (2010). Heavy alcohol use, alcohol and drug screening and their relationship to mothers' welfare participation: A temporal-ordered causal analysis. *Journal of Social Policy, 39*(4), 543–559.

Cherpitel, C. (2007). Alcohol and injuries: A review of international emergency room studies since 1995. *Drug and Alcohol Review, 26*(2), 201–214.

Clarke, A. E., Mamo, L., Fosket, J. R., Fishman, J. R., & Shim, J. K. (Eds.). (2010). *Biomedicalization. Technoscience, health and illness in the US.* Durham, NC: Duke University Press.

Clarke, A. E., Shim, J. K., Mamo, L., Fosket, J. R., & Fishman, J. R. (2003). Biomedicalization: Technoscientific transformations of health, illness, and U.S. Biomedicine. *American Sociological Review, 68*, 161–194.

Cohen, C. I. (1993). The biomedicalization of psychiatry: A critical overview. *Community Mental Health Journal, 29*, 509–521.

Corrigan, M. J., Bill, M. L., & Slater, J. R. (2009). The development of a substance abuse curriculum in a Master's of Social Work program. *Journal of Social Work Education, 45*(3), 513–520.

Council on Social Work Education. (1994). *Handbook of accreditation standards and procedures.* Alexandria, VA: Council on Social Work Education.

Dent, C., Grube, J., & Biglan, A. (2005). Community level alcohol availability and enforcement of possession laws as predictors of youth drinking. *Preventative Medicine, 40*, 355–362.

Des Jarlais, D. C. (1995). Harm reduction—A framework for incorporating science into drug policy. *American Journal of Public Health, 85*(1), 10–12.

Edwards, G. (1997). Alcohol policy and the public good. *Addiction, 92*(Suppl. 1), S73–S79.

Elder, R., Shults, R., Sleet, D., Nichols, J., Zaza, S., & Thompson, R. (2002). Effectiveness of sobriety checkpoints for reducing alcohol-involved crashes. *Traffic Injury Prevention, 3*, 266–274.

Estes, C. L., & Binney, E. A. (1989). The biomedicalization of aging: Dangers and dilemmas. *Gerontologist, 29*(5), 587–596.

Fishman, J. R. (2010) The making of Viagra. In A. E. Clarke, L. Mamo, J. R. Fosket, J. R. Fishman, J. K. Shim (Eds.), *Biomedicalization. Technoscience, health and illness in the U.S.* (pp. 289–306). Durham, NC: Duke University Press (Chapter 10).

Fitzgerald, H. E., & Das Eiden, R. (2007). Paternal alcoholism, family functioning, and infant mental health. *Zero to Three, 27*(4), 11–18.

Frankel, S. (1990). What is unique about social work: A brief think piece. *The Social Worker, 58*(2), 61–68.

Frans, D. (1994). Social work, social science and the disease concept: New directions for addiction treatment. *Journal of Sociology and Social Welfare, 21*(2), 71–89.

Gomory, T., Wong, S. E., Cohen, D., & Lacasse, J. R. (2011). Clinical social work and the biomedical industrial complex. *Journal of Sociology and Social Welfare, 38*(5), 135–165.

Greenfield, T. K., Ye, Y., Kerr, W. C., Bond, J., Rehm, J., & Giesbrecht, N. (2009). Externalities from alcohol consumption in the 2005 US National Alcohol Survey: Implications for policy. *International Journal of Environmental Research and Public Health, 6*(12), 3205–3224.

Grossman, M., Chaloupka, F., Saffer, H., & Laixuthai, A. (1994). Effects of alcohol price policy on youth: A summary of economic research. *Journal of Research on Adolescence, 4*(2), 347–364.

Grossman, M., & Markowitz, S. (2001). Alcohol regulation and violence on college campuses. In M. Grossman & C. R. Hsieh (Eds.), *Economic analysis of substance use and abuse: The experience of developed countries and lessons for developing countries* (pp. 257–289). Cheltenham, United Kingdom: Edward Elgar.

Gruenewald, P., Ponicki, W., & Holder, H. D. (1993). The relationship of outlet densities to alcohol consumption: A time series cross-sectional analysis. *Alcoholism: Clinical and Experimental Research, 17*(1), 38–47.

Gruenewald, P., & Remer, L. (2006). Changes in outlet densities affect violence rates. *Alcoholism: Clinical and Experimental Research, 30*(7), 1184–1193.

Hammond, D., Fong, G. T., Borland, R., & Cummings, K. M. (2007). Text and graphic warnings on cigarette packages: Findings from the international tobacco control four country study. *American Journal of Preventive Medicine, 32*(3), 202–209.

Hingson, R. W., Heeren, T., Winter, M., & Wechsler, H. (2005). Magnitude of alcohol-related mortality and morbidity among U.S. college students ages 18–24: Changes from 1998 to 2001. *Annual Review of Public Health, 26*, 259–279.

Hingson, R. W., Wenxing, Z., & Weitzman, E. R. (2009). Magnitude of and trends in alcohol-related mortality and morbidity among U.S. college students ages 18–24, 1998–2005. *Journal of Studies on Alcohol and Drugs,* Sup. 16, 12–20.

Hogan, S. R., Unick, G. J., Speiglman, R., & Norris, J. C. (2008). Social welfare policy and public assistance for low-income substance abusers: The impact of 1996 welfare reform legislation on the economic security of former supplemental security income drug addiction and alcoholism beneficiaries. *Journal of Sociology and Social Welfare, 35*(1), 221–245.

Holder, H. D. (2009). *Policies to prevent alcohol problems: A research agenda for 2010–2015.* Princeton, NJ: Robert Wood Johnson Foundation.

Humphreys, C., Regan, L., River, D., & Thiara, R. K. (2005). Domestic violence and substance use: Tackling complexity. *British Journal of Social Work, 35*(8), 1303–1320.

Jellinek, E. M. (1960). *The disease concept of alcoholism.* New Brunswick, NJ: Hillhouse Press.

Jernigan, D., & DeMarco, V. (2011, May 20). How Marylanders beat the alcohol lobby. *The Washington Post.* Retrieved from http://www.washingtonpost.com/opinions/how-marylanders-beat-the-alcohol-lobby/2011/05/18/AFVVF17G_story.html.

Johnston, L., O'Malley, P., Bachman, J., & Schulenberg, J. (2010). *Marijuana use is rising; ecstasy use is beginning to rise; and alcohol use is declining among US teens.* Ann Arbor, MI: University of Michigan News Service.

Jones, N., Pieper, C., & Robertson, L. (1992). The effect of legal drinking age on fatal injuries of adolescents and young adults. *American Journal of Public Health, 82,* 112–115.

Ker, K., & Chinnock, P. (2008). Interventions in the alcohol server setting for preventing injuries. *Cochrane Database of Systematic Reviews, 3.* doi: 10.1002/14651858.

Kreitman, N. (1986). Alcohol consumption and the preventive paradox. *British Journal of Addiction, 81,* 353–363.

Laixuthai, A., & Chaloupka, F. (1993). Youth alcohol use and public policy. *Contemporary Economic Policy, 11*(4), 70–81.

Landen, M. G., Beller, M., Funk, E., Propst, M., Middaugh, J., & Moolenaar, R. L. (1997). Alcohol-related injury death and alcohol availability in remote Alaska. *Journal of the American Medical Association, 278*(21), 1755–1758.

Larimer, M. E., & Cronce, J. M. (2007). Identification, prevention, and treatment revisited: Individual-focused college drinking prevention strategies 1999–2006. *Addictive Behaviors, 32,* 2439–2468.

Lens, V., & Gibelman, M. (2000). Advocacy be not forsaken! Retrospective lessons from welfare reform. *The journal of Contemporary Social Services, 81*(6), 611–620.

Lyman, K. A. (1989). Bringing the social back in: A critique of the biomedicalization of dementia. *Gerontologist, 29*(5), 597–605.

MacCoun, R., & Caulkins, J. (1996). Examing the behavioral assumptions of the national drug control strategy. In W. Bickel & R. DeGranpre (Eds.), *Drug policy and human nature: Psychological perspectives on the prevention, management, and treatment of illicit drug abuse* (pp. 177–197). New York: Plenum Press.

MacKinnon, D. P., & Nohre, L. (2006). Alcohol and tobacco warnings. In M. Wogalter (Ed.), *Handbook of warnings.* Mahwah, NJ: Erlbaum (Chapter 54).

MacKinnon, D. P., Nohre, L., Cheong, J., Stacy, A. W., & Pentz, M. A. (2001). Longitudinal relationship between the alcohol warning label and alcohol consumption. *Journal of Studies on Alcohol and Drugs, 62*(2).

MacKinnon, D. P., Nohre, L., Pentz, M. A., & Stacy, A. W. (2000). The alcohol warning and adolescents: 5-year effects. *American Journal of Public Health, 90*(10), 1589–1594.

MacMaster, S. A. (2004). Harm reduction: A new perspective on substance abuse services. *Social Work, 49*(3), 356.

Mann, R. E., Macdonald, S., Stoduto, G., Bondy, S., Jonah, B., & Shaikh, A. (2001). The effects of introducing or lowering legal per se blood alcohol limits for driving: An international review. *Accident Analysis & Prevention, 33*(5), 569–583.

Markowitz, S., & Grossman, M. (1998). Alcohol regulation and domestic violence towards children. *Contemporary Economic Policy, 16*(3), 309–320.

Markowitz, S., & Grossman, M. (2000). The effects of beer taxes on physical child abuse. *Journal of Health Economics, 19*(2), 271–282.

McCardell, J. M. J. (2004, September 13). What your college president didn't tell you. *The New York Times.*

McQueen, J., Howe, T. E., Allan, L., & Mains, D. (2009). Brief interventions for heavy alcohol users admitted to general hospital wards. *Cochrane Database Systematic Review, 8*(3).

Midanik, L. T. (2004). Biomedicalization and alcohol studies: Implications for policy. *Journal of Public Health Policy, 25*, 211–228.

Midanik, L. T. (2006). *Biomedicalization of alcohol studies. Ideological shifts and institutional challenges*. New Brunswick, NJ: Aldine Transaction.

Moyer, A., & Finney, J. W. (2004/2005). Brief interventions for alcohol problems: Factors that facilitate implementation. *Alcohol Research & Health, 28*(1), 44–50.

Moyer, A., Finney, J. W., Swearingen, C. E., & Vergun, P. (2002). Brief interventions for alcohol problems: A meta-analytic review of controlled investigations in treatment-seeking and non-treatment seeking populations. *Addiction, 97*, 279–292.

Mulia, N., & Schmidt, L. A. (2003). Conflicts and trade-offs due to alcohol and drugs: Client's accounts of leaving welfare. *Social Service Review, 77*(4), 499–522.

Nadelmann, E., Cohen, P., Locher, U., Stimson, G., Wodak, A., & Drucker, E. (1994). *The harm reduction approach to drug control: International progress*. Unpublished document. New York, NY: Lindesmith Center.

Namyniuk, L., Brems, C., & Kuka-Hindin, C. (2001). Ethnic differences in substance use patterns in a sample of pregnant substance-using women in treatment. *Journal of Addictions & Offender Counseling, 21*(2), 50–67.

National Highway Traffic Safety Administration. (2010). *Traffic Safety Facts 2009: Highlights of the 2009 motor vehicle crashes*. Washington, DC: NHTSA.

National Institute on Alcohol Abuse and Alcoholism. (2005). Brief interventions. In *Alcohol alert* (Vol. 66). Bethesda, MD: National Institute of Health.

National Institute on Alcohol Abuse and Alcoholism. (2011). *Women and alcohol*. Bethesda, MD: National Institute of Health.

New York State Department of Children and Family Services. (2008). *Gearing up to improve outcomes for families: New York state collaborative practice guide for managers and supervisors in child welfare, chemical dependency services, and court systems*. New York: Rensselaer.

O'Brien, J., Ingoglia, C., & Jarvis, D. (2010, September 21). *Healthcare reform: Implications for behavioral health providers*.

O'Malley, P. M., & Wagenaar, A. C. (1991). Effects of minimum drinking age laws on alcohol use, related behaviors and traffic crash involvement among American youth: 1976–1987. *Journal of Studies on Alcohol, 52*(5), 478–491.

Office of National Drug Control Policy. (2010). *The new healthcare reform law: Helping to close the 'treatment gap'*. Retrieved June 6, 2011, from http://www.whitehousedrugpolicy.gov/publications/html/healthcare.html.

Ofosu, A. (2011). *The implications of healthcare reform for the social work profession*. Washington, DC: United States House of Representatives Congressional briefing.

Orr, J. (2010) Biopsychiatry and the informatics of diagnosis. In A. E. Clarke, L. Mamo, J. R. Fosket, J. R. Fishman, J. K. Shim (Eds.), *Biomedicalization. Technoscience, health and illness in the U.S.* (pp. 353–379). Durham, NC: Duke University Press (Chapter 13).

Ponicki, W., Gruenewald, P., & LaScala, E. (2007). Joint impacts of minimum legal drinking age and beer taxes on US youth traffic fatalities, 1975 to 2001. *Alcoholism: Clinical and Experimental Research, 31*(5), 804–813.

Rehm, J., Mathers, C., Popova, S., Thavorncharoensap, M., Teerawattananon, Y., & Patra, J. (2009). Global burden of disease and injury and economic cost attributable to alcohol use and alcohol-use disorders. *The Lancet, 373*(9682), 2223–2233.

Room, R., Babor, T., & Rehm, J. (2005). Alcohol and public health. *The Lancet, 365*(9458), 519–530.

Saffer, H., & Grossman, M. (1987). Beer taxes, the legal drinking age, and youth motor vehicle fatalities. *Journal of Legal Studies, 16*(2), 351–374.

Searle, J. P., Shellenberger, S., & Spence, J. (2006). Alcohol problems in Alaska Natives: Lessons from the Inuit. *American Indian and Alaska Native Mental Health Research, 13*(1), 1–31.

Shah, M. F., Mancuso, D., He, L., Estee, S., Felver, B. E. M., Beall, K., et al. (2010). *Behavioral health risk among TANF parents: Links to homelessness, child abuse, and arrests*. Olympia, WA: Washington State Department of Social and Health Services.

Shults, R., Beck, L., & Dellinger, A. (2010). *Self-reported alcohol-impaired driving among adults in the United States, 2006 and 2008*. Paper presented at the Safety 2010 World Conference, London, England.

Shults, R., Elder, R., Sleet, D., Nichols, J., Alao, M. O., Carande-Kullis, V. G., et al. (2001). Reviews of evidence regarding interventions to reduce alcohol-impaired driving. *American Journal of Preventive Medicine, 21*(4), 66–88.

Slayter, E. (2010). Disparities in access to substance abuse treatment among people with intellectual disabilities and serious mental illness. *Health & Social Work, 35*(1), 49–59.

Social Service Manual. (2006). *Alcohol and other substance abuse in substantiated investigations*. Georgia: Georgia Department of Human Resources.

Social Work Reinvestment Initiative. (n.d.). *Reinvesting in social work*. Retrieved March 21, 2011, from http://www.socialworkreinvestment.org/SWRA/.

State of Maine. (2007). Universal substance abuse screening for families in the child welfare system: Policy and practice for family assessments and alternative response. Retrieved from http://www.ncsacw.samhsa.gov/files/Maine-Pamphlet-Universal-Substance-Abuse-Screening-for-Familie-in-the-Child-Welfare-System.pdf.

Substance Abuse and Mental Health Services Administration (Producer). (2010). Materials to Support Presentations. Retrieved March 21, 2011, from http://www.uclaisap.org/Affordable-Care-Act/assets/documents/health%20care%20reform/General/64-Speakers%20Bureau%20Master%20Set%20-%2012-1-10.pdf.

Toomey, T., Lenk, K. M., & Wagenaar, A. C. (2007). Environmental policies to reduce college drinking: An update of research findings. *Journal of Studies on Alcohol and Drugs, 68*, 208–219.

Treno, A., Grube, J., & Martin, S. (2003). Alcohol availability as a predictor of youth drinking and driving: A hierarchical analysis of survey and archival data. *Alcoholism: Clinical and Experimental Research, 27*(5), 835–840.

Wagenaar, A. C. (1993). Minimum drinking age and alcohol availability to youth: Issues and research needs. In M. Hilton, & G. Bloss (Eds.), *Economics and the prevention of alcohol-related problems*. National Institute on Alcohol Abuse and Alcoholism Research Monograph No. 25. Bethesda, MD: NIAAA.

Wagenaar, A. C., & Holder, H. D. (1996). The scientific process works: Seven replications now show significant wine sales increase after privatization [A Letter to the Editor]. *Journal of Studies on Alcohol, 57*(5), 575–576.

Wagenaar, A. C., Murray, D., Gehan, J., Wolfson, J., Forster, J., Toomey, T., et al. (2000). Communities mobilizing for change on alcohol: Outcomes from a randomized community trial. *Journal of Studies on Alcohol, 51*(1), 85–94.

Weisner, C., Matzger, H., & Kaskutas, L. A. (2003). How important is treatment? One-year outcomes of treated and untreated alcohol-dependent individuals. *Addiction, 98*(7), 901–911.

Widom, C. S., & Hiller-Sturmhofel, S. (2001). Alcohol abuse as a risk factor for and consequence of child abuse. *Alcohol Research & Health, 25*(1).

Willis, C., Lybrand, S., & Bellamy, N. (2004). Alcohol ignition interlock programmes for reducing drink driving recidivism. *Cochrane Database of Systematic Reviews, 3*. doi: 10.1002/14651858.

Wood, D. S., & Gruenewald, P. J. (2006). Local alcohol prohibition, police presence and serious injury in isolated Alaska Native villages. *Addiction, 101*(3), 393–403.

Woodcock, J., & Sheppard, M. (2002). Double trouble: Maternal depression and alcohol dependence as combined factors in child and family social work. *Children & Society, 16*(4), 232–245.

Young, N., Gardner, S., Whitaker, B., Yeh, S., & Otero, C. (2003). *A preliminary review of alcohol and other drug issues in the states' children and family service reviews and program improvement plans*. Irvine, CA: National Center on Substance Abuse and Child Welfare.

Zabkiewicz, D., & Schmidt, L. A. (2007). Behavioral health problems as barriers to work: Results from a 6-year panel study of welfare recipients. *The Journal of Behavioral Health Services and Research, 34*(2), 168–185.

Chapter 15
Drug Control Policies: Problems and Prospects

Maayan Lawental Schori and Eli Lawental

According to the most recent national studies, over 22 million people ages 12 and older—nearly 9% of the U.S. population—suffered from a substance use disorder (abuse or dependence) in the last year [Substance Abuse and Mental Health Services Administration (SAMHSA) (SAMHSA), 2009]. This number is based on criteria specified in the 4th edition of the Diagnostic and Statistical Manual of Mental Disorders [DSM-IV] (American Psychiatric Association, 1994). Of these 22 million, 68% abused or were dependent on alcohol, 17% on illegal drugs, and 14% on both. These numbers have remained relatively steady since 2002. The same survey classified over 23 million persons as needing treatment. Needing treatment was operationalized as having a substance use disorder or receiving treatment in a specialty facility—hospital inpatient, drug or alcohol rehabilitation facilities—inpatient or outpatient, or mental health centers—in the past year. Thus, the classification of needing treatment includes the people who are already in treatment, who may have not used drugs in the past year (and therefore so not necessarily suffer from a substance use disorder according to DSM criteria). However, only four million of them received any, and for over half of these the treatment was provided by self-help groups. The vast majority of people who need treatment for drug abuse in the USA do not receive it (SAMHSA, 2009).

M.L. Schori, PhD (✉)
University of Pennsylvania, Philadelphia, PA, USA
e-mail: mschori@sp2.upenn.edu

E. Lawental
Tel Hai College, Haifa, Israel
e-mail: lawental@hdatc.co.il

M.G. Vaughn and B.E. Perron (eds.), *Social Work Practice in the Addictions*,
Contemporary Social Work Practice, DOI 10.1007/978-1-4614-5357-4_15,
© Springer Science+Business Media New York 2013

Economic Costs of Drug Abuse

According to the latest data available, the estimated economic costs associated with drug abuse disorders were over $180 billion in 2002 (Harwood, 2004). The estimated costs associated with alcohol abuse were $185 billion in 1998 (Harwood, 2000). Despite these seemingly high costs, only $21 billion has been spent on any form of treatment (roughly $10.5 billion for alcohol and $10.2 billion for drug abuse) (Harwood, 2004; Mark et al., 2007). These estimates, based on guidelines set forth by the U.S. Public Health Service, suggest that drug abuse is a major health problem, comparable in cost to heart disease, alcohol abuse, mental illness, smoking, cancer, obesity, and diabetes (Harwood, 2004). The majority of treatment spending (77%) came from public sources, including federal, state, and local governments (French, Popovici, & Tapsell, 2008; Mark et al., 2007). This financial commitment is strikingly low considering the ample research detailing the efficacy of treatment and the economic benefits it yields (e.g. Kimberly & McLellan, 2006; McLellan, Lewis, O'Brien, & Kleber, 2000; NIDA, 2006; Scott, Dennis, & Foss, 2005).

In 2002, 71.2% of the total costs of drug abuse were attributed to loss of productivity, 8.7% to health costs (which include all treatment efforts), and 20.1% to other costs, including criminal justice and welfare. These costs of drug abuse are both direct and indirect. Direct costs of illnesses can be defined as expenditures for prevention, detection, treatment, rehabilitation, research, training, and capital investment in medical facilities. Indirect costs of illness represent the loss of output to the economy (Rice, 1967; Segel, 2006). In our case, direct costs are the sum of the total health-care costs and the costs of other effects; indirect costs are the costs of the loss of productivity. In 2002 the estimates for these costs were $52.2 billion and $128.6 billion, respectively (Harwood, 2004).

It is important to note that each of the three components (health-care costs, costs associated with productivity losses, and costs associated with other effects of drug abuse) contain subcomponents that are crime-related. When added up across all three categories, these crime-related costs represent 57.5% of the total cost of drug abuse in 1992 ($61.8 billion). This percentage increased to 59.6% in 2002 ($107.8 billion). Incarceration and crime careers constitute more than 50% of these crime-related costs. In fact, incarceration of drug offenders was the highest single economic cost of drug abuse in 2002, representing over a fifth of all drug abuse costs ($39 billion). This cost had increased 8.1% annually in the previous decade as a result of the increase in incarceration rates for drug offenders (from 431,000 people in 1992 to 663,000 in 2002) (Harwood, 2004).

Within the field of illegal drug abuse, cost of illness studies have been criticized for being conservative rather than presenting ranges or best estimates (Moore & Caulkins, 2006). They have also been accused of inherent conceptual limitations—for example, a COI study might take a health-related approach to an illness whose costs of health care are relatively low (Moore & Caulkins, 2006).

Reuter (1999) argued that COI estimates are limited due to uncertainty and ambiguity in some of the subcategory calculations. For instance, various national surveys estimate cost associated with loss of productivity differently. Similarly, when a component is deemed too difficult to measure, it is set to zero (i.e., not included). For example, Harwood's (2004) report does not include costs attributed to motor vehicle accidents, operating reimbursement systems, or income generating crimes committed by nonaddicted users. Furthermore, as noted above, health-care costs often represent a tiny component of the total cost of illness of drug abuse. Estimates take into account only a handful of diseases such as HIV/AIDS, tuberculosis, and hepatitis B and C, ignoring the additional medical complications associated with addiction, including, but not limited to, premature death, liver damage, mental health issues (i.e., comorbidity), prenatal effects and cardiovascular problems. COI's failure to account for these complications and several others lends further force to the accusation that COI underestimates the costs associated with drug abuse (Cartwright, 2008).

In sum, cost of illness studies contain much information but do not suggest a course of action, nor do they favor one policy over another. In order to explore how U.S. policy makers have been addressing the issue of drug abuse, we now turn to explore the history of the U.S. national drug control policy.

A Historical Perspective: The War on Drugs in U.S. Social Policy

The war on drugs refers to a wide array of public policies and programs designed to address the problem of illegal drug use. It is a prohibition campaign undertaken by the U.S. Government with the assistance of participating countries intended to "combat" the illegal drug trade—to curb supply and diminish demand for certain psychoactive substances deemed harmful by the government (Marlatt, 1998; Shohov & Lamazi, 2004). Though the terms are not mutually exclusive (or inclusive), in general, efforts to reduce supply include foreign as well as domestic law enforcement activities, while demand reduction efforts include treatment, prevention, and research [National Drug Control Strategy (NDCS), 2007, 2008]. Thus, the war on drugs is, in essence, an initiative, which includes a set of laws, policies, and programs that are intended to eliminate the production, distribution, and consumption of targeted psychoactive substances (Marlatt, 1998; Shohov & Lamazi, 2004). Though the USA has been waging this war for many decades, the term itself was coined only in 1971 by President Richard Nixon to describe a new set of initiatives designed to enhance drug prohibition and battle "America's public enemy number one" (Fisher, 2006; Shohov & Lamazi, 2004).

The historical origins of the war on drugs can be traced back to 1880 when the USA and China signed a treaty prohibiting the shipment of opium between the two countries. In 1887, the U.S. congress implemented legislation on this matter, and citizens found in violation were subject to high fines (Shohov & Lamazi, 2004). The first recorded instance of the USA enacting a ban on the domestic distribution of drugs is the Harrison Narcotic Act of 1914 (Fisher, 2006). This ban set the stage for U.S. drug policies in the years to come (Gossop, 2003). However, it was not until 1924 that heroin (frequently used in cough syrup) was banned from medical practice. Cocaine, which was a substance in Coca-Cola until 1903 and in many other wines and medicines, was prescribed for medicinal purposes until the late 1920s (Fisher, 2006).

The United States alcohol prohibition from 1920 to 1933 is the most widely known historical period of drug prohibition (Fisher, 2006; Shohov & Lamazi, 2004). Alcohol prohibition in the USA first appeared as the Volstead Act of 1919, having been approved by 36 of the 48 U.S. states. This, the 18th amendment to the United States Constitution, remains the only major act of prohibition to be repealed, having been struck down in 1933 by the 21st amendment, which determined the laws constructed under the former unconstitutional (Marlatt, 1998).

In 1937, congress passed the Marijuana Tax Act, modeled after the Harrison Act. This law called for a $1 tax on the distribution of marijuana, and required anyone distributing it to submit a detailed account of his transactions. It was also, however, a "catch 22," as obtaining a tax stamp required individuals to first present the marijuana, an act tantamount to a confession of possession of an illegal substance. Thus, no tax stamps were ever produced. Although by this time there was ample scientific research to contest the claim that marijuana caused insanity, criminality, or death, the basis for these laws shifted to the notion that marijuana use would lead to the use of "hard" drugs (i.e. heroin). The 1951 Boggs Act first created mandatory sentencing, which were later hardened in the Narcotics Control Act (Daniel Act) of 1956, which allowed for a death sentence to persons distributing heroin to minors (Fisher, 2006; Marlatt, 1998).

As demonstrated above, the U.S. congress passed several legislative acts concerning illegal substances. In 1970, following the return of many heroin-addicted soldiers from the Vietnam War, the U.S. congress, under President Nixon, passed the Comprehensive Drug Abuse Prevention and Control Act, which replaced and updated all previous legislation and added new policies. This act is the foundation for modern U.S. drug policy to this day and was the basis for Nixon to declare "The [modern] war on Drugs." Responsibility for enforcement of this new law was given to the Special Action Office of Drug Abuse Prevention and then in 1973 to the newly formed Drug Enforcement Agency (DEA). President Nixon also appointed the first Drug Czar in an effort to coordinate the war (Fisher, 2006; Marlatt, 1998).

Presidents Ford and Carter both took little interest in the issue of drugs, though during his camping, President Carter proposed to eliminate penalties for those in possession of less than an ounce of marijuana, yet his attempt did not materialize. By the time President Reagan entered office, cocaine and crack dependence were of major concern in the USA. In 1986 he passed the Anti Drug Abuse Act, which included minimum sentencing for selling and using crack and cocaine (Fisher, 2006).

In 1988, towards the end of President Reagan's second term in office, the Office of National Drug Control Policy (ONDCP) was created for central coordination of drug-related legislative, security, diplomatic, research and health policy efforts.

In recognition of his central role, the director of ONDCP is commonly known as the Drug Czar. The position was raised to cabinet-level status by President Bill Clinton in 1993. The USA has then seen several drug czars, including one that disliked the analogy of "war" (General Barry McCaffrey who served from 1996 to 2000; Fisher, 2006), though the policies remained the same and the USA has not wavered in its zero tolerance stance (Fisher, 2006; Gossop, 2003; Riley & O'Hare, 2000).

On the state level, several attempts have been made by individual states to implement policies decriminalizing illicit substances. For example, in 1996, a majority of California voters voted for the legalization of growing and use of marijuana for medical purposes. This created much tension between the federal government and the state. Several other individual states have laws authorizing the use of marijuana for medical and research purposes. However, these laws do not protect from federal prosecution (Harrison, 2004).

The U.S. National Drug Control Strategy: Curbing Supply and Reducing Demand

According to the latest National Drug Control Strategy (NDCS, 2010) budget summary for fiscal year 2011, President Obama requested $15.5 billion in order to reduce use and availability of drugs (including alcohol and tobacco), a 3.5% increase from the 2010 enacted budget. These funds are to be spent on (1) prevention—$1.7 billion; (2) treatment efforts—$3.9 billion; (3) domestic law enforcement—$3.9 billion; (4) interdiction—$3.7 billion; and (5) international efforts—$2.3 billion. As in previous years, these funds are to be distributed among various government agencies that focus on demand reduction (including the drug control programs of the Departments of Education, Health and Human Services, Interior, Small Business Administration, and Veterans Affairs) and supply reduction (the Departments of Defense, Homeland Security, Justice, State, Transportation and Treasury). Demand reduction includes treatment and prevention (requested budget of $5.2. billion, or 34% of the budget), while supply reduction includes interdiction, international efforts, and law enforcement (requested budget of $9.9 billion, or 66% of the budget).

In the past several years, while efforts to reduce supply have been increasing, efforts to reduce demand have been decreasing as a percent of the total budget. This can be attributed largely to increases in funding for interdiction efforts and decreases in funding for prevention efforts (NDCS, 2010). It is important to note that the most recent budget requested shows a very slight reverse of that trend (NDCS, 2010). Though the final budget for 2011 is not yet available, the budget request might be suggestive of a shift yet to come.

The numbers above show that the USA spends roughly two thirds of its budget on supply reduction, while the remainder is spent on prevention and treatment. This allocation of funds can be attributed to approaches that have dominated the field of substance abuse in the USA for many decades. In the next section we introduce these approaches.

Three Approaches

Traditionally, two approaches have dominated the field of substance abuse in the USA. These approaches have been applied in all aspects of policy and practice. One is the moral approach. As its name suggests, this approach assumes that substance abuse is morally wrong. Under this model the use and distribution of certain substances is a crime and therefore deserving of punishment. Thus, the criminal justice system and the legislative system collaborate to establish a society without drugs. This collaboration takes the form of practices demanding zero-tolerance and policies collectively termed the war on drugs. The moral approach demands complete abstinence as a condition for receiving treatment. The other, the medical model, views addiction as a biological or genetic (acute) disease that should be cured or prevented. This approach emphasizes treatment and rehabilitation. Interventions based on this approach target individuals' desire for drugs; are concerned with demand reduction (French, Homer, & Nielsen, 2006; Marlatt, 1998). Despite the apparent differences (and at times competition) between the two models, both are based on the premise that the only acceptable goal should be abstinence. In addition, they both tend to focus on the individual drug user, and as such differ from harm reduction approaches which focus on public health (Bertman, Blachman, Sharpe, & Andreas, 1996; Marlatt, 1998).

Recently, researchers have suggested that substance abuse is comparable to other chronic disorders, such as diabetes, hypertension, and asthma (McLellan et al., 2000; O'Brien & McLellan, 1996). The rationale behind this notion is threefold: First, similar to many other chronic conditions, the etiology for substance abuse includes genetic, environmental, and personal factors. Second, akin to other chronic conditions, only some forms of substance abuse can be treated effectively by medication. Third, substance abusers show rates of adherence, early dropout and relapse similar to those associated with many other chronic conditions. Thus, researchers have called for long-term care practices, such as those utilized in the treatment of various chronic conditions, in addition to insurance policies and evaluation strategies to match them (McLellan et al., 2000; O'Brien & McLellan, 1996).

In the last few decades, one of the most serious damages caused by behaviors associated with drug addiction—such as risky sexual behavior and needle sharing—has been the contraction of infectious diseases such as HIV, hepatitis, and tuberculosis (McLellan et al., 2000; NIDA, 2006). These diseases do not remain within substance abusing populations; rather, they quickly find their way to the rest of society, mainly through sexual intercourse (it has been estimated that at least 40% of injecting drug users maintain sexual relationships with non-users) (Riley & O'Hare, 2000).

Since the 1980s, with the emergence of HIV/AIDS and other infectious diseases among injecting substance abusers as well as the population as a whole, many countries worldwide have recognized the need for more pragmatic approaches to substance abuse (McLellan et al., 2000; NIDA, 2006). Harm reduction is a term used to refer to "policies, programs and practices that aim to reduce the adverse health, social and economic consequences of the use of legal and illegal psychoactive drugs." These policies are "based on a strong commitment to public health" [International Harm Reduction Association (IHRA), 2009, p. 1].

The underlying assumption of harm reduction approaches is that people always have and probably always will engage in risky behaviors (i.e., drug use, unsafe sex). Harm reduction approaches aim to reduce the damages caused by these risky behaviors. They recognize that substance use lies on a continuum between serious abuse and dysfunction and complete abstinence, and that some forms of use are preferable to others. For example, they contend that occasional use is preferable to daily use (Fisher, 2006; Inciardi & Harrison, 2000; Marlatt, 1998).

Harm reduction approaches regard quality of life as the desired outcome of policies, and they take a nonjudgmental stand towards users. One of the main principles of harm reduction is the recognition that poverty, past experience, race, class and gender affect peoples' ability to cope with harms associated with substance use. Harm reduction advocates see prohibition and criminalization of substance abuse as ineffective and counterproductive, since substance use and abuse are very common despite countless laws and billions of dollars devoted to battling it. Advocates of these pragmatic approaches argue that "zero tolerance" policies criminalize many people who could otherwise be productive members of society (Inciardi & Harrison, 2000; Marlatt, 1998).

Many harm reduction advocates argue that the need to decrease HIV rates must take precedence over the moral reactions to drug use. Some also argue that prohibition and criminalization are simply not effective and that more pragmatic measures should be explored. Despite the US government's tough stance on drugs, some treatment is available and harm reduction programs are not unheard of. In addition, many public health-related programs are in place, needle exchange programs are expanding with state support and many cities are adapting these programs to their own at-risk residents (Schori, 2010).

Each of the three approaches discussed in this section leads to different policies, practices, and distributions of resources. The moral model tends to suggest that most resources should be allocated to law enforcement. To advocates of the moral model, prevention is secondary, and treatment tertiary. Alternatively, advocates of the medical model tend to put treatment first (primarily abstinence based or medication based), followed by prevention and finally by law enforcement. Finally, similar to the medical model, the harm reduction model tends to favor spending on treatment and prevention versus spending on law enforcement. However, this model also stresses the need for additional funds for interventions that are not necessarily abstinence-based, but that help to reduce the cost of illness to society and to increase quality of life for addicts and their families (Schori, 2010).

Discussion, Conclusions, and Implications for Social Work

Despite the significant costs associated with illegal drug abuse and the ample evidence suggesting that treatment is effective and beneficial to individuals as well as to society, the amount spent on treatment remains relatively low. In other words, despite the apparent potential to decrease costs to society and to help more addicts reach better results, society's efforts remain concentrated elsewhere—mainly in efforts to disrupt the drug market (i.e., reduce the supply through prohibition and law enforcement). These efforts seem to suggest that decisions regarding drug abuse strategy, policy, and resource allocation stem from the moral model, which views drug use as a moral wrong deserving of punishment. In fact, as mentioned above, incarceration of drug offenders is the highest single economic cost associated with drug abuse. However, the third of the budget intended for treatment and prevention suggests the influence of medical approaches as well. Despite their effectiveness and benefits for society, harm reduction interventions remain essentially unsupported in the current funding structure. Studies that detail the benefits and effectiveness of treatment and harm reduction interventions may serve to inform policy makers and shift public opinion (Schori, 2010).

Miron (2003) pointed out that cost of illness estimates are often used in support of prohibition policies. While any specific policy implemented may be desirable, be it prohibition, treatment or harm reduction, COI studies provide no basis for making this determination. In order to declare one policy preferable to another, one must examine how the various categories differ among competing policies (not simply the rates of drug abuse related harms). In addition, one would have to take into account any secondary consequences. Thus, in the case of prohibitionist policies, examples might include increased violence and corruption, diminished civil liberties, heightened racial tensions, distorted foreign relations, added restrictions on medicinal drug use, the transfer of wealth to criminals, and civil unrest within drug-producing countries (Miron, 2003). Cost of illness estimates, which are frequently utilized to measure various health and social problems, provide important information, but they are insufficient to determine which policy or practice might be a wiser investment of societal resources (Schori, 2010).

Despite efforts to eradicate drug abuse using "zero tolerance" policies, there has been no substantial decrease in substance abuse and the costs attributed to it (Brocato & Wagner, 2003; Currie, 1993; Cussen & Block, 2000; Huggins, 2005). In some cases, prohibition can even lead to risk behaviors such as associating with criminals, sharing needles due to inability to attain clean needles, and shifts to unsafe environments whenever using (Elliot, Csete, Wood, & Kerr, 2005). This possibility exists regardless of the pattern of use or abuse. Users and addicts also contract diseases that might be prevented if they were not forced to hide and to buy their drugs through illegal channels. As mentioned above, these diseases do not remain within substance abusing populations (Riley & O'Hare, 2000).

Yet it is clear that no real policy change can occur without a shift in public opinion towards drug use, without research translated into effective practices, and without education about the true nature of substance use and abuse. Furthermore, harm reduction programs/policies and other new forms of treatment should be put into effect with careful consideration of public opinion, and they must take into account the diversity of the population that is in need (French et al., 2006).

The implications of current policies and practices on our profession are profound. The National Association of Social Workers (NASW, 1999) Code of Ethics states that:

> The primary mission of the social work profession is to enhance human wellbeing and help meet the basic human needs of all people …. A historic and defining feature of social work

is the profession's focus on individual wellbeing in a social context and the wellbeing of society. Fundamental to social work is attention to the environmental forces that create, contribute to, and address problems in living.

Social workers promote social justice and social change with and on behalf of clients. … Social workers are sensitive to cultural and ethnic diversity and strive to end discrimination, oppression, poverty, and other forms of social injustice. These activities may be in the form of direct practice, community organizing, supervision, consultation administration, advocacy, social and political action, policy development and implementation, education, and research and evaluation. Social workers seek to enhance the capacity of people to address their own needs. Social workers also seek to promote the responsiveness of organizations, communities, and other social institutions to individuals' needs and social problems.

This suggests that as a profession, we should not be judging, punishing, or trying to cure our clients, but rather advocating for them, treating and helping them in achieving self-determination. Though most of us can probably agree that abstinence is a desired outcome, we must recognize that not everyone is ready, willing or able to set this as his or her only goal. Meeting our clients where they are, rather than where we want or think they should want to be, will serve to expand our repertoire of available interventions and advocacy solutions. Remembering that society has played a part in creating and maintain the social problem of drug abuse, might offer some insight into possible solutions.

The principles of harm reduction seem to be a better fit with the values of social work; more than the notions of the medical model and certainly more than those of the moral model. Harm reduction programs and policies take on many forms. Some are widely established such as HIV and substance use prevention efforts, designated driver campaigns and methadone maintenance programs. Others are highly controversial such as condom distribution in schools, providing injecting drug users with clean needles (Needle Exchange Programs, NEP), establishing safe injection sites, and heroin maintenance programs and drug legalization or at the very least decriminalization (Fisher, 2006).

While methadone maintenance and needle exchange programs typify harm reduction efforts, there are several other ways in which substance abuse treatment programs can adopt practices that are in accordance with the underlying principles of harm reduction. For instance, "low-threshold" approaches to SAT maintain that services should be offered to all those who seek them, regardless of continued use (Marlatt, 2002). Offering clients the option of gradual tapering from various substitution therapies (such as methadone or buprenorphine) is another example (Eversman, 2009). Working with clients to achieve treatment goals other than abstinence, teaching substance use management techniques (education about safer use), and advocating for policy change are also construed as harm reduction efforts (Marlatt, 2002).

Proponents of harm reduction stress that it is important to keep in mind that adopting a single harm reduction strategy does not mean adopting them all. Programs should be implemented where they are needed and adapted to the populations they serve. Not every program can be successful in all environments, and they must be culturally sensitive, as well as sensitive to gender, socioeconomic background and many other factors (Fisher, 2006; Marlatt, 1998), ideas that our profession was built upon. Some have also argued for the integration of abstinence and harm reduction into one continuum in an attempt to play to the strengths of both (e.g., Kellogg, 2003).

Riley and O'Hare (2000) summarized some of the main barriers to harm reduction practices. The main argument is that people who would not otherwise use drugs might begin doing so if they perceive that it is safe and legal (or at the least not criminalized). They also argued that currently society does not except drug use as a "legitimate form of risk taking," thus the moral stance is prevalent. People with strong religious beliefs also tend to oppose any attempt to modify current policies in the direction of what they perceive as moral looseness. These notions, in addition to laws already in place and to lack of knowledge in the general public regarding the true nature of substance abuse, lead to a political climate which is less than supportive of efforts to implement harm reduction measures (Riley & O'Hare, 2000).

Considering the ample research indicating that substance abuse treatment (SAT) programs operating under the harm reduction paradigm are often effective in reducing health disparities, rates of overdose, incarceration, HIV, hepatitis, and other infectious diseases as well as in improving the quality of life of many addicts and their families, many countries worldwide have incorporated a wide array of harm reduction practices into SAT. Yet, the USA has been slow to follow. Social workers can work to better the lives of substance abusers, their families, and society:

1. As a profession we must advocate for and with our clients and take on the role of social change agents. By adopting some of the principles of harm reduction, already compatible with those of our profession, we can help educate, prevent, and develop a wider and more comprehensive array of interventions for our clients and for society.
2. Social workers who work with users and addicts must be able to offer alternatives to the abstinence model, even if temporary, when clients seek these services.
3. Social workers who do not work directly with substance using populations should be trained to recognize persons with substance use disorders, be aware of the alternatives available to them, and be able to offer them referral to appropriate services.

We conclude with a word of caution: it is clear that no real policy change can occur without a shift in public opinion towards drug use, without research translated into effective practices, and without education about the true nature of substance use and abuse. Furthermore, harm reduction programs, policies and other new forms of treatment should be put into effect with careful consideration of public opinion, and they must take into account the diversity of the population that is in need (French et al., 2006; Schori, 2010).

References

American Psychiatric Association. (1994). *Diagnostic and Statistical Manual of Mental Disorders, 4th edition (DSM-IV)*. Washington, DC: American Psychiatric Association.

Bertman, E., Blachman, M., Sharpe, K., & Andreas, P. (1996). *Drug war politics: The price of denial*. Berkeley, CA: University of California Press.

Brocato, J., & Wagner, E. E. (2003). Harm reduction: A social work practice model and social justice agenda. *Health and Social Work, 28*, 117–125.

Cartwright, W. S. (2008). Economic costs of drug abuse: Financial, cost-of-illness, and services. *Journal of Substance Abuse Treatment, 34*, 224–233.

Currie, E. (1993). *Reckoning: Drugs, the cities, and the American future*. New York: Hill & Wang.

Cussen, M., & Block, W. (2000). Legalize drugs now!: An analysis of the benefits of legalized drugs. *American Journal of Economics and Sociology, 59*, 525–536.

Elliot, R., Csete, J., Wood, E., & Kerr, T. (2005). Harm reduction, HIV/AIDS, and the human rights challenge to global drug control policy. *Health and Human Rights—Emerging Issues in HIV/AIDS, 8*, 104–138.

Eversman, M. (2009). *Harm reduction in outpatient drug-free substance abuse treatment settings*. Available form ProQuest Dissertations and Theses database (AAT 3359005).

Fisher, G. L. (2006). *Rethinking our war on drugs*. Westport, CT: Praeger.

French, M. T., Homer, J. F., & Nielsen, A. L. (2006). Does America spend enough on addiction treatment? Results from public opinion surveys. *Journal of Substance Abuse Treatment, 31*, 245–254.

French, M. T., Popovici, I., & Tapsell, L. (2008). The economic costs of substance abuse treatment: Updated estimates and cost bands for program assessment and reimbursement. *Journal of Substance Abuse Treatment, 35*, 462–469.

Gossop, M. (2003). *Drug addiction and its treatment*. New York: Oxford University Press.

Harrison, L. D. (2004). The medicalization of marihuana. In J. A. Inciardi, & L. D. Harrison (Eds.), *Harm reduction: National and international perspectives* (pp. 69–88). Thousand Oaks, CA: Sage.

Harwood, H. (2000). *Updating estimates of the economic costs of alcohol abuse in the United States: Estimates, update methods, and data*. Report prepared by The Lewin Group for the National Institute on Alcohol Abuse and Alcoholism. Bethesda, MD: National Institutes of Health.

Harwood, H. (2004). *The economic costs of drug abuse in the United States: 1992–2002*. Report prepared by The Lewin Group for the Office of National Drug Control Policy (ONDCP). Bethesda, MD: National Institutes of Health.

Huggins, L. E. (Ed.). (2005). *Drug war deadlock: The policy battle continues*. Stanford, CA: Hoover Institution Press.

Inciardi, J. A., & Harrison, L. D. (Eds.). (2000). *Harm reduction: National and international perspectives*. Thousand Oaks, CA: Sage.

International Harm Reduction Association (IHRA). (2009). *What is harm reduction? A position statement from the International Harm Reduction Association*. London: IHRA.

Kellogg, S. (2003). On "gradualism" and the building of the harm reduction-abstinence continuum. *Journal of Substance Abuse Treatment, 25*, 241–247.

Kimberly, J. R., & McLellan, T. A. (2006). Introduction: The business of addiction treatment: A research agenda. *Journal of Substance Abuse Treatment, 31*, 213–219.

Mark, T. L., Levit, K. R., Coffey, R. M., McKusick, D. R., Harwood, H. J., King, E. C., et al. (2007). *National expenditures for mental health services and substance abuse treatment, 1993–2003*. DHHS Publication No. SMA 07-4227. Rockville, MD: Substance Abuse and Mental Health Services Administration.

Marlatt, G. A. (1998). *Harm reduction*. New York, NY: Guillford Press.

Marlatt, G. A. (2002). *Harm reduction: Pragmatic strategies for managing high-risk behaviors*. New York, NY: Guillford Press.

McLellan, T. A., Lewis, D. C., O'Brien, C. P., & Kleber, H. D. (2000). Drug dependence, a chronic medical illness: Implications for treatment, insurance, and outcomes evaluation. *Journal of the American Medical Association, 284*, 1689–1695.

Miron, J. A. (2003). *A critique of estimates of the economic cost of drug abuse. Manuscript.* Boston: Department of Economics, Boston University.

Moore, T. J., & Caulkins, J. P. (2006). How cost-of-illness studies can be made more useful for illicit drug policy analysis. *Applied Health Economics and Health Policy, 5*, 75–85.

National Association of Social Workers. (approved 1996, revised 1999). *Code of Ethics of the National Association of Social Workers.* Washington, DC: National Association of Social Workers.

National Drug Control Strategy: FY 2008 Budget Summary. (2007). Washington, DC: The White House.

National Drug Control Strategy: FY 2009 Budget Summary. (2008). Washington, DC: The White House.

National Drug Control Strategy: FY 2011 Budget Summary. (2010). Washington, DC: The White House.

National Institute on Drug Abuse (NIDA). (2006). *NIDA InfoFacts: Treatment approaches for drug addiction.* Retrieved from: http://www.drugabuse.gov/infofacts/treatmeth.html.

O'Brien, C. P., & McLellan, T. A. (1996). Myths about the treatment of addiction. *Lancet, 347*, 237–240.

Reuter, P. (1999). Are calculations of the economic costs of drug abuse either possible or useful? *Addiction, 94*, 635–638.

Rice, D. P. (1967). Estimating the cost of illness. *American Journal of Public Health, 57*, 424–440.

Riley, D., & O'Hare, P. (2000). Harm reduction: History, definition and practice. In J. A. Inciardi, & L. D. Harrison (Eds.), *Harm reduction: National and international perspectives* (pp. 1–27). Thousand Oaks, CA: Sage.

Schori, M. (2010). Valuation of drug abuse: A review of current methodologies and implications for policy making. *Research on Social Work Practice, 21*, 421–431.

Scott, C. K., Dennis, M. L., & Foss, M. A. (2005). Utilizing recovery management checkups to shorten the cycle of relapse, treatment reentry, and recovery. *Drug and Alcohol Dependence, 78*, 325–338.

Segel, J. E. (2006). *Cost-of-illness studies—A primer.* Durham, NC: RTI-UNC Center of Excellence in Health Promotion Economics, RTI International.

Shohov, T. P., & Lamazi, F. (Eds.). (2004). *War on drugs: Issues and development.* New York: Novinka.

Substance Abuse and Mental Health Services Administration (SAMHSA). (2009). *Results from the 2008 National Survey on Drug Use and Health: National Findings.* Office of Applied Studies, NSDUH Series H-36, HHS Publication No. SMA 09-4434. Rockville, MD: SAMHSA.

Chapter 16
Conclusions and Future Directions

Brian E. Perron and Michael G. Vaughn

The contributing authors have skillfully summarized and integrated a large body of literature on various topics. The readers will find many of the citations to be key resources for further development. Furthermore, many of the journals containing these citations are ones that can help social workers remain current with the latest developments in the field. Thus, we hope that this collection of works serve not only to inform readers on critical issues in the field of substance use disorders, but that it will also be useful point of departure for lifelong learning.

It would be disingenuous to claim that this volume contained all the information required to be a skilled and effective social worker in the field of substance use disorder treatment. The sheer brevity of the volume, and the finite amount of time that social workers realistically spend in training, has necessarily excluded some important content. Moreover, the authors were directed to focus their efforts on what is known about the various topics, which takes away from opportunities to speculate on the likely (and needed) changes in the field. Thus, in offering concluding remarks to this volume, we thought it would be fruitful to present a few integrative and speculative themes. We hope this these concluding remarks will be helpful in guiding the process of lifelong learning.

B.E. Perron (✉)
University of Michigan, Ann Arbor, MI, USA
e-mail: beperron@umich.edu

M.G. Vaughn
Saint Louis University, St. Louis, MO, USA
e-mail: mvaughn9@slu.edu

M.G. Vaughn and B.E. Perron (eds.), *Social Work Practice in the Addictions*,   261
Contemporary Social Work Practice, DOI 10.1007/978-1-4614-5357-4_16,
© Springer Science+Business Media New York 2013

Technology Will Play an Increasingly Important Role in All Aspects of Substance Use Disorder Treatment

Technology is defined as "the practical application of knowledge especially in a particular area (Merriam-Webster, 2011). With this definition in mind, the contents of each chapter can be rightfully considered a form of technology. That is, we are using knowledge from various areas to meaningfully affect change in lives of people affected by substance use disorders. This volume would have looked much different if it were written ten years ago. And it will look much different ten years from now. Our technology for preventing and treating substance-related problems is an ongoing, dynamic, and a complex process. Social workers involved with the care of persons who have substance-related problems face the ongoing challenge of remaining current with the latest change-related technologies, which is vast, complex, and continually evolving.

It is necessary to consider the change-related technologies in the broader context of information and communication technologies (ICTs) that are shaping our broader culture, education, and provision of services (see Perron, Taylor, Glass, & Margerum-Leys, 2010). ICTs are technologies used to convey, manipulate, and store data by electronic means. This can include e-mail, SMS text messaging, video chat (e.g., Skype), and online social media (e.g., Facebook). It also includes all the different computing devices (e.g., laptop computers and smart phones) that carry out a wide range of communication and information functions. While remaining current with ICTs adds further complexity to the challenge of remaining current with the advances in the prevention and treatment of SUDs, it is important to consider these as integrated rather than separate challenges. That is, much of what we learn about substances and related problems is disseminated and discussed electronically (e.g., online databases, open access journals). We are increasingly reliant on scheduling, coordinating, and documenting care electronically (e.g., electronic medical records). The methods of communication among professionals and clients are also changing, with the most notable changes being advances in the underlying electronics.

Although the current social work curriculum passively instructs students on the use of ICTs, we believe that effective social work practice in the area of substance use disorders requires a seamless integration of new technologies into the daily work routines of social workers. The use of ICTs also raises further issues related to information security. As a starting point, we encourage social workers to begin exploring different strategies for using different devices for rapidly accessing the latest information. For example, social workers can subscribe to *RSS feeds* to nearly every major journals that have been cited in this volume to the various journals. This gives immediate access to the latest developments in the field, at a time and on a device (e.g., smart phone, tablet computer) that is most convenient. Open access journals are also a new way to freely access high quality information. These are just a few examples that will prove to be useful but ultimately will change over time.

We Will See Increased Importance of Substance-Related Problems in Non-specialty Substance Use Disorder Treatment Settings

The knowledge contained in this volume will undoubtedly be of value to social workers working in specialty treatment settings—that is, treatment centers that have a primary focus on treating substance-related problems. However, knowledge of substances and related problems will become increasingly important to social workers in non-specialty treatment settings. These are settings in which substance-related problems may be present, but not the primary focus of treatment—e.g., nursing homes, family service programs, after-school youth programs, and criminal justice programs. For example, problems of prescription medication misuse, abuse, and dependence are receiving increased attention in substance use disorder treatment settings. However, the significance of this problem has emerged in public schools and university settings, the child welfare system, and medical settings.

As noted throughout this volume, substance-related problems can emerge in almost any social work setting, and readers will no doubt recognize that simply ignoring them will result in barriers to meaningful change in other domains of functioning. Thus, even if the reader chooses a social work career in a non-specialty treatment setting, the information contained in this volume will undoubtedly be important. We are also confident that the importance of this knowledge will be increasingly important in non-specialty settings over time for a few reasons.

One important factor underlying this speculation is the rapidly changing racial and ethnic composition of the USA. Persons with substance-related problems may ultimately be seeking or receiving services in other settings due to language barriers, lack of access to specialty treatment services, and preferences for treatment. Thus, social workers in non-specialty settings will likely be the first point of contact for persons with substance-related problems. Another factor to consider is the continued integration of health, mental health, and substance use disorder treatments. Social workers will play a key role in helping coordinate the care for individuals with comorbidities and complex psychosocial needs.

It also comes as no surprise that the economic climate has made access to specialty treatment increasingly limited. Thus, the care needs of persons with substance-related problem will inevitably be redistributed in some fashion to social workers in a variety of other settings. This requires social workers to be skilled at assessment and brief interventions, in addition to establishing effective referral processes with other service agencies.

With Respect to Treating Substance Use Disorders, Social Workers in Direct Practice Will Have Encountered Increased Responsibility and Opportunities for Making Macro-level Decisions

Chapters 14 and 15 reveal considerable complexity with respect to alcohol and drug policies. It is not uncommon for social workers to consider policy related issues as a form of macro-level practice that is not part of the provision of direct services. However, with respect to substance-related problems, macro-level practice activities are important for direct service providers. And the importance of such activities will increase with time.

One notable example is the current changes in marijuana policy. For example, at the time of preparing this volume, many states have provisions for the use of medical marijuana, with a number of other states with pending legislation. With the increased access to marijuana and its legal sanctions, social workers will have to determine how to interpret and implement this policy. For example, substance use disorder treatment centers need to determine under what circumstances this substance is considered a prescription medicine or an illicit drug. Unfortunately, the current research isn't at a place that can help sort out such issues. Social workers will ultimately need to be involved in the writing of service-related policies that takes into consider broader policy changes at the state and federal level.

At the same time, social workers involved in macro-level activities need to have an intimate awareness of what occurs in frontline treatment settings. For example, with increased attention to outcome measurement, it is important to consider the capacity of organizations to collect, summarize, and meaningfully use outcome data. Social workers with macro-level responsibilities need to be aware of not only the innovations and developments of the field, but the extent to which organizations are ready to innovate. Innovations in the field will ultimately require more effective strategies to build communication channels among social workers engaged in micro- and macro-level activities. While this holds true for social work practice in general, we believe that it is especially critical for practice issues involving substance-related problems.

Of course, these integrative and speculative themes only begin to touch upon the full range of possibilities. It would be our delight to continue filling in the gaps by discussing more extensively about other important and related topics, including (but not limited to) etiology, brain functioning, the science of personality and individual differences, classification, service systems, law, and international issues. However, we are feel most satisfied with the work of the contributing authors who have brought together some of the most pertinent information that ultimately serves as a foundation for lifelong learning.

References

Merriam-Webster. (2011). *Technology*. Retrieved December 30, 2011 from http://www.merriam-webster.com/dictionary/technology.

Perron, B. E., Taylor, H. O., Glass, J. E., & Margerum-Leys, J. (2010). Information and communication technologies in social work. *Advances in Social Work, 11*(1), 67–81.

Index

M.G. Vaughn and B.E. Perron (eds.), *Social Work Practice in the Addictions,*
Contemporary Social Work Practice, DOI 10.1007/978-1-4614-5357-4,
© Springer Science+Business Media New York 2013

CPSIA information can be obtained
at www.ICGtesting.com
Printed in the USA
LVOW09s0742080118
562208LV00008B/171/P